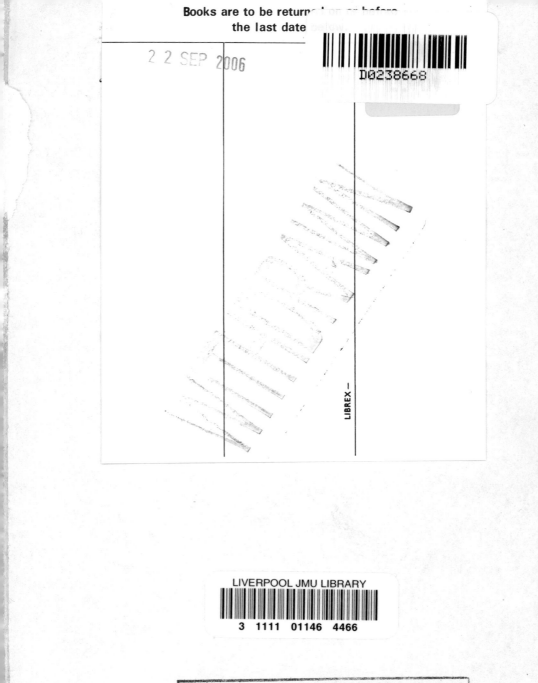

From Russ Reising:

To Alma, Maggie, Natasha, and James,
Who all make it so easy not to be afraid to care.
And,
To the memory of our dear CubbyBear,
Who actually preferred *Meddle* (for 'Seamus') and *Animals* (for 'Dogs').

From all the contributors:

Heartfelt thanks to Pink Floyd
For bring such stimulation and immense joy to our lives.

'Speak to Me': The Legacy of Pink Floyd's *The Dark Side of the Moon*

Edited by

RUSSELL REISING
University of Toldeo, USA

ASHGATE

Published by
Ashgate Publishing Limited
Gower House
Croft Road
Aldershot
Hampshire GU11 3HR
England

Ashgate Publishing Company
Suite 420
101 Cherry Street
Burlington, VT, 05401-4405
USA

Ashgate website: http://www.ashgate.com

British Library Cataloguing in Publication Data
'Speak to me' : the legacy of Pink Floyd's The dark side of the
    moon. – (Ashgate popular and folk music series)
    1. Pink Floyd (Group). The dark side of the moon 2. Rock music –
    History and criticism
    I. Reising, Russell
    782.4'2166

Library of Congress Cataloging-in-Publication Data
Speak to me : the legacy of Pink Floyd's The dark side of the moon / Russell Reising,
editor.
        p. cm.—(Ashgate popular and folk music series)
    Includes bibliographical references (p.   ) and index.
    ISBN 0-7546-4018-3 (alk. paper)—ISBN 0-7546-4019-1 (pbk.) 1. Pink Floyd
    (Musical quartet). The dark side of the moon. 2. Rock music—History and criticism.
I. Reising, Russell. II. Series

    ML421.P6S74 2004
    782.42166'092'2—dc22

                                                                        2004013258

ISBN 0 7546 4018 3 (HBK)
ISBN 0 7546 4019 1 (PBK)

Typeset by IML Typographers, Birkenhead, Merseyside
Printed and bound in Great Britain by MPG Books Ltd, Bodmin

Contents

Part III: 'There's no dark side of the moon': Theoretical discussions

Part IV: 'Speak to me': The influence of *The Dark Side of the Moon*

'Assorted lunatics': Contributors' biographical notes

Matthew Bannister, University of Auckland, New Zealand
I used to be a rock star in a minor way, as a member of Sneaky Feelings, who were part of the 'Dunedin Sound' Flying Nun axis in 1980s New Zealand, and I still play live music with my current band The Weather. In 1999 I published 'Positively George Street – a personal history of Sneaky Feelings and the Dunedin Sound' and started research on my presently-being-examined PhD 'White Man's Soul: Pakeha (white) Masculinities and NZ popular music' (2002). I have also published articles on the influence of 1960s girl groups on the Beatles ('Beatlestudies 3', 2001), NZ popular music ('Perfect Beat' July 2000), the Bonzo Dog Band and George Harrison. I live in Auckland with my wife and two children.

The Dark Side of the Moon was the record that all our older brothers had in the 1970s, and they assured us that when we were old enough and serious and mature enough, we would stop listening to Abba, glam rock, and the Sex Pistols and finally appreciate some *real* music. I'm still waiting. (Gilmour's solo on 'Money' is pretty fab, however; though I wouldn't mention this in mixed company.)

Lee Barron, University of Northumbria, UK
I am a Lecturer in Sociology at the University of Northumbria. My doctoral research considers the role and significance of angels within contemporary cinema, and my teaching areas include research methods, sociological theory, cultural studies, and criminology. I have published in the areas of sport, crime and society, teaching and learning via computerized technology, research methods, popular music, and the nature of celebrity. Most recently, I contributed a chapter concerning the nature of soundtrack albums for the book *Popular Music and Film* (2003).

My introduction to *The Dark Side of the Moon* actually came in the early 1990s, when, as a fledgling bass guitarist, I was introduced to the album by musician friends who forcefully argued that there was more to music than a constant diet of heavy metal. They assured me of its quality and significance and, sure enough, the album soon became a favorite. Listening to it today, it retains the power to instantly recall particularly fond memories of lengthy jam sessions built around the track 'Money'.

Mathew Bartkowiak, Bowling Green State University, USA
I received my Bachelor's degree at the University of Wisconsin-Green Bay, where I had an independent major in Music and Society. I am now a Masters candidate in

the Popular Culture Department at Bowling Green State University focusing primarily on popular music history and cultural studies. I plan to pursue a PhD in American Studies or History.

The Dark Side of the Moon for me has always been a building crescendo, which peaks brilliantly with the lines, 'and everything under the sun is in tune / but the sun is eclipsed by the moon'. I like that as the needle leaves the groove, even though the sonic journey has allowed the listener to descend into madness and perhaps see moments of joy, Pink Floyd in the end doesn't promise the listener a damn thing. A savagely fun trip ...

Kevin J. Holm-Hudson, University of Kentucky, USA

I received my Doctor of Musical Arts degree in Composition (with Ethnomusicology concentration) from the University of Illinois at Urbana-Champaign. I am now Assistant Professor of Music Theory at the University of Kentucky where my ongoing research interests include the semiotics of recorded popular music, harmonic/formal/timbral analysis of popular music, and American experimental music (post-1945). I edited *Progressive Rock Reconsidered* (2002) and have published articles in *Music Theory Online*, *Popular Music and Society*, *Leonardo Music Journal*, *Genre*, and *Ex Tempore*.

I first encountered *The Dark Side of the Moon* at the age of 11 in the summer of 1973, when I saw a radio station's chart listing for 'Money' and surmised that Pink Floyd was the name of a soul singer. Not long afterward, my older brother brought the record home and my mind was warped in a prog direction forever afterward.

Ian Inglis, University of Northumbria, Newcastle upon Tyne, UK

After a year or so as a cub reporter on a regional newspaper (during which my most memorable achievement was to turn down the opportunity to interview Jimi Hendrix), I entered the world of higher education and have remained there ever since, currently as Senior Lecturer in Sociology at the University of Northumbria. My books include *The Beatles, Popular Music and Society: A Thousand Voices* (2000) and *Popular Music and Film* (2003), and I am currently preparing *The Performance of Popular Music: Traditions and Transitions* for Ashgate. My doctoral research considered the significance of social psychological, sociological, and cultural theory in explanations of the career of the Beatles. I am a member of the editorial board of *Popular Music And Society*, and have had articles published in numerous journals, including *Popular Music*, *Journal of Popular Culture*, *International Review of the Aesthetics and Sociology of Music*, *Visual Culture in Britain*, *American Music*, *Popular Music And Society*, and *Journal of Popular Music Studies*.

Back in 1973, when *The Dark Side of the Moon* was released, I was one of a small group of young, newly-appointed members of staff in the Department of Sociology at Leicester University. With Derek Layder, Neil Mercer, John Muncie, Mike Fitzgerald et al., much of my time was spent in discussions, analyses, and arguments about music, football and (very occasionally) sociology. *The Dark Side of the Moon* provided a consistently beguiling soundtrack to many of our activities. The track that caught my attention more than any others was 'Money' – possibly because few of us had any at that time. Within a few years, we had all gone our separate professional ways, but the album has always retained its capacity to evoke a particular place and period in my life.

Kimi Kärki, University of Turku, Finland
Following a year as the coordinator of the Graduate School of Cultural Interaction and Integration in the Baltic Sea Region, I am back for a second time working as an Assistant at the Department of Cultural History, University of Turku, Finland – same department, different perspective. I am doing research on the stage performance of Pink Floyd and the rise of audiovisual 'Gesamtkunstverk' 1965–94.

The first time I heard *The Dark Side of the Moon* was when I was 11 years old, living in a small village called Karjalohja, in southern Finland. My good friend raved about the obscure sounds of this Pink Floyd LP he had, and sure enough when he put the needle on the record and the ambient-like intro of 'Time' filled the room, I was completely hooked. Right now, gradually working on my PhD on Pink Floyd's stage performance as a case study of audiovisual stadium aesthetics, I can still recall that moment clearly: the excitement on my friend's face, and me there staring at that enigmatic prisma-cover, silently wondering 'what the heck is VCS-3?'.

Peter Mills, Leeds Metropolitan University, UK
I am currently Senior Lecturer in Media and Popular Culture at Leeds Metropolitan University, specializing in Popular Music Studies with responsibility for introducing the subject to the degree programme there.

A graduate of the School of English at the University of Liverpool, I have written and published books on Olaf Stapledon and Samuel Beckett, and am working on a book on Van Morrison and self-mythology. I visited Hungary in 1993 and stayed for three years, enthralled to find a nation for whom music was the dominant creative principle. Once upon a time I was the singer and lyricist for Liverpool group 'Innocents Abroad' who toured Britain and Europe and recorded three albums, *Quaker City*, *Eleven*, and *Map*. My earliest memory is of sitting in front of my sister's Dansette with the 45s of 'Mr. Tambourine Man' and the 'Twist and Shout' EP on repeat play.

I first encountered *The Dark Side of the Moon* as a 10-year-old, finding it both terrifying and compulsive, a view I still stand by. I'd like to thank Jonathan and Clare Lynas for their help and their piano.

Shaugn O'Donnell, City College, City University of New York, USA
I have written on topics ranging from 18th-century chromaticism to metaphor theory in rock music. Pink Floyd holds a special place for me as the soundtrack of my youth, defining the socio-political views of my teen years, and influencing my

career as I abandoned the clarinet of my childhood for the more emotive electric guitar. I am currently an Associate Professor of music theory at The City College and Graduate Center of the City University of New York.

As for so many fans, *The Dark Side of the Moon* was my portal into the band's universe; I even remember painting the prism on the back of my denim jacket in junior high school.

Russell Reising, University of Toledo, Ohio, USA

After studying Asian languages and English literature in college and spending a year wandering the Dharma Trail in Asia, I earned my PhD in American literature from Northwestern University. A Professor of American Literature and Culture at University of Toledo, I also teach, lecture, and publish on Japanese literature, on popular music, and on psychedelic culture. My most recent book, *'Every Sound There Is': The Beatles'* Revolver *and the Transformation of Rock and Roll*, was published in 2002 by Ashgate. I have lived in Taiwan, Japan, and Finland, but now reside in Toledo, Ohio with my wife, Alma, my children, Maggie, Natasha, and James, and many pets.

I've been listening to *The Dark Side of the Moon* since its release in 1973, and I guess I'd have to count myself among those who have experienced it in about as many different states of mind as possible. In the obsessive-compulsive list of the '50 Greatest Songs of All Time' which I compiled for my 50th birthday, 'Time' chimed in at #7, the second highest ranked Pink Floyd number, 'Echoes' came in at #2, just behind the Jimi Hendrix Experience's 'Voodoo Chile (Slight Return)'. *Electric Ladyland* is the next book!

Ben Schleifer, Colorado College, Boulder, Colorado, USA

My interest in music was encouraged by my loving family. Now majoring in Neuroscience, with a minor in music, I play the bassoon, piano, and saxophone. In Colorado, I belong to five musical groups. My idea of fun is performing music. I am 19 years old, and I hope this paper helps me further my musical career and interests. I would like to thank my father, and my 'Uncle' Russ for setting up this great gig.

I first heard *Dark Side* when I was 13, and since then, I have always been surprised at how many people I can relate to through just this album. My high school chemistry teacher, Mr. Richardson, could spend 20 minutes talking about how this album changed his life – all during class. Pink Floyd takes me to a place that artists of today refuse to go. And I like it here, on the dark side of the moon.

Nicola Spelman, University of Salford, Greater Manchester, UK

Over the past eight years I have been involved in developing effective strategies for the teaching and assessment of popular music composition, while teaching accompanying courses in style and genre, and music video. Now Programme Leader for the BA (Hons) degree in Popular Music & Recording at Salford, I am currently finishing my PhD which explores constructions of madness, and focuses upon the relationship between anti-psychiatry and 1970s rock.

As an undergraduate on the UK's first popular music degree in 1991, there were certain classic albums, deemed 'essential listening,' a certain familiarity with which was integral to establishing one's credibility as a worthy popular music scholar. Needless to say, Pink Floyd's *The Dark Side of the Moon* was one such album, although my experience of it up until that time had been sadly limited to snapshots of individual tracks. By the end of my first year, with the aforementioned situation remedied, I began to appreciate the more intricate musical and textual elements that ensure the album as a whole adds up to more than the sum of its separate parts. Today, I remain thoroughly impressed by the high level of musicianship exhibited, and the variety of influences it encompasses.

Ger Tillekens, University of Groeningen, The Netherlands

After I finished school at 18, not yet prepared and ready for a job, I decided to go on studying sociology at Leiden University. It was 1968 and since the Beatles' triumphant visit to The Netherlands in 1964, a feeling that something new was on its way, had overcome Dutch youth in general. I certainly was not immune to it. Soon, as this feeling grew, the academy itself was to experience the impact of waves of students demanding a democratisation of the university. Again, I was among them, but from then on it seemed something did change. In 1970, the optimism, which started it all, began to show its first cracks. The Sixties clearly had ended and slowly life began to take a more serious turn. I finished my studies, specializing in the relation between education and the labor market, and went on as a researcher to work on these and related matters at the University of Groningen. Only years later did my mind return to the period and I spent some time studying it from a sociological perspective, pondering over its ethos and its ending.

As a product of the 1960s myself, it seemed quite logical to me to look for answers in the music. And, just as the start of that peculiar period for me is connected to the Beatles, the end of it is associated with Pink Floyd. I can clearly remember myself in 1973, sitting in a record store and listening to *The Dark Side of the Moon* with Sennheiser earphones, and being overcome with that feeling of gloom that I'm now trying to explain.

Sheila Whiteley, University of Salford, Greater Manchester, UK

Now Chair of Popular Music at the University of Salford, Greater Manchester, I am also Publications Officer of the International Association for the Study of Popular Music (IASPM), having previously been their General Secretary (1999–2001). I am General Editor of the IASPM series (Ashgate) and co-editor, with Stan Hawkins and Andy Bennett of *Music, Space and Place. Popular Music and Cultural Identity* (2004). My other publications include *The Space Between the Notes: Rock and the Counter Culture* (1992), *Women and Popular Music:*

Sexuality, Identity and Subjectivity (1998), and *Too Much Too Young. Popular Music, Age and Gender* (2003). I also edited *Sexing the Groove: Popular Music and Gender* (1998) and contributed chapters to *Reading Pop. Approaches to Textual Analysis in Popular Music* (2000), edited by Richard Middleton, and to *'Every Sound There Is'. The Beatles'* Revolver *and the Transformation of Rock and Roll* (2002), edited by Russell Reising.

In 1972, and after an incredible journey across America, from Connecticut to California and back to Hamilton, Ontario we had returned to England where, in September 1971 my daughter Anni was born. *The Dark Side of the Moon* seemed, at the time, to encapsulate my feelings, not least the madness surrounding the deaths of Jim Morrison, Jimi Hendrix and Janis Joplin, but also the general awareness that the ideals of the counter-culture were under attack and that war, the continuing power of capitalism and a general feeling of unease had replaced the heady optimism that was prevalent when we first left for Canada in 1968. At the same time, the strange beauty of *The Dark Side of the Moon* provided both a sense of summing-up and a vision of metaphysical transformation, a heady mix that has remained a constant source of inspiration, not least in these troubling times. The lessons are still there. War, greed and man's inhumanity to man continue unabated and 'The Great Gig in the Sky' remains, for me, one of those very real places that offers both serenity and escape.

As Professor of Popular Music at the University of Salford, I am fortunate in working in an environment that believes strongly in the power of music, the arts and the humanities to effect cultural and social regeneration. My research continues to focus on issues surrounding gender, sexuality, identity and subjectivity, albeit that I still take the occasional excursion into psychedelia and drug-related music. My chapter is dedicated to my grandchildren in the hope that they may contribute towards a more tolerant and forgiving world.

Kenneth Womack, Penn State University, Altoona, USA
Currently Associate Professor of English and Head of the Division of Arts and Humanities at Penn State, I have published widely on 20th-century literature and popular culture. I serve as Editor of *Interdisciplinary Literary Studies: A Journal of Criticism and Theory* and as Co-Editor of Oxford University Press's celebrated *Year's Work in English Studies*. Together with Ruth Robbins and Julian Wolfreys, I co-authored *Key Concepts in Literary Theory* (2002), and I co-edited (with Todd F. Davis) *Mapping the Ethical Turn: A Reader in Ethics, Culture, and Literary Theory* (2001). In 2001, I published *Postwar Academic Fiction: Satire, Ethics, Community*.

I 'discovered' *The Dark Side of the Moon*, as it were, on a lengthy family car trip during the 1970s. After experiencing the unbounded musical terrain of 'Brain Damage' and the intense lyrical rush of 'Eclipse,' I restarted my Panasonic mini-cassette recorder and played the album over and over again for the duration of the holiday and beyond.

Foreword: The Floydian slip

Craig Bailey

That *The Dark Side of the Moon* is one of the most celebrated and successful albums in the history of recorded music is without dispute. In fact, if Pink Floyd had never made an album before *Dark Side*, and never recorded a single note afterward, the band would still end up on rock's shortlist of all-time overachievers.

No one debates the numbers: 741 weeks on the Billboard Hot 200 chart, upwards of 34 million units sold, the third most popular album of all time. The quandary, more often than not, is: Why?

What is it about this particular album, these 10 tracks, this 43-minute aural experience that could possibly justify such truly freakish success? To put it in perspective, compare the 14- to 15-year chart life of *Dark Side* to a more typical 'popular' album, which might measure its longevity in weeks or months, if lucky. How could an album produced more than 30 years ago possibly continue to appeal to enough people today to account for 8,000 new copies sold each year in the new millennium in America alone?

Yet it does.

I have my own notions, though I hesitate to expound too deeply lest anyone accuse me of taking things Floydian too seriously. The truth is this: Anyone who says they have an answer is a liar. Let's face it, if I really knew, I'd surely be too busy *making* the next *Dark Side* to find the time to write about it.

There are theories – some even offered by the Floyd's members, who certainly must be tired of being asked about it by now. To paraphrase: 'The album's eternal, cross-cultural themes, such as money, death and war, tap into a Jungian, archetypal consciousness.'

Then again, 'It just plain rocks,' has a certain poetry, too.

For me, like many, it all started with *Dark Side*. My introduction in earnest to one of rock's most enigmatic bands began with a casual suggestion from a friend outside a bar. The Floyd, he told me one chilly Vermont night, was something worth checking out.

Coincidentally, I tried to return the favor by suggesting he give a listen to *The Alan Parsons Project*. The connection between the two groups – Parsons engineered some Floyd albums, including *Dark Side* – wasn't immediately obvious to me. He eventually passed me a cassette of *Dark Side*, dubbed from his LP. (That dull roar you hear is the grinding teeth of blue-blooded audiophiles everywhere.)

Never one to suggest that home taping – a term that sounds so freckle-faced and pig-tailed in today's age of MP3 and broadband – should be encouraged, I like to think I've paid back with interest any debt to the band and its business associates. The following year I started 'Floydian Slip™,' a weekly radio show devoted to all things Floyd. Fifteen years later, I've probably spent more time listening to *Dark Side* than the band has. And I'd like to think at least a few of those copies of *Dark Side* sliding across the checkout scanner each year are helped along by my show and its associated Web site, floydianslip.com.

It's not an album to be played in small bits. That much is obvious. Not to mention ironic, coming from a jock who has produced several hundred radio shows devoted to a band infamous for making track numbers nearly irrelevant. (The story of *Dark Side* is full of irony, as you'll read.)

In the days of vinyl, determining where one song ended on *Dark Side* and the next began was all but impossible. Drop the needle just about anywhere on Side 2, for example, and your listeners were treated to the entire balance of the album, whether you planned it that way or not. And it was good.

Compact discs have helped many DJs navigate the album, but they haven't changed the fact that this isn't a collection of neat and tidy three-minute hit singles. This is the whole nut. The meaning of life. On a half-shell.

While the album's broad themes might be understood by anyone with an interest in paying attention – requisite pothead jokes aside, Floyd is a thinking person's band before anything else – the effect is quite personal. Floyd might have been playing to a universal audience, but like we say in broadcasting, 'There is no mass audience – only a massive audience of individuals.' When Roger Waters sings, 'I'll see you on the dark side of the moon,' more than a few heads have knowingly nodded in agreement over the years.

Deep themes, brilliant production, and rich, layered compositions aside, it's the mystery of *Dark Side* that, for me, is one of its strongest selling points. The same holds true for the band as a whole. For example, if the cover had featured a posturing studio shot of the band, would the whole package be as appealing? The Floyd's absence from their albums' artwork became one of the band's trademarks. The story is told that back in the day the group's longhaired members could mill about the longhaired crowd before their shows, without ever being recognized. One has to wonder what Floyd would have been like if it had been born in the age of MTV instead of the Age of Aquarius.

The cover of *Dark Side* opts for an image much more open for interpretation than any band photo. The prism – a simple yet elegant demonstration of a basic principle of physics: Light directed through it is split into its basic components. That's the way it is. That's the way it's always been. That's the way it'll always be. Universal.

It's only been on more recent pressings that the album has occasionally included the title and band name printed on the front. That's particularly silly since the prism, one of many designs created throughout the band's history by

Hipgnosis and that design firm's co-founder Storm Thorgerson, has become one of the most familiar icons in the history of rock.

Whatever the album might mean to its listeners, to the band, *Dark Side* represented a beginning and an end. That's only appropriate when you consider the heartbeat that ties the end of *Dark Side* to its beginning – the visual manifestation of which is achieved when opening gatefolds of multiple copies and placing them end-to-end. (Give it a try. It's better documented than trying to pound this round album into the square hole of *The Wizard of Oz* – and it won't take nearly as long.)

Beginning: In 1973, after eight albums, *Dark Side* hoisted Floyd to a plane of popularity few bands experience. The hit single 'Money,' which peaked at number 14 during a 15-week stay on the Billboard chart, helped introduce hordes of people to the band and has become a staple of rock radio.

End: At the same time, *Dark Side* was the last album the band recorded while truly working together as a group. And that hit single? With so many potential dollars at stake when it came to royalty revenues, 'Money' helped stir within the band the very same devilish problems of protecting one's stash that it had set to music. Determining songwriting credits on future projects became more emotional and divisive for the band. When they returned to the studio for 1975's *Wish You Were Here*, the albatross hanging around their collective necks was spelled s-u-c-c-e-s-s.

Floyd would complete four more albums with Roger Waters. The last, 1983's *The Final Cut*, is considered by many to be a Waters solo effort in all but name. A few years following his departure among bad feelings and bruised egos, the remaining members re-formed under the Pink Floyd name. Waters's subsequent legal action and bickering between the two camps threatened to overshadow the band's impressive catalog of work.

Readers who belong to a generation that might have thought it preposterous to spend time analyzing anything as base as a rock record, might be surprised by a book like this. But aside from the level of excitement the album continues to generate so long after its release, I'm not sure there's any better testament to the validity of *The Dark Side of the Moon* than these 14 educated minds from all over the globe waxing philosophic about its place in music history.

A virtue of the creative world seems to be that great works beget great works. If that's the case, savor the rest of these pages.

Craig Bailey produces 'Floydian Slip'™ for Classic Rock Champ (WCPV/WCVR) in Burlington, Vermont. His Web site, floydianslip.com, is one of the most popular and longest running sites devoted to Pink Floyd.

General Editor's preface

The upheaval that occurred in musicology during the last two decades of the twentieth century has created a new urgency for the study of popular music alongside the development of new critical and theoretical models. A relativistic outlook has replaced the universal perspective of modernism (the international ambitions of the 12-note style); the grand narrative of the evolution and dissolution of tonality has been challenged, and emphasis has shifted to cultural context, reception and subject position. Together, these have conspired to eat away at the status of canonical composers and categories of high and low in music. A need has arisen, also, to recognize and address the emergence of crossovers, mixed and new genres, to engage in debates concerning the vexed problem of what constitutes authenticity in music and to offer a critique of musical practice as the product of free, individual expression.

Popular musicology is now a vital and exciting area of scholarship, and the Ashgate Popular and Folk Music Series aims to present the best research in the field. Authors will be concerned with locating musical practices, values and meanings in cultural context, and may draw upon methodologies and theories developed in cultural studies, semiotics, poststructuralism, psychology and sociology. The series will focus on popular musics of the twentieth and twenty-first centuries. It is designed to embrace the world's popular musics from Acid Jazz to Zydeco, whether high tech or low tech, commercial or non-commercial, contemporary or traditional.

Professor Derek B. Scott
Chair of Music
University of Salford

Visit Project Pop:
http://www.music.salford.ac.uk/music2/web/projects/FDTLpop/welcome.htm

Introduction: Life on the dark side of the moon

Russell Reising

> We wanted to come down to earth a bit. I had something I definitely wanted to say.
> – Roger Waters, *Q Magazine*, April 1998

I've been listening to *The Dark Side of the Moon* for more than half of my life, and I find Roger Waters's remark both perfectly understandable and utterly bizarre. My own *Dark Side of the Moon* T-shirt confirms that Pink Floyd is 'still the first in space', and what could be more credible than a mass-produced consumer item? That Waters's vision of coming 'down to earth' results in an album that shifts into the interstellar overdrive within seconds of those first heartbeats and sound collage, and one that almost single-handedly defined the genre of 'space rock', already captures part of *The Dark Side of the Moon*'s visionary complexity, the core of its immense and enduring appeal. Of course, *Dark Side of the Moon* does address the quintessential dilemmas, hopes, and fears of the human condition, and does, therefore, represent a return to earth from the circumambient, and often wordless, heights visited during pieces such as 'Astronomy Domine', 'Interstellar Overdrive', 'Set the Controls for the Heart of the Sun', and 'Saucerful of Secrets'. But the paradox remains, as do the many paradoxes and tensions of the album itself.

For those of us who have worn out vinyl LPs (five different versions exist – original stereo, quadraphonic, and two different picture discs, one with pyramids and one with the prism, and a 30th-anniversary vinyl pressing), and bought the original compact disc, the 20th-anniversary edition, the *Shine On* boxed set, the *Echoes* 'greatest hits' set, and, most recently, the new 30th-anniversary vinyl and SACD editions of *The Dark Side of the Moon*, our repeated listenings have probably etched those 42 minutes and 58 seconds into our heads as deeply and with as many nuances as the fresh grooves on a virgin vinyl pressing. We hear the exact timbre of every note, feel the precise timing of every sound there is on that album, sense the slight pauses between tracks, vibrate to Waters's lyrics and bass strums, soar with Gilmour's guitar solos, glide on Wright's organ and synthesizer waves, and ricochet with Mason's rim shots, roto-tom syncopation, and cymbal crashes. We're convinced that David Gilmour, Nick Mason, Roger Waters, and Richard Wright are not, after all, 'ordinary men'. There's *someone* in *our* heads, and it's probably Clare Torry. For us, Tony Parry's short, intense sax solos take us higher than do those of Clarence 'Big Man' Clemmons. And the roadies and doormen who complement *The Dark Side of the Moon* with their laughs and pithy remarks are rivaled in their contribution to the final experience only by Neil Young's 'road-eyes', who play their vital, albeit hooded, roles in his brilliant *Rust Never Sleeps* performance and video. In retrospect, 1973 probably represents the apogee of the 'prog rock' tradition, with the release of some remarkable (and not all positively so!) prog rock albums, including Emerson, Lake, and Palmer's *Brain Salad Surgery*, Jethro Tull's *A Passion Play*, King Crimson's *Larks' Tongues in Aspic*, Genesis's *Selling England By the Pound*, and Yes's monumental *Tales from Topographic Oceans*, although, even among these milestones, *The Dark Side of the Moon* still reigns supreme.

I personally can't help thinking of the album every time I gaze at a full moon, a lunar-terrestrial fusion of two worlds, one soundless and frigid and the other musical and warm, a fulfilling experience of sensory, if not *exactly* interstellar, overdrive. In a like fashion, those prismatic light waves on the album's cover as well as those dusky pyramids realized by Storm Thorgerson and Hipgnosis on the inside of the album jacket, lurk with the same kind of persistence of memory in the minds of millions of people, like Monet's water lilies, Dali's melting clocks, or Magritte's clouds. In fact, Thorgerson's album cover is regarded as one of the most immediately recognizable and brilliant designs in that genre's history. An amazon.com reviewer known as Brainiac goes so far as to claim that *Dark Side of the Moon* owes its success completely to Thorgerson's design, 'if [*Wish You Were Here*] had [*The Dark Side of the Moon*'s] album cover, *it* would have been the biggest selling album of all-time'. As Thorgerson himself notes in the documentary DVD, his prism and pyramid design responded to three themes: Pink Floyd's famous light shows, a society driven by ambition and greed, and Richard Wright's urging that the art be simple, bold, and dramatic. The resulting concept has provided the motif for prism neckties by Ralph Marlin, tattoos, custom van paint jobs, posters, flags, banners (at flagline.com), T-shirts, lunch boxes, coffee mugs, wall clocks, quartz wristwatches, lapel pins, light-switch backing plates, screen savers, computer monitor wallpaper, and even a stainless steel flask which, the ad assures you, will save you the purchase price in one night if you take your own alcohol rather than paying exorbitant club prices![1] So ubiquitous are the visual traces of Pink Floyd's opus and Thorgerson's design that the on-line science journal *The Scientist* recently featured an article entitled 'The Dark Side of the Genome', a piece that focuses on the fact that we don't really understand the huge majority of the human genome, which is comprised of random shards of genetic information, called 'junk'. Author and Pink Floyd fan Brendan A. Maher even went so far as to title a section of his essay about the 3-gigabase mammalian genomes, 'Three Big Gigs in the Sky'. Accompanying Maher's piece was a tribute to Storm Thorgerson's original album art (reproduced below by kind permission of *The Scientist*).

The members of Pink Floyd might not think about those images much these days, but they constitute a variety of collective unconscious and an archive of images for millions of their fans worldwide.

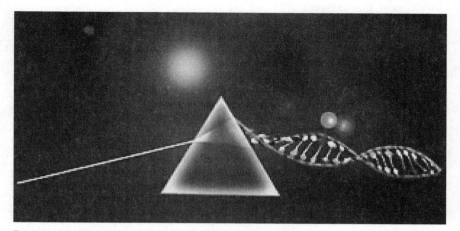

Image reproduced by kind permission of Erika P. Johnson

Like many denizens of the *Dark Side*, I remember the first time I listened to the album as though it were yesterday (30 years have got behind me!). A sophomore at Miami University in southwest Ohio, I was brought back from both the flatlining of the post-1960s doldrums and the (often vacuous) glittering posturings of the then flourishing glam rock by the increasingly vital heartbeat that opens the album. Brian Eno still performed with Roxy Music in those days (also before the release of the other 1973 accomplishments mentioned above), and, in my experience, social circles were defined by whether one slapped Mott the Hoople's *All the Young Dudes*, Stevie Wonder's *Innervisions*, or the Grateful Dead's *Europe 1972* on the turntable at a party (or whether one wore satin or flannel and denim). I still wear denim and still like those albums, but, for me, they represent musical cul-de-sacs, not portals into another dimension. I probably didn't even realize I had become comfortably numb until 'Time' jolted me into a new realm of musical ambition and excitement with its barrage of bells, chimes, alarm clock screams, ominous chords, compositional excess balanced with restraint, and Nick Mason's new roto-toms. That was a new kind of starting gun, an update on the thunderous chords that wake John Lennon on *Revolver*'s 'I'm Only Sleeping'. Indeed, in my own experience, only the Beatles' *Revolver* comes close for sheer musical, emotional, spiritual, and intellectual overload; both albums still leave me simultaneously and equally sapped, inspired, introspective, optimistic, curious, convinced, confused, and provoked.[2] *The Dark Side of the Moon* hit me with all the might of the funkiest riffs from 'Money,' and yet it tantalized me with the deliciously enigmatic yearning common to dream quests. It felt like James Brown's 'Get Up Off of That Thing,' the Beatles' 'Tomorrow Never Knows', and the Rolling Stones' 'Street Fighting Man' fused into one totalizing intellectual and emotional vision. It fused 'music so high you can't get over it' and 'music so low you can't get under it' (the Temptations, 'Psychedelic Shack'). Whether high or low, I, like many listeners, have found *The Dark Side of the Moon* a near perfect soundtrack, almost a perfect *place*, for the many phases of my own moons, and I suspect that most of its listeners, even those, like Johnny Rotten, that wear (or wore) 'I hate Pink Floyd' T-shirts, still do as well.

On a darker side, I also suffered through *The Dark Side of the Moon* ruining a Sonny Rollins performance in Chicago. During the late 1970s and early 1980s, ChicagoFest was held at Chicago's Navy Pier, on which several different stages hosted performers from various musical genres. One night, Rollins's scorchingly cool performance on the jazz stage had to be interrupted for a pre-programmed laser extravaganza flashed through the hot summer night in psychedelic glory to selections from *The Dark Side of the Moon* played at astonishing volume. The moment was fantastic, with Chicago's skyline illuminated in the background and multi-hued laser lights piercing the darkened extension into Lake Michigan, but, when Rollins returned after the interruption to finish his set, he couldn't get it back together and, after a couple of clumsy attempts at rekindling his inspiration, simply walked off the stage in disgust, clearly not liking any of Pink Floyd's colours.

As *Revolver* was for the Beatles, *The Dark Side of the Moon* was Pink Floyd's pivotal album, the fulcrum both for their careers and for the history of popular music. With respect to their earlier work, *The Dark Side of the Moon* represents the culmination of everything they had done before, fusing the individual psychedelic pop gems of *Pipers at the Gates of Dawn* with the extended compositional experiment of *Atom Heart Mother* and the soundscapes and ethical musings of 'Echoes'. Roger Waters notes in the documentary DVD that everything interesting Pink Floyd did after *The Dark Side of the Moon* was about issues and problems that arose for and within the group as a result of what they achieved on *Dark Side*. Of course, the significance of the album hardly depends on its placement within the Pink Floyd corpus. As Craig Bailey puts it on his Floydian Slip website:

> If Pink Floyd had never recorded an album before *Dark Side of the Moon*, and never recorded another after, this 1973 classic would have been more than enough to keep the band in the record books (and in the money) for years to come. (http://www.floydianslip.com/discs/ dsotm.htm)

Rock journalist David Fricke notes during the DVD documentary that *The Dark Side of the Moon* is the ultimate concept album: 'the concept is there; the songs are there; the space between the songs is there, but it doesn't take away any of the imagination.'

In a recent posting on amazon.com, Bill Goldstein (from Stone Mountain, Georgia, USA) indicates the fanaticism that *The Dark Side of the Moon* inspires in its listeners:

> I don't need to ramble on, but this album tells a deep story. I have listened, made love (perfect for that), heard a deep story, and tried to figure why this band made one album out of 10 songs that most bands could have made 5 albums and 50 songs from. It's a

testament to genius, who didn't know that genius existed. These guys give you so many movements in one album that a lesser group would have made several albums out of. I'm 48 years old and I have listened to DARK SIDE OF THE MOON each and every day for the last 30 years. And each time I listen to it, I never fail to hear something new. I'm not stuck in time … the album is.

Another amazon.com listing, this one by 'ChiefSanch' of New Hartford, New York, offers a truly obsessive encapsulation of the album and of each song:

> There is no denying, *Revolver* is a close second to *Dark Side Of The Moon*. There has never been a longer lasting, more popular album ever. Maybe *The White Album*, but more *Dark Side* gets airplay, every college kid I know owns it or has downloaded some of its songs. The fact is, after Sid, Pink Floyd got technically better. Their music was just as memorable, but now it was better. When Roger and David were finally able to collaborate outright, this was what they came up with first. Coincidence, I think not.

ChiefSanch also provides song-by-song commentary, stressing the salient features of each track. For example, 'Speak To Me/Breathe' 'are like something you can't get in a solid drug. It's mellow and just makes you slip into the cushions of your couch, relaxing and just going on some kind of great trip, setting you up for the rest of the album'. '"The Great Gig In The Sky" is like an aria from some rock opera. This chick has some pipes and she sounds like some kind of musical instrument, like Jim Morrison on LA Woman's Cars Hiss By My Window'. 'Any Colour You Like,' ChiefSanch notes, 'is more Wright and this guy is some kind of virtuoso. I would love to make him sit down with a book of Chopin and say "Here, make him look bad." And he could.' Finally, '"Eclipse" is not a song, it is a poem to music. Read the lyrics in the booklet and it is in the form of and is unmistakably a poem.' Of all the online *Dark Side* commentary, David Woods's 'How to Listen to Dark Side of the Moon' (http://alum.wpi.edu/+chekov/ds-howto.html) is, by far, the most engaged and passionate, if not always the most articulate. Running to about nine full typed pages, double-spaced, Woods's site offers a brief history of the album, a breakdown of various ways to experience the album, an anatomy of how to listen to the album for the first time and for many subsequent times, and an analysis of the album into four sections (beginning, early middle, home stretch, and conclusion). To sum up his guidelines, Woods urges us to enjoy the album:

> Once you've gone through all of the main experiences, Dark Side does not then become a boring, run of the mill album. Dark Side is an album you can enjoy over and over again. Listen carefully to the background speech. Pay attention to the incredible details in 'On the Run' and 'Any Colour You Like'. Fall asleep to 'Great Gig in the Sky'. Investing in a CD version of this album is a definite must for those who do not have it. Dark Side is sometimes regarded as the best album ever made. There is good reason. Listen and find out for yourself.

Woods might regard 'Great Gig in the Sky' as a perfect song for falling asleep to, but other Floyd fans from around the world have found *The Dark Side of the*

Moon the perfect album for getting drunk, getting stoned, tripping, having sex, testing new stereo systems (I personally fried the dome tweeter from one of my classic ADS L-810s with the beginning of 'Time' played at showboating volume), meditating, even, a fanatic coterie claims, for watching *The Wizard of Oz*.

Of course, the pulsing heartbeat that opens and closes the album, the frenzy of clocks ticking and alarm blaring from the introduction to 'Time,' the cash register and coin sounds that open 'Money,' and the eerie laughter and background dialogue have all become standard sound effects for radio economic reports, for promotions, and for segues from one commercial pitch to another. In spite of such commercial spin-offs, David Sinclair suggests the apparent lack of commercial potential in the musical dimension of Floyd's masterpiece:

> Plainly unsuitable as an accompaniment for the snappy advertising of beer or jeans, it seems entirely appropriate that the one track from *Dark Side Of The Moon* which has found its way into a TV commercial – keyboard player Richard Wright's haunting interlude for piano and voice, 'The Great Gig In The Sky' – was adopted for a surreal Nurofen painkiller advertisement.

However, *The Dark Side of the Moon* is not everybody's cup of tea. One amazon.com reviewer, 'a music fan from Queens, NY', sums up a whole host of negative reviews that believe *The Dark Side of the Moon* to be boring, overrated, anachronistic, and so on:

> I used to listen to Pink Floyd in High School and college. It is music that is meant to be listened to in an altered state, if you know what I mean :-) But, the fact is, now at the age of 33, I would never pop in a Pink Floyd album. The music is dull, pessimistic, and it drones on folks … All Pink Floyd can say is 'I'll see you on the Dark Side of the Moon.' – Real uplifting. Bottom line: If you are under 22, still in college – buy it. Adults with any Self-worth and sense of hope = don't buy it!

For a bizarre and confused trashing of Pink Floyd in general, consult George Starostin's Reviews website (http://starling.rinet.ru/music/pink.htm), which starts off with the following remarks:

> I HATE PINK FLOYD. No, ladies and gentlemen, my name is not Johnny Rotten. And my motives for disliking this greatest symbol of the Seventies (second only to Led Zeppelin, it seems) differ greatly from those of the Sex Pistols. The Pistols and their kinsmen hated Pink Floyd because of their pretentiousness and overbearing complexity, and in this, it seems, their hate was purely conventional – in fact, they just experienced the same kind of things that they felt towards any other mature or non-mature prog rock band. Me, I have nothing against prog rock in general. But I do have something against Pink in particular. What I honestly feel is that the Floyders are probably the most overrated rock band in man's history. Certainly, they are worthy. A very worthy band – even me, who's not a fan, could go on speaking of their advantages for hours.

By the time he reaches *The Dark Side of the Moon* in his album-by-album evaluation, Starostin's contradictory assessment simply collapses under the weight of its own inconsistencies and buffoonery. For a broad sampling of recent, unprofessional comments on *The Dark Side of the Moon*, browse through any of the 849 user reviews (as of 1/23/2004) posted on amazon.com, and also check out the hundreds of fan ratings on these two sites: http://rateyourmusic.com/ view_album_details/album_id_is_976 and http://www.epinions.com/content_ 28847804036, both of which are web pages devoted to listeners' ratings of the album. There, the passion, adulation, inspiration, awe, incoherent babbling, and sometimes vitriolic loathing surrounding Pink Floyd's magnum opus still evoke much of the excitement that accompanied the album's release in 1973.

Lists of the 'greatest albums of all time' predictably include *The Dark Side of the Moon*, usually near the top. In 1987, *Rolling Stone* ranked *The Dark Side of the Moon* number 35 in its list of the 'Top 100 Albums of the Last 20 Years'. By the edition of 17 October 2002, Floyd's classic had jumped to #11 in *Rolling Stone*'s reader's poll of 'the 100 Greatest Albums of All Time'. *MOJO* readers voted it #8 in their pantheon of 'The 100 Greatest Albums Ever Made' (January 1996 Edition, #27). In *Q*'s 'Top 100 Albums of All Time' list, *Dark Side* charted at #10. The 'Classic Rock 101' radio station in Vancouver, British Columbia places *The Dark Side of the Moon* at the very top of its list of the 'Top 101 Classic Rock Albums' of all time, just ahead of *Led Zeppelin IV* and *Sgt. Pepper's Lonely Hearts Club Band*, *Led Zeppelin II*, and *The Wall* (http://207.34.118.180/station/classic_rock_ albums.cfm). On Springfield (MA), Rock 102's list of the 'Top 102 Albums of All Time, *Dark Side* comes in second, just behind *Sgt. Pepper's* and just ahead of *The Beatles*; *The Wall* ranks sixth (http://www.rock102.com/extra1.shtml). *Dark Side* sits atop the list by KINK FM, with *Abbey Road*, *The Beatles*, and *Sgt. Pepper's* coming in at 2, 3, and 4 (http://www.kink.fm/specials/33Main.asp). Stuart Madow, who lists his credentials as 'co-author of the critically acclaimed book *The Colour of Your Dreams*, former columnist for the popular music magazine *The Indie File*, aspiring Rock Music historian, visionary music producer (at least in his own mind) and all around nice guy!!', ranks *The Dark Side of the Moon* eighth in his pantheon of his favorite and the greatest albums ever made: 'I must have worn out a hundred stylus's playing this album. "Money" is my favorite. Listening to this album on acid is a trip. *Dark Side of the Moon* is possibly the best album ever recorded.' Of course, what Madow doesn't acknowledge is that listening to William Shatner sing 'Mr. Tambourine Man' while on acid is also a trip!

The following website includes *The Dark Side of the Moon*'s ranking in almost 50 polls by writers, critics, musicians, and fans from around the world, many of them hyperlinked to the sites themselves (http://hem.bredband.net/b135745/ A273.htm):

New Musical Express (UK) – All Times Top 100 Albums (1974):   92
Paul Gambaccini – The World Critics' Best Albums of All Time (1977):   135
Dave Marsh and Kevin Stein (USA) – The 40 Best of Album Chartmakers by
    Year (1981):   25

Paul Gambaccini – The World Critics' Best Albums of All Time (1987): 15
Rolling Stone (USA) – Top 100 Albums of the Last 20 Years (1987): 35
Epoca (Italy) – The 100 Best Albums of All Time (1988): 3
Hot Press (Ireland) – The 100 Best Albums of All Time (1989): 47
Slitz (Sweden) – The 50 Best Albums of All Time (1990): 30
Entertainment Weekly (USA) – The 100 Greatest CDs of All Time (1993): 5
The Times (UK) – The 100 Best Albums of All Time (1993): 17
Musik Express/Sounds (Germany) – The 100 Masterpieces (1993): 79
Guitarist (UK) – The Top 50 Most Influential Guitar Albums of All Time
    (1994): 29
Nieuwe Revu (Netherlands) – Top 100 Albums of All Time (1994): 80
Radio WXPN (USA) – The 100 Most Progressive Albums (1996): 15
Alternative Melbourne (Australia) – The Top 100 Rock/Pop Albums
    (1996): 15
Viceversa (Italy) – 100 Rock Albums (1996): 3
Guardian (UK) – The 100 Best Albums Ever (1997): 37
Max Magazine (Germany) – The 50 Best Albums of All Time (1997): 9
Rolling Stone (Germany) – The Best Albums of 5 Decades (1997): 101
Q (UK) – The 50 Best Albums of the 70s (1998): 2
Berlin Media (Germany) – The 100 Best Albums of All Time (1998): 70
Amazon.com (USA) – The 10 Best Albums by Decade (1999): 6
Gear (USA) – The 100 Greatest Albums of the Century (1999): 22
Aftenposten (Norway) – Top 50 Albums of All Time (1999): 35
Panorama (Norway) – The 30 Best Albums of the Year 1970–98 (1999): 3
Aloha (Netherlands) – The 50 Best Albums of All Time (1999): 17
Wiener (Austria) – The 100 Best Albums of the 20th Century (1999): 32
Showbizz (Brazil) – 100 CDs of All Time (1999): 19
Q (UK) – The 100 Greatest British Albums Ever (2000): 11
Plásticos y Decibelios (Spain) – The 80 Best Albums of All Time (2000): 7
The Review, University of Delaware (USA) – 100 Greatest Albums of All Time
    (2001): 20
VH1 (USA) – The 100 Greatest Albums of R 'N' R (2001): 51
Classic Rock (UK) – The 50 Greatest Rock Albums of All Time (2001): 2
Complete Book of the British Charts (UK, 2001) – Neil Warwick's Top 10
    Albums: 4
Platekompaniet (Norway) – Top 100 Albums of All Time (2001): 37
CDNOW (Japan) – 100 Essential Albums (2001?): 25
Rod Underhill (USA) – The Top 100 Rock/Pop Albums (2003): 29

No particular order in the following lists:

Zig Zag (UK) – Gillett & Frith's 100 Essential Rock Albums (1975)
Popster (Italy) – The 100 Best Albums of the 70s (1979)

Rolling Stone Album Guide, 5 Stars Albums (USA, 1983)
Bill Shapiro (USA) – The Top 100 Rock Compact Discs (1991)
Life (USA) – 40 Years of Rock & Roll, the Album of the Year 1952–91 (updated 1995)
Rolling Stone (USA) – The Essential 200 Rock Records (1997)
List by Asian Critics – 100 Essential Albums (1998?)
List by Japanese Critics – 200 Essential Albums (1998?)
Mauro Ronconi (Italy) – The 200 Best Albums of the 20th Century (1998)
IE (USA) – 50 Great Albums, a Rock Time Capsule (1999)
Pause & Play (USA) – Albums Inducted into a Time Capsule, One Album per Week
The Recording Academy Grammy Hall of Fame Albums and Songs (USA, 2001)
Rock & Folk (France) – The Best Albums from 1963 to 1999 (1999)
Allan Kozinn, AVGuide (USA) – The 100 Greatest Pop Albums of the Century (2000)
MOJO (UK) – The Mojo Collection, The Ultimate Music Companion (2000)
The Sun (Canada) – The Best Albums from 1971 to 2000 (2001)
Stuart Maconie's Critical List on BBC Radio 2 (UK) – One Album Added Each Week
Blender (USA) – 500 CDs You Must Own Before You Die (2003)
Pause & Play (USA) – 10 Albums of the 70's (2003)

Various rating systems:

Robert Christgau (USA) – Consumer Guide: Album Grade B
Rolling Stone Album Guide, Ratings 1–5 Stars (USA, 1992):   5 Stars
José Ramón Pardo (Spain) – *The 1000 Best Pop-Rock Albums*, Ratings 1–5 (1997):   5
MusicHound Rock and R&B (USA) – Album Ratings 0–5 Bones (1998–99):   5
Paul Roland (UK) – CD Guide to Pop & Rock, Album Ratings 1–5 Stars (2001):   5
All Music Guide (USA) – Album Ratings 1–5 Stars: 5
Martin C. Strong (UK) – *The Great Rock Discography*, 6th edition, Ratings 1–10:   10
Virgin Encyclopedia of Popular Music (UK) – Album Ratings 1–5 Stars (2002):   5

All in all, a strange and mixed set of results for an album that still sells hundreds of thousands of copies per year (400,000 in 2002), everything from several #1 rankings to lists that don't include *The Dark Side of the Moon* at all. For example, *New Musical Express*'s Writers Poll voted *Dark Side* #92 in 1974 (just above

Doctor John's *Gris-Gris* and just below Big Brother and the Holding Company's *Cheap Thrills*), but the album didn't even make the top 100 in either the 1985 or 1993 polls. Recall that in 1987, *Rolling Stone* had ranked *Dark Side* only the 35th greatest album of the last 20 years, but their readers pushed it up to #11 in 2002, making it a much bigger fish in the largest possible pond! And in 'Paul Gambaccini – The World Critics' Best Albums of All Time' polls listed above, *The Dark Side of the Moon* charted only #135 in 1977, but by 1987 had soared up to #15. Either Gambaccini finally listened to the album, or the 120 previously listed 'above' *The Dark Side of the Moon* lost whatever sonic Viagra had previously pumped them up. Or, maybe he simply caught up to the millions of fans worldwide who believe *The Dark Side of the Moon* is one of, if not the, greatest accomplishments in popular music.

The present collection includes essays by men and women who remember the day *The Dark Side of the Moon* was released in 1973, some by scholars and critics who may have been conceived during particularly intimate experiences of 'Great Gig in the Sky' (it has, of course, been voted 'best song to make love to'), and by many in between. Our contributors are men and women from Canada, England, Finland, the Netherlands, the United States, and New Zealand. Most, but not all, teach at universities, others are students. We range in age from 19 to 60-something, with representatives of every decade in between. Our essays address musical, philosophical, psychological, historical, thematic, and performative dimensions of *The Dark Side of the Moon*, and many fertile intersections link these various strong contributions. Four essays of a historical, evaluative, and narrative emphasis come under the rubric '"Any colour you like": General discussions'. These pieces all, albeit loosely, address large questions about *The Dark Side of the Moon* and its historical significance and influence. They establish some of the themes and issues to which many of the other essays will return. '"Everything under the sun is in tune": Musical and structural discussions' includes three technical, though eminently accessible, musicological essays, all by music theorists. While the terminology of some of these contributions may seem daunting, we have done all we can to make them of interest to the general reader as well as to the musical specialist. Finally, '"There's no dark side of the moon": Theoretical discussions' joins together four remarkable essays on the humanistic dimension of Pink Floyd's accomplishment on *The Dark Side of the Moon*.

Each section's essays speak to each other in productive ways. In Part I, for example, Kimi Kärki and Matthew Bannister both address the significance and implications of Pink Floyd's technological mastery and their innovative stage presence/ performances, while the essay by Lee Barron and Ian Inglis meshes with Ben Schleifer's discussion by situating *The Dark Side of the Moon* with other significant cultural artifacts. Likewise, in Part II, Nicola Spelman's essay on anti-psychiatry and Kenneth Womack's discussion of Levinas's ethics intersect in fascinating and important ways. Finally, for those wishing to read virtually every substantial discussion ever written about *The Dark Side of the Moon*, Matthew Bartkowiak's substantial and carefully annotated bibliography summarizes and evaluates scores of influential (and some obscure) reviews, interviews, and general discussions of the album.

These essays occasionally contradict each other, and, like the critics and reviewers quoted above, the contributors don't necessarily agree on any particular interpretation or evaluation of *The Dark Side of the Moon*. Rather than trying to smooth out differences, disagreements, and contradictions among these essays, I have chosen to let them stand on their own, speaking to each other, provoking dialogue and debate among ourselves and, we all hope, among you, our readers. To paraphrase Walt Whitman, 'do we contradict ourselves? Very well then, we contradict ourselves. We are large, we contain multitudes' (apologies to *Song of Myself*). Actually it's *The Dark Side of the Moon* that reaches both upward into the cosmos and downward into our collective souls. We, the contributors to *'Speak to Me': The Legacy of Pink Floyd's The Dark Side of the Moon*, have embraced those energies and have done our best to illuminate them. That Pink Floyd's masterpiece has spawned differences of opinion for over 30 years is only one testament to its ambitions and its importance.

Notes

1. See websites such as half.com and ebay for examples of products *The Dark Side of the Moon* has inspired.
2. See Russell Reising (ed.) (2002), *'Every Sound There Is:' The Beatles' Revolver and the Transformation of Rock and Roll* (Aldershot: Ashgate), for my collection of essays on that Beatles masterpiece. Many of the contributors to this volume participated in that project as well.

Part I

'Any colour you like'
General discussions

Chapter 1

On the waxing and waning: a brief history of *The Dark Side of the Moon*

Russell Reising

> The Goddess Astarte ... had more phases than the moon. She knew the dark side of the moon like the palm of her hand.
>
> – Tom Robbins, *Skinny Legs and All*

What is this thing called *The Dark Side of the Moon*? And how did Pink Floyd readjust their controls, steering away from the sun and towards the dark side of the moon? How did they transport themselves from the lush submarine environments of 'Echoes', the final cut on *Meddle*, to the airless aridity of lunar space? Surely, titles like 'Interstellar Overdrive', 'Astronomy Domine', and 'Set the Controls for the Heart of the Sun', had already established the Floyd as spacey, otherworldly? The essays in this collection address this question in various ways, but I think fundamental questions will remain as to the album's significance, endurance, appeal, and essence. Is it a mere collection of fragments pieced together over a couple of years, or is it the apotheosis of album coherence and grand unification? Sound or light? Group effort or realization of individual genius? Morbid descent into lunacy or inspiring testament to transcendence and empathy? Adolescent psychodrama or mature ethical statement? Frenzied rush or mellow soporific? Frigidly esoteric, impersonal, and abstruse 'space music' or pumped-up blues funk? Despairing personal wail or bracing political statement? Erotic or violent or spiritual or philosophical or ethical or psychological or existential or solar or lunar or terrestrial? None of these either/or propositions does any justice to *The Dark Side of the Moon*, and the case is better understood as both both/and and either/or for each of these dichotomies. Like the Beatles in *Revolver*, Pink Floyd on *The Dark Side of the Moon* set their controls for the heart of the moon, settling for nothing less than a total apprehension of life and what it means to be human. And that means that no dividing lines are tidy; perhaps none is possible.

The Dark Side of the Moon, like many great artistic achievements, cannot be rendered as regular and predictable as the groove on vinyl, the magnetic clusters on a VHS tape, or the digital bits 'burned' on a CD or DVD. In fact, the suite waxed and waned into and out of its 1973 realization in several distinct phases, many of which exist in easily found (and often downloaded) commercial audio and video forms. As David Gilmour noted in an interview with Chris Welch in 1973, 'A lot of the material had already been performed when we recorded it, and usually we go into the studio and write and record at the same time. We started writing the basic idea ages ago, and it changed quite a lot. It was pretty rough to begin with' (MacDonald, 1997, p. 300). Beginning with the tentative experiments we see and hear on Pink Floyd's *Live in Pompeii* video, through the Earls Court *Pulse* and Roger Waters's *In the Flesh* audio and video documents, *The Dark Side of the Moon* has morphed through a series of phases as lively and fecund as anything found this side of the Sea of Fertility. My goal here is to organize and account for the significance and meaning of the phases *The Dark Side of the Moon* has passed through and to speculate on what they reveal about the overall impact of Pink Floyd's accomplishment. Since most of the other essays in this collection focus on the 1973 recorded version of *The Dark Side of the Moon*, approaching it from various cultural, musicological, and thematic perspectives, I will focus on the earlier and later performances of Pink Floyd's suite, including those performed after the official breakup of Pink Floyd. Of course, my commentary on these alternative moons carries with it my sense of the work's essence.

One small step for Floyd

The video *Pink Floyd Live at Pompeii* (dir. Adrian Maben, 1972) contains the earliest recorded traces of Pink Floyd's work on *The Dark Side of the Moon*. In addition to documenting their performance amidst the ruins of the ancient stadium, the video captures the band members chatting, responding to interview questions, and, most importantly for our purposes, in the recording studio, experimenting on guitar, keyboard, and synthesizer riffs that will eventually become *The Dark Side of the Moon*. Beginning and ending musically with 'Echoes', *Live at Pompeii* captures Pink Floyd at the apogee of their pre-*Dark Side* power, basking in their sense of significance and playing such early classics as 'Set the Controls for the Heart of the Sun' and 'Saucerful of Secrets' as well as much of *Meddle*, all for an audience of their sound and recording assistants, a film crew, and the breathless ghosts from the Vesuvian-scorched city. In an interview included as an extra feature of the 'Director's Cut' DVD, Maben refers to his film as an 'anti-Woodstock', indicating that he believed the audience-less quality of his *Live at Pompeii* broke away from the clichéd concert film convention of focusing on audience reactions to ordinary stage performances. Interview footage incorporated into the film plumbs the group's and each individual member's identity, their sense of nostalgia for their earliest days together, and their sense of where they're heading musically. Roger Waters muses on the group's relationship to technology, and David Gilmour assures viewers that Pink Floyd isn't a 'drug orientated group'. At other times, the entire production suggests nothing more than a parodic Floydian revisitation of the Beatles' early stadium shows or Grand

Funk Railroad's sold-out stadium extravaganzas. Pink Floyd, however, play to an empty coliseum where, could their echoes still be heard, the agony of dying gladiators would have surpassed the din of screaming fans. The Beatles and the Monkees capered, as though joined at the hip, for cameras in movies and television shows. Pink Floyd, however, cavort among lava vents and bursts of steam from the still volatile topography and play their inimitable brand of psychedelic music to film footage of ruined Pompeii mosaics and exploding volcanoes. This is clearly rock documentary with a difference, filmed even before Pink Floyd themselves explode with the release of *The Dark Side of the Moon*.

Punctuating his presentation of Pink Floyd playing Pompeii, filmmaker Maben inserts several snippets of early *Dark Side* materials from Waters, Gilmour, and Wright, tucking them amid Floyd's performances, interviews, and endless shots of Nick Mason's drumming and an equal number of their equipment, clearly stenciled 'PINK FLOYD. LONDON'. The film documents Pink Floyd playing and reproducing their unearthly sounds without any of the appurtenances of studio technology, and the version of 'Saucerful of Secrets' performed entirely live on guitar, drums, gong, grand piano, bass, and organ is a bracing reminder that Floyd, unlike many highly technologized groups with elaborate recording regimens, could always perform their work on stage.

Maben juxtaposes such exciting live footage with their preliminary work on materials that eventually become *The Dark Side of the Moon*, filming those scenes, quite understandably, under the artificial lighting and within the confines of recording studios, signaling, perhaps, a new departure in Floyd's musical and technological odyssey. A significant amount of the interview footage addresses the possibility that the band have become extensions of their equipment rather than the other way around. Waters comments: 'it's just a question of using the available tools when they're available. And more and more there are all kinds of electric goodies which are available for people like us to use.' Gilmour expands on Waters's notion by adding, 'I mean it's all extensions of what's coming out of our heads. You've got to have it inside your head to be able to get it out at all anyway.' Then, during Roger Waters's experimenting with a synthesized portion of 'On the Run', the first actual musical references to *The Dark Side of the Moon*, he comments, 'it's like saying give a man a Les Paul guitar, and he becomes Eric Clapton. It's not true. Give a man an amplifier and synthesizer and he doesn't become … us.' Slightly later in the film, the camera lingers on Rich Wright playing some of the piano line to 'Us and Them', with Wright and Waters then discussing precisely what it is that Rick is doing in that section.

The most remarkable and extended passages in which the film samples *The Dark Side of the Moon* occur in tandem with the group's commentary about their past and future as a group. The segment begins with Waters recording the bass line to 'Eclipse', a scene that fades into him also discussing the general economics of the rock music industry. The film then morphs into Nick Mason discussing the way in which Pink Floyd still, for many people, functions as a nostalgic reminder of 'their childhood of 1968, the underground in London, free concerts in Hyde Park, and so on'. David Gilmour then counters the common notion that Pink Floyd was a very 'drug-orientated group' by assuring the viewers, 'Of course, we're not. You can trust us.' Back to Nick Mason, once again, who notes that Pink Floyd is 'doing other things [now], cause [they] want to do other things'. At that point, the film returns to Rick Wright recording the final piano lines to 'Us and Them'. Quite a remarkable retrospective portion of the film, and, quite significantly, Maben chooses to frame the most extended and serious commentary on the group's history and sense of themselves with their work on *The Dark Side of the Moon*. Just before the final two live numbers, Maben includes one more view of the *Dark Side* recording sessions, this time, David Gilmour recording two different guitar sections for 'Brain Damage'. Gilmour and Waters discuss whether the work is too 'toppy', Gilmour asks for a second take, and then, providing a coda for the *Dark Side* footage included in *Pink Floyd: Live at Pompeii*, Gilmour complains that he has to re-record another section by asking, 'Christ, where would rock and roll be without feedback?'

It is in his framing of the 'Director's Cut' of *Live at Pompeii* that director Maben most clearly accentuates his film's relationship with *The Dark Side of the Moon*. In fact, virtually every significant difference between the original VHS and the DVD version adds to the sense of Pink Floyd on the verge of the *The Dark Side of the Moon*. Even the blasted landscapes of Pompeii come more and more to resemble scenes from the dark side of the moon. Most notably, however, Maben frames his film with a sonic tribute to *The Dark Side of the Moon*, and the only sounds heard against a totally black screen at the very beginning and very ending of the film are a heartbeat and slow rhythmic breathing, clearly recalling the album's first two tracks, 'Speak to Me' and 'Breathe'. In another framing device, Maben includes spacey shots of planets and various forms of cosmic debris flying through space, finally resolving into a close-up of the lunar surface and the earth emerging from behind the moon. In other words, *Pink Floyd Live at Pompeii, The Director's Cut* begins and ends with the earth being eclipsed by the moon.

For their pre-1973 live performances of what was then called *Eclipse*, Pink Floyd open with the signature heartbeat effects and some industrial rumblings before opening up to David Gilmour guitar strums and Roger Waters's thunderous bass rumbles. Absent is Richard Wright's keyboard work that eventually comes to dominate the earliest minutes of *The Dark Side of the Moon*. Pink Floyd perform, and Gilmour certainly sings, 'Breathe' at what seems, in retrospect, glacial slowness, a pace relieved by the guitar-strum dominated transitional piece 'On the Run', which sounds more like a jazzy guitar jam, or like something reminiscent of 'Interstellar Overdrive'. Gilmour's guitar work is unrelated to the heavily synthesized work Wright contributed to the recorded version. In 1972, however, the keyboardist limits his input to a very jazzy piano accompaniment punctuating Gilmour's frenetic strums, while Waters and Nick Mason set down a rapid, yet conventional beat, with Mason's few flourishes coming on the high-hat cymbals.

As the suite moves towards 'Time' (without any of the airplane crash effects or jangling clock sounds!), Wright contributes more synthesized machine-like effects, all of which fade out of audibility, giving way to Mason's roto-tom percussive introduction to 'Time', when Gilmour's and Wright's playing builds up to the vocals. Mason complicates his roto-tom work, by adding a backbeat that industrializes the opening bars of his drumming. Floyd protract the instrumental introduction to 'Time', but the piece never quite escalates in intensity of foreboding, and Gilmour and Waters sing a vocal duet that lumbers out in mournful, nearly lugubrious, strains. The pace of these early versions shocks the listener used to the album and subsequent performance versions, a pace that Gilmour's guitar solo reproduces. Most of the notes are there, as is the general trajectory of the solo, but Gilmour slurs most of his playing, and the pace sounds like a 45rpm record played at 33⅓ rpms. Gilmour and Waters achieve interesting vocal effects, with one frequently either singing slightly behind the other or adding wordless harmony to the primary vocal line. The reprise of 'Breathe', with Gilmour's 'Home, home again' line, maintains this pace before easing into what constitutes one of the most remarkable differences between these preliminary versions and the 1973 recorded piece.

As the 'Breathe' reprise fades out, Wright fades in playing what can only be described as funereal church music with pipe organ strains accentuated by rolling bass. In the background of what was then called 'the mortality piece', Waters chants in prayerful tones and inserts televangelistic solicitations, before actually reciting 'The Lord's Prayer' to Wright's organ work. As he concludes the so-called mortality section, Wright's playing resembles Keith Jarrett's work on *Hymns and Spheres*, surging with spiritual atmospherics and intricate keyboard work. Prior to the 1973 recording, no Clare Torry or any other female vocal work eases the performance out of 'Time' and into the syncopated coin sounds introducing 'Money', with rhythmic complexity added by a tambourine. Again, the vocal presentation proceeds in carefully modulated and very slow pace until Wright sets out on a solo that will eventually be replaced by Dick Parry on the saxophone. Here also, Gilmour's guitar solo, which bursts out on the record and in post-1973 concert performances, eases out of Wright's keyboard work. Gilmour eventually does rise to some soaring intensity near the end of the solo and approximates the jazzy rendition he played live, up to and including the *Pulse* performance. These 1972 performances already reveal a Pink Floyd experimenting with their opus. In the Sapporo, Japan versions, they eliminate the final vocal verse of 'Money', and the conclusion of Gilmour's solo more or less coincides with the end of the song. In one of the London shows, however, the structure of 'Money', and the segue from 'Money' into 'Us and Them' have already taken on the colouring and embellishments of the recorded version.

'Us and Them' begins with Gilmour playing more than he will by 1973, and both Gilmour and Waters provide vocal effects that will be replaced by more of Wright's keyboards and synthesizers. It is in the bridge sections of 'Us and Them' that the suite approaches the edge and intensity of the recorded performance. Gilmour and Waters's voices, as well as the entire instrumentation, surge out of the mellow vocals and keyboard melody with a sense of uncontrollable rage and bitterness. In these moments, we can hear the glimmerings of the more symphonic presentation that will come to define 'Us and Them' from 1973 onward.

At this point, Pink Floyd seems to have begun realizing the potential of the manic juxtapositions that characterize their mature realization of *The Dark Side of the Moon*. They don't fully exploit the tonal potential of these shifts and surges, but they have clearly discovered what will become the musical and atmospheric essence of their vision. Their total vision for *Dark Side* lurks within these 1972 performances, but not until Pink Floyd harness the manic, nearly bipolar, shifts in tone, intensity, and musical interplay does the emotional and psychological resonance of their opus emerge.

The moon in full

Pink Floyd closed their *Pulse* tour by performing and filming *The Dark Side of the Moon* in its entirety, recovering what must have been some of the excitement of their initial 1972 and 1973 inaugural shows, while altering the piece with a beefed-up ensemble, new lighting effects, and films. Of course, Roger Waters is conspicuously absent. Nevertheless, Pink Floyd and director David Mallet re-create much of *The Dark Side of the Moon*'s essence, with Dick Parry still working his sax magic and a trio of brilliant background singers wailing away on 'The Great Gig in the Sky', which actually surpassed the versions I heard in 1974 and 1975. As spectacle and as musical performance, the *Pulse* rendition of *The Dark Side of the Moon* leaves little to be desired; moreover, the filmed version might be the greatest concert video ever made – an honor often reserved for the Talking Heads' *Stop Making Sense* (1984) or, since its 2002 release on DVD, Neil Young's *Rust Never Sleeps* (1979).

Directed by David Mallet, with lighting designs by Marc Brickman and screen footage directed by Storm Thorgerson and Caroline Wright, *Pulse* utilizes dazzling yet unobtrusive camera work and editing to re-create the concert experience of *The Dark Side of the Moon*. Mallet presents his vision from something akin to an omniscient, we might call it psychedelic, point of view. Cameras zoom in for close-ups of intricate fret work of guitar solos, percussion flourishes by Nick Mason, the emotional delight of vocalists in action, the pointedly satisfied facial expressions of the band as they communicate throughout the performance, and frequently of the round screen upon which they project Thorgerson's accompanying video segments. Wider-angle shots capture groups of performers – Rick Wright and Jon Carron on keyboards, all three backing vocalists, Nick Mason and Gary Wallis doing their percussion groove thing. Still wider shots illuminate the vast space of Earls Court for views of the entire stage ensemble and spectacular lighting and laser effects that contribute to the concert experience. Even Pink Floyd's stage design contributes to the overall impact, with an arch creating a half-moon environment, and the large, circular screen poised overhead symbolizing the moon at its fullest, though certainly not darkest. *Pulse*, as film, gives viewers every possible best seat in the house for every possible musical and visual moment.

What those moments amount to is the definitive statement of *Dark Side of the Moon* and its complex vision of human existence. As in the 'old days', Floyd performs *The Dark Side of the Moon* as the second half of their show, with the intermission silence broken by the increasingly vital heartbeat pulsing and the active electrocardiogram projected on the large circular screen just above and behind the performers. Adding equally to the illusion, Pink Floyd close out their first set with a tour de force performance of 'One of These Days', setting the stage for something resembling the Floydian experience circa 1973. At some point during the introductory sonic gestures of 'Speak to Me', the heartbeat graphic morphs into a human eye that in turn expands into a visual of cosmic starfields before settling into the signature image of the cratered surface of a full moon at the first notes of 'Breathe'. Such blending of visceral human imagery with interstellar spaces sets the tone of *The Dark Side of the Moon*, which traffics in paradox and contrast until the heartbeat returns to close the album at the finale of 'Eclipse'.

The full complement of this greatly beefed-up 'Pink Floyd', consisting of Gilmour, Mason, and Wright, each supplemented by an additional player (one each on keyboards, guitar, and percussion), Guy Pratt on bass, Dick Parry on sax, and three female backup singers, doesn't appear until 'Time'. In fact, during 'On the Run', performed to the original video scenes from a hospital and an airport, the only band members we see are Richard Wright and Jon Carron backlit and perched behind their keyboards and synthesizers, looking like a Tangerine Dream concert from 1973.

The musical buildup in 'Time' is accompanied by a video of clock mechanisms, Daliesque timepieces, and a skeletal robotic figure striking a drum in a pose that exactly mimics one of Nick Mason's during the concert. This transformation of the human into the machine, this memento mori reminder of death at the heart of 'time' meshes perfectly with the menacing guitar and roto-tom lead-in, setting the anxious tone that lurks behind this song and much of the album. But when Pink Floyd explode in full musical and visual grandeur, the performative brilliance of the audio/visual extravaganza overwhelms any morbidity with sensual saturation and excitement. Gilmour's vocals maintain the ferocity of his more youthful days, and Richard Wright's mellow vocal interludes perfectly balance the emotional complexity of the song.

The lighting and filming of 'Time' reveal the essence of its place within the emotional and conceptual economy of *The Dark Side of the Moon*. At various times, the camera lingers on the very sensuous figures of the backup singers, now clad entirely in black (during the first half of the *Pulse* show, they wear all-white), and the iconographic complexity of this simultaneously erotic and deathly trio (almost like the Three Fates of Greek mythology) captures the contradictory pulls of Pink Floyd's composition. However, it is the lighting (and filming) of Nick Mason's drumming that links 'Time' with the general dynamic of the suite. Part of the light show captured by the *Pulse* cinematographers situates Mason within a chromatic and geometric scheme that resembles nothing so much as a cathedral's stained glass vibrating with the music, and it is this insinuation of the sacred within the earthly, the erotic, and the mortal nature of human existence that captures the philosophical (and, I would argue, quintessentially psychedelic) thrust of Waters's lyrics in their explosive synergy with the musical performance and the illumination of Pink Floyd's stage show. All this even before the explicit, though wordless, meditation on death and mortality of 'The Great Gig in the Sky'.

Pink Floyd and their cinematographers exploit and develop the same conceptual and thematic synergy throughout the *Dark Side* set. The erotic charge added visually by the black-clad trio of Sam Brown, Durga McBroom, and Claudia Fontaine is surpassed only by their soulful wailing during 'The Great Gig in the Sky', where each, bathed exclusively in either blue or red light, takes her turn at a segment of Clare Torry's original. Like a choir in a Baptist church *and* the celebrants of a pagan ritual, the singers feel each note with an intensity that transcends either spirituality or sexuality. We can't tell if the gigantic waves projected on the screen above them promise orgasm or threaten obliteration, but we do realize that these women hold the keys to the infinite reaches of the cosmos as well as to the fluid fields and tidal forces out of which human life emerged. During one lovely moment, the camera captures David Gilmour gazing in awe (perhaps desire) up at the women, joining the concert or cinematic audience in their delicious appreciation of the performances.

The general direction of *The Dark Side of the Moon* up to 'Money' is primarily personal and individual. With the flip of the original LP, the suite itself switches into communal concerns – the power of money and the overtly political visions of 'Us and Them' and 'Brain Damage'. Indeed, after flashing images of coins, gold bars, and other varieties of filthy lucre to accompany the sound collage at the beginning of 'Money', the film projected overhead reflects befurred women, financial district bankers, Rolls Royces, yachts, and opulent estates, with an occasional glimpse of the original LP spinning on a turntable. In 'Money', the same women who just completed the spiritual exercise of 'The Great Gig in the Sky' turn sultry as they slither, dip, and dance around Dick Parry during his sax parts. In a matter of seconds, then, the stage is transformed from a site of spiritual, almost religious, devotion into a scene of debauchery, an orgy celebrating the debased world of money, status, and corruption. Adopting a pose that recalls his admiring gaze at Claudia Fontaine near the end of her segment of 'The Great Gig in the Sky', David Gilmour, turned hipster, snaps his fingers and leers at the trio as they transform the spiritualized wails of 'Great Gig' into the overtly seductive moans and purrs they add to a vocal interlude. To invert a biblical aphorism, the way up ('The Great Gig in the Sky') was the way down ('Money').

'Us and Them', of course, bewails various dichotomies that plague what is obviously envisioned as a fallen social world – us/them, with/without, war, power, and all the inequitable hierarchies that such divisions entail. However, it does so in the quietest, most elegant, majestic, and austere composition on the album. Perhaps owing to its original conception as the soundtrack to Antonioni's *Zabriskie Point*, where it was composed for 'the violent sequence', 'Us and Them' works its musical magic through litotic simplicity. As opposed to the images of glamorous affluence or political power that accompany 'Money' and 'Brain Damage', film footage of ordinary people, workers, and miners, all in huge crowds, yet all walking in what appears to be lonely insularity runs throughout 'Us and Them'. Hanging on in quiet desperation seems still to be the English way, but, given the wide range of global imagery that accompanies the *Pulse* performance of *The Dark Side of the Moon*, suggesting that quiet desperation is now, pandemically, the modern way. Moreover, this footage captures crowds rather than individuals without lingering on any particular face or expression. Given this separation between the viewer and the reflected masses of humanity, we're never sure if we are 'Us' or 'Them'. It is in this montage of visual images that the video accompaniment to *The Dark Side of the Moon* and the ineluctably visual nature of the *Pulse* video complicate the very essence of the work. Is *Dark Side* an internal document, mirroring the alienation we all feel, or is it ideological critique from a detached perspective? In other words, are we among the crowds feeling as they feel, or are we somehow above it all, yet compassionately feeling for them?

'Any Colour You Like' is Pink Floyd's most explicitly nostalgic performative gesture. Whereas dazzling, state-of-the-art light and laser effects complement their playing throughout the rest of their *Dark Side* performance (indeed, the entirety of their *Pulse* presentation), 'Any Colour You Like' receives a much simpler treatment, a 1960s-style light show, created with oil, bubbles and glass, reminiscent of Jefferson Airplane or Big Brother and the Holding Company concerts at the Fillmore or Winterland in 1968, primarily in the same pastels refracted in stained-glass style during 'Time'. In other words, such visual imagery pre-dates even the original performances of *The Dark Side of the Moon* and position Floyd's masterpiece relative to the history of experiments in sound and color from the entire psychedelic era. Like the thematic complexity of *The Dark Side of the Moon*'s lyrics and music, the *Pulse* light show, then, aims at nothing less than a totalizing vision, a history of sorts, of psychedelic concert production, from the simplest experiments of the mid- and late sixties to the perfectly synchronized light, film, and laser sophistication of the 21st century. In another historical gesture, Pink Floyd updated the video montage that accompanies 'Brain Damage' to include such post-1973 villains as Richard Nixon, Idi Amin, Ronald Reagan, George Bush, Margaret Thatcher, John Major, Bill Clinton, Imelda Marcos, Saddam Hussein, Pol Pot, and Oliver North; and, to tell the truth, they make the images of Stalin and Castro seem almost benign by comparison, especially when the video shows Bill Clinton playing the saxophone and Imelda Marcos singing during uncomfortably synchronized moments of the song. The interplay between the nostalgic psychedelic imagery of 'Any Colour You Like' and the updated and very political imagery of 'Brain Damage' again anchors the powerful synthetic dimension of *The Dark Side of the Moon* just prior to its magnificent culmination in 'Eclipse' when a close-up image of the moon is superimposed over the entire stage.

By the way, which one's dark?

Roger Waters's *In the Flesh* tour, CD, and video represent what remains, at this point, the final Floydian presentation of *The Dark Side of the Moon*. While editing his opus slightly, Waters and his band introduce and frame their second set with the dominant themes from *Dark Side*, 'Breathe (In the Air)', 'Time', and 'Money', followed by selections from Waters's solo projects, especially a series of pieces from *Amused to Death*, including 'The Bravery of Being Out of Range', and the shimmeringly beautiful and poignantly enraged 'It's a Miracle' and 'Amused to Death', then followed by 'Brain Damage', and finally 'Eclipse'. The *Dark Side* selections come on after the intermission, just as in Floyd shows I saw, with the heartbeat and sound effects breaking the chaotic silence between sets. The omission of 'On the Run', 'The Great Gig in the Sky', and 'Us and Them' more or less erases Rich Wright from audibility in Waters's sampling, eliminating the keyboard magician's lyrical and synthesized arrangements and segues. Waters's vocals sound a bit labored, even strained, after all these years, detracting from the affirmative overture to *The Dark Side of the Moon*, but the backing vocals warm each song up quite a bit.

'Speak to Me/Breathe' opens with what sounds like the original tapes from the album, before giving way to Waters's combo easing in with big and lush waves of instrumental sound, highlighted by acoustic guitar strums and pronounced bass thumps. An ensemble of male and female voices defines the vocal presentation throughout the performance, softening it greatly, not only through the harmonics but also through the presence of women singing lines originally handled by Gilmour and/or Waters. Waters's performance holds some surprising shifts from one song to another that violate the expectations we've had for almost 30 years. In one such example of unorthodox sequencing, 'Breathe' runs right into 'Time', without the segue of 'On the Run' building suspense and setting the tone. Other differences also abound. On 'Time', in particular, a thunderously busy combination of drummers complicates the interesting simplicity of Mason's original roto-tom offerings. Waters's vocals lack the lacerating intensity and force of Gilmour's, but they gain in depth and understanding, coming from the mouth of the man who, at age 28, 'suddenly realized that I wasn't going to wake up one morning and find that, now, my life was going to start. I realized that it was happening for a long, long time without me noticing it' (MacDonald, 1997, p. 275). The mix of Waters's performance submerges the guitar solo into backing instruments, and, while the solo captures much of Gilmour's original and even adds some interesting embellishments, the production (as well as the Detroit performance I attended) prevents it from exploding and dominating the sonic space. Waters also allows the backing voices to figure more prominently, again mellowing the overall impact of the piece. Waters's vocal embellishments, such as his singing the word 'breath' in two syllables in the line 'Shorter of br-eath, one day closer to death', provide occasional nice touches, especially compared to the clipped enunciation in other versions. Moreover, when, during the title track from *Amused to Death*, Waters sings the lines, 'Bartender, what is wrong with me? Why am I so out of breath?', he echoes 'Time' and signals the return of *The Dark Side of the Moon* even before he actually performs 'Brain Damage' and 'Eclipse' to close out his second set.

In the most jarring transition of his performance, Waters and crew launch right into 'Money' after the line 'softly spoken magic spell'. Again, Waters relies on the original coin and cash register tape-effects, but then departs with a different male vocalist and with his female backup singers once again carrying much of the singing. As one might expect, Waters and his production team keep the vocals right up front, clean, and uncharacteristically audible. While the *In the Flesh* 'Money' borrows some of its originally jazzy flavor, its rock essence dominates the number rather than erupting in the oft-noted change of time signatures. When Waters and company return to conclude *The Dark Side of the Moon* with 'Brain Damage' and 'Eclipse', they don't quite capture any of the epochal feel or intensity that these concluding pieces have on the album, a testament, perhaps, to how synergistic the original creation was. Waters's vocals can't quite sustain the lugubrious intensity, and both tunes, even with the seamless segue linking them, seem stranded, amputated from their proper environment. The pieces feel 'final' in one sense, but they lack the cumulative force they possess when fully integrated with the rest of *The Dark Side of the Moon*.

Overall, Roger Waters accentuates the symphonic grandeur of *The Dark Side of the Moon*, with lusher instrumentation and lovely vocals throughout the performance (listen, for example, to his backup singers doing the line 'far away across the field ...' at the end of 'Time'). Waters filters his *In the Flesh* version of *Dark Side* through the sounds, lyrical innovations, and musical evolution of his post-Floyd solo career. One wonders if these differences between Gilmour's and Waters's visions of the suite aren't what members of Floyd discussed in the *Uncut* special issue (June, 2003) that interviewed each of them on the subject of *The Dark Side of the Moon*.

The instrumental interludes in 'Money' reveal important differences. Waters's provides a rhythmic funk bottom, but Floyd's, with the entire band, pump up the funkiness of 'Money,' providing a soulful, even jazzy intermission before the album surges toward its conclusion. *The Dark Side of the Moon* frames the second set, surrounding some of Waters's most important and beautiful solo work (especially 'It's a Miracle' and 'Amused to Death'). By so sandwiching these more recent pieces, Waters recasts the emotional valence of the abbreviated *Dark Side*, emphasizing the darkness, maybe even the futility, of human endeavor in the face of growing social collapse, greed, and ennui. Waters's solo work explores the same pressures that impinge on humanity – time, death, religion, war, money, and greed. But, whereas in *The Dark Side of the Moon*, these threatening aspects of the contemporary human condition were examined and criticized from the perspective of a core of resilience and optimism ('don't be afraid to care'), Waters's *In the Flesh* reinterpretation heaps the general social malaise atop the struggling individual, obscuring and almost annihilating whatever personal effort and commitments refracted rays of hope on *The Dark Side of the Moon*. When Waters does begin singing 'Brain Damage', his clipped vocal presentation suggests a more matter-of-fact acceptance of lunatics in one's head and halls, completely eliminating the playfully mellifluous presentation from *Dark Side*. If humanity has amused itself to death *and* the sun is eclipsed by the moon, what else to be but 'Comfortably Numb' (the first encore number both for *In the Flesh* and *Pulse*)?

So, what is this thing called *The Dark Side of the Moon*? The synergy that is *The Dark Side of the Moon* links individual songs with album concept; lyrics with music; music with noise; speech with song; sound with silence; ambient with dominant sound; performers with audience; artistic creation with listener experience; the theater, concert hall, or stadium crowd with the solitary individual sitting headphoned in the dark; the sober with the ecstatic; the political with the personal; the morbid with the inspirational; sex with death; time with time-lessness; the lunar with the terrestrial; the cosmic with the local; and, especially given Roger Waters's emphasis on the empathetic nature of his lyrics, self with other(s), 'us' with 'them'. As if to stress the suite's layering and balancing of alternative meanings, the film backdrop to Pink Floyd's concert performances of *The Dark Side of the Moon* concludes by juxtaposing a human eye, its black pupil surrounded by a beautiful iris, with the moon gliding in to eclipse the sun and, finally, of a total eclipse, the sun's penumbra escaping from behind the moon's rim. Us and them, to be sure.

Chapter 2

'Matter of fact it's all dark': audiovisual stadium rock aesthetics in Pink Floyd's *The Dark Side of the Moon* tour, 1973

Kimi Kärki

> There is just so much more that you can do t⸺ it a complete experience than watching four, long-haired youth⸺ , beating their banjos. Not that I'm saying that's w⸺ ⸺lf a bit further.
>
> – Roger Waters[1]

It ⸺ ⸺on of original mastermind
⸺ ⸺se of this feature of their
⸺ ⸺s of rock-audiovisuals. It
⸺ ⸺ning mask and, as Deena
W⸺ ⸺pessimism (Weinstein,
20⸺ ⸺*rk Side of the Moon*, as
it s⸺ ⸺opened up a dark path
for⸺ ⸺e, but the sun was still
ecli⸺ ⸺ladison, Wisconsin's
Dane⸺ ⸺ated a new era in the
unific⸺ ⸺iovisual technology
into a⸺

Pink ⸺ ⸺nnovations from its
early d⸺ ⸺of the 1970s and
beyond,⸺ ⸺heir biggest seller,
The Da⸺ ⸺in recording history. Not
surprising⸺ ⸺ormances of *Dark Side* raised rock-
audiovisu⸺ ⸺ights. Early live versions of the concept had already been
performed in 1972 under the title *Eclipse*, but not until the 1973 *The Dark Side of the Moon* tour did the show reach its zenith.

I will discuss these performances from four points of view. First, the development of and most important changes in Pink Floyd's stage performance prior to the tour; second, the technology Pink Floyd used in their live concerts at the time; third, the dystopic narratives of Pink Floyd's stage performance of *The*

Dark Side of the Moon as it was executed in the 1973 tour; and, fourth, I will consider the position of the group as a definer of the stadium rock aesthetics. What emerges is a paradoxical vision of Pink Floyd as both critics of modern culture, and commercially led spectacle. Still, innovative attitudes towards performing have also produced vigorous criticsm against stadium spectacles; even Pink Floyd's 1970s mastermind Roger Waters himself spoke out against the massive spectacles.[3] Pink Floyd's original stage performances of *The Dark Side of the Moon* thus provides a good musical example of the multifaceted and complicated relation between modern culture and technology.

Eclipse

The Dark Side of the Moon was played live, under the name *Eclipse*, for the first time on 20 January 1972 at The Dome, in Sussex, England, and the official press introduction gig was 17 February 1972 at London's Rainbow Theatre (Schaffner, 1992, p. 173; Fitch, 1997, p. 377). The path to mega stardom surely opened when the actual album was released, but there was a long pre-history that led Pink Floyd to world fame.

Pink Floyd began to be associated with audiovisual technology at the very beginning of their career. According to Syd Barrett biographer Julian Palacios, it's really difficult to determine precisely 'who' did 'what' first when discussing the use of light and backdrop images in England. Dozens of people had been working with light already in the 1950s. However, Palacios is certain that at least Mark Boyle, Peter Wynne-Wilson, John Marsh, Mike Leonard, and Joe Gannon must be considered among the pioneering light men of London in the psychedelic 1960s (Palacios, 1998, p. 81). Each also worked for Floyd, mainly between 1966 and 1967, the hottest period of London underground, with John Marsh staying on the longest, throughout 1966–68 (Fitch, 1997, pp. 43, 112, 171, 186, 345–6).

Pink Floyd, assisted by light men Mike Leonard and Peter Wynne-Wilson, performed with some of the first psychedelic light shows in Britain during the early days of their London underground club gigs (Cunningham, 1999, p. 15). Roger Waters remembers that Floyd's first audiovisual gig was at Essex University, when someone showed a film on the wall while the band was playing. The band members immediately noticed and appreciated this powerful synergy between light and sound. Soon afterwards they saw a really spectacular background, when someone used bubbles and oil to create a psychedelic pulsating effect at Powis Garden (*Disc and Music Echo* (UK), 8 Aug. 1970; Fitch, 2001, p. 77). John 'Hoppy' Hopkins, one of the best known underground figures of Swinging London, thinks that the first real psychedelic light show was produced at the *International Times* magazine launch party: 'And these Americans I knew called Joel and Toni Brown, who were friends of Timothy Leary, did some slide projections to go with what the Floyd were doing. I'm pretty certain that was the first psychedelic light show to be seen in Britain' (Williamson, 2001, p. 60).[4]

Joe Gannon, Pink Floyd's earliest official light man, built the first light show designed specifically for and by the band. His role in the early Pink Floyd shows was so big that he was sometimes called 'the fifth Floyd' (Williamson, 2001, p. 112). Gannon, then only 17 years old, told a local newspaper inteerviewer about the slides and lights Pink Floyd used in 1966:

> I design the slides, basing them on my idea of the music. The lights work rhythmically. I just wave my hand over the micro-switches and the different colors flash. We have only been using the lights for one month. But before that, we were concentrating on starting with the right equipment. The lighting is so much a part of the group that it had to be good before it could be blend properly with the music. (*The Herald*, Kent (UK), 23 Nov. 1966; Fitch, 2001, pp. 10–11)

The band decided to abandon the whole idea of a light show after Syd Barrett left, partly because the psychedelic 'happenings' started to fade out of fashion. In 1972 drummer Nick Mason stated that the whole idea had become stagnant and lost its appeal. Pink Floyd had not acquired new lighting equipment, but, instead, *had* added dramatically to the quantity and quality of their sound equipment. But by the time of early versions of *Eclipse*, Pink Floyd was again taking the light show back on the road on a much larger scale: 'It won't be the same sort of light show, but we've just bought our own complete lighting set up. And it's six times as strong as our original effort' (*New Musical Express*, 12 Feb.1972; Fitch, 2001, pp. 120–21).

So, by the *Eclipse* era in 1972, the whole idea of a Pink Floyd light show had changed dramatically, as had their music. In 1973, at the same time that Pink Floyd replaced their signature dissonant soundscaping chaos with tight structures, Roger Waters commented that he had gotten bored with the whole idea of a 'random' light show. He felt that the lights were supposed to work in a specific way in an appropriate situation. Waters thought that Pink Floyd's music had become so precisely timed in performance that all of the visual effects needed to be synchronized with it. Musically intensive parts needed to have some big special effect to celebrate the peak, some orange smoke or rockets perhaps (*Zig Zag Magazine 32*, **3** (8) (UK), May 1973; Fitch, 2001, p. 154). Floyd's visual equipment thus began serving the idea of a modern mass spectacle.

Pink Floyd's live performance style changed for the first time after Syd Barrett's departure in 1968. The band started to explore the possibilities of the long and structured pieces, for example *Saucerful of Secrets* (1968) and *Atom Heart Mother* (1970), and it did not take long for the theme-developing improvization to migrate from stages to studio. Another fundamental change occurred between *Meddle* (1971) and *The Dark Side of the Moon* in 1973. As David Gilmour noted in an interview for *Relix Magazine* in 1979:

Yes, just after *Meddle*, there was a turning point. There was a specific direction change when we made 'Dark Side of the Moon,' and that was one of bringing lyrical and idea content up to being on an even footing with the musical content. The ideas had always been subservient to the music. A lot of the lyrics before that time were just being treated rather like instruments, and quite pretty at times, but not of any great significance. (*Relix Magazine* (US), Feb. 1979; Fitch, 2001, p. 254)

As I have noted, Pink Floyd performed the *Dark Side of the Moon* concept live significantly before the album's release. This was a great way to get rid of the weak parts.[5] The concept was then called *Eclipse*, because there was another band called Medicine Head who were using the title *Dark Side of the Moon* – luckily for Pink Floyd, Medicine Head flopped, and Floyd readopted the original title (Di Perna and Tolinski, 1997, p. 47; Schaffner, 1992, p. 173). Roger Waters's lyrics reached new heights of complexity and sophistication, and this new turn excited Nick Mason, for one: 'It was very new to us and seemed like a wonderful idea' (*The Dark Side* (1996), 00710–00715). David Gilmour clarified the concept soon after the release of the album:

The effects are purely to help the listener understand what the whole thing is about ... 'The Dark Side of the Moon' itself is an allusion to the moon and lunacy. The dark side is generally related to what goes on inside people's heads, the subconscious and the unknown. (*Melody Maker* (UK) 19 May 1973; Fitch, 2001, p. 162)

Technical ecstasy

Post-Barrett Pink Floyd's greatest obsession must have been the best possible gig-sound. The goal of the band was always to get the best possible gear, hence their reputation as technology freaks. According to Barrett's replacement guitarist/vocalist David Gilmour, the amount of Pink Floyd's stage technology was huge already in 1973. To be able to make a concert happen perfectly, Pink Floyd had to send people from their organization to the venue two weeks before the scheduled concert date. Their task was to make sure that every single detail of the yet to be constructed stage was going to be just as demanded. The stage needed two separate electric systems, one for the lights and one for the PA equipment.[6] If this instruction was not followed, the lighting system caused a loud hum to come out from the speakers. In most cases it was also necessary to build a properly sized and proportioned stage. By this point, the band had 11 tons of equipment that had to be transported with special trucks. Gilmour certainly saw the problems in the new bombastic scale of the events: 'Oh yes, it's the death of rock and roll. Big bands are coming back' (*Melody Maker* (UK) 19 May 1973; Fitch, 2001, p. 163).

Organizing a stadium concert always meant that additional workers had to be employed for a few days to build the stage. Peter Watts, who had begun working as a roadie for Floyd in 1967 and who worked as the Road Manager for *The Dark Side of the Moon* tour, commented on some pre-concert arrangements done by him and his assistants. Like the band members, he was committed to creating the best possible sound, and thus had not only acquired a great deal of Pink Floyd's sound technology, but had also designed and built some of the equipment himself. Between the tours he searched for state-of-the-art equipment, and, during the tours, he made sure that Pink Floyd's demands were always satisfied. Most importantly, the stage and the power supply had to meet their requirements. Watts described a usual concert day: the trucks brought the stage equipment to the venue around 10 am. He himself arrived by plane at the same time, and it took the rest of the day to supervise the building of the stage. This took at least six hours, so Pink Floyd was able to begin their sound check around 4 pm (Torker, 1990, p. 9).

The *Dark Side* tour also saw the advent of the complicated mixing technology for their shows. The mixing desk was positioned in the hall, so that the audience was able to hear the most balanced sound possible. Nick Mason thought the most important thing was to adapt the mixing system to be as easy to use and transport as possible, but without losing any versatility – they had to be able to plug in organs, guitar, drums, or any sound source, and also affect the sound with the mixing equipment. Especially important was to be able to transport any sound through the mixing desk in four channels, stereo, or double track. Developing functional technology proved daunting: 'It's enormously expensive and time consuming to get involved in it' (*New Musical Express* (UK), 19 Feb. 1972; Fitch, 2001, p. 121). Alan Parsons, the engineer of *Dark Side of the Moon* album, was also mixing some of the Pink Floyd gigs, most notably the whole American tour. In 1976, he told *Recording Engineer/Producer* magazine about the 1973 tour PA-equipment, and its order in the mixing desk:

> I think it was 24 in, a four-way stereo out, plus the quad buss. So when you selected the quad outputs, it didn't reach the P.A. If it was in a hall with two levels, then you would have two levels of quad speakers ... Another thing was the fact that the poor people that had to sit near the speakers had to endure that loudness. (Fitch, 2001, p. 219)

What really took Pink Floyd's mixing desk miles away from the other desks of the time was the separate output to quadraphonic system. Thus there were 24 channels coming from the instruments to mixer, and four continued to the hall PA-system. The speakers were placed all around the hall, enabling the mixer to pan any sound all around the venue in three-dimensional fashion. The best sound was always in the middle of the venue, where the PA-sound and quad-sound were best balanced. According to Parsons, the quadraphonic system that Pink Floyd had already pioneered in the late 1960s was an early and technological solution, which got old fashioned as soon as people started to build mixing desks with quad pots. He admitted, though, that Azimuth Coordinator was the first quad-system he was aware of (Fitch, 2001, p. 219).

Pink Floyd's music has always been highly technical, both in the means of playing – even if some of the historians of progressive rock disagree here – and the usage of latest equipment.[7] A common misunderstanding was that the music was entirely created by machines. David Gilmour commented this famous idea during a break from the recordings of *The Dark Side of the Moon*:

> I mean it's all extensions of what's coming out of our heads. I mean you got to remember you've got to have it inside your head to get it out at all anyway. And the equipment isn't actually thinking of what to do any of the time. It couldn't control itself … It would be interesting to see exactly what four people could do, just give them the equipment, who didn't know anything about it really. And just tell them to get on with it and do something. It would be an interesting experiment. I think we'd come off better. (*Live at Pompeii* (1994), 01531–01550, 01646–01700)[8]

The thought of music created entirely by machines was, at that time, new and fascinating, but it could be argued that Pink Floyd never had much to do with actual synthesizer-based music, even if electrical sound effects were often used to enhance their music. When performing their concept albums, they utilized a wide variety of special tape-recordings, such as helicopter sounds, ringing bells, sound of running steps, a heartbeat, and so on. Originally these were created for the actual albums, but the effects could be played from the tape in live situations, and thus there was no need to reproduce them. The effects were created in studio by recording different everyday sounds or by experimenting with the VCS3-synthesizer. The results were mixed into the band sound during the gigs. David Gilmour emphasized the fact that there isn't too much special technology involved in the process: 'most of them are recorded by using all the old regular equipment. There are millions of different effects you can produce just by using a tape recorder or two. You can do phasing, automatic double tracking, sound on sound, most things in fact' (Cooper, 1985, p. 77). Keyboard player Rick Wright mentioned in a 1972 interview that they were not yet able to use the quadraphonic system for anything else but the tape effects. He was hoping there would be a system which would cover the whole band, so that the stage would cease to be the centre of the sound. On the other hand, he admitted he was missing the simple gigs, where the band would only go to the venue and play. As the band was constantly worried about hitting the right timing cues, it sometimes affected the playing and thus the whole performance (*Sounds* (UK), 3 June 1972; Fitch, 2001, p. 129). Wright later remembered the technical details of the *Dark Side* tour as a massive nuisance:

> We were one of the first bands to do that, click-tracks they call them now. It was a massive headache because the equipment was pretty unreliable. The film would snap or the projector would break down or the click would suddenly come blasting out of the PA in the middle of the piece because someone had turned the wrong knob. There was a lot of missing cues and trying to get back in time, whereas today with everything digital it works like clockwork. (Sutcliffe, 1995, p. 73)

The visual solutions developed for the *Dark Side of the Moon* tour and *British Winter Tour* were soon obsolete. The arenas that were offered to Pink Floyd for their American tour in 1975 were so huge that the scale of the visual accompaniment had to grow almost geometrically. Pink Floyd hired two architectural designers, Mark Fisher and Jonathan Park, who had some experience on pneumatic mobile architectural structures (architecture of floating objects, that is!). Park later commented on the assignment: 'We saw this as part of the moving spirit of the age, you know, a bit of mobile architecture' (*Behind the Wall* (2000), 01430–01436). From this cooperation rose, for example, the famous flying pig, not to mention the brick wall that was built for *The Wall* stage performance.

In Paul Stump's opinion, the central achievement of Pink Floyd was the wide usage of technology: The group's utilization of technology in recording, both of the crudest lo-fi and the most futuristic hi-fi varieties, became part of their legend. Furthermore, it's hard to conceive nowadays of the sheer wonder that Pink Floyd's light shows – which virtually invented the look of the modern rock show – evoked at the time (Stump, 2001, p. 45). Stump also sees Pink Floyd as imprisoned by the new technological equipment ever since *The Dark Side of the Moon*: 'Henceforward, the band were trapped as prisoners of new technology they had helped to bring about, and they would be required to use this technology to make more money off the people whose alienation they had tapped into' (Stump, 2001, p. 47). The technology aside, the band became also prisoners of the market expectations. Commercial success brought new pressures, and thus the brand called Pink Floyd gradually became a producer of technological nostalgia, which instead of new ideas brought forward references to its own past. This is most evident in their two latest studio albums, *A Momentary Lapse of Reason* (1987) and *The Division Bell* (1994). I'm not trying to imply this has too much to do with the departure of Roger Waters, as he too has sounded sometimes tired and with a definite emphasis on the lyrics rather than the music in his solo albums.

Staged dystopy

In a Canadian press conference in 1972, Pink Floyd's members remarked that they were not primarily stage performers, because they felt their personalities became irrelevant during the concerts. As they didn't even try to reflect their personalities to the audience, the size of the audience was irrelevant to a successful gig: 'If the band is together personally, and the sound is together; then we do a good show' (*The Vancouver Free Press* (Can.), 28 Sep. 1972; Fitch, 2001, p. 139). Could this be one reason for their success as a huge stadium attraction, besides the spectacular audiovisual show? The fact that they never focused on dishing up their innermost feelings and personalities on a tray might account for the relatively long duration of the band. It's more difficult to burn out when one is not constantly trying to be in the spotlight, and anonymity has been one of the key features in the publicity strategy of Pink Floyd since the Barrett days. Perhaps there was enough warning in his mental burnout for the rest of the band.

I'd like to suggest that, while Pink Floyd members were not very personable on stage and lacked overmuch typical star-like quality in their performance, their shows actually benefited from that anonymity. This particular lack of star quality on stage added a great deal to their techno-spectacle and fed the space-age image they had and which they hated. Thus anonymity became a part of the group's authenticity: essayist Walter Benjamin's idea on the 'here and now' value of the work of art is reversed – Pink Floyd is not 'Hier and Jetzt', it's 'out there behind their wall of spectacle' (Benjamin 1989, pp. 127–8, 142–4, 147, 165–7). They *are* but 'are not' present on stage. The star of the show is the audio-visual spectacle itself, not the performers of the music. This technological mask is what defines the group and, paradoxically, while covering and surrounding them with modern phantasmagoria, gives them their special place in the field of rock performance.

In a 1982 interview, David Gilmour confirmed that Pink Floyd's relation to their fans changed completely after *The Dark Side of the Moon*. He remembered how irritated the whole band was in the middle of their gigantic success, when the stadiums were filled with the kids shouting 'Money!' all the way through the gigs. Band members were used to playing to silent, almost worshipful, audiences, calmly celebrating their cult reputation. One could almost hear a needle drop to the floor during quieter numbers. All that had now changed once and for all (*Musician Magazine* (US), Dec 1982; Fitch, 2001, p. 296). Nick Mason felt that only the outdoor shows suffered from the new fanbase, while indoor shows remained under control (*The Dark Side* (1996), 01750–01820). Most furious of all was Roger Waters, with the alienated atmospherics of *Wish You Were Here* (1975) representing the direct artistic fruit of his anger, and his megalomaniac concept of *The Wall* (1979) finally encapsulating his distaste for spectacle (Schaffner, 1992, pp. 198–9, 225). The period after *The Dark Side of the Moon*'s release was mentally hard for Waters, who felt the former contact and the interaction with the audience was now lost:

> I've been through a period when I've not wished to do any concerts with the Floyd ever again. I felt that very strongly, but the last week I've had vague kind of flickerings, feeling that I could maybe have a play. But when those flickerings hit the front of my mind I cast myself back into how fucking dreadful I felt on the last American tour with all those thousands and thousands of drunken kids smashing each other to pieces. I felt dreadful because it had nothing to do with us – I didn't think there was any contact between us and them. (Sedgewick, 1985, p. 19)

The early hippie utopia permeating Syd Barrett's lyrics had, by 1973, all but disappeared. Instead, pessimism and cynical observations triumphed. The change is most dramatic between the *Meddle* album and *The Dark Side of the Moon*. The dreamy landscapes of 'Echoes' ('Overhead the albatross / hangs motionless upon the air / and deep beneath the rolling waves / in labyrinths of coral caves / the echo of the distant times / willowing across the sand / and everything is green and submarine') were replaced by dark visions of walking towards death, as in 'Time'

('And you run and you run to catch up with the sun, but it's sinking / and racing around to come up behind you again / the sun is the same in a relative way, but you're older / shorter of breath and one day closer to death').

Roger Waters went through a sort of an age crisis in between these two albums. He had waited for his 'real life' to begin until he was about 28 years old (1971), expecting to turn from a chrysalis to a butterfly, but nothing happened. 'Time passes, and you are what you are, you do what you do' (*Rolling Stone* (US), 16 Sep. 1982; Fitch, 2001, p. 287). At the same time, the hippie movement had descended into the crisis from where it never rose again. The well-known events of the Rolling Stones' Altamont concert and increased violence at other rock festivals, harder drugs, and also the tighter attitudes towards the drugs in general were all effecting the re-evaluation of the utopian nature of the hippie movement in public (Whiteley, 1992, pp. 101–3). But also these dark clouds have a longer history. Dystopias – or counter-utopias – have had a firm tradition within 20th-century cultural history, a tradition that can easily assimilate Roger Waters, mainly because of his science fiction hobby.[9]

In the 20th century, as Italian philosopher Gianni Vattimo suggests, the different radical counter-utopias, such as Friz Lang's *Metropolis* (1926), Aldous Huxley's *Brave New World* (1932), and George Orwell's *1984* (1948), became common in Western culture (Vattimo, 1999, p. 60). Science fiction literature, especially, has had its share of dystopias since the 1950s. According to utopia researcher Krishan Kumar, science fiction as a genre was then abandoning science utopias as story material, even seeing science as the road to chaos and destruction. Science fiction moved from outer space to inner space, and at the same time the interest in historical utopias diminished (Kumar, 1987, pp. 403–4). In a way, science fiction turned more psychological, it became 'head literature' just as Pink Floyd was considered 'head music'. Deena Weinstein compares Waters to the earlier cultural pessimism of such authors as Ruper Brooke and Thomas Hardy, but also sees in his writing traces of Rousseau-styled existentialism (Weinstein, 2002, pp. 96, 101–5). Waters was expressing his concern over the world situation as early as 1971:

I work to keep my mind off a doomy situation. All over the globe, it gets crazier every day. And the craziness seems to be accelerating at a fantastic rate. But it might just be that, as you get older, your perception gets faster, until the whole thing seems unreal, as I leaf through my Guardian each morning. (*Melody Maker* (UK), 9 Oct. 1971; Fitch, 2001, p. 111)

Paradoxically Pink Floyd's armchair, left-wing countercultural attitude – or more clearly the cultural pessimism of Roger Waters – was not really manifested before their concept albums of the 1970s; when the hippie movement triumphed, they were only providing the background music to the happenings. Thus one could argue the band became countercultural when such posturing was already anachronistic. The constructive critique had been replaced with somewhat more fatalistic undertones. Waters's cultural pessimism grew in the years following *The Dark Side of the Moon*, yet he was able to turn his anxiety into a creative force with the concept albums *Wish You Were Here, Animals* (1977), *The Wall*, and *The Final Cut* (1983). Concerts were staged to reflect the bitter undertones of Waters's lyrics. 'It looks like hell,' commented journalist Derek Jewell in the *Sunday Times* review of the premiere of *The Dark Side of the Moon* (Schaffner, 1992, p. 173). Another example of Jewell's reviews, from a series of concerts at the Empire Pool, Wembley, from 15 to 19 March 1977, during the *Animals in the Flesh* tour, has similar notions on the pessimistic quality of the performance:

> Entertainment? Scarcely. Arguably, it's closer to sombre modern conservatoire music ... Rarely, if ever, can so-called popular music have dealt so relentlessly in images of bleakest pessimism ... Their presentation is the ultimate in brilliantly staged theatre of despair (*The Sunday Times* (UK), 20 March 1977; Fitch, 2001, pp. 230–31)

If we consider the popular musical culture of the late 1970s, especially in its disco and glam-rock finery, it is no wonder that the pop journalists of the time felt Pink Floyd concerts to be endlessly pessimistic, almost desperate happenings.

Defining stadium rock aesthetics

Andrew Goodwin has summed up the essential facts about a stadium-scale performance:

> Indeed, most stadium concerts are now accompanied by simultaneous video replay onto large screens. Attending a live performance by a pop megastar these days is often roughly the experience of listening to prerecorded music (taped or sequenced) while watching a small, noisy TV set in a large, crowded field. (1990, p. 269)

Stadium-scale performance is based on the architecture of light and sound, where the space, when needed, disappears, and gives way to new reflected worlds that are easily transformed to meet the demands of each song and the general themes and narratives of the tour.

The reflected video image changes the live concert to an even more multi-layered event: it fortifies the sensory experience of the audience. The 'star' or 'artist' on the stage is not alone, just behind and all around him is a mediated and simultaneous representation of the very same stadium star. Mass-stardom is thus a powerful mix of physical presence and media construction. This kind of stadium aesthetics was developed during the 1970s, and pioneered by Pink Floyd.

The new and hugely more powerful PA-systems of the early 1970s made stadium performances technically possible. The new bloated scale of things also required new visual solutions, so that the people at the back of the venues had something to look at. Pink Floyd started to use reflected film material behind the stage in a few shows in France during 1973, and most notably from *British Winter* tour 1974 onward (Jones, 1996a, p. 95; Povey and Russell, 1997, pp. 134, 136–7). 'Mr. Screen', Pink Floyd's 'giant eye into another universe', as journalist and Pink Floyd biographer Nicholas Schaffner called it, has later become a distinctive element in Pink Floyd shows. The simple, circular screen behind the band enabled them to project film during the songs, thus creating the new visual narratives to accompany the musical performance. Eric Holding emphasizes the high quality of Pink Floyd performances by reminding us that they have always used film and projectors instead of videos, even when the video technology became good enough. Film has a better resolution, and, according to Holding, the 'arty' connotations that come with the film images don't look strange at all on Pink Floyd (Schaffner, 1992, p. xviii; Holding, 2000, p. 39, 44). The period from 1972 to 1974 was a hugely innovative time for the band, in both a narrative and technological sense.

The acquisition of a visual canvas to express narratives in a new sensory way can be seen as one of the most important developments of Pink Floyd's spectacles. One of the Pink Floyd concert's visual highlights was then to project Britain's former Prime Minister Alec Douglas Home and other politicians – including, for example, Richard Nixon, and Fidel Castro – on the screen during 'Brain Damage' and 'Eclipse'. The insane laughter coming from the speakers completed the analogy between the politicians and the lunatics (Povey and Russell, 1997, pp. 138–9). The films made for the *British Winter* tour included images of the moon, clocks, city lights, car lights, police lights, cloud tunnel, alien planets, some clips from an underwater movie *Crystal Voyager*, and of course some money too (*Sounds* (UK), 9 Nov. 1974; Fitch, 2001, p. 187). The planning of the films required intricate planning and coordination, according to Rick Wright:

> It was hard work for Roger, Nick, and Arthur Max, the sound engineer, but it's still not right. I think we are still at the experimental stage in finding out what visuals work, and which don't, even after all these years … People always expect Floyd to come up with something different, new and better, when it comes to visuals. And it's very difficult to keep thinking of new ideas. (*Melody Maker* (UK), 16 Nov. 1974; Fitch, 2001, p. 188)

Eventually, Pink Floyd incorporated other big innovations and extra stage gimmicks, of which the later flying pig must be the most famous. Exaggeration is a must when the stage does indeed look like a small television from the back of the venue. One might go so far as to claim that Floyd shows had become as much circus as rock concert. Roger Waters had already in 1968 expressed some thoughts on possible rock-circus, and he was asked about that during the *Dark Side* tour. He felt the show had lots of similar elements. When he had watched the setting up of the stage with all the wires, he felt it was nearing the circus. Even the model aeroplane Pink Floyd was using at the Earls Court shows was a little like circus space rockets: 'It was silver and red and about six foot long, like a bloody great aluminium paper dart, flashing lights and smoke, amazing' (*Zig Zag Magazine*, 32, **3** (8) (UK), May 1973; Fitch, 2001, p. 154).[10]

Spectacular entertainment and mass-culture have had a field day from the 1970s onward. The use of gigantic venues changed rock performances into total or 'totalitarian' mass-art, in which rock stardom was preserved and created by technological means. Aesthetics of the stadium spectacle have grown from this need to exaggerate and fortify audiovisual gestures through technology. One could thus compare a rock concert to a propaganda meeting where a dictator gives orders to the worshipping audience, an analogy supported by Roger Waters within *The Wall* narrative, for example. Without this cultural technology there wouldn't be any stadium stardom: by showing the close-ups of the facial expressions of the artists in the video screen it is possible – even if this happens only partly – to restore the intimacy that has been lost because of the huge scale, or spectacle, of the events.

One central feature of the technical world is spectacle. Cultural theorist Guy Debord has discussed the spectacle-like nature of the whole western world in his influential and polemic book *La Societé du Spectacle* (*The Society of the Spectacle*). For him, the spectacle means social human relations, which are mediated through pictures. However, it has nothing to do with communication, this phenomenon is disrupting the world and emphasizing the autonomy of the visual. So, spectacle for Debord is definitely something inherently negative. As we live in the society of spectacle, everything appears as visual surface without any deeper substance. Spectacle demands passive approving: everything that appears is good, and everything good appears. Here we have an obvious tautology, which is no accident. For me, this is the real core of the cultural pessimism and anxiety of the 1970s Pink Floyd. Spectacle feeds on itself, and the technological dimension of Pink Floyd only brings new levels to the ritualistic visual quality of the group's performances. Debord claims that spectacle is a direct continuation of religion, or, more precisely, a materialistic reconstruction of a religious illusion (Debord, 1995, pp. 12–15, 17–18). If we are supposed to find the essence of a spectacle from this deceiving and pacifying visual surface and new substitute for religious practices, we can find the cultural roots to the idea from the concept of *Phantasmagoria*. According to art historian Anna Kortelainen, this concept refers to the illusory and futureless nature of our culture, its products and technologies (Kortelainen, 2002, pp. 43–5). I'd like to argue that the Pink Floyd live show could be seen as the ultimate spectacle or phantasmagoria, as even the band members themselves have been aware of the dystopic undertones of Waters's ideas in the narrative of *The Dark Side of the Moon*.

Stadium technology was innovated to provide means for modern *Gesamtkunstwerk,* a complete work of art.[11] The technology connects the performer's theatrical gestures to wider, elaborately planned thematic structures. This is what large venues and their disposable architecture are all about these days: connecting sound, light, and material surfaces with popular imagery, and, in the case of Pink Floyd, also with popular nostalgia and the historical references of the audiovisual narratives. This band was – at least almost – solely pioneering the usage of stadium-scale audiovisual technology. But after the enormous success of *The Dark Side of the Moon*, Roger Waters felt his bombastic dreams had failed. He felt that the idea of a stadium spectacle was foundationally empty. I find it enormously ironic that this man had tried – with the complete weight of his willpower – to make these large theatrical spectacles happen, but after achieving some success with them he turned against the whole idea of this kind of a mass art (*Is There Anybody Out There?*, 2000, p. 5).

Conclusion

According to journalist Paul Stump, Pink Floyd was one of the first legends of the 1960s who realised how to exploit their huge masses of fans by the nostalgia paradoxically created in large arena tours. There was a huge fanbase for the band immediately in the 1960s and especially in the 1970s, ready to worship the audiovisual spectacle and at the same time relive their youth. The exploitation of this popular nostalgia was perhaps the key element of their shows in the 1980s and 1990s, but the knowledge of the possibility was there already when *The Dark Side of the Moon* was being made. As Nick Mason commented: 'Unfortunately, really, we mark a sort of era. We are in danger of becoming a relic of the past. For some people we represent their childhood of 1967, I mean the underground in London, free concert in Hyde Park and so on' (*Live at Pompeii* (1994), 03956–04020). Stump feels that the group have in their later years invited their fans to worship their myth in a ritualistic fashion. Nothing more was needed than that the myth was kept alive in a right way. Stump sees special irony in the fact that this band, which had once been one of the leaders of musical counterculture in England and later the harsh critic of the high-culture fortresses, had now become a satire of itself. Stump has no mercy in his critique: '[t]hree-quarters of one of the most imaginative rock outfits in history plodding through yet another evening of Industrial Light and Magic' (Stump, 2001, p. 50).

David Gilmour had already commented on this paradox of Pink Floyd stadium-scale spectacles in a 1978 interview for the Italian *Ciao 2000* magazine. He saw the group becoming a monstrous machine, the technology of which suffocated the feelings of the music. Thus he felt they had sometimes lost the control: 'If you only rely on the technique alone, there isn't any real purpose to the music. At times, we may have gone a bit too far' (*Ciao 2001*, 13 Aug. 1978; Fitch, 2001, p. 252). Funnily enough, Gilmour was the one to strive towards even bigger stadium-scale shows in the 1980s and 1990s, with his *Delicate Sound of Thunder*, and *Division Bell* tours.

I've often wondered about the nature of the technological space that Pink Floyd created for themselves or, more precisely, for their anonymous and expressionless stage personas. Perhaps the group was a side act in their own live performance. Their voluntary retreat behind orange smoke, steel cranes, animations, flying planes, floating giant figures and – as a last extreme straw – the wall hiding the whole stage does not leave too much room for differing thoughts. Roger Waters in particular seemed to first want his spectacle and then, when he was given one, he seemingly hated the whole dark circus.

Even if Pink Floyd were propelled into megastardom by the success of the *Dark Side of the Moon* album, their reputation as an inspired live band was much older. However, only after this album were they able to conquer the huge stadiums in the United States. It is interesting to note how Pink Floyd were both an album-oriented band and, at the same time, one of the hugest live attractions of the 1970s. When observing the career of Pink Floyd from the early avant-garde psychedelia to more and more gigantic productions, it's easy to trace the development of this band into a product and a brand. Pink Floyd's market value grew out of proportion during the 1970s, and this impacted also on their stadium performances as they pioneered the bloated technology of the stadium aesthetics that we have later seen with bands like the Rolling Stones and U2 (Stump, 1997, p. 12). Even today, almost ten years after their latest – last? – performances, they remain almost unchallenged as synonymous with the ultimate stadium spectacle. Pink Floyd will remain a part of the history of the concept album, and they will always be remembered for their efforts to bring about the marriage of lyrics, music, and visual aspects. The band is thereby connected to historical tradition – the traces lead back to Wagner's operas, and even to the ancient mystery plays. 'Deus Ex Machina' is today a rock megastar.

Notes

1. Pink Floyd bassist and sometimes vocalist Roger Waters expressed his ambitions in an interview. *Melody Maker* (UK), 5 Dec. 1970; Fitch (2001), p. 98.
2. I wrote my MA thesis on the stage performance of Pink Floyd 1965–81. See Kärki (2002).
3. *The Wall*, being an album (1979), a stage show (1980–81), and a movie (1982), was Waters's most explicit attempt to comment on the isolation he felt had begun with the commercial success of the *Dark Side* album.
4. The *IT* launch party took place on 15 October 1966 (Fitch, 1997, p. 355).
5. In a live bootleg from 1972 one can hear some of the material differing dramatically from the album versions, for example 'The Great Gig in the Sky' is almost unrecognizable. Listen to Pink Floyd: *Crackers* (s.a.).
6. PA meaning public address or power amplification; the system that includes microphones, mixer, and the hall speakers (Bacon, 1981, p. 214).
7. On the debate whether Pink Floyd is progressive rock see, for example, Martin (1998), pp. 17, 102.
8. Schaffner has quoted the same source, but has also edited Gilmour's speech. See Schaffner (1992), p. 169.
9. Pink Floyd later maintained a certain countercultural flavor with their album *The Wall*; South African black youth protested against their compulsory education system with the slogan 'We don't need no education'. In England, the song was heavily

protested against, as it was misunderstood to be against education in general (Frith, 1996, p. 165; 'Another Brick In the Wall pt. II' (*The Wall*), Pink Floyd 1979). During the worst moral panic even the Archbishop of Canterbury took a stand against the song (*Shine On* (1997), 01720–01730).

10.   The visual spectacle of the progressive rock bands of the time could also be compared to Disneyland, as in Macan (1997), p. 157.
11.   For more on Wagnerian *Gesamntkunstwerk*, see Salmi (1999), pp. 74–80.

Works cited

Interviews and articles in magazines

Cooper, Gary (1985), 'An Interview with David Gilmour', in *The Wish You Were Here Song Book*. London: Pink Floyd Music Publishers, pp. 73–81.
Di Perma, Alan and Tolinski, Barad (1997), 'Wall of Sound', (*Guitar World Presents*) *Guitar Legends*, no 22, pp. 46–7, 95.
Fitch, Vernon (2001), *Pink Floyd. The Press Reports 1966–1983*, Burlington, Ontario: Collector's Guide Publishing.
Sedgewick, Nick (1985), 'A Rambling Conversation with Roger Waters Concerning All This and That', in *The Wish You Were Here Song Book*, London: Pink Floyd Music Publishers, pp. 9–23.
Stump, Paul (2001), 'The Incredible Journey', *Uncut*, Take 54, pp. 42–50.
Sutcliffe, Phil (1995), 'The 30 Year Technicolour Dream', *Mojo*, 20, 64–80.
Torker, Frank (1990), 'Peter Watts, Road Manager interviewed by Frank Torker', in *The Dark Side of the Moon Song Book. Guitar Tablature Edition*, London: Pink Floyd Music Publishers, pp. 9–15.
Williamson, Nigel (2001), 'Notes From the Underground', *Uncut*, Take 54, pp. 52–62.

Videos

Pink Floyd Live at Pompeii (1994), Director: Adrian Maben. Music: Pink Floyd. Producer: Michele Arnaud Production. Polygram Video 080 730 3.
Pink Floyd. The Dark Side (1996), Picture Profiles. File 04.
Pink Floyd. Shine On. Interviews (1997), Picture Profiles. File 05.
Pink Floyd. Behind the Wall (2000), documentary for Finnish Television, Channel 4, 30 August 2000. Director/Producer: Bob Smeaton. Initial (GMG Endemol Entertainment).

Records

Pink Floyd (1968), *Saucerful of Secrets*, Columbia (EMI) SCX 6258.
Pink Floyd (1970), *Atom Heart Mother*, Harvest (EMI) SHVL 781.
Pink Floyd (1971), *Meddle*, Harvest (EMI) SHLV 795.

Pink Floyd (s.a.), *Crackers. Live at Hollywood Bowl Los Angeles CA September 22, 1972*, Limited edition bootleg CD.

Pink Floyd (1973), *The Dark Side of the Moon*, Harvest (EMI) SHVL 804.

Pink Floyd (1975), *Wish You Were Here*, Harvest (EMI) SHVL 814 9.

Pink Floyd (1977), *Animals*, Harvest (EMI) SHVL 815.

Pink Floyd (1979), *The Wall*, Harvest (EMI) SHVL 822.

Pink Floyd (1983), *The Final Cut*, Harvest (EMI). SHPF 1983.

Pink Floyd (1987), *A Momentary Lapse of Reason*, EMI EMD 1003.

Pink Floyd (1994), *The Division Bell*, EMI 8 28984.

Pink Floyd (2000), *Is There Anybody Out There? The Wall Live. Pink Floyd 1980–81*, limited edition, EMI, LC0542 7243 5 23562 2 5 (5 23563–4 2).

Chapter 3

Dark side of the men: Pink Floyd, classic rock and white masculinities

Matthew Bannister

In his autobiography, *Lost in Music*, musician Giles Smith describes his adolescent initiation into *The Dark Side of the Moon* at an all-male gathering presided over by an older, 'more experienced', hippie peer: 'Each of us sat there in the black-out, overawed. Even at the end of side one ... there was silence' (Smith, 1995, p. 81). *Dark Side* is best listened to 'in absolute silence and in the dark, the better to soak up its mind-boggling oddity' (ibid., p. 80). In other words, like a classical audience – this is *serious* music. Moreover, as Smith points out, in the 1970s, the ritual of listening to *The Dark Side of the Moon* and other progressive rock concept albums, like one's first joint or sexual experience, was a 'rite of passage' that marked out 'the men from the boys' (ibid., pp. 22–3; Raphael, 1988). This was adult music, our older brothers told us. Forget glam rock – it's time to put away childish things and become, in the words of Steely Dan, 'part of the brotherhood', a fraternity that was coded as both countercultural and homosocial.[1]

In this essay I want to outline two possible approaches to masculinities in popular music generally and in particular Pink Floyd: in terms of high culture and popular culture. The first discourse I discuss in terms of 'rock as art' – the use of high cultural ideologies ('seriousness', hierarchization, autonomy) by participants within popular music and the degree to which this can be read as a gendered discourse. The second identifies rock, in contrast, as 'music of the people' (counter)culture, a means of popular creative expression, in which value is attributed to music according to the degree of 'authenticity' it has for a particular, non-dominant social group (usually youth) – the history of *The Dark Side of the Moon* in terms of its audiences. But clearly different audiences may have different investments – the hippie counterculture of the 1970s heard a different *Dark Side* than does a 'classic rock' radio listener today. However, both audiences share a predominantly male demographic, and to some extent a shared canon that cursorily acknowledges blues as 'roots' (and thereby attendant ideologies of black masculinity as instinctive potency), but mainly focuses on the emergence of rock in the 1960s as a type of self-composed music played by groups of white men with electric instruments and guitars, opposed to mainstream pop, and countercultural. Along with other 1970s white rock bands like the Rolling Stones and Led Zeppelin, Pink Floyd is central to both audiences' understanding of 'rock' (Willis, 1978, pp. 107–8; Radio Hauraki, 2003).

The concept of a canon conventionally refers to high culture and thus draws us back towards 'rock as art', emphasizing that the culture/art distinction I made initially is by no means clearcut. It suggests that popular culture is stratified like high culture, and has its own forms of (sub)cultural capital (Thornton, 1995, p. 11); for example, Giles Smith's older brothers' disdain for Marc Bolan, who represents teenybopper pop, in contrast to rock (Smith, 1995, pp. 22–3). Rock is canonical – pop is not. Canonism can also suggest masculinities, firstly because histories of popular music often privilege a patriarchal lineage of 'great' artists: 'Without Hank Williams and Arthur Crudup, there would be no Elvis Presley; without Little Richard and James Brown, no Prince; without Chuck Berry, Buddy Holly and Lonnie Donegan, no Beatles' (Dafydd and Crampton, 1996, p. 4; *Rolling Stone*, '100 Greatest'). And without the Beatles, no Pink Floyd, we might add. Pop, in contrast, is constructed as feminine and ephemeral (Smith, 1995, pp. 22–3). Canonism constructs culture as competitive and hierarchical, with 'absolute' standards of excellence, an emphasis not exclusive to rock historians. The working-class bikers Paul Willis studies in *Profane Culture* also have a strong investment in a canon of past greats that constitute for them 'classic rock'. The music has changed, but the social similarities with the classic rock audience are striking, in suggesting how canonism and male culture are related.[2]

In general, however, past studies of rock masculinities are not particularly useful for my present undertaking. Why not? Many studies of masculinities in popular music focus on 'machismo' or 'men behaving badly' – masculinity in performance ('cock rock'), that is articulated in strongly homophobic or misogynistic terms, or in terms of genres or artists that are recognizably 'masculine', such as heavy metal or Bruce Springsteen.[3] Such studies would include many rock artists in the canon I identified above. However, progressive rock and Pink Floyd tend not to feature prominently in its pantheon. Ethnographic and subcultural studies, such as Willis (1978) and Hebdige (1979), focus on minority audiences specific to a time and place – Pink Floyd's audience(s) is much larger and more heterogeneous, including non-working-class elements. Progressive rock performers do not display 'machismo' as much as other rock performers. More generally, while these studies are useful sources of information and ideas about rock masculinities, they do not theorize gender as such, rather they tend to presume it as a norm (Thornton, 1995, p. 93). Such studies risk essentializing masculinities in terms of a resistant, proletarian, male 'otherness' that is both exotically alluring and fundamentally alien to the, often male, middle-class academic researcher. On the other hand, ethnographic studies of popular music that focus on gender generally deal with the experience of women and gays. Mary-Anne Clawson writes, 'such studies do not sufficiently problematise the "normality" of masculine musicianship, and thus fail to understand rock as a gendered activity' (1999, p. 99).

Pink Floyd do not relate specifically to a subculture. They are not macho. They don't rock. They don't play the blues (okay, Gilmour sometimes). They don't have powerful bodies, and they don't smash their instruments. They're not sexy, and they don't even pretend to be working class. So where do they get their mojo?

Rock as art

Elite modernist and Romantic ideologies of high and low culture are relevant to Pink Floyd because of their association with progressive rock, which leaned heavily on discourses of 'rock as art', and its creators as artists, as part of its self-legitimation.[4] The attempted elevation of rock to the pantheon of great art echoes in such early 1970s writing as Richard Meltzer's *The Aesthetics of Rock* (1970), and articulates the 'maturing' of the first generation of baby boomers, their attempts to legitimate in more 'conventional' and socially acceptable terms the music they had grown up with, and the related growth of FM AOR in the USA (the playlists of which anticipate classic rock). Progressive rock also links to the emergence in the late 1960s of a 'superstar culture' of a small circle of white male US and UK 'virtuoso' musicians, the 'all-star' jam, 'supergroups' such as Blind Faith, ELP, Crosby Stills Nash & Young, and the like. It should be noted, however, that Pink Floyd's members were not particularly identified with this superstar culture – indeed the band were noted rather for their anonymity. Moreover, they were not 'virtuosos'. I will comment on this further below.) Both countercultural and progressive values might include the ideology of rock as 'art' and its players as 'great' musicians or artists.

Apart from the raised social status of rock, the material and economic conditions of the early 1970s record industry may have contributed to changes in the way the rock was both produced and received. In relation to the UK, which is generally recognized as the 'cradle' of progressive rock, Allan Moore argues:

> The most important feature of mid-1960s Britain in enabling the development of these [progressive] styles was the economic situation of the record companies ... Not only did they see the world market expand rapidly, but the consumer boom in the UK yielded them large returns, enabling them to invest in their artists without requiring an immediate financial return (a return they continued to enjoy well into the 1970s) ... this both enabled and encouraged artists to experiment with music that was not immediately and widely accessible. (2001, p. 65)

Thus, 'progressive musicians [developed] ... an ideology of artistic freedom and self-expression ... within what was considered a freedom from the constraints of the immediate, dancing audience: the term progressive connoted a concern with aesthetic and individual rather than immediate or communal qualities' (ibid.,

p. 65). Progressive rock musicians were certainly keen to extend this upwardly mobile development of rock into the areas of conception and composition: 'to establish a degree of aesthetic unity greater than that of the individual song' (ibid., p. 92). Hence the concept album. Such a stress on intellectual, individual and aesthetic qualities can be seen as typical of high art and also as a strategy for social hierarchization through 'taste' – creating 'cultural capital', a set of strategies by which the upper classes differentiate themselves from 'the masses'.[5] Hence the designation 'art' becomes one of the highest forms of cultural capital, and works primarily in the interests of the most powerful group generally to maintain the status quo. Art, far from being autonomous, is actually ideological, and patriarchal.

Lucy Green explains how the high cultural discourse of classical music is gendered masculine. In terms of performance, she notes how the performer is always displaying him/herself and becoming the object of a gaze.[6] Male classical musicians dress uniformly, minimizing individuating display – women musicians, by contrast, are relatively highlighted, emphasizing their singularity and sexuality. Historically, in musical performance, some female delineations have been more acceptable than others – the singer, for example, is acceptable because she presents a 'natural' ability that is already gendered (it is usually easy to tell sex from a voice) and because singing is seen as deriving from the body rather than from technology. Green argues that the feminine is admissible in music as long as it does not challenge masculine dominance in the areas of composition and technology (1997, pp. 27–30, 60–62).

Similar processes occur in popular music – the association of woman primarily with voice rather than technology, and with sexual display (which is often seen as compromising musical ability). *Dark Side* features women but only as voices: namely, the session singers Doris Troy, Leslie Duncan, and Liza Strike. Their contribution is largely non-verbal, consisting of wordless 'aahs', cries, and moans. This has the effect of situating them as non-rational, expressive subjects. We might say that, if the theme of the album is madness (represented by the moon), then female voices express it most clearly. On the other hand, the technological control of the album – its composition, performance and (studio) production are all in male hands. 'The Great Gig in the Sky' may be mainly memorable for its vocal performance by Clare Torry, but the song is credited to Rick Wright, and the singer herself saw no royalties from it. Notably, Torry was also asked to improvise her part, and claims she had no idea what they wanted and no idea what she was actually doing (Lambert, 1998).

Women supply the body, men the mind. This is not to say that women *are* body, but rather that control is here associated with a mental mastery, and that this is associated with masculinity: 'For male instrumentalists throughout history, the delineation of gender has been nearly always metaphorically transparent: it is there, but we do not see it, we see through it … we do not hear it, we hear through it' (Green, 1997, p. 54). Masculinity is normative in relation to music, and thus it is invisible, in contrast to women, whose sexuality tends to be highlighted because of the male gaze.

Pink Floyd are marked by such discourses of impersonality – their studio-based works privilege an overall sound picture rather than the personalities of the musicians, and even their live performances privilege technical excellence and spectacular visual effects over the performance personae of the band members. In this sense they are perhaps more like an orchestra than a rock band – their individuality is subjugated to the collective project of realization of a 'masterwork'. Indeed, in general, the group is remarkably 'faceless'. Observing Pink Floyd tribute bands, which often recreate 'works' such as *Dark Side* and *The Wall*, one is tempted to comment that the personalities of the players are irrelevant as long as they have the technology under control: 'In concert they [Pink Floyd] are more like engineers than musicians, sitting at great consoles turning knobs and flicking switches rather than actually playing instruments' (Willis, 1978, p. 159). In contrast, a Rolling Stones tribute band would more or less require performers who looked and sounded like Mick Jagger, Keith Richards, and the rest.

Green goes on to consider how masculinity is normalized in relation to music by its association with composition:

> Composition itself is gendered through its association with mind, and through its impersonal control of a large ensemble . . . with composition it is *a metaphorical display of the mind* of the composer which enters into delineation ... Whilst we listen to music, it is not just the inherent meanings that occupy our attention, but also our idea of the composer's mental processes ... The masculine delineation of music is articulated through . . . the cerebral control of knowledge and technology which is implicit in the notion of composition. (1997, pp. 84–5; author's emphasis)

A comparison may be made with film auteur theory – the value of a work is related to the 'mind' that 'created' it, which is not directly present but is articulated through technical elements of mise-en-scène, editing, cinematography (Sarris, 1968). But who is the auteur of *The Dark Side of the Moon*?

Roger Waters as auteur

Most accounts of the band agree that *The Dark Side of the Moon* marked the beginning of Roger Waters's domination of Pink Floyd: 'All the words were written by Roger Waters and ... his lyrical achievement would ensure his future dominance over the band's output' (Welch, 1994, p. 89). Waters's lyrics display a thematic coherence from *Dark Side* on that arguably give him the status of auteur, plus the fact that he writes the majority of the songs, and seems to have originated the concept of this and other Floyd albums (for example, *Animals*, *The Wall*) (Jones, 1996b, pp. 94, 112, 120). His control of the band in visionary, and other terms places him close to the discourse of the composer outlined above by Green.

Deena Weinstein describes Waters's affiliation to high art (2002, p. 69) and Paul Stump remarks of him: 'Clearly what was at stake here was no longer simply music but the entire artistic realm, a striving towards *Gesamtkunstwerk* that the modernist pioneer and archangel of Romanticism, Richard Wagner, would have recognised: music ... sat at the center of a multi-artistic endeavour' (1997, pp. 26–7).

Such control involved manipulation of the other musicians in the band, and, when they didn't measure up, Waters replaced them or attempted to alienate them – Rick Wright, for example. In Waters's view, the band became increasingly a vehicle for what he had to say, rather than a cooperative enterprise. In his view, 'What was important [about *Dark Side*] was what it was *about* ... The recording was very ordinary, *really*' (quoted in Resnicoff, 1992). The album marked the point at which he began to assume control.

It would be unfair, however, to single out Roger Waters for criticism (although many have) and to reduce gender to the reported behaviour of individuals (to argue *ad hominem*, so to speak). Moreover, even though Waters may see himself (and be seen) as an auteur, it is fairly clear that rock music (like film) is collaborative and that authorship is probably better understood in collective terms. Foucault suggests that it is misleading to read power discourses, for example gender, only in terms of authorship. In Foucault's terms, what matters most is not so much what is 'in' the discourses (for example, representations), or who 'authors' them, but the overall 'economy' of discourses: 'their intrinsic *technology* ... this and not a system of representations, determines what they have to say' (Foucault, 1974, pp. 68–9; 1991, p. 462). In other words, not who did it, but how it was done. This leads towards a consideration of *Dark Side* in terms of technology and gender (I am not suggesting that technology is only oppressive, but rather that, in specific instances, it can be used in the interests of a dominant group).

Technology and power

Paul Théberge describes how the multitrack studio produces and reproduces a hierarchical model of labour relations, in which technological and aesthetic expertise are combined in the producer or musician/producer's manipulation of individual parts and players.[7] The studio becomes to the rock artist/producer as an orchestra is to a composer, with each multitrack channel becoming an individually scored part. It is thus possible for an individual to use multitracking to achieve a total musical vision, adjusting parts by overdubbing, like the composer rewrites a score to make each part 'perfect'. Such painstaking studio perfectionism was a hallmark of 1970s AOR, especially Pink Floyd.[8]

This 'rock elite' of aesthetically *and* technically competent music makers was reinforced in its position by the onward development of technology. As the complexity of equipment increased, so too did the cultural and financial capital required to gain access to the means of production. In effect the record industry had ceded control to a coterie of established rock-masters. (Toynbee, 2000, p. 93)

This coterie involved both the 'superstar culture' mentioned above, but it also gave a new status to the 'technological expert', the usually faceless technologist whose knowledge of complex technology and 'abstract systems' is essential to the maintenance of production – in the case of rock, the 'producer'. For example, *The Dark Side of the Moon* as a technological achievement – setting new standards of studio production, employing cutting-edge technology (sequencers, for example), the role of producer Alan Parsons, who subsequently and not unrelatedly enjoyed success with his own band, the Alan Parsons Project, and, finally, mixer Chris Thomas, who subsequently produced the Sex Pistols' album *Never Mind the Bollocks* – an example of how technological considerations can complicate notions of 'authenticity' (given punk's derision of 'dinosaur' bands like Pink Floyd). Control of technology allows 'the technical apparatus and the social groups which administer it a disproportionate superiority to the rest of the population' (Adorno and Horkheimer, 1994, p. xiv). Masculinities in modernity, I would argue, are marked by their association with discourses of power: rationalization, industrialization and technological knowledge (Giddens, 1990, pp. 16–17). Power in Western industrialized society increasingly 'expresses itself not directly as authority but indirectly as the transformation of all relationships into objective, instrumental, depersonalised forms' (Benjamin, 1978, pp. 35–6; see also Weber, 1970, pp. 15–16; Hearn, 1994, p. 168). Authority is asserted through the implementation and adjustment of 'abstract systems' and their manipulation and control, rather than through direct performativity or 'machismo'.[9]

> Pink Floyd are a cult of unpersonality, a band who, after the departure of Syd, were bereft of a personal focal point and so let the icons and imagery of their albums do the job for them. This created one of the great marketing strategies of all time – the anti-image image ... think about the powerful icons the band have created ... These are amongst the most recognised and evocative images on earth ... yet their creators could walk through any shopping mall in any country unrecognized. (Jones, 1996b, p. 6)

This passage strongly suggests a rather different sort of male power to that usually associated with rock performers, not 'star' power, but the impersonal, organizational and financial power of successful capitalist entrepreneurs. It also suggests how 'high art' values segue neatly into consumerism. Yesterday's concept album is tomorrow's 'high concept'. 'The concept album ... far from vanishing, has grown to the extent that all rock tours have acquired particular identities, existing largely to promote a particular album' (Moore, 2001, p. 92). Pink Floyd in this sense have become a very much a 'corporate' entity, marked by the same anonymity that we often find in modern multinationals, what Jeff Hearn describes as a 'public' masculinity (1994, p. 1). I think this aspect has not been sufficiently emphasized in discussions of rock masculinities, perhaps because of the emphasis on rock as resisting or rebelling 'against the system'.

The association of masculinity with mental control of process through technology reproduces a mind/body dichotomy. In classical music, body is subservient to mind – the mental concept of the composer, as articulated in the score, is central, and the orchestra is like a machine which translates this into sound. Bodily display is kept to a minimum – both orchestral players and audiences may not physically respond to the music except within tightly controlled limits – the movements necessary to play, the applause at the end of the piece. As I pointed out above, the band perform in a way that minimizes their bodily presence, and, although I would not go so far as to suggest that audiences are obliged to respond to the same way, it is, however, true that the affect of Pink Floyd is often described in terms of a similar mind/body dichotomy, a mental response, as 'head' music (you can't dance to it). Moore describes the affect of a typical Floyd track as 'almost solipsistic', which again emphasizes the subjective aspect of 'inner space' (2001, p. 111). Paul Willis's account of hippie culture stresses that hippies prefer LPs (to singles), especially concept albums because they were 'clearly for listening to' (that is, taking drugs to) as opposed to dancing or as a background to other activities (Willis, 1978, p. 156).

Live, Pink Floyd showed a strong interest in controlling audience experience, rapidly moving from the 'freak-out, into the more controlled, refined atmosphere of the arts festival', where they could experiment and improve their sound – the technological sophistication of their presentation clearly required a more upmarket, bourgeois setting than the average rock concert. 'The sort of thing we do doesn't fit in to the environment we are playing in' (Roger Waters, quoted in Welch, 1994, p. 63). Their response was not to change themselves, but to change their environment. Floyd's concern with 'quality control' led to a highly structured concert experience in which the band's 'works' were often faithfully reproduced in their entirety, including *Dark Side* (Welch, 1994, p. 88). Such an approach is more redolent of classical than popular music, and perhaps it is unsurprising that Waters eventually became frustrated with the 'passivity' of audiences (leading to *The Wall*). But one has to say that the band put up the wall themselves, by buying into the high-art ethos, which is based around controlling dichotomies that reproduce patriarchal structures.

Rock and popular culture

Rock as popular culture emphasizes resistance to, rather than complicity with, dominant social groups, a creative form 'listened to and made by the same group of people' (usually working-class youth) (Landau, 1972, p. 40). In academia, the work of the Birmingham School of subcultural studies (Hebdige, 1979; Willis,

1978) articulates this broadly left-wing agenda, but it is also a founding tenet of rock criticism (hence the Landau quote). Central is the idea that rock music legitimates itself by articulating the voices of repressed groups, particularly, I would argue, in terms of age, class and ethnicity (rather than gender). Hence arises the concept of homologies between musics and repressed social groups, mythologies of rock's working-class 'street credibility' and, perhaps most importantly, of its African-American origins. For instance, Dick Hebdige treats Mods as emulating the 'cool' of the potent 'immaculate' African-American man, placing them squarely in a masculine lineage (1979, p. 45).

Similar themes of gender and race also occur in relation to rock performance. Writing on the electric guitar as a cultural signifier in rock music, Steve Waksman suggests:

> a racial subtext ... within which the primitive stands for the African-American influence upon electric guitar performance, whereas the technological stands for white contributions. For it was during this period [the mid-1960s] that the electric guitar came to embody a certain set of countercultural desires that hinged upon the transference of sexual identity between African-American and white men. (1999, p. 4)

Or, as Floyd's compatriots and contemporaries The Bonzo Dog Band put it: 'Can blue men sing the whites, or are they hypocrites?' (rhyming with 'whites', of course).[10] A question that was central to the developing rock aesthetic, and Pink Floyd's place within it.

Waksman argues that the emergence of Jimi Hendrix in London in 1966 (the same time and place as Pink Floyd) crystallized a set of anxieties about the authenticity of white rock music – for here was a 'primitive' black blues-man, charged with earthy sexuality, who was simultaneously a virtuoso, not only instrumentally but also in terms of his overall technological mastery of sound production, traditionally the 'white' domain. Thus Hendrix made even 'superstar' white musicians such as Eric Clapton, Mike Bloomfield and Pete Townshend, feel inadequate and 'emasculated' (Waksman, 1999, pp. 196–201).

One possible reaction to this by contemporary white artists was simply to remove black/blues influences from their music, and this I would argue was more or less what early Floyd did – early singles like 'See Emily Play' are marked by a pervasive 'Englishness' and whiteness: 'Syd's early singles unconsciously shunned the US blues roots of artists like Bo Diddley and Muddy Waters ... Instead, Syd's music brought forth a white middle class art school agenda' (Jones, 1996b, p. 15).[11] On a broader level, the developing progressive rock movement typically consisted of musicians who had started playing blues, but gradually moved away from it and towards an 'eclecticism' which was, however, mainly composed of primarily white Western musical forms, such as classical music, European folk musics and so forth (Chambers, 1985, pp. 85, 90). A crucial intermediary genre in this process was psychedelia, which encouraged such experimentation in the first place, and became, especially in the UK, a way of articulating a new kind of rock masculinity that did not depend for its legitimation upon African-American musical forms.

Pink Floyd as 'psychedelic mummy's boys'

Psychedelia, argue Simon Reynolds and Joy Press in *The Sex Revolts*, is a key to understanding changes in the ways masculinities were articulated in 1960s rock music, offering a 'way out' for white masculinities who felt that they could not compete with the perceived authenticity of African-American musicians, whose claims to be 'the people' were always going to be more compelling than those of middle-class English white boys.[12]

Press and Reynolds distinguish between active and passive masculinities in rock: on the one hand, the 'rebel' ethos of men 'breaking away', asserting their individuality, boasting about their sexual and other prowess, which in turn suggests a strong debt to African-American musical forms, especially blues; and on the other a counter-discourse of male passivity, a subjective rebellion of the mind, what are called the 'psychedelic mother's boys' (Reynolds and Press, 1995, p. 156). 'Underneath, say, the pastoralism of the Byrds, the born-again blues of Van Morrison, the oceanic-cosmic flux of Can and Pink Floyd is a nostalgia for the primal we of the mother/infant dyad' (ibid., p. 157), a nostalgic and regressive psychedelia, a resurgence of Romanticism's pastoralism and pantheism, a quest for a lost state of grace and childhood innocence. 'In psychedelia rock lost its hardness, became a medium in which the listener is suspended and enwombed.' Expanding on this metaphor, Reynolds and Press claim that psychedelia was a feminization of rock, in that it expressed 'a longing to come home, to return to the womb' (p. 184).

Pink Floyd fit the model in a number of ways – they were clearly psychedelic in terms of their audiences and milieux and also their music, which favoured drones (which Reynolds sees as a fundamental element of psychedelic music), 'weird' sound effects, mind-expanding light shows, and Barrett was certainly infantile. Later they lost Barrett's quirkiness, but adopted the slow tempos and hypnotic effect that characterized their 1970s sound, rock pastoralism, a kind of 'relax and let it all wash over you' effect, which Reynolds and Press find womblike and embracing. Also many of their song and album titles reference mothers and children: for example, 'Embryo', *Atom Heart Mother*, 'Matilda Mother'.

I would suggest that this model is a simplification. What psychedelia did, I would argue, is rearticulate a masculine myth of rock authenticity by moving it away from African-American 'origins' and finding an alternative source of authority in the past, literally – the myth of paradise, of original innocence, childhood. This return to Eden was effected through psychedelic drugs that 'destroyed' the masculine superego and restored a primitive naivety. It also connected strongly to Romantic ideologies about the 'true' vision of childhood, and the nostalgic, regressive Arcadianism that is a recurring theme in English middle-class culture.[13]

It is not difficult to find evidence of such themes in the early Pink Floyd, particularly in the work of Syd Barrett, but also, Reynolds and Press argue, in post-Barrett Floyd (pp. 170–75). Notably, however, their discussion stops abruptly short of *Dark Side*, and we might wonder why this is the case. Perhaps it is because its lyrical themes are implicitly critical of the whole psychedelic mummy's boy thesis. Clearly the group's involvement with Barrett is at least partially responsible for the band's lyrical preoccupation with madness and marginality, but their take on such themes is far removed from Reynolds's giddy Utopianism. Although, like Reynolds, they identify 'madness' with visions of lost innocence and childhood: 'remembering games and daisy chains and laughs' ('Brain Damage'), their conclusion is far more downbeat and 'realistic': 'Got to keep the loonies on the path.' There is no place in the modern world for 'inspired lunacy'. Presumably their involvement with an acid casualty gave them a rather more sober assessment of the revolutionary possibilities of psychedelia, and the associated sexual revolution, which Reynolds relates to a new, 'soft' rock masculinity. More broadly, to hear psychedelic music purely as an expression of 'male passivity' overlooks the aspects of technological mediation and performance, aspects very much to the fore on *Dark Side*.

Indeed, the growth of psychedelia is inextricable from discourses of technological progress and mastery of the recording studio. The Beatles' psychedelic period coincided with and was inseparable from their growing mastery and manipulation of studio technology, assisted by George Martin and the other Abbey Road sound engineers. Tracks like 'Strawberry Fields Forever' were the product of many hours of overdubbing, of varying tape speeds to achieve unusual timbres, of phasing, limiting and backwards recording. Although the Beatles shared the evocation of childhood and passivity that Reynolds describes as typical of psychedelia, this vision was achieved through technological mastery. Floyd in turn were profoundly influenced by the Beatles, and they even shared studios (Abbey Road) and the same recording engineer (Norman Smith).

Discourses of innocence and primitivism in psychedelia are, on closer examination, inseparable from the development of musical technology, and the way that buys into a rather different type of masculinity: Pink Floyd's well-documented studio perfectionism, and the hugely technological spectacle of their live shows. Pink Floyd then, as well as being psychedelic, also construct themselves as technological authoritarians, masters of a huge array of equipment (as on the cover of *Umma Gumma*), which in turn makes their diatribes against authoritarianism like *The Wall* and, to some degree, *The Dark Side of the Moon*, seem unintentionally ironic. They may have been mummy's boys, but they were playing with daddy's toys.

However, Reynolds has also pointed to the more recent trend in dance culture of artists like the Orb who constantly refer to and sample Floyd's works ('The Back

Side of the Moon') to create a 'chillout' ambience of beatific relaxation after the exertions of the dancefloor. Combined, again with hallucinogenics, in this case Ecstasy, the affect achieved, according to Reynolds, is a unique state of jouissance and innocence in a Second Summer of Love. Doesn't this confirm his earlier suppositions (1999, pp. 181–9) about the band as in some sense 'psychedelic/ feminine/regressive'?

Not necessarily. Rather than seeing the resurgence of Floyd in dance culture solely in terms of a regressive desire for pre-Oedipal bliss, perhaps what is more relevant is how the band's use of technology predicts dance culture – basically habituating audiences to a performance spectacle which highlights technology and de-emphasizes the role of the performer, in which the performers are less important than the whiz-bang effects, and the 'humanity' of the music is persistently made subservient to the medium. A second point of similarity is the perceived 'anonymity' of dance producers, which could be seen as continuing a tradition of 'retiring', non-performative masculinities, hiding behind their machines, like Pink Floyd in live performance: super techno boffins, whose physical (non)appearance belies their mental (and financial) mastery and control. Direct masculine dominance has been replaced by discourses of technology and corporatization: 'However depersonalised or obscured, the new form of rationality which has superseded patriarchal religion and the visible role of pater familias should be understood as the embodiment of male domination in the culture as a whole ... we could think of this as patriarchy without the father' (Benjamin, 1978, p. 36). The second way in which this relates to Pink Floyd is in relation to African-American culture – the black masculinity (paternity) that is central to the development of rock is repudiated, and replaced by a white discourse of technological superiority, just as the body in Floyd's music is subservient to a primarily mental experience.

Notes

1. 'Chain Lightning', Steely Dan, *Katy Lied* (1975).
2. Another more recent study is Will Straw's 'Sizing Up Record Collections' (1997).
3. Frith and McRobbie (1990); Reynolds and Press (1995); Palmer (1997); Frith (1988); Walser (1993).
4. Marsh (1999), p. 338; Moore (2001), p. 69; Sheinbaum (2002), p. 21.
5. Bourdieu (1984), p. 3; Green (1988), p. 111.
6. Mulvey (1989), p. 20; Green (1997), pp. 22–6.
7. Theberge (1989), p. 106; Toynbee (2000), p. 69.
8. Of course, any musician who is familiar with multitracking knows that machines, like human beings, introduce new errors of their own and that, while often annoying, system errors can sometimes suggest new possibilities. Some studio auteurs such as Eno attempt to incorporate such discrepancies into their studio practice – 'honour thy error as a hidden intention' (Eno).
9. 'Abstract systems' deal in information rather than material goods, like the phone network or the stock exchange, in which we invest trust in unseen others or faceless

experts who maintain these systems, thereby replacing a direct social interaction with an indirect, mediated one (Giddens (1990), pp. 83–6).

10. 'Can Blue Men Sing the Whites', Bonzo Dog Band, *Urban Spaceman* (1968).

11. Admittedly the B-side of their first single, 'Candy and a Currant Bun', steals the riff of Howlin' Wolf's 'Smokestack Lightnin' '. But the effect is hardly blues.

12. It must be acknowledged that Hendrix himself played music that was profoundly psychedelic, which is a point that Waksman misses. The way he describes Hendrix's impact centres around the impact of Hendrix's early live performance persona, an image which is in many ways at odds with the kind of music Hendrix created in the studio, especially *Electric Ladyland*.

13. But such a regression to childhood was more socially acceptable for men than women, perhaps because female passivity and 'childishness' invite too much sexual attention. The psychedelic little boys of the 1960s are many (consider Syd Barrett, John Lennon, Brian Wilson and Jimi Hendrix, for example) but we look in vain for their female counterparts.

Chapter 4

'We're not in Kansas any more': music, myth and narrative structure in *The Dark Side of the Moon*

Lee Barron and Ian Inglis

1939 has been described as Hollywood's greatest year. Production and consumption were at record levels, with the major studios releasing nearly 400 movies, which were watched by average weekly worldwide audiences of more than 200 million. They included such memorable films as *Gone With The Wind* (Victor Fleming), *Ninotchka* (Ernst Lubitsch), *Mr Smith Goes to Washington* (Frank Capra), *Stagecoach* (John Ford), *The Roaring Twenties* (Raoul Walsh), *Dark Victory* (Edmund Goulding), *Wuthering Heights* (William Wyler), *Goodbye Mr Chips* (Sam Wood), *Destry Rides Again* (George Marshall), and *The Wizard of Oz* (Victor Fleming).

1973 was an equally buoyant year for popular music. Global sales figures in excess of two billion dollars continued the annual upward momentum stimulated by the impact of the Beatles and the subsequent 'British invasion' of ten years earlier, and significant future trajectories were signalled by the debut recordings of performers such as Bruce Springsteen, Barry White, Bob Marley, and the New York Dolls. The year's album releases included Mike Oldfield's *Tubular Bells*, Paul McCartney and Wings' *Band on the Run*, Led Zeppelin's *Houses of the Holy*, the Eagles' *Desperado*, David Bowie's *Aladdin Sane*, John Lennon's *Mind Games*, Elton John's *Goodbye Yellow Brick Road*, The Who's *Quadrophenia*, Stevie Wonder's *Innervisions*, and Pink Floyd's *The Dark Side of the Moon*.

Separated by several decades, and ranging across two distinct, if related, areas of the entertainment industry, the above sets of facts would seem to have little in common, other than to provide confirmation of professional achievements and activity. Indeed, for more than 30 years, Pink Floyd's album – marked by its 'acute balance of opposites ... full of great big noises and quietness that's almost subsonic' (Sutcliffe and Henderson, 1998, pp. 68–9) – has been one of popular music's greatest commercial successes.[1] More recently, however, its reputation has been augmented by the addition of a meticulous and complex theory which claims that the album was conceived, constructed, and produced as a deliberate and calculated musical accompaniment to the narrative of *The Wizard of Oz*, and that its noises and silences will, if correctly decoded, reveal explicit and specific congruences with key scenes from the movie.

The origins of the theory can be traced to the mid-1990s, when 'various Pink Floyd fan websites started getting excited about the synchronicities that happen when you watch the movie and listen to the album simultaneously' (Fielder, 2003, p. 68). These fansites (and there are many) contain detailed instructions for the newcomer to follow in order to explore and experience the audio-visual parallels.

Typically, the viewer is told to begin the film, but almost immediately to engage the pause button, stopping the video or DVD at the precise moment that the pre-credit MGM trademark lion reaches its third roar. Then he/she should reduce the sound of the television, activate the CD (setting it on repeat), and restart the film. If the music begins at the exact moment that the credit 'Produced by Mervyn Leroy' appears on screen, then the musical-visual parallel is on track. And the coincidences begin:

- Seconds after the words 'look around' during 'Breathe', Dorothy turns around.
- As the band sings 'no one told you when to run', Dorothy breaks into a trot.
- The chimes on 'Time' coincide with the arrival of the Wicked Witch of the West.
- 'The Great Gig In The Sky' starts just as the tornado begins and ends just as it ceases.
- To the lyric 'balanced on the biggest wave', Dorothy is seen to be balancing upon a fence.
- During 'On The Run', helicopter sounds on the album cue Dorothy looking into the sky, as if hearing the noise.
- Against the lyric 'tired of lying in the sunshine', Dorothy's dog Toto is seen lying on a bed, bathed in sunshine.
- The Munchkins dance in time to 'Money'.
- The lyric 'and everyone you meet' cues Dorothy meeting the Tin Man.
- As the album ends to the sound of fading heartbeats, Dorothy is listening to the Tin Man's chest to see if he has a heart.
- The first letters of the opening three lines of 'Money' ('Money, get away / Get a good job with more pay and you're OK / Money, it's a gas') spell out MGM, the studio that produced *The Wizard of Oz*.

The exact number of such musical-visual coincidences is uncertain, but this very vagueness only serves to compound the mystique of the phenomenon. Different websites claim between 70 and 100 synchronicities between the album and the film. And while some provide 'definitive' lists of the parallels, others only provide selections, so as not to spoil the thrill of the search for new participants. In this way, the process of discovery is *active*: those who consult the sites are encouraged to complete the exercise, report back with their results and, in so doing, strengthen the circulation of the myth.

The imposition of such subversive or alternative 'meanings' on any cultural text is always likely to be labeled as a disruptive, even destructive attack on the status of the text – and, by implication, its original author(s): 'textual meaning still holds privilege over readers' meanings; fan activities are still defined primarily through relations of consumption and spectatorship rather than production or participation' (Tulloch and Jenkins, 1995, p. 4). Yet the enthusiasm with which the story has been, and continues to be, circulated suggests that there are many such 'textual poachers' prepared to challenge 'official' discourses.

The claimed associations between *The Dark Side of the Moon* and *The Wizard of Oz* constitute an example of an 'urban myth' or 'urban legend'. Urban legends are 'tales circulated widely in modern society … they are generally transmitted orally … although some are also picked up and disseminated, usually unattributed, by mass media, and told as "true stories", often attributed to a friend of a friend' (Jones, 1995, p. 439). It has been suggested that they 'belong to the subclass of folk narratives, legends … believed, or at least believable' (Brunvald, 1981, p. 3). They are often fantastical stories that are told and re-told, and that, however unlikely, achieve an enviable longevity: 'The Hook', 'The Spider in the Beehive Hairstyle', 'The Snake in the Blanket' and 'Alligators in the Sewers' are among the most dramatic.

Significantly, it has been noted that 'whatever the origins of urban legends, their dissemination is no mystery … groups of age-mates, especially adolescents, are one important American legend channel, but other paths of transmission are among office workers and club members, as well as among religious, recreational, and regional groups' (ibid., pp. 4–5).

Fans – in this case, the fans of Pink Floyd – represent one such group. The 'rumour' about the musical-visual interplay between *The Dark Side of the Moon* and *The Wizard of Oz* has been disseminated in the same ways in which traditional urban legends have gained widespread credence. Initially generated through a casual process of 'word of mouth' between peers, such tales may eventually come to the attention of a member of the mass media who then passes on the story – either as news or entertainment – to a wider audience. And, as total global sales of *The Dark Side of the Moon* are in excess of 30 million, there are considerably more opportunities than is normal for the 'friend of a friend' rationale to be employed in advertising this story. Fanzines are additional vehicles of transmission. Localized, independent, and often highly idiosyncratic, they are ideal mediums for the publication of novel or alternative readings. Occupying a cultural terrain that lies 'somewhere between a personal letter and a magazine' (Duncombe, 1997, p. 10), they provide fertile ground for the transmission of musical urban myths.

However, through the 1990s, many of the traditional sites of fan literature began to give way to the Internet and, as noted above, it was at this point that the connections between Pink Floyd's album and Victor Fleming's movie spilled out from a relatively small and exclusive community to a wider general public. In so doing, it provided a concise illustration of Manuel Castells' observations about the nature of contacts and communications within 'the network society':

> For all the science fiction ideology and commercial hype surrounding the emergence of the so-called Information Superhighway, we can hardly underestimate its significance. The potential integration of text, images and sounds in the same system, interacting from multiple points, in chosen time (real or delayed) along a global network, in conditions of open and affordable access, does fundamentally change the character of communication. (1996, p. 328)

An early demonstration of the consequences of the Internet's effective transformation of communication was the generation and circulation of the urban legend that *The Blair Witch Project* (Daniel Myrick and Eduardo Sanchez, 1999) was a true story. In fact, the myth had considerable commercial repercussions and 'fostered tremendous sub-cultural interest in the phenomenon' (Best and Kellner, 2001, p. 241), Those who enter the key words 'Wizard Of Oz & Dark Side Of The Moon' into a search engine are likewise directed to numerous sites in which the story is presented and discussed; indeed, many of the sites have been established for this sole purpose. By taking advantage of the Internet's capacity for global instantaneous transfers of information, stories which previously may have passed from a friend to a friend have been supplemented by stories passing from a site to a site:

> In the past, rumoring has been discussed as a type of communication that was only possible with people who were already involved in the same social network or by way of direct physical contact. The Internet has changed the ways rumoring can happen and has made possible rumoring between people who have never met or communicated before. (Fisher, 1998, p. 159)

In almost all cases, attempts to trace the sources of the classic, perennial urban myths, many of which continue to circulate today, are impossible. The doctor who treated the woman fatally bitten by the exotic snake lurking in the blanket, the cheated wife who sold the husband's Porsche for $50, the unsuspecting motorist who picked up a phantom hitch-hiker, and other familiar characters can rarely, if ever, be located. However, *The Dark Side of the Moon's* status as an eccentric soundtrack to *The Wizard of Oz* soundtrack *can* be directly traced to its supposed source: Pink Floyd. Nonetheless, its members have always dismissively refuted any association:

> David Gilmour has spoken of 'some guy with too much time on his hands', and Waters finds it 'amusing'. But it's Nick Mason who has really let the cat out of the bag. 'It's absolute nonsense,' he replied when asked about it, 'it has nothing to do with *The Wizard Of Oz*. It was based on *The Sound Of Music!*' (Fielder, 2003, p. 68)

Such blunt denials from the band have been supported by comments from the album's sound engineer, Alan Parsons, who has pointed to the absence in the early 1970s of the video technology which would have been needed to fashion such complex musical-visual links. Furthermore, the recording history of the album reveals that Pink Floyd were forced to schedule their studio sessions over nine months between extensive tours of Europe, America and Japan, and commitments to film soundtracks – which would leave little time or space for the kind of detailed planning required for deliberate movie/album synchronization. But such objections fail to discourage the theory's proponents. In fact, the protestations from Gilmour, Mason, and Parsons have encouraged an alternative 'sub-theory' that the correspondences were, therefore, purely the creation of Roger Waters alone, who fabricated and inserted them without the knowledge of the other band members. His fascination with background sound effects, spoken dialogue, and other narrative components, illustrated on post-Pink Floyd solo albums like *The Pros and Cons of Hitch Hiking* and *Radio Kaos*, and his precise instructions to the listener who wants to fully experience the 'Qsound' of *Amused To Death* have been presented as illustrations of an overarching desire to adorn his albums with additional layers of information and meaning.

Along with the Pretty Things' *S. F. Sorrow*, The Who's *Tommy*, the Beatles' *Sgt Pepper's Lonely Hearts Club Band*, David Bowie's *The Rise and Fall of Ziggy Stardust & The Spiders From Mars*, the Kinks' *Arthur*, and Mike Oldfield's *Tubular Bells*, *The Dark Side of the Moon* is generally, if inexactly, perceived as one of popular music's first 'concept albums':

> Concept albums (and rock operas) are unified by a theme, which can be instrumental, compositional, narrative or lyrical. In this form, the album changed from a collection of heterogeneous songs into a narrative work with a single theme, in which individual songs segue into one another. (Shuker, 1998, p. 5).

Through the 1980s and 1990s, the 'concept' album gradually became less fashionable, although examples such as Queensryche's *Operation Mindcrime*, Marilyn Manson's *Antichrist Superstar*, and Dream Theater's *Scenes from A Memory* have retained its commercial presence. However, around those albums where such a 'concept' or 'message' is believed to exist, audiences remain more than ready to search out and expose additional, often 'hidden' aspects of the information or instructions it contains. Claims by fans of Pink Floyd that the cover of the band's post-Waters 1995 live album, *Pulse*, reveals images of Dorothy's red shoes, the Wicked Witch of the West's bicycle, and the Tin Man's axe (Fielder, 2003, p. 68) have therefore been incorporated into the original thesis. And assertions that some of the band's other albums, such as *Meddle*, *Wish You Were Here*, and *Animals*, were similarly constructed to act as musical accompaniments to films as varied as *Fantasia* (James Algar and Samuel Armstrong, 1940), *Blade Runner* (Ridley Scott, 1982), *Videodrome* (David Cronenberg, 1983), and *Contact* (Robert Zemeckis, 1997) – or that the directors of those movies consciously fashioned movies which studiously reflected the rhythms and tempos of those albums – have added to the identification of the band as possessing a prescient, not to say preternatural, creative impulse. Equally, of course, they may have also added to a wider public perception of fans who engage in such discussions as irrational and/or obsessive:

> Fandom is conceived of as a chronic attempt to compensate for a perceived personal lack of autonomy, absence of community, incomplete identity, lack of power and lack of recognition ... the inadequate fan is defined as someone who is making up for some inherent lack. He or she seeks identity, connection and meaning via celebrities ... the fan has fragile self-esteem, weak or non-existent social alliances, a dull and monotonous 'real' existence. (Jenson, 1992, pp. 17–18)

From this perspective, fans' immersion into the labrynthine world of Pink Floyd, the search for hidden clues, the announcement of revelatory discoveries, and the construction of an 'imagined community' can thus be seen as attempts to galvanize and refashion the meaningless and unsatisfying routines of their own mundane lives.

In passing, it should be noted that the contemporary and commonplace invalidation of fans, as reported by Jenson, has been a persistent feature in sociological analyses of musical consumption for many decades. Adorno's belief that pre-war listeners to popular music were 'not merely turned away from more important music, but confirmed in their neurotic stupidity' (1991, p. 41) and Hoggart's description of the post-war audience for rock'n'roll in the United Kingdom as 'living to a large extent in a myth-world ... they form a depressing group ... perhaps most of them are rather less intelligent than average ... they have no aim, no ambition, no protection, no belief' (1957, pp. 248–9) may merely be two of the more familiar accounts that have sought to undermine fans and their activities.

Struggles at an ideological level between the 'superiority' of products of 'high' culture and the 'inferiority' of products of 'popular' or 'mass' culture will not be resolved by resorting to accusations of elitism. It has been suggested, however, that 'one major distinction between "popular" art forms and academically "canonized" works could be that fans of popular art and artists engage in their connoisseurship or scholarship voluntarily, and not in school' (Hawkins, 1990, p. 109). In this respect, there is little doubt that *The Dark Side of the Moon* (and *The Wizard of Oz*) categorically belong in the realm of the popular – which might explain why the scholarship surrounding them (and its effective scholars) are not accorded any formal status.

But, however outrageous or abnormal the behaviour and explanations of fan communities might appear to Adorno, Hoggart et al., their interpretations – *any* interpretations – are not inherently invalid. The belief that any album or play or novel or movie – whether it be Pink Floyd's *The Dark Side of the Moon*, William Shakespeare's *The Taming of the* Shrew, J.D. Salinger's *The Catcher in the Rye* or

Sam Peckinpah's *The Wild Bunch* – possesses a single, absolute 'meaning' is difficult to sustain, since it rests on the assumption that the text contains a deliberate message, which is decoded by the reader in the way it was encoded by the producer, and which is accepted uncritically. The recognition that texts generate multiple meanings that free the reader from the tyranny of imposed definition is one of the principal tenets underlying the relocation of the consumer as *active* rather than *passive*. The implications of this have been neatly described by Wolff:

> The reader, viewer or audience is actively involved in the construction of the work of art, and without the act of reception/consumption, the cultural product is incomplete. This is not to say that consumption is simultaneous with production, but that it complements and completes it. (1981, p. 95)

Such completions, expansions and extensions serve to illustrate the more general patterns of myth circulation, as predicted by Brunvald: 'the telling of one story inspires other people to share what they have read or heard, and in a short time a lively exchange of details occurs and ... new variants are created' (1981, p. 5).

Popular music is by no means the only, or even the principal, area of contemporary social life in which such urban myths have taken root and flourished. We suspect there are very few people in the Western world who have not heard, in some guise or other, the story of the vanishing hitch-hiker, or the baby-sitter menaced by the madman in the upstairs room, or the funeral ashes mistakenly used as exotic spices, or the moon mission that was actually carried out in a Hollywood film studio. The function of such myths, it is often alleged, is to provide vehicles through which 'symbolic expression is given to the unconscious desires, fears and tensions that underlie patterns of human behaviour ... mythology, in other words, is psychology misread as biography' (Campbell, 1949, p. 256).

But the deficiency in such explanations is, as Campbell correctly recognizes, that it is clear that the patterns through which myths are generated and circulated are *consciously* articulated. They are not spontaneous or irrational assertions, but 'controlled and intended statements' (ibid., p. 257) which might function, in a similar way to fairy tales, to allow members of a community (particularly the young) to access the wisdom and experience of past generations in order to learn of the dangers that exist in the wider world. Thus, the encounter with a vanishing hitch-hiker teaches us to be wary of strangers; the fate of the unsuspecting baby-sitter reminds us to be vigilant at all times; the eating of the funeral ashes tells us to avoid rash actions without full knowledge of the facts; the deception of the faked moon mission warns us not to trust those in authority.

However, the urban myths of popular music are not so easily explained in these terms. Many of them seem to contain little in the way of warning or guidance, but stand by themselves as independent narratives. Consider the following examples:

- *Bob Dylan's unannounced visit*   On a trip to London, Bob Dylan contacts Dave Stewart of the Eurythmics, who invites him to use his studio. However, Dylan goes to the wrong address, the house of a plumber whose name is also Dave. When the plumber returns from work, his wife greets him with the words, 'Bob Dylan's here to see you – he's in the kitchen, having a cup of tea.'

- *Paul is dead*   At the height of the Beatles' success, Paul McCartney is killed in a car crash, and replaced by an actor named William Campbell. The Beatles are able to continue their career (with the impostor) for several years, but provide numerous clues about the circumstances of Paul's death – on their album covers, in the lyrics of their songs, in films and photographs of the group.

- *The Rolling Stones, Marianne Faithfull and a Mars bar*   In May 1967, the police raid Keith Richards' home in Sussex, and arrest Richards, Mick Jagger and art gallery owner Robert Fraser on drugs charges. During the raid, the police discover a naked Marianne Faithfull lying across the sofa, while Jagger eats a Mars bar that is protruding from her vagina.

- *The Beatles' lost album*   Shortly before the release of *Abbey Road*, the master tapes of another planned album by the Beatles ('Hot As Sun'), are stolen from the home of George Martin, and the offices of EMI and Apple. They are held to ransom. Of the three sets of tapes, two are destroyed and the third is accidentally wiped clean while being brought through the X-ray security equipment at Heathrow.

Like these, and many other, examples, the reported connection between *The Dark Side of the Moon* and *The Wizard of Oz* seems to provide neither guidance nor warning to those who hear of it. To fully understand the continued propagation of the story – despite the refutations of the members of Pink Floyd themselves – it is important therefore, to focus attention not only on the substantive details of the story, but also on the motivations of those who relate it. We suggest there are four major categories into which the story-tellers may be placed.

1. *The believer*   This is the person who genuinely believes – or hopes – that the story is true. Repeated examinations of the album's soundtrack and the movie's narrative have convinced him/her that the correspondences are too exact to be coincidental. The group's denials are dismissed as playful attempts to confuse audiences and which, ironically, only add to the conviction with which the story is believed. The believer's revelations of the story serve to concentrate attention on the musical inventiveness of Pink Floyd and the astonishing intricacy of the album.

2. *The cynic*   Conversely, the cynic knows, or believes, the story to be false. In telling the story, he/she intends to illustrate the absurdity of the myth and the gullibility of those who subscribe to it. Cynics outside Pink Floyd's

immediate fan base may relate the story as a means of undermining and questioning the maturity and judgement of those fans and, by implication, of the group itself; those within the group's fan base may create and exacerbate divisions between believers and non-believers.

3. *The entertainer* The accuracy or inaccuracy of the claims is irrelevant to the entertainer, for whom the story is merely a diverting or unusual tale to be told to others; it is related in the same way that a joke is told. He/she may expect to gain a reputation as a raconteur of amusing and provocative anecdotes. Repetitions of the story for social reasons will inevitably lead to a wider circulation of its components, and there is no guarantee that those to whom it is presented as 'mere' entertainment will accept it as such.

4. *The expert* For the expert, each retelling of the story increases the stock of 'cultural capital' he/she possesses. The apparent access to knowledge and insights not shared by others may be employed as a specific attribute which lends the expert a mark of distinction. That sense of authority is further increased if the expert can claim (as he/she often does) a more personal association with the source of the story. Cultural capital may, of course, be associated with material capital; the acquisition of exclusive information is often seen to follow naturally from the collection of rare or valuable materials.

Thus, the continued distribution to ever-wider audiences of the alleged intersections between Pink Floyd's 1973 album, MGM's 1939 musical and (by extension) L. Frank Baum's 1900 novel on which the movie was based, can be seen to derive from a variety of reasons, both personal and social. In this sense, attempts to 'prove' or 'disprove' the assertions are irrelevant, since those who claim to investigate the myth may be motivated by shifting combinations of self-aggrandizement, group membership, and socio-cultural status, more than they are by the spirit of objective enquiry.

Whether the coincidences between *The Dark Side of the Moon* and *The Wizard of Oz* are regarded as deliberate, accidental, contrived or fanciful, each of the types of story-teller discussed above retains a vested interest in preserving its circulation. More importantly, the acts of deconstruction and reconstruction which have surrounded *The Dark Side of the Moon* may be seen as an anti-authoritarian act that is entirely justified:

> The reader is always right, and no one can take away the freedom to make whatever use of a text which suits him ... the right to leaf back and forward, to skip whole passages, to read sentences against the grain, to misunderstand them, to reshape them, to embroider them with every possible association, to draw conclusions from the text of which the text knows nothing. (Enzensberger, 1992, p. 11)

Moreover, the narrative that they have developed has failed to damage either the sales of the album or the reputation of its creators. More than 30 years after its release, it still continues to sell between 250,000 and 500,000 copies annually; music magazines regularly revisit the album to confirm it as one of the most significant in rock and roll's history;[2] and Pink Floyd tribute bands recognize it as a lucrative way of making contact with the group's older fans as well as cohorts of newer listeners deprived of the opportunity to attend the original live performances.[3]

Much of the extraordinary longevity of *The Dark Side of the Moon* can be ascribed to the pervasive mystery and powerful emotional impetus that are intrinsic to its music – soaring vocals, electronic innovations, instrumental virtuosity, quirky eccentricities, and disturbing lyrics. That these attributes might be compounded by the addition of a myth which attempts to unite two of the 20th century's most significant cultural inventions – cinema and rock and roll – does not detract from, but adds to the complexity with which the production and consumption of the album has been, and continues to be, invested. The desire to totalize, or unify, artistic forms in this way exemplifies Eco's insights into the manner in which contemporary culture views reality.

> The closed, single conception in a work by a medieval artist reflected the conception of the cosmos as a hierarchy of fixed, preordained orders. In the modern scientific universe ... the whole construct expands towards a totality which is near to the infinite. It refuses to be hemmed in by any ideal normative conception of the world. It shares in a general urge toward discovery and constantly renewed contact with reality. (1981, p. 57)

Finally, it has to be recognized that, however we may come to evaluate the 'truth' or 'untruth' of the myth, there are undeniable similarities of production between the 'electronics, technology, sound effects, synthesizers, space and intellectuality' (Sutcliffe and Henderson, 1998, p. 68) that permeate the album, and 'the intensity of color and special effects ... [and] ... aggregation of elements designed to appeal to a range of different viewers' (Maltby, 1995, pp. 26–7) that characterize the movie. Lyrically too, there is little difference between Pink Floyd's declaration that 'home, home again ... I like to be here when I can ... when I come home cold and tired, it's good to warm my bones beside the fire' and Dorothy's realization on her return from Oz that 'if I ever go looking for my heart's desire again, I won't go looking any further than my own back yard, because if you can't find it there, then you probably never lost it in the first place.'

In her account of the golden age of Hollywood, during which *The Wizard of Oz* was produced, Stacey has suggested that 'Hollywood cinema offered audiences the possibility to be part of another world far away from the difficulties of everyday life' (1994, p. 125). Whether that other world lies in the land of Oz or on the dark side of the moon, it would appear that Dorothy and Pink Floyd offer remarkably similar conclusions about the advantages that exploration, discovery, and travel (physical, emotional, or intellectual) are likely to produce.

In nothing else studied can more delight be experienced while in the pursuit of knowledge. Where can our hearts and brains and courage be more enriched than on the yellow brick road to the Emerald City of Oz? (Hawkins, 1990, p. 183)

In the light of such commonalities of sentiment and intent, it may not be surprising that the road from Kansas to the dark side of the moon remains a route along which many travellers are prepared to journey.

Notes

1. It has sold more than 30 million copies since its release in 1973. Only three albums – Michael Jackson's *Thriller*, Fleetwood Mac's *Rumours*, and *Saturday Night Fever* – have sold more.
2. See, for example, 'The First Men on the Moon', *Mojo*, 52, March 1998, pp. 66–89; 'Dark Side of the Moon', *Classic Rock*, 51, March 2003, pp. 64–8.
3. The Australian Pink Floyd Show's 'Dark Side Of The Moon 30th Anniversary Tour' in 2003–4 advertised itself as offering 'live note-for-note recreation of the greatest rock album of all time'.

Part II

'Everything under the sun is in tune'
Musical and structural discussions

Chapter 5

'Worked out within the grooves': the sound and structure of *The Dark Side of the Moon*

Kevin J. Holm-Hudson

The Dark Side of the Moon (1973) introduced Pink Floyd to a mass rock audience, especially in America (then the world's largest market for popular music). Because the group was largely still an 'underground' or 'cult' band in America prior to its release, the album was received as stunningly avant-garde 'head music' by American listeners in the mid-1970s, much as a previous generation had embraced *Sgt. Pepper* as some new oracle of the electronic age.

However, *The Dark Side of the Moon* did not emerge from a musical vacuum. It is best understood in the context of developments in popular music in the late 1960s and early 1970s, especially the development of the concept album. Its diverse influences are not only drawn from the group's previous work but also from the Beatles' *Sgt. Pepper*, the lesser-known work of American electronic pioneers Paul Beaver and Bernard Krause, and even Marvin Gaye's *What's Going On*.

In its review of *The Dark Side of the Moon* upon its release, *Rolling Stone* noted, 'The sound is lush and multilayered while remaining clear and well-structured ... *The Dark Side of the Moon* is a fine album with a textural and conceptual richness that not only invites, but demands involvement' (Grossman, 1973, p. 57). Thirty years later, Phish's bassist Mike Gordon speaks with admiration of 'how well the songs on the album flow from one to the next to create an overall experience greater than the sum of its parts' (see p. 219 of this volume).

Alan Parsons, the *Dark Side* engineer, remembers that:

> performing it as a complete piece [as the group had done in their concerts since early 1972] had an effect on the way they structured it for the studio. Most of it was actually recorded as an album; the songs weren't separated. Most of the two sides [of the album] were recorded as they were eventually mixed. The final running order was pretty much determined from the first days. (Lambert, 1998)

Parsons attributes its unprecedented success to its compatibility with the then-emerging American 'Album Oriented Radio' FM format. 'It was very programmable. If a jock wanted to play two or three tracks one after the other,

he'd had his work done for him because all the segues were carefully worked out within the grooves' (MacDonald, 1997, p. 245). The variety of segues – timbral, harmonic, metric – between tracks give the *Dark Side* album a multidimensional unity that is lacking in Pink Floyd's later concept albums, with the exception of *Dark Side*'s successor *Wish You Were Here* (1975).

In discussing how the segues work to enhance the dramatic effect of *The Dark Side of the Moon*, I will draw upon analogies from film theory. Rebecca Leydon (2001) has applied aspects of film editing to account for transitions in the music of Debussy; I propose that the cinematic qualities of Pink Floyd's segues, coupled with the dramatic unity that is characteristic of the concept album, combine to striking effect in *The Dark Side of the Moon*.

Patrick McDonald (1997) has remarked on the 'filmic quality' of Pink Floyd's music, a quality no doubt observed by film makers such as Michelangelo Antonioni and Barbet Schroeder, who sought the group's services for soundtracks in the late 1960s and early 1970s. (The group's last Schroeder soundtrack, for the 1972 film *La Vallée,* was recorded concurrently with the first *Dark Side* sessions and released as *Obscured by Clouds*.) The cinematic aspects of Pink Floyd's music, and *The Dark Side of the Moon* in particular, came to the fore again in 1997 as rumors spread that the album was a soundtrack to the first 43 minutes of *The Wizard of Oz*. Such rumors had been circulating on the Internet for several years, by some accounts as early as 1994 (*MTV.com News,* 1997). When WZLX-FM in Boston and WNEW-FM in New York reported the story on the air in the spring of 1997, audience response was overwhelming. George Taylor Morris, the disk jockey for WZLX-FM in Boston, said, 'I just mentioned it, just briefly on the air' (*MTV.com News,* 1997). Helen Kennedy's (1997) *New York Daily News* article on the *Dark Side/Oz* connection was widely circulated in the mainstream media; within a few weeks sales for *The Dark Side of the Moon* had doubled. EMI-Capitol's response was a delighted laissez-faire; they had benefited from a similar situation in 1976 when rumors circulated that an album by the Toronto studio band Klaatu, also Capitol artists, was in fact the long-lost Beatles' 'Sun album' (Bradley, 2000). Bruce Kirkland, chief of EMI-Capitol, said, 'It's happening at an organic, grass-roots level, but we're into fueling it … Why not? It's not harmful, it's not exploitative, and nobody died. It's just fun. Yeah, let's get into it' (Gunderson, 1997, p. 2D).

Band members denied any connection, and engineer Alan Parsons has said that no one in the band mentioned *The Wizard of Oz* while the record was being made (Gardner, 2002): 'There simply wasn't mechanics to do it. We had no means of playing videotapes in the room at all. I don't think VHS had come along by '72, had it?' (*MTV.com News,* 1997). Nevertheless, the fact that so many fans believed (and may still believe) that *The Dark Side of the Moon* was a hidden 'soundtrack' to *The Wizard of Oz* is testimony to the novelty and effectiveness of the segues that give the album its continuity and dramatic shape.

Several species of small schizophrenic soundbites ...

The Dark Side of the Moon was (and is) also widely acclaimed for its novel use of electronics and sound effects. By 1973, Pink Floyd already had a well-established underground reputation for 'wielding an arsenal of sound effects with authority and finesse', and they were noted for 'their dazzling and potentially overwhelming sonic wizzardry [*sic*]' (Grossman, 1973, p. 57). Although the group had used sound effects since their first album (1967's 'Bike' even ends with a clock-chimes collage that anticipates 1973's 'Time'), by *The Dark Side of the Moon* such effects were used as integral, unifying elements of the music rather than for distracting transitions. Even Robert Christgau, amidst his patronizing post-punk assessment of the album in 1981, grudgingly concedes the skill with which such effects were used: 'It may sell on sheer aural sensationalism, but the studio effects do transmute David Gilmour's guitar solos into something more than they were when he played them. Its taped speech fragments may be old hat, but for once they cohere musically' (McDonald, 1997, p. 61).

Pink Floyd's early use of electronics and sound effects may be compared with the contemporaneous work of American electronic musicians Paul Beaver and Bernard Krause, who released three albums for Warner Brothers in the early 1970s – *In a Wild Sanctuary* (1970), *Gandharva* (1971), and *All Good Men* (1972) – as well as recording the instructional record *The Nonesuch Guide to Electronic Music* (1968) for the classical Nonesuch label. Although their recordings were at the time considered pioneering in their use of electronics, Beaver and Krause tended to downplay its electronic aspects, preferring to think of their music as 'a new form of audio-expressionism' (Logan and Woffinden, 1977, p. 28). *Rolling Stone* recognized this in its review of *In a Wild Sanctuary*:

> Unfortunately, the electronic music synthesizer ... often invites the generating of some cerebral and boring music ... So it's nice to find *In a Wild Sanctuary* ... which avoids the pitfall ... *Sanctuary*, although full of (invisible) electronic prowess, shows the Moog relegated to the position of a 'sideman,' playing its sounds when needed, never a dictating or lead instrument. (Amatneek, 1970, p. 46)

In a Wild Sanctuary was praised as 'a tasteful mixture of concrete sounds, instrumental music and the vibrations from technological artistry' (ibid., p. 46). Similar remarks were made in *Rolling Stone*'s review of *The Dark Side of the Moon*: 'Throughout the album the band lays down *a solid framework which they embellish* with synthesizers, sound effects and spoken voice tapes' (Grossman, 1973, p. 57; emphasis added).

Beaver and Krause met in April 1967, at about the same time as Pink Floyd's first UK chart success with 'Arnold Layne'. They had a singularly eclectic background between them. Paul Beaver was 13 years Krause's senior, and had been working with electronic sound for a number of years (in 1953 he contributed electronic effects to *The Magnetic Monster*, one of the first films to use an electronic soundtrack) (Logan and Woffinden, 1977, p. 28). His early musical experiences involved playing in jazz clubs in the 1940s and 1950s. Krause began as a folk singer (including a brief stint with the Weavers in 1963) and eventually drifted to explore techniques of electronic music at the San Francisco Tape Center in 1967 (Fong-Torres, 1972, p. 18). The Tape Center was at that time a hotbed of experimental music activity, attracting composers such as Terry Riley, Pauline Oliveros, Steve Reich, and Joseph Byrd, who also worked in the rock field as a member of the psychedelic-experimental United States of America (Holm-Hudson, 2002). In other words, much of the tape-music experiments taking shape at the San Francisco Tape Center parallel similar experiments in Pink Floyd's early music, especially evident in their use of *musique concrète* effects on *Ummagumma* and other albums.

Investing in one of the first commercially marketed Moog synthesizers, Beaver and Krause set up a booth at the Monterey Pop Festival in June 1967 (Krause, 1998, pp. 49–50). This led to a steady stream of session work between 1967 and 1970, contributing electronic music and effects to songs by Simon and Garfunkel ('Save the Life of My Child'), the Doors ('Strange Days'), the Byrds ('Space Odyssey'), and even the Monkees ('Daily Nightly') (Fong-Torres, 1972, pp. 16, 18). Their work was also heard in films, including *Performance*, *Rosemary's Baby*, and *Catch-22*. Among their clients was George Martin (at whose AIR Studios Pink Floyd would record part of *Meddle* a few years later) (Krause, 1998, p. 53). George Harrison reportedly released a tape of Krause's synthesizer sounds, made during a teaching session, as the second side of his second solo recording *Electronic Sound* (Fong-Torres, 1972, p. 18). Their burgeoning reputation in the rock and film worlds eventually led to a contract with Warner Brothers.

In a Wild Sanctuary was essentially an ecological concept album, the idea for which came from fellow Warner Brothers artist Van Dyke Parks (Krause, 1998, pp. 55–6). The record was completed in the late spring of 1969; its release the following year coincided nicely with the public environmental *zeitgeist* in the wake of the first Earth Day on 20 April 1970. The album's liner notes describe the music as 'environmental impressions recorded with Moog synthesizer, Hammond organ, congas, cuicas, tablas, tambourines, drums, piano, guitar, wooden and metal flutes, the sea, live voices, live lions, birds, monkeys, cable car tow cable clicks and San Francisco muni buses' (Krause, 1970). Most of the latter named sounds were featured in an instrumental called 'Walking Green Algae Blues'. According to Krause: 'We spent a month walking around the San Francisco area with a portable stereo tape recorder taking in sounds of streams, birds, people and animals at the zoo, and machinery' (ibid.). 'Walking Green Algae Blues' culminates in a rapidly edited 'survey' of people speaking the word 'war', sometimes matter-of-fact, sometimes nervously, sometimes gleefully. The method of gathering these sound samples – in which Krause apparently stopped visitors at the zoo and asked them to simply speak the word 'war' – recalls the 'interview' methods that Roger Waters used to obtain the memorable spoken-word clips on *The Dark Side of the Moon*:

I still glow with pleasure at how well that worked ... I devised a series of about 20 questions on pieces of card. They were in order and ranged from obscure questions like, What does the phrase 'the dark side of the moon' mean to you?, to a series of questions that related to each other like, When was the last time you were violent? and then, Do you think you were in the right? We asked people to just go into an empty studio, look at the top card, respond to it, move on to the next card and respond to that, and so on until they'd done all the cards. We showed them to everyone from Paul McCartney to Jerry Driscoll, the Abbey Road doorman. (Henderson et al., 1998)

What's more, 'Walking Green Algae Blues' even features a (synthesized) heartbeat which begins at [5:16] into the song and persists for a minute and a half, underlying the 'war' collage in the process.[1]

Their second album, *Gandharva* (1971), is even more eclectic than *In a Wild Sanctuary*. Although it is not explicitly a concept album, Krause later described it as a 'progressive musical journey of "noise" to the ethereal' (Krause, 1998, p. 69). It is significant to note here, in light of Pink Floyd's 'cinematic' musical style, that Krause also described *Gandharva* in the liner notes as 'a score from a non-existent film' (Krause, 1971).

The album was structured as a gradual decrescendo, using 'a poorly recorded rock and roll cut at the beginning as an example of aural pollution, then gradually making the album quieter and more peaceful to the fading echo of the last lingering note at the end' (Krause, 1998, p. 68). The first side of the album ranges from experimental electronic soundscapes to blues-rock and even a choral gospel number with piano accompaniment. It is the second side, however – recorded live on two evenings at San Francisco's Grace Cathedral with the assistance of jazz notables Gerry Mulligan, Bud Shank, and Howard Roberts – that holds up today. A spacious set of improvisations, Side 2 of *Gandharva* was one of the first quadrophonic recordings; it also made use of the cathedral's natural seven-second reverberation, becoming in the process one of the earliest examples of 'new age' or ambient music.

Although no Beaver and Krause album ever sold more than 30,000 copies (Fong-Torres, 1972, p. 18), both *In a Wild Sanctuary* and *Gandharva* were acclaimed by industry insiders, who rewarded the duo with further film and session work in Hollywood, New York, and London (Krause, 1998, p. 60). Evidently a copy of *Gandharva*, at least, made its way into the right hands. It was observed in the early 1970s that David Gilmour was 'the one member of Floyd who keeps in touch with the music "scene"; the only one ever seen in clubs' (Logan and Woffinden, 1977, p. 182). During the overdub sessions for 'Us and Them' in October 1972, it was Gilmour who urged Dick Parry – an old bandmate from his student days in Cambridge – to pattern his playing after Gerry Mulligan's contributions to *Gandharva* (Henderson et al., 1998). Gilmour may have had in mind the 'very breathy' tone Mulligan used on 'By Your Grace' and 'Good Places' from that album. *Gandharva* may have influenced *The Dark Side of the*

Moon in other ways. Like Pink Floyd's album, *Gandharva* opens with an essentially 'abstract' piece of electronic music ('Soft/White'). There is also a song, 'Walkin',' with a gospel vocalize that uncannily anticipates Clare Torry's famous performance on 'The Great Gig in the Sky'. Krause wrote on the album notes,

> 'Walkin'' is an a cappella performance by Patrice Holloway. She came into the studio in Los Angeles and sang the track in one take. So perfect was her pitch that Paul [Beaver] was able to lay a piano track in Satie fashion some weeks later without altering the speed of the tape to change the pitch. The voice was then processed with Moog, VSO [oscillator] and Echoplex on 16-track. (Krause, 1971)

The Dark Side of the Moon, then, was directly influenced by *Gandharva* in at least some respects. The work of both groups – with their parallel interests in sound effects and spatial aspects of sound production such as quadrophonic sound – may be seen as evidence of rock's gleeful adaptation of John Cage's maxim that 'everything we do is music, and everywhere is the best seat'. *The Dark Side of the Moon* went one step further than *Gandharva*, however, in use of continuous segues from song to song to facilitate an unbroken trip.

Frame by frame, measure by measure – the art of the segue

Although Roger Waters has asserted that 'there will never be a film of *Dark Side of the Moon*. It would be madness' (MacDonald, 1997, p. 195), its songs are connected using rhetorical devices that have counterparts in film: fades, dissolves, direct cuts, montage. Such techniques are so associated with *The Dark Side of the Moon* that Capitol Records used them on the band's compilation albums as well. *Works* (Capitol, 1983) even begins with a collage of *Dark Side* sound effects, recalling *Dark Side*'s opener 'Speak to Me.' *Echoes* (Capitol, 2001) uses cross-fades (or 'dissolves') and tonal segues (songs related by key or chord progressions that extend from one song to the next) to replace a simple chronological arrangement with a more cohesive flow. Both of these compilations can be regarded to be a tribute to *Dark Side*'s staying power.

Rebecca Leydon has written that the 'techniques and practices' of the motion-picture camera in the early 20th century gave 'expression to a new kind of visual logic'. She itemizes some of these devices:

> the 'fade', in which the screen gradually turns black; the 'dissolve,' in which one image gradually disappears while another emerges; the 'cut-in,' an instantaneous cut to a close shot; the juxtaposition of different camera angles; and the varieties of special effects involving stop-motion tricks, adjustment of film speed and direction, double-exposure of the film, and matted images. (2001, p. 218)

The 'fade', of course, has a long-standing counterpart in popular music as the ubiquitous 'fade-out'. In the mid-1960s, however, rock musicians and their producers and engineers – in a clear effort to enhance the synaesthetic qualities of psychedelia – began to appropriate the devices of the cinematic avant-garde into their recordings. Accordingly, analogies to many of the latter-named techniques – adjustment of speed and direction, double-exposure – can be found in psychedelic rock music of the 1960s. For example, McDonald and Kaufman (2002) have detailed many of the Beatles' experiments with altered tape speeds and tape reversal during the making of *Revolver* in 1966. Engineers Ken Townsend and Geoff Emerick also experimented with unusual microphone arrangements (McDonald and Kaufman, 2002, pp. 141–2), a clear parallel to juxtaposing different camera angles. The Beatles' widespread use of ADT (automatic double tracking), not only for vocals but instruments, can be considered to be analogous to the technique of double-exposure in film.[2]

Of the film-editing devices listed by Leydon above, however, the 'dissolve' and the 'direct cut' – an 'instantaneous shift to a new shot' (Leydon, 2001, p. 225) – were somewhat later in coming in rock music. Perhaps the most famous early 'direct cut' in rock is the rooster-into-electric-guitar-note splice that joins 'Good Morning, Good Morning' with the reprise of 'Sgt. Pepper's Lonely Hearts Club Band' on the Beatles' *Sgt. Pepper*. Just a few months later in 1967, Pink Floyd used a similar direct-cut segue on their first album *The Piper at the Gates of Dawn*, cutting from the stampede of percussion and detuned electric guitar strings concluding 'Interstellar Overdrive' to the bass harmonics and temple blocks that introduce 'The Gnome'.[3]

The direct cut at the end of Roger Waters's solo track 'Grantchester Meadows' (*Ummagumma*, 1969) demonstrates the rapid shift of perspective – from close-up to long shot – that was enabled by the cinematic direct cut. The loud, close crack of a flyswatter is spliced to the sound of distant birds at the beginning of 'Several Species of Small Furry Animals Gathered Together in a Cave and Grooving with a Pict'. This ability to instantaneously shift perspective was celebrated by film critic Emile Vuillermoz, writing in 1916. Vuillermoz extolled 'this ability to juxtapose, within several seconds, on the same luminous screen, images which generally are isolated in time and space, this power (hitherto reserved to the human imagination) to leap from one end of the universe to the other' (Leydon, 2001, p. 222).

Still another early film technique involved superimposition, 'in which a second image is inserted into a portion of the frame through a matting process or through double exposure of the film' (ibid., p. 229). This multiple-exposure technique is used by Pink Floyd in the recapitulating collage of earlier song fragments just before the 'remergence' section [17:59–19:09] of 'Atom Heart Mother' (1970) (O'Donnell, 1999).

By the time Pink Floyd recorded *The Wall* in 1979, technology and the group's musical maturity had developed considerably. Direct cuts are used to join 'The

Happiest Days of Our Lives' between parts 1 and 2 of 'Another Brick in the Wall.' In the first instance the cut is jarring, the abrupt shrill call of the teacher and the helicopter noise changing abruptly to the bass and drum hits that begin the next song. The second cut is smoother, building on the violent climax of the 'Happiest Days of Our Lives' and segueing – in mid-scream, and without a lapse in meter or tempo – to 'Another Brick in the Wall (Part 2)'.

As the second *Wall* example indicates, direct cuts may be joined more 'smoothly' by similarities in tempo or key. *Tonal segues* result from the beginning of a song being in the same key as the previous song. More indirect *tonal relationship segues* may be created by joining two songs that are in closely related keys for a 'similar-yet-different' effect, much like the relationship between movements in a Classic-era multimovement work such as a symphony or sonata. Occasionally one may encounter *tonal completion segues*, transitions in which the end of one song is left incomplete, to be 'resolved' by the first chord of the next song. *Temporal segues* flow from one song to the next without changes in tempo; usually there is no change of meter as well (dance-music DJs have perfected the art of such transitions).

To a certain extent, the above categories overlap. The transition between 'The Happiest Days of Our Lives' and 'Another Brick in the Wall (Part 2)' is a good example. A tonal relationship segue occurs, as the close of the first song is in F major while the beginning of the next in the relative-minor key of d minor. It is also a tonal completion segue, in that 'Happiest Days' ends on its dominant chord of C major, which is then 'resolved' deceptively to the d minor of 'Another Brick in the Wall (Part 2)'. Lastly, the transition is also a temporal segue because there is no change of tempo.

The *dissolve*, or cross-fade, eliminates the fissure that is perceived in even the smoothest tonal or temporal segue. In cinematic terms, a dissolve occurs when one shot fades in as another is fading out. Its counterpart in recorded music, to fade one track down as another is faded in, was made possible with advances in multitrack recording and mixing in the 1960s. Still, the recorded evidence seems to indicate that dissolves that would work musically – by sharing the same key, or being synchronized in tempo and meter – were either beyond the capabilities of 1960s technology or the pitch-recognition sensibilities of most recording engineers.[4] Early examples of the 'dissolve' tended to involve ambient noise rather than musical links per se. The Beatles, for example, faded in 'Dear Prudence' over the fading jet noise of 'Back in the U.S.S.R.' on the *White Album* (1968), and linked 'You Never Give Me Your Money' to 'Sun King' on *Abbey Road* (1969) with the sound of crickets and cow bells.[5] Similarly, Pink Floyd used the sounds of lighting matches, frying eggs, and dripping faucets to link the various instrumental interludes on 'Alan's Psychedelic Breakfast' (*Atom Heart Mother*, 1970). Wind was the dissolve of choice on 1971's *Meddle* (linking 'One of These Days' with 'A Pillow of Winds', and 1975's *Wish You Were Here* (joining the title track with part 6 of 'Shine On You Crazy Diamond').

How suite it is … Marvin Gaye and the album-length concept album

Each of the examples discussed so far, however, only involves a pair of songs. In joining more than two songs into unbroken (or virtually unbroken) strands, the Beatles once again led the way, with the interrelated suite of songs on Side 2 of *Abbey Road* (1969). To link an album's entire collection of songs, however, demonstrating the power of segues as a unifying device, it took Marvin Gaye's *What's Going On*, released in 1971. An early example of a soul concept album, *What's Going On* was a marked departure for Motown. Gaye's biographer David Ritz has written:

> *What's Going On* enjoys a unique position in and out of its time frame. Written from a distinctly African-American point of view, the work evokes an era, directly responding to what was happening at the end of the sixties, one of the most tumultuous decades in American history. But it also transcends those issues by drawing upon a powerful spiritual base. Beyond that, the songs project the extremely personal vision of its creator, an artist deeply divided between body and soul. The music reflects similar cross-currents, strands of rhythm-and-blues, silky pop and biting avant-garde jazz. (Ritz, 1994, p. 4)

Predictably, the concept-album structure of *What's Going On* led to attention from the white press; *Rolling Stone,* for example, did its first major article on Marvin Gaye in early 1972 (Ritz, 1991, p. 156).

Gaye used *What's Going On* to chronicle the state of Black America at the turn of the decade. Economic hard times, pollution, and drug abuse were the subjects of songs such as the title track, 'What's Happening Brother', 'Mercy Mercy Me (The Ecology)', and 'Inner City Blues (Make Me Wanna Holler)'. Interspersed among these social statements are songs of uplifting spirituality that seem to offer a way out: 'God is Love,' 'Right On', 'Wholy Holy'. As Ritz has written, 'the music and meanings in *What's Going On* crisscross between the flesh and the spirit, the material and the metaphysical' (1994, p. 12).

What is especially impressive about *What's Going On*, however, are the ways in which its music is used to impart a continuity to the whole that transcends the many dichotomies presented by its lyrics. Table 5.1 reveals the degree to which tonal, temporal, and timbral relationships in *What's Going On* are carefully controlled.

Casual listeners to *What's Going On* might notice the recurrent musical cues: an ascending string theme first heard in the bridge to 'What's Going On', the reprise of the opening song in the closing moments of 'Inner City Blues', and the ubiquitous conga grooves (sometimes with reverb added) that drive the album. As Table 5.1 shows, however, *What's Going On* also flows from track to track by relying on a limited number of interrelated tempi: 96 bpm (beats per minute), and its slightly slower variant, 92 bpm, are contrasted with the more leisurely 72 bpm. The first appearance of 72 bpm occurs in 'Flyin' High', which features a 3:2

Table 5.1 Tonal/metric/segue structure of Marvin Gaye, *What's Going On*

Song	Meter	Tempo	Key	Distinctive musical features
What's Going On	4/4	♩ = 96	E	*Conga groove, ascending string theme* at [1:39–1:56]
		FADE		
What's Happening Brother	4/4	♩ = 92	~	Modulatory (some cadential arrivals at c minor); introduction begins with *ascending string theme* in backing vocals
		DIRECT CUT (TONAL SEGUE)		
Flyin' High	2/4	♩ = 72; triplet q = 108 polyrhythmic	~	Modulatory (some prolongation of g minor); begins with same chord as end of 'What's Happening Brother'
		DIRECT CUT (TEMPORAL SEGUE)		
Save the Children	2/4	♩ = 72; triplet q = 108 polyrhythmic	C	Same meter and 3:2 polyrhythmic feel as 'Flyin' High' until [3:13]; active *congas* return at [0:21]; arrival at C major avoided until [2:41]
	4/4	♩ = 96		Reprise of opening in same tempo and meter as 'What's Going On,' featuring *conga groove*
		DIRECT CUT (TEMPORAL SEGUE)		
God is Love	4/4	♩ = 96	E♭	Begins on B♭11 chord; *conga groove*
		DIRECT CUT (TONAL/TEMPORAL SEGUE)		

Song	Meter	Tempo	Key	Distinctive musical features
Mercy Mercy Me	4/4	♩ = 92	E F at [1:56] to c at [3:03]	Begins on same B♭11 chord as 'God is Love' before shifting up a half step to new key; *conga groove*[1] with reverb; *ascending string theme* at [2:13–2:34]
			FADE (end of Side 1)	
Right On	4/4	♩ = 108	g	Guiro, *conga groove* with reverb until [4:59]
			DIRECT CUT at [4:59]	
		TONAL (COMPLETION) SEGUE		New theme, texturally similar to 'Save the Children'; guiro returns at [6:00]; conga-led groove returns at [6:45]; ends on G7 chord to facilitate tonal (completion) segue
Wholy Holy	6/8	♪ = 144	C	Metric feel not pronounced
		RUPTURE		
Inner City Blues	4/4	♩ = 92	e♭ c♯ at [3:41] C♯ at [4:30]	*Conga groove*; reprise of 'What's Going On' verse 3 at [4:30]; *ascending string theme* at [4:55] on f♯ (ii of E), over *conga groove*
			FADE (end of Side 2)	

[1] According to session percussionist Jack Ashford, the 'conga' on 'Mercy Mercy Me' was actually a hollow block: 'It was wooden and shaped like a tube. It was concave, with a middle section that had a hole, 'bout one inch in diameter, running all the way through it. I've got very big hands, so when I cupped it and hit it, you got that very unusual *pow pow* sound you hear on the record. It came out that way because my hand was acting like an echo chamber. That gave it such a sound!' (Edmonds, 2001, p. 167).

polyrhythmic feel throughout to highlight the mood of drug-induced disorientation; the triplets thus clock in at 108 bpm, a tempo that returns in 'Right On'. These temporal relationships allow the seamless medley of 'Flyin' High', 'Save the Children', and 'God is Love,' for example. One of the mixing engineers for *What's Going On*, Steve Smith, remembers that '[Gaye's] direction to me was to mix it as rhythmically as possible ... He wanted the voices and the percussion to be emphasized, and to keep the rhythm going through it like the *heartbeat* of a late-night party' (Edmonds, 2001, p. 197; emphasis added).

From the beginning, Gaye had intended the album to flow from beginning to end. Initially, arranger David Van De Pitte had suggested composing musical interludes to link the tracks (ibid., p. 167); this technique had been used in the Moody Blues' 1968 album *Days of Future Passed*. Ultimately, however, it was decided to splice all of the basic tracks together in the album's running order, then apply overdubs to the entire album rather than to individual songs (ibid., p. 168).[6]

Other segues occur strategically in *What's Going On*. 'Mercy Mercy Me' begins with the same chord, in the same voicing, as 'God is Love', allowing a more deceptive kind of segue – the listener might be initially tricked into hearing the opening of 'Mercy Mercy Me' as yet another verse of 'God is Love'. 'Right On' ends on a G7 chord that resolves into the radiant C major of 'Wholy Holy', providing an instance of a tonal completion segue.

Discounting the break between 'Mercy Mercy Me' and 'Right On' that was imposed by the temporal limitations of the vinyl recording format, only two songs on *What's Going On* – the first and the last – do not make use of segues. The title track is nevertheless linked to what follows as a kind of overture, its ascending string theme and conga grooves reappearing later in the album (and, indeed, at the beginning of the next song). On the other hand, 'Inner City Blues', which takes us out of the celestial realms of C major ('Wholy Holy') into the stark ghetto darkness of $e^\flat$ minor, has no segue at all. The effect here is that of a rupture in the musical fabric, made all the more pronounced by how seemingly effortlessly everything before had been joined; this rupture gives 'Inner City Blues' particular dramatic power as the closing number on the album, the antithesis of 'Wholy Holy's spiritual joy. In summary, *What's Going On* 'revolutionized soul music by expanding its boundaries' (Ritz, 1991, p. 152) – not only in its subject matter, but in its form as a full-length concept-album suite of interconnected songs.

In lingering on this discussion of *What's Going On*, I am not arguing that Pink Floyd were aware of and directly influenced by this album. In fact, both the album and title song failed to chart in the UK, where Gaye's change of style was not as enthusiastically received (Rees and Crampton, 1996, p. 53). (It is possible that the American inner-city concerns he addressed so starkly were somewhat removed from the everyday experience of his British fan base.) Nevertheless, Lawrence Miles, engineer for *What's Going On*, recalls that 'it was to be an intimate listening experience. We were mixing it for people sitting in their living rooms listening to the album straight through' (Edmonds, 2001, p. 196) – and *The Dark*

Side of the Moon was meant to be experienced in the same listening context. *The Dark Side of the Moon* is thus structured in a similar way, incorporating similar devices to again unify an entire album into two sidelong suites. The recurring features here include the heartbeat (returning in 'On the Run', 'Time', and 'Brain Damage') and the so-called ' "Breathe" theme' (heard explicitly at the close of 'Time', implicitly in 'The Great Gig of the Sky' and 'Any Colour You Like'). The tempos in *The Dark Side of the Moon* are not rigidly controlled as they seem to have been in *What's Going On*; instead, almost all of the songs gravitate in a kind of lazy cluster about the 60 bpm that is established by the album's opening heartbeat (see Table 5.2). Tonally, *Dark Side* is much more consistent than *What's Going On*; with the exception of 'The Great Gig in the Sky', all of the songs are in D major or keys closely related to D (e minor, f# minor, b minor). Like *What's Going On*, however, the songs are linked in a continuous fashion in two sidelong suites by a variety of segues.

Other correspondences are introduced between tracks by recurrent themes in the lyrics, especially in the first side of the album. Running, for example, is referred to in 'Breathe' ('Run, rabbit, run' – a likely reference to John Updike's 1960 novel) as well as 'Time' ('and you run and you run …'). Running was also literally incorporated into 'On the Run'; Parsons recorded assistant engineer Peter James running around Abbey Road's Studio #2 (Lambert, 1998). 'Poor Peter had the job of running back and forth while I recorded him. I remember instructing him to do things like "breathe harder"' (Tolinski, 1993, p. 79). The line 'shorter of breath and one day closer to death' toward the end of 'Time' establishes a link between the theme of running and the theme of death, the topic of 'The Great Gig in the Sky'. The 'softly spoken magic spells' in the 'Breathe' reprise were originally recorded prayers in the early performances of 'Great Gig' (then a collage of organ and church sound effects called 'The Mortality Sequence').

The most striking of Pink Floyd's segues on *The Dark Side of the Moon* is the slow (13-second) dissolve between 'Money' and 'Us and Them.' Over a walking <B–D> bass pattern that effectively links the keys of the two pieces, Richard Wright's organ chords slowly fade in as Gilmour's guitar-scat vocal interchange from 'Money' fades away. The dissolve was to become the technique of choice in linking the tracks on *Dark Side*'s successor, *Wish You Were Here* (1975). As Dick Parry's sax solo at the end of 'Shine On You Crazy Diamond (Part 5)' fades away, adding reverb in the process under Wright's ascending string synthesizer, the low hum underlying 'Welcome to the Machine' begins – some 28 seconds before 'Welcome to the Machine' begins. An even longer dissolve is used to reintroduce the 'Shine On' suite after 'Wish You Were Here'. Synthesized white noise (simulating wind) enters at [4:31], with 'Wish You Were Here' slowly fading for another 46 seconds. At [0:06] into 'Shine On You Crazy Diamond (Part 6)', Waters's bass tentatively enters (this moment recalls the famous beginning of 'One of These Days' from *Meddle*). Gilmour's guitar enters at [0:22], while the wind that effectively linked these two songs does not disappear until [1:05]. In

Table 5.2 Tonal/metric/segue structure of Pink F;oyd, *The Dark Side of the Moon*

Song	Meter	Tempo	Key	Distinctive musical features
Speak to Me	3/4	♩ = 180	n/a	heartbeat, three clocks (one 1/2 speed) spoken 'madness' dialogue, 'Money' tape loop, loony laugh, VCS3 buzz, Clare Torry's scream, two backward chords (one with echo) (Henderson et al., 1998)
			TONAL SEGUE / DISSOLVE @ 1:08	
Breathe	4/4	♩ = 63	e	*'Breathe' progression*
			TONAL COMPLETION SEGUE / DISSOLVE	
On the Run	2/4	♩ = 168	e	VCS3 synthesizers, *heartbeat*
			DISSOLVE	
Time intro	2/4	♩ = 120	f♯	As 'On the Run' explosion fades out, ticking clocks fade in for 0:19 before chimes. *Heartbeat* duplicates first two ♪'s of muted bass 'tick-tock' pattern. First note of VCS3 bass @ [0:54] is E, reinforcing link with previous track. F♯ asserts metric primacy @ [1:58].
verse (Gilmour vocal)	4/4	♩ = 63	f♯	

Song		Meter	Tempo	Key	Distinctive musical features
	bridge (Wright vocal)		♩=60	A	
			TONAL COMPLETION SEGUE		
	Coda @ [5:55]		♩=60	e	'Breathe' reprise
			FADE/DISSOLVE; TONAL SEGUE		
Great Gig in the Sky	piano intro	4 / 4	♩=56	B♭ → g	→ B♭ Piano begins on same b minor chord as final organ chord of 'Time,' before organ has faded away; 'Breathe' reprise in g @ [0:18]
	full band, Clare Torry @ [1:07]		♩=63	g	'Breathe' progression
	piano, Clare Torry @ [2:31]		slows down to ♩=56 by [2:52]	B♭ → g	→ B♭ Reprise of piano intro
	piano, Clare Torry @ [3:36]		continual slowdown	g	'Breathe' progression
			FADE (end of Side 1)[1]		
Money		7 / 4	♩=114	b	
		4 / 4	♩=136[2]	b	12-bar blues jam

Table 5.2   *concluded*

Song	Meter	Tempo	Key	Distinctive musical features
Money [cont.]	7/4	♩ = 114	b	Organ fades in at [6:23]; 'Money' fade-out persists 0:10 into 'Us and Them'; total time of dissolve = 0:13.
		DISSOLVE		
Us and Them	4/4	♩ = 72	D	
		TONAL/TEMPO SEGUE		
Any Colour You Like	4/4	♩ = 72	d	*Breathe' progression*
		TONAL COMPLETION SEGUE		
Brain Damage	2/4	♩ = 66	D	*heartbeat duplicates first two x's of measure*
		TONAL SEGUE/TEMPO NEAR-SEGUE		
Eclipse	3/4	♩ = 138	D	q almost equivalent to e of 'Brain Damage'; *heartbeat at fade-out*
		FADE (end of Side 2)		

[1] Later EMI-remastered CDs of *The Dark Side of the Moon* have an added dissolve between 'The Great Gig in the Sky' and 'Money', capitalizing on the continuous play afforded by the CD format. Engineers James Guthrie, Doug Sax and Alan Parsons added the new cross-fade to make the transition flow more smoothly; the first sound effect of 'Money' is heard before the final chord of 'Great Gig in the Sky' has completely faded away ('Echoes FAQ').

[2] Waters: 'One of the ways you can tell that it was done live as a band is that the tempo changes so much from the beginning to the end. It speeds up fantastically' (Henderson et al., 1998).

short, through the deliberate pacing of staggered entrances and exits of sounds, the dissolve between 'Wish You Were Here' and 'Shine On You Crazy Diamond (Part 6)' is made to last for nearly two minutes. The dissolve is thus used to enhance the symmetrical form of *Wish You Were Here*; given the cinematic associations of temporal displacement associated with the dissolve (Leydon, 2001, p. 226), 'Welcome to the Machine', 'Have a Cigar', and 'Wish You Were Here' can be interpreted as one long flashback.

Conclusion

Today, in rock critic and fan discourse, *The Dark Side of the Moon* has come to be associated with both its crystalline high-detail sound production and its segues. For example, a search on the Internet for the phrase 'Dark Side of the Moon', along with the word 'segue,' yields hundreds of hits. Interestingly, a significant number of these references only refer to Pink Floyd's album as a model to compare the use of segues on another recording. This suggests that even though each of *The Dark Side of the Moon*'s transitional techniques had been used on previous Pink Floyd albums, it is the memorable segues on *Dark Side* that seem to forever link the techniques with this specific album. When critics compared Radiohead's *OK Computer* (1997) to *The Dark Side of the Moon*, for example, they were referring to the continuity of its transitions between songs more than any perceived similarities in musical style.

Rebecca Leydon observes that:

> the first proponents of the cinema valued it most for its verisimilitude, its ability to depict 'things as they really are,' particularly things in the natural world. And many critics were quick to see the poetic possibilities in cinema, a potential for a kind of *psychological* verisimilitude. Writers such as [film critic Emile] Vuillermoz were interested in the way that devices such as the dissolve could evoke dreams, hallucinations, or imitate real human perception. (2001, p. 222).

The recurrence of spoken-word soundbites, heartbeats, insane giggles, and so on in *The Dark Side of the Moon* has a similar function, creating competing temporalities as segments of the heard 'past' keep impinging upon the sounding 'present' like a hallucinogenic flashback. Such superimpositions were commonly employed in the early cinema, by inserting one image into a portion of another through matting or multiple exposure, to represent a character's dreams or hallucinations (ibid., p. 229).

The cinematic dissolve is also somewhat hallucinogenic in nature, in that 'for a brief moment, the cinematic spectator sees two images at the same time' (ibid., p. 224); the musical equivalent results in momentarily experiencing placement in two simultaneous musical *spaces* (ibid., p. 224). Leydon significantly describes the dissolve as 'one of the most salient devices specific to the cinematic medium' (ibid., p. 223). Thus – in spite of Waters's protestations that a film of the album would be 'madness' – *The Dark Side of the Moon* is, along with *Wish You Were Here*, among the most cinematically constructed rock albums ever made.

Notes

1. Krause learned in the early 1970s that 'Walking Green Algae Blues' had been adopted by Daniel Cohn-Bendit, formerly a leader in the 1968 student rebellion in France, as the anthem for Europe's Green Party (Krause, 1998, p. 60).
2. See McDonald and Kaufman (2002, p. 141) for a discussion of ADT and its use by the Beatles.
3. O'Donnell (2002) has detailed a number of ways in which Pink Floyd were influenced by the Beatles' groundbreaking sonic explorations.
4. For Yes's 'Perpetual Change', released in 1971, engineer Eddie Offord synchronized two group performances employing different metric groupings of a 14-beat pattern, fading one in above the other. Todd Rundgren went one better in 1974, juxtaposing an audience sing-along from a San Francisco performance over a New York live performance (and synchronizing the tempos) for 'Sons of 1984'. Such feats of engineering virtuosity were rare, however, and perhaps more resemble musical analogs for multiple-exposure in film technique.
5. One of the engineers for the Beatles' *Abbey Road* was Alan Parsons.
6. Alan Parsons recalls a similar intent in the making of *The Dark Side of the Moon*, although the much more complex layering – including 'bouncing' of tracks onto other unused tracks to make room for more overdubs – presented considerable challenges. 'The final running order was pretty much determined from the first days. Obviously, we had to record and mix it in sections, which made it a nightmare for track allocation' (Lambert, 1998).

Chapter 6

'On the path': tracing tonal coherence in *The Dark Side of the Moon*

Shaugn O'Donnell

One of the most popular rock albums of all time, Pink Floyd's *The Dark Side of the Moon* is a late 20th-century masterwork, and perhaps the quintessential 'concept album'. Long acclaimed for its stunning studio production and literary coherence in the popular press, the often-ignored musical details of *Dark Side* also merit attention from scholars and critics. The individual musical components of the album – such as the chord progressions and vocal melodies – are quite simple, but the complete work is greater than the sum of its parts. While most of the songs on *Dark Side* can stand alone and have received extensive radio airplay in that format, hearing them in the context of the complete cycle can alter a listener's experience of the individual songs. Numerous elements – segues, *musique concrète*, and poetic themes – serve to unify the work, but it is the projection of a single tonal arch that generates much of the album's musical continuity and linear power. Beginning with 'Breathe,' and culminating in 'Eclipse', a tonal and motivic coherence unifies the musical structure of this modern song cycle. In this chapter, I explore the complete tonal path of *The Dark Side of the Moon*.

Dark Side is the first album of Pink Floyd's mature style, spanning 1973 through 1977, which also includes the albums *Wish You Were Here* and *Animals*.[1] David Gilmour's guitar work and Roger Waters's lyrics both slowly emerged from Syd Barrett's shadow between *A Saucerful of Secrets* (1968) and *Obscured by Clouds* (1972).[2] There were brilliant moments during that period, such as the epic song 'Echoes' (*Meddle*, 1971), but quality control and polish reached a new level with *Dark Side*. While the Floyd were previously known for their experimental – almost avant-garde – work, *The Dark Side of the Moon* is a collection of less obviously radical rock songs. Nonetheless, the songs remain Floydian in style, bearing important signature traits, and, while the album lacks one of their dramatic 20-minute tracks, the effectiveness of the complete cycle achieves a comparable scope. Despite the importance of the instrumental passages in this and in all of Pink Floyd's music, this chapter focuses on the songs as rock is primarily a vocal musical genre. As I examine each of the eight songs, I begin with an outline of the form in order to place the harmony and melody into a local context. The form also helps highlight Floydian characteristics, such as the frequent lack of that typical pop/rock staple – a chorus. After outlining the formal organization of each song, I examine the local melodic construction.[3] As I progress through the cycle, I illustrate the large-scale linear structure to place each song back into the context of the album.

'Breathe'

'Speak to Me', the long overture of *musique concrète* that precedes 'Breathe', generates enough momentum that the song's first chord, a reverse-strummed Em9 chord, immediately becomes the local tonic and the structural downbeat of the album. The song's construction is simple, a binary form that is a variation of the twelve-bar blues. Table 6.1 outlines the form of 'Breathe'. The first and second rows list the formal sections; the third row indicates measure numbers; and the final row gives approximate CD start timings.[4] It consists of an eight-bar progression (labelled A in the table) containing two chords, tonic and subdominant, followed by a four-bar turnaround (labelled B in the table).[5] 'Breathe' becomes more rock than blues via its long introduction (which repeats the eight-bar progression), its through-composed lyrics, and its uncommon turnaround, which has the quality of a refrain owing to the repeated text 'for long you live and high you fly' that begins the two verse occurrences. In rock, B sections are often choruses, but one of the driving forces of *Dark Side* is the lack of repeated text associated with a chorus. In fact, the band withholds a true chorus until 'Brain Damage' at the conclusion of the cycle.

Table 6.1   'Breathe'

Introduction			Verse 1		Verse 2	
A	A	B	A	B	A	B
1–8	9–16	17–20	21–28	29–32	33–40	41–44
0:01	0:31	1:01	1:16	1:46	2:01	2:31

Harmonically, as an isolated entity, 'Breathe' is in an unambiguous E dorian mode. The A sections consist of a persistent alternation of Em7 (often with an added 9th) and A7.[6] This common dorian progression (i7–IV7) constitutes the bulk of the song, as shown in the form table. The turnaround | Cmaj7 | Bm7 | Fmaj7 | G – D7♯9 – D♯dim7 | is the only contrasting progression, and, despite the prominent C♮ that signals its beginning, or the F♮ that soon follows, it creates a strong and convincing motion back to Em7 and the dorian progression. By the time the vocals enter at measure 21, the turnaround confirms E minor as the tonic.

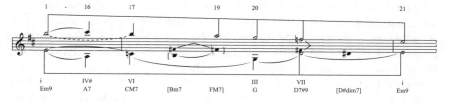

Example 6.1   'Breathe', introduction

Example 6.1 offers a linear representation of this process.[7] Here, the bar lines mark the formal boundaries between the A and B sections. The upper line represents Gilmour's slide guitar melody, while the bass supplies the harmonic roots.[8] For visual clarity, Table 6.1 omits the slide guitar cover tones F♯5 and E5, which sound over the Em7–A7 progression. The graph reveals an interesting blend of traditional and rock tendencies. The descending melodic fifth establishes the tonic in a traditional fashion. The phrygian, or natural, scale-degree 2 is slightly unusual, but the more typical diatonic scale-degree 2, F♯, sounds simultaneously in the harmony, merely displaced into an inner voice. On the other hand, the natural VII supporting scale-degree 2 as the modal dominant, is purely rock, as is the plagal chain of ascending harmonic fifths in the turnaround (C–G–D) leading to the rock dominant. However, even the rock cadence VII–i receives a traditional twist with the addition of the passing D♯dim7 harmony, the conventional leading-tone chord of E minor.[9]

In addition to establishing the tonic, the turnaround introduces one of the most significant musical motives that occurs throughout the album: the cross-relation F♯ versus F♮ (henceforth F♯–F). The angle brackets in the graph highlight this surface conflict, but they merit some elaboration. A cross-relation (C♯ versus C♮) first occurs over the bar line in the graph, as A7 moves to Cmaj7, marking the boundary between sections. The more significant F♯–F motive first occurs as part of the tritone progression, Bm7–Fmaj7, that also recurs on the album.[10] Finally, the motive becomes even more critical as the two tones sound simultaneously as part of the rock dominant VII♯9, the sonority that establishes the E-minor tonic and drives the music forward.

While the instrumental introduction establishes the tonic and the cycle's defining musical motive, the vocals are the focus of this chapter. The projection of the album's tonal arch occurs in the vocal melodies rather than in the instrumental interludes. The graphic analysis of Example 6.1 serves to provide the foundation for my subsequent discussion.

Once the vocals enter, the clarity of the E-minor tonic weakens slightly. The primary melodic tone over A7 remains C♯, but Gilmour approaches it from above, singing D4 over Em7 most of the time. Despite being in E dorian, the melodic motion D–C♯ begins to emphasize D as a possible tonic, as though the A-section progression was ii7–V7 in D major, rather than i7–IV7. The vocal melody of the turnaround further weakens the E minor tonic. Unlike the slide guitar, Gilmour's vocal line does not complete a conclusive descent to E, stopping instead on A. Example 6.2 illustrates the linear structure of the verses. The harmonic progression is the same as the introduction shown previously in Example 6.1, though I omit the stemless notes for clarity. The melodic organization, however, is markedly different. A descending fourth from D4 to A3 replaces the earlier fifth-span from B to E. The melodic descent in the turnaround, C♮ through A, includes several neighbor-tone embellishments characteristic of the vocals on *Dark Side*. The middleground reductions shown in my examples exclude these surface features despite their local foreground significance.

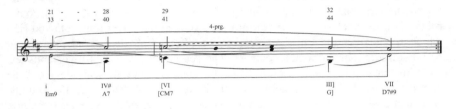

Example 6.2   'Breathe', verses

The underlying descent from D to A again seems to project a sense of D major rather than E dorian. Locally, E minor remains the tonic, and the harmonic accompaniment still includes the instrumental line that previously established the tonal center, but the vocal line is not entirely in agreement. The initiating D is so prominent, and the descent so incomplete, that a desire for continuity arises that drives the music forward beyond the frame of the song. The D-oriented descending fourths, heard twice in the vocals, displace the earlier E-minor closure of the slide guitar introduction. By the end of 'Breathe', a desire for resolution to D major is already in place.

'Time'

Functioning like the overture that precedes 'Breathe', the instrumental track 'On the Run' links the songs 'Breathe' and 'Time'. The early concert versions of this tune, 'Travel' or 'The Travel Sequence/Section', were simply a dorian vamp on an E pedal.[11] Early in the 1972 tour, Gilmour emphasized a B♭ harmony, which – though it was a simple neighbor to A, reminiscent of a blues inflection – resonated with the harmonic tritone motive of the 'Breathe' turnaround. Later in the year he omits this embellishment. The polished album version of 'On the Run' departs from the keyboard and guitar modal improvisation, and focuses instead on electronic timbres, with filter sweeps and stereo panning providing the primary source of forward motion. However, all the versions of the track suspend tonal motion until the beginning of the song 'Time'.

In the introduction of 'Time', the alternating bare E and F♯ are tonally ambiguous, as though the music is re-emerging from some harmonic morass. At first, E still seems to be the tonic and the F♯ sounds like its upper neighbor, but the passing E♯ in measure 10 (1:34) reverses the harmonic roles. Earlier concert versions introduced the chromatic passing tone sooner, but this was less successful as it decreased the harmonic suspense. E♯ acts as a leading tone to F♯, and is an enharmonic manifestation of the F♯–F motive from 'Breathe'. After the E♯ sounds, F♯ becomes the tonic, making E sound like a rock dominant VII. The second iteration of the passing E♯ (m. 14) confirms this reinterpretation, and the repetition of F♯ (m. 17) completes this process.[12] The rest of the introduction is the core verse progression, F♯m–A–E–F♯m, in augmentation. Table 6.2 outlines the form of 'Time', illustrating both its binary (row 2) and ternary (row 1) characteristics.

Table 6.2 'Time'

Introduction		Verse 1		Guitar solo		Verse 2	
E – F♯	A' aug.	A	B	A (2x)	B	A	B
1–16	17–24	25–32	33–40	41–56	57–64	65–72	73–80
0:54	1:58	2:30	2:59	3:29	4:26	4:55	5:25

The vocal melodies for 'Time' are very simple, as Gilmour sings the A sections almost entirely on F♯4 and a neighboring E4. In early concerts, Gilmour sang these sections an octave lower, creating a dramatically different affect. The drop in energy from the pitch range of 'Breathe' depicted the tedium of the 'Time' lyrics, but it destroyed the tonal arch and forward motion of the *Dark Side* song cycle. The album's higher F♯4 generates a sense of urgency that emphasizes the fleeting nature of time, and drives the music forward by reaching higher than the 'Breathe' range. Wright's vocals in the B section return to the range of 'Breathe', and bring back the neighbor-tone figuration of its B section. Harmonically, the B section (Dmaj7–Amaj7 :‖ Dmaj7–C♯m7–Bm7–E) leans toward A major, though the final ii7–V is deceptive, becoming iv7–VII leading back to the F♯ minor tonic of the A section via the rock dominant VII. Example 6.3 shows a graph of the complete

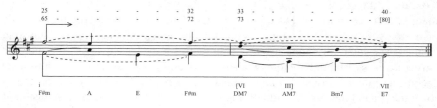

Example 6.3 'Time'

'Time' verse. The A section arpeggiates up to F♯4 from the top D4 of 'Breathe', while the B-section vocals are an inner voice, continuing the lower range of 'Breathe'. Gilmour's backing vocals further this interpretation as he prolongs F♯ over the B section with his upper-third harmonization. In essence, 'Time' is a prolongation of the single melodic tone F♯4! Locally, this prominent F♯ is scale-degree 1 in F♯ minor, but after the emphasis on D4 and the descending D4–A3 fourths in 'Breathe', it sounds like an arpeggiation of a D-major triad over the span of two songs.

'Breathe (Reprise)'

The transition back to 'Breathe (Reprise)' occurs by replacing the final E chord of the B section in 'Time' with Bm7–F, another instance of the previously-mentioned tritone progression. This one is even more significant since the F♯–F motive sounds in the vocal line, although it is still only the upper backing vocals. The modulation back to an E center occurs through F, just as it did back in the introduction of 'Time'. The reprise compresses the 'Breathe' form as shown in Table 6.3.

Table 6.3   'Breathe (Reprise)'

Introduction	Verse 1	
A (1/2)	A	B
1–4	5–12	13–16
5:55	6:11	6:42

The melody and harmony remain the same as 'Breathe' with the exception of the final Bm chord. Rose (2001, p. 24) points out the 'unsettling effect' of this unusual resolution of D♯dim7, but, despite its harmonic ambiguity, the cadence has a melodic coherence. Instead of truncating the turnaround descent at A3 as in 'Breathe', the vocal line now plummets all the way down to F♯3, completing the octave descent from the F♯4 of 'Time'. Example 6.4 summarizes the melodic activity over the first three songs. While the discrete harmonic areas of each song make sense internally, they are less coherent as a cycle. However, the melodic structure is substantially more goal-oriented and seems to strongly outline D major, despite the absence of any songs in that key. This characteristic continues over the span of the album, withholding the implied D tonic until the conclusion of the cycle.

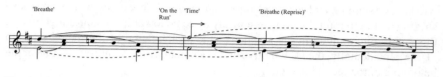

Example 6.4 'Breathe' through 'Breathe (Reprise)'

'The Great Gig in the Sky'

Like the other songs in the *Dark Side* cycle, 'The Great Gig in the Sky' evolved over the course of the 1972 performances. Its early incarnation as 'The Mortality Sequence/Section' was quite unlike its final version, but even as 'The Great Gig in the Sky' began to take shape in late 1972, it continued to lack energy. It was not until Clare Torry added her improvised vocals in early 1973 that the track achieved its full power and became the climax of the album's tonal arch. Table 6.4 outlines the form of 'The Great Gig in the Sky'.[13]

Table 6.4 'The Great Gig in the Sky'

Introduction	Band & vocals	Bridge	(mostly) Piano & vocals	
A	B	C	A	B
1–16	17–34	35–38	39–54	55–67
0:00	1:07	2:16	2:30	3:36

The A section begins with the by now familiar tritone progression Bm–F, and proves to be the most harmonically active segment of the song cycle. Establishing F major as the tonic over the first nine bars, the song quickly modulates to B♭ major by the end of the A section. The B section returns to the dorian vamp that generated 'Breathe', though now transposed to i7–IV9 in G dorian. This progression occurs briefly in the A section also, though it is ii7–V9 (mm. 5–6) as part of the phrase that establishes F major. Despite that earlier occurrence, the band's dramatic entrance at the downbeat of the B section, as well as Torry's scat singing, reorients the progression to a G-minor tonic.[14] The virtuosic vocal part spans an incredible range, roughly a thirteenth, sometimes in the span of a couple of measures. The rapid ascending and descending registral sweeps create a jagged contour that, along with the repetitive dorian progression, revels in surface-level sensuality, rather than directed linear progress. While the B section remains static in many ways, it is the repeated orgasmic climax of Torry's line on the high G5 and its upper neighbor A that propels the song cycle forward. She reaches it within two bars of singing, and reiterates it throughout her improvisation. The note is so striking that I interpret this song as entirely directed toward, and a prolongation of, this single pitch, much in the manner of the prolongation of the melodic F♯4 in 'Time'. Incidentally, the F♯–F motive arises again in Torry's improvised line at the beginning of the second A section.

'Money'

'Money' is an elaborate 12-bar minor blues in 7/4. Other than the odd meter, the three verses are very traditional, with eight bars of tonic harmony supported by the famous B-minor riff from the introduction, followed by a four-bar turnaround, v7–iv7–i7. Though the lyrics are through-composed, the repetition of the word 'money' in bars 1 and 5 of the pattern evokes the blues convention of repeating the first line before the payoff line, that is, the lyrical structure aab. The subsequent turnaround introduces a brief metric hitch, as an 8/4 riff supports the v7 chord and a 6/4 riff supports the iv7 chord, before resuming the steady 7/4 of the tonic harmony (O'Donnell, 2002, p. 77). The most prominent case of the F♯–F motive thus far occurs here as it sounds in unison in the guitar parts and lead vocal on the words 'daydream', 'travelling', and 'no sur-(prise)' in the three verses respectively. In fact, the passing F♮ stands out as the extra quarter note 'stolen' from the subdominant measure, creating the 8 + 6 syncopation. Table 6.5 outlines the form of 'Money'.

Table 6.5   'Money'

Intro.	Verses 1–2	Sax solo	Guitar solo	Verse 3	Coda
7/4 Bm riff	12-bar 7/4 blues	7/4 aug. blues	4/4 aug. blues	7/4 blues	4/4 Bm vamp
1–8	9–32	33–52	53–122	123–133	133–150s
0:12	0:40	2:01	3:05	5:11	5:43

As the table makes clear, the bulk of the song consists of solos by Gilmour and saxophonist Dick Parry. The sax solo continues the 7/4 blues, though now in rhythmic augmentation. The first eight bars are doubled, becoming sixteen bars, and include the more conventional blues move to the subdominant. The turnaround is not augmented, and the final tonic shifts to 4/4 with the triplets generating a sense of haste signalling the impending guitar solo. The long composite guitar solo (there are three individual solos) represents Gilmour's most polished work to date, just as this album marks the start of the band's mature style.

The solo continues the augmented blues pattern, but now for a full 24 bars and in 4/4 time. Instead of sounding relaxed, the more regular, common meter creates tension in comparison to the previous 7/4 sections, thereby increasing the excitement generated by the guitar solo.

In terms of the long-range melodic arch, 'Money' returns to a prolongation of F♯. The verses essentially arpeggiate a B-minor triad, with a few neighbor tones and blues inflections, but the crucial 'money' leading off each line of text returns to F♯4. Example 6.5 presents the linear structure. The turnaround also reaches that climactic pitch with 'new car, cav-(iar)', 'high fidel-(ity)', 'but if you ask',

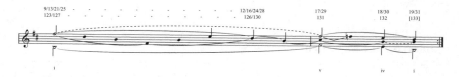

Example 6.5   'Money'

respectively for each verse. Gilmour then sings through the passing F♮ to a prolonged E, finally arriving at D with the return of the B-minor tonic. This would be a very conclusive progression in D, and like 'Breathe' and its reprise, it leans toward D major without actually being in that key. Gilmour lands on the local tonic B minor very convincingly at the coda, especially with the repeated text 'away' arriving on B3 each time. However, the F♯–E–D line of the 12-bar verses maintains a background sense of D major despite the local tonic B minor. Even the climax of the guitar solo, the third segment (beginning at 4:30 or m. 101), reaches a cover tone D6, Gilmour's highest possible note on the 22-fret Fender Stratocaster he played at the time. He dramatizes this climax by bending the note up a whole step to reach a neighbouring E, but D remains the consonant structural tone.

'Money', in returning to a prolongation of the tone F♯ as in 'Time', and by maintaining a sense of D major, creates the retrospective interpretation of 'The Great Gig in the Sky' as a large-scale neighbor tone. Example 6.6 illustrates this long-range motion. The line begins at D in 'Breathe', arpeggiates up to F♯ in 'Time', reaches even higher to G in 'The Great Gig in the Sky', and falls back to F♯ in 'Money'. This very common melodic pattern in D major sustains the unfulfilled desire for D major initiated in the Em7–A7 progression of 'Breathe'.

Example 6.6   'Breathe' through 'Money'

'Us and Them'

'Us and Them' finally delivers D major, and, though it does not resolve all of the tonal and motivic issues, it begins the release of harmonic tension generated and prolonged throughout the album thus far. The D pedal in the guitar accompaniment makes D the unambiguous tonal center through sheer persistence, but the added tones in each harmony, D(add 9)–E(add9)/D–Dm(maj7)–G/D, cloud the sense of harmonic arrival.[15] The F♯–F motive is prominent in the progression via the Dm(maj7) chord. Table 6.6 outlines the simple, but long, binary form of 'Us and Them'.

Table 6.6   'Us and Them'

Intro.	Verse 1		Verse 2		Piano & sax solo		Verse 3	
A	A	B	A	B	A	B	A	B
1–20	21–40	41–48	49–68	69–76	77–96	97–104	105–124	125–32
0:25	1:33	2:40	3:06	4:12	4:36	5:44	6:09	7:15

Rather than continuing with the F♯4 of 'Money', the vocal line drops into the inner register for the A section of the verses. In the first verse, Gilmour's echoing voice climbs from A3 up to C♯4, striving for D, yet falls back to B3 before achieving its goal. The A sections of the second and third verses reach the goal D4 with the upper third harmonization, spelling out an ascending fourth from A3 to D4; the retrograde of the descending fourth heard earlier in 'Breathe'. The ascending tetrachord strongly outlines D major, but a G/D chord accompanies the arrival on D4, rather than a root-position D chord. The dissonant 6/4 voicing keeps the music unstable despite the melodic arrival.

I show the B sections as part of the verses because of their through-composed lyrics, however, they have the aural impact of a chorus. The triadic vocal harmonization and the strong downbeat arrival of a thicker instrumental texture help create this effect. These chorus-like B sections interrupt the A-section ascending tetrachords with a dramatic return to the upper line F♯4 heard previously in 'Time' and 'Money'. Notably, the foreground figuration even recalls the F♯–G–F♯ neighbor figure projected over the span of the album (see Example 6.6). The B-section progression, Bm–Gmaj7–C, supports the melodic motion F♯4 to E4, or the arrival of the structural scale-degree 2. Unlike traditional harmony, in which V usually supports scale-degree 2, the rock dominant VII supports its arrival here. Example 6.7 illustrates the linear progression in 'Us and Them'.

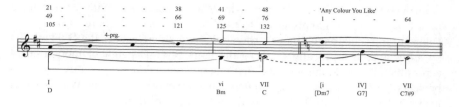

Example 6.7 'Us and Them'

'Any Colour You Like' links 'Us and Them' to the grand finale 'Brain Damage'–'Eclipse'. This instrumental interlude is a second reprise of 'Breathe', but transposed down a whole step. Therefore, locally it is yet another instance of the dorian progression i7–IV7, but now on Dm7 and G7. The turnaround, transposed to | B♭maj7 | Am | E♭maj7 | F–C7♯9–C♯dim7 |, occurs only once, at the conclusion of the track. Table 6.7 outlines the form of 'Any Colour You Like'.[16]

Table 6.7 'Any Colour You Like'

Vamp	Turnaround
A	B
1–60	61–64
0:00	3:13

The tonal function of 'Any Colour You Like' is a prolongation of the crucial C chord that concludes 'Us and Them'. Just as the Em7–A7 progression in 'Breathe' implies D major, the transposed progression in 'Any Colour You Like' suggests C major.[17] The many iterations of the progression lack directed tonal motion, but tension increases as the desire for a literal C grows until the turnaround delivers it. The track's penultimate chord finally provides us with the literal C, once again a dominant chord. Just like the 'Breathe' turnaround, this concluding C7♯9–C♯dim7 motion combines traditional (the passing C♯dim7 chord) and rock dominant (VII) characteristics. The album's structural dominant, supporting scale-degree 2, is thus dramatized via prolongation from the final chord of 'Us and Them' through the final chord of 'Any Colour You Like'.

'Brain Damage'

While 'Us and Them' obscured the arrival of the long-expected D major tonic, 'Brain Damage' begins with a bright, clear, unaltered D major triad. Gilmour's guitar melody at the conclusion of 'Any Colour You Like', with its prominent final G4, resolves smoothly down to the F#4 of the open D chord in the 'Brain Damage' introduction. Gilmour's slide guitar work here echoes the G–F# motion up an octave, again locally recalling the large F#–G–F# neighbor motion heard across the album. Along with the first unambiguous D major tonality, the song presents the first blatant verse/chorus formal structure, as well as Waters's first lead vocal on the album. Table 6.8 outlines the form of 'Brain Damage'.[18]

Table 6.8 'Brain Damage'

Intro.	Verse 1	Verse 2	Chorus 1	Verse 3	Chorus 3	Postlude
A	A	A	B	A	B	A
1–4	5–12	13–21	22–30	31–43	44–52	53–64
0:00	0:15	0:44	1:16	1:48	2:35	3:07

'Brain Damage' recalls and resolves many of the desires generated earlier in – and sustained throughout – the album. The F#–F motive occurs in all eight songs as part of the foreground harmonic accompaniment, but it gains increasing emphasis in the vocal lines over the course of the complete cycle. First, it occurs as part of the harmonizing voice at the end of 'Time', then it sounds briefly in the vocal improvisation in 'The Great Gig in the Sky', and it eventually becomes the lead line in the 'Money' turnaround. This process culminates in 'Brain Damage' as the first half of each verse (mm. 5–8, 13–16, 31–34), consists almost entirely of F#3 and F3.[19] The second half of each verse (mm. 9–12, 17–21, 35–42) also evokes the beginning of the cycle, as Gilmour's upper harmony part returns to the D4–C#4 of 'Breathe', though now locally in the context of the long-desired D major. Most significantly, this pitch reminiscence accompanies Waters's lead vocal as it completes a contrapuntal motion left unrealized at the beginning of the cycle. As shown back in Example 6.2, Gilmour's vocal line in 'Breathe' outlines a descending tetrachord D4 through A3, never completing the motion down to D as the melodic line seems to desire.[20] In measures 9–12 of 'Brain Damage', Waters's vocal line regains A3 and descends a fifth to D3, thereby complementing the earlier tetrachord of 'Breathe' and completing the octave descent from D4 to D3. Waters's descending fifth convincingly establishes D major as the tonic, finally reaching closure with the text 'on the path'. Example 6.8 illustrates this cross-album relation. Accompanying the phrase 'got to keep the loonies on the path' with the most conventional cadence on the album is rich with word-painting irony.

Exercise 6.8   Completing the octave descent

While the first verse provides tonal closure with the descending fifth, the long upper line from F♯4 in 'Time' and 'Money' to E4 in 'Us and Them' still yearns for a prominent resolution to D4, that is, a return to the obligatory register. Gilmour's upper harmony briefly provides us with that pitch, but it is clearly the secondary vocal line at the time, overshadowed by Waters's lower voice. In the next two verses Waters does not even complete the descent to D3, stopping instead on F♯3, also maintaining the desire for resolution. The chorus melody seems to provide the necessary D4, going as far as recalling the previous E4 as well, but the harmony does not support the resolution because it modulates to the subdominant, G major. However, the brief vocal 'ah's that conclude the chorus, and bring us back to the key of D major, do in fact employ E4 as scale-degree 2 once again. Rather than occurring over the rock dominant VII, as it did earlier in 'Us and Them' and 'Any Colour You Like', this scale-degree 2 occurs over the traditional dominant V7, as part of a ii7–V7 progression (mm. 30 and 52). This again recalls the beginning of the cycle as it literally places the Em7–A7 progression of 'Breathe' in the context of D major. After hearing this prominent scale-degree 2, Gilmour's upper harmony D4 in the third verse is slightly more convincing than it was in the first two verses, but it is still too deep in the mix to be completely satisfying. Example 6.9 outlines the linear structure of 'Brain Damage'.

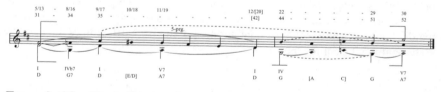

Example 6.9   'Brain Damage'

'Eclipse'

With 'Brain Damage' achieving tonal closure, 'Eclipse' functions as a coda to *The Dark Side of the Moon*, serving to conclude the cycle and to reach the obligatory vocal register D4. A simple passacaglia in 6/4 accompanies Waters's litany, with the ground bass outlining a descending minor tetrachord D–C–B♭–A. There are eight iterations of this four-bar pattern, with the first being an instrumental introduction. Table 6.9 outlines the form of 'Eclipse'.

Table 6.9 '**Eclipse**'

Introduction	Litany
A	A (7×)
1–4	5–32
0:00	0:10

The F♯–F motive recurs throughout 'Eclipse' via the conflict between the D major tonic and the lament bass tetrachord, with F♯ sounding in the first two bars, and F♮ sounding in the third bar of each repetition. Waters's initial lead vocal is a recitative on A3 with minimal neighboring embellishments, but Gilmour's upper vocal line, entering on the fourth vocal iteration (m. 17, 0:42) delivers D4 and its neighbor E4. Unlike the chorus of 'Brain Damage', which was in the key of the subdominant, this melody occurs over tonic harmony. And unlike the backing vocal part in the verse of 'Brain Damage', Gilmour's harmonization in 'Eclipse' is not buried in the mix, making it a much more convincing arrival on D4. However, despite several repetitions of this line, these D4s sound detached from the long arch of the whole cycle. At this point, it still needs a more direct link to the structural dominant and scale-degree 2. Such a link finally arrives in the last two iterations, specifically in measures 28–29 (1:11–1:15) with the text 'everything under the sun is in tune'. At that moment scale-degree 2 arrives in the long-expected register, E4, over traditional dominant harmony, V7, and resolves to D4 over tonic harmony![21] This is also the point of metric resolution in the litany, as Waters extends his phrase across the boundary of the repeating four-bar passacaglia progression (Stephenson, 2002, p. 162). The single remaining line of text, 'but the sun is eclipsed by the moon', is recited on D4 with a concluding D-major chord replacing A7 in the final iteration. Example 6.10 outlines the melodic arch spanning the entire album.

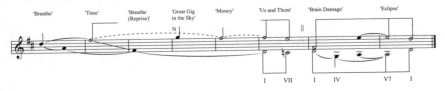

Example 6.10   Background structure of *The Dark Side of the Moon*

Conclusion

The Dark Side of the Moon is more than a collection of independent rock songs linked by related literary themes and cobbled together with slick production. The music itself makes the album a unified song cycle in three significant ways: consistent foreground motivic development, middleground associations, and a comprehensive linear structure spanning the entire background. In the foreground, the F♯–F motif binds all eight songs together. This is more than a shared characteristic, it is also a process of development, as the motivic role of F♯–F evolves from accompaniment ('Breathe') to lead vocal melody ('Brain Damage') over the course of the album. The ubiquitous dorian progression of 'Breathe' also unifies the work, occurring in five of the eight songs, as well as in one of the instrumental tracks. This is also more process than trait, as the progression moves through a series of transpositions and reinterpretations from E dorian in 'Breathe' and 'Breathe (Reprise)', through F major and G dorian in 'The Great Gig in the Sky', through D dorian in 'Any Colour You Like', and finally reaching D major in 'Brain Damage'. Similarly, middleground associations play an important role in the musical continuity. Most significant among these relations are the phases of the descending 'Breathe' tetrachord as it projects D major throughout the album. It travels its own path of expansion in 'Breathe (Reprise)', inversion in 'Us and Them', and finally complementation and completion as it keeps 'the loonies on the path' in 'Brain Damage'. At that point it migrates to become, in minor form, the bass line for the 'Eclipse' passacaglia. Finally, the prolongation of an extended melodic arch over the entire album generates a continual sense of forward motion, even across the boundaries of the discrete songs. The simplicity of each song's individual melodic line coalesces into a single cohesive musical gesture. This fundamental line is essential to the success of *The Dark Side of the Moon*'s long-range narrative structure, and it is, in essence, the album's musical path.

Notes

1. Many fans would include *The Wall* (1979) in this period, but I use Waters's 'spitting incident' (Olympic Stadium, Montreal, 6 July 1977) as the dividing line between the band's mature and late styles. The incident, which inspired Waters to write *The Wall*, is discussed in most Pink Floyd references (for example, see Schaffner, 1991, pp. 219–20).
2. For detailed information about this early transitional period, see any of the standard references, especially Hodges and Priston (1999). For information about Syd Barrett, see Watkinson and Anderson (1991), Palacios (1998), or Parker (2001). Pink Floyd's film *Live at Pompeii* (1972) clearly portrays Gilmour's emergence from Barrett's shadow. 'One hears the last vestiges of Barrett in "A Saucerful of Secrets", witnesses the emerging guitar hero in "Echoes", and gets the first glimpse of the mature Gilmour recording tracks for *Dark Side of the Moon*' (O'Donnell, 2002, p. 86, n. 34).
3. There are several *Dark Side of the Moon* songbooks available, as well as numerous guitar tablature versions on the Internet, but they are best used as mere guides in making one's own transcriptions. Both Pink Floyd ([1992b] 1995) and (1973b) were useful references in beginning my analytical transcriptions.
4. CD timings throughout the essay are from the remastered *The Dark Side of the Moon* included in the *Shine On* CD boxed set (Pink Floyd, 1992).

5. Both *Dark Side of the Moon* songbooks cited above in note 3 double the number of measures for 'Breathe', 'Time', and 'Breathe (Reprise)'. The 1995 book notates these songs in a quick 4/4, while the 1973 book notates them in cut time. The drums clearly contradict such interpretations, and converting both transcriptions to 4/2 (or a half-tempo 4/4) corrects the error.

6. This dorian mode progression is typical enough that Frank Zappa (1981) referred to it as the 'Carlos Santana Secret Chord Progression'.

7. This graph, and the others throughout this essay, use modified Schenkerian analytical techniques. The examples include tones that I hear as significant structural events, and omit other embellishing tones. However, it is worth noting that the cyclical nature of much rock music often makes graphs representative of a single pass through a progression, rather than a model of a complete through-composed work. Also, foreground and background interpretations are often less distant in rock music than that of the 'classical' repertoire for which this analytical technique is designed. Regardless of these significant differences, I find that the hierarchy and musical notation of Schenker's methods remain useful to illustrate my reading of this music. For an introduction to Schenkerian analysis, see Cadwallader and Gagné (1998). For a successful application of these techniques in rock analysis, see Everett (1999).

8. As is standard in music notation, the guitar lines and male voices in all my graphs are written an octave higher than they sound. However, the bass lines represent harmonic roots rather than literal bass parts, and I represent them in convenient registers to simplify the musical examples. When referring to specific pitches in the text, I use the Acoustical Society of America's standard middle C = C4.

9. Gilmour's rhythm guitar part further emphasizes VII as the structural chord in this turnaround, rather than the more traditional D♯dim7. He plays a D7♭9, which incorporates an enharmonic spelling of the important leading tone D♯, but retains D as his root, so one hears both notes simultaneously.

10. Macan (1997, pp. 258–9, n. 37) suggests that 'numerous cross relations' are characteristic of Pink Floyd's style from 1971 through 1975. He also mentions the role of the tritone progression later in the album as part of 'The Great Gig in the Sky'. Rose (2001, p. 25) also mentions the tritone progression.

11. For more information about Pink Floyd's performance history, see Povey and Russell (1997), particularly pp. 106–31 for information about the *Dark Side* tours.

12. Rose (2001, p. 20) discusses the tonal ambiguity of this introduction, and similarly marks measure 17 as the defining moment, though he does not relate the harmonic shift to the leading-tone E♯ or the F♯–F motive.

13. Proper metric notation begins with this song in both Pink Floyd (1973b) and (1995).

14. Rose (2001, p. 26) still hears this section as ii–V desiring resolution to F, not unlike my interpretation of the equivalent progression in 'Breathe' creating a desire for D.

15. Rose (2001, p. 29) also comments on this ambiguity, and uses the conflict between the pedal and the harmonic progression to support his interpretation of the lyrics.

16. Curiously, Pink Floyd (1995, pp. 98–107) notates 'Any Colour You Like' in the proper slow 4/4 despite the metric errors in 'Breathe' and 'Breathe (Reprise)'.

17. Rose (2001, p. 32) again comments on the desire for 'resolution to a C modality' as he did for F in 'The Great Gig in the Sky'. Surprisingly, he does not associate 'Breathe' or 'Breath (Reprise)' with this progression, and therefore he never desires a resolution to D. As a result, all of his expectations remain unfulfilled over the course of the album, and that, in turn, negatively influences his interpretation of the lyrics.

18. Pink Floyd (1973b) and (1995) once again incorrectly notate the meter, doubling the number of measures for 'Brain Damage' and 'Eclipse'.

19. Stephenson (2002, pp. 159–60) relates the F♯–F duality in 'Brain Damage' to schizophrenia, reading F♯ as 'normal' and F♮ as 'pathological'.

20. 'Breathe (Reprise)' takes the melodic line further, but still falls short of completing the octave as it stops at F♯3.

21. Whiteley (1992, p. 116), without citing specific reasons, also mentions 'the finality of the V–I cadence supporting the vocal line "and everything under the sun is in tune"'. She goes on to suggest that the subsequent plagal cadence provides no reprieve from madness, as though the album's concluding musical gesture contradicts the tonal closure achieved just seconds earlier. However, a closing plagal cadence is quite common after a work reaches its final authentic cadence, and it usually has the opposite effect of granting reprieve or final rest, hence its colloquial label as the 'Amen cadence'. Despite her interpretation, Whiteley even hints at this possibility with her description of its 'hymn-like effect'.

Chapter 7

The keys to quiet desperation: modulating between misery and madness

Ger Tillekens

Hanging on in quiet desperation is the English way.

– Roger Waters, 'Time'

From the mid-1960s on, pop musicians succeeded in loosening some of the constrictions of the music industry. Willing to do their own thing, they eagerly used their newly-won freedom to extend the expressive powers of their trade. As a result, what once had started as sheer amusement for the young, now suddenly turned into an art form. Not all of it, of course. Just like Western music had done during the 19th century (Mellers, 1988, p. 592), popular music split up into the separated fields of an 'artists' music' and a 'people's music'. The latter simply kept to the label of pop music, though some people now denounced it by giving it derogatory names like MOR, short for 'Middle of the Road'. The former, the artists' branch, made itself known as 'progressive rock', 'prog-rock' or just plain 'rock' (Frith, 1981). It all happened rather quickly, as one might expect from such a rapidly-evolving style of music. If we take 1956, the year of rock and roll, as its beginning, the whole process took about ten years. The outcome was epitomized by two albums, appearing in what became known as the Summer of Love. One was the Beatles' album *Sgt. Pepper's Lonely Hearts Club Band*, released on the first day of June, 1967, and the other was Pink Floyd's first album *The Piper at the Gates of Dawn* that hit the shelves two months and a few days later.

In their own ways, both these albums marked the birth of psychedelics. They were recorded in the same studio complex of Abbey Road, at roughly the same time of year. Looking at the names of those involved, one can see that by then a scene of real pop artists had formed, meeting each other during tours and festivals and attending the concerts of their peers in the budding club circuit of Swinging London, at venues like the Marquee and the UFO Club. Musical experiments led to lengthier and more complex compositions, while artists shifted their attention from the single to the album and hipper deejays abandoned the AM-frequencies for FM radio. Meanwhile, the attitude of the audience also changed. With pop music its natural environment, youth culture itself evolved into a counterculture, presenting and declaring itself as a self-sufficient, alternative lifestyle. For those who then and there were at the right places, it might have seemed as if the 1960s would never stop. The rock music experience exploded in big concerts and festivals, after the stage was set by the Monterey Pop Festival (1967), the first Isle of Wight festival (1968), and Woodstock (1969). At the same time, however, many things seem to take a wrong turn. Some serious cracks were shining through the many-coloured varnish of psychedelics and, as a group, Pink Floyd would be among the first to be affected by it on a personal and artistic level.

Six years and an impressive number of albums – including a singles collection and two film soundtracks – after their first album, the group released *The Dark Side of the Moon* (1973). This number nine in the Pink Floyd series of records proved to be a rather sad album. As such it reflected the general atmosphere of the time as, undeniably, there was some sadness in the air – 'a peculiar emptiness', as pop journalist Greil Marcus once called it (1975, p. 45). Indeed, an uneasy feeling had been hanging around for some time, as many people acknowledged the deaths of Janis Joplin and Jimi Hendrix in 1970 as signalling the closure of a period, symbolically representing the countless minor incidents by which youth culture lost its professed innocence. Some people experienced the waning optimism even earlier on. Writing about the Band, Marcus located the turning point already in 1968, just one year after the Summer of Love. Next to the Band, he could have mentioned Pink Floyd – the group had lost its main driving force, Syd Barrett, that very same year due to a psychosis.

This loss hit hard, as Barrett had been largely responsible for the group's initial musical successes (Kent, 1974; Palacios, 1998). Moreover, the Floyd had started their career right at the artistic turn. As the initial thrust of the counterculture faltered, many groups returned to their roots. This option, however, was not readily available for Pink Floyd. Progressive rock was their trade, and they couldn't fall back to the earlier standards of sheer pop-craftsmanship as easily as bands and artists who had started before them. Looking for a way out, David Gilmour, Nick Mason, Richard Wright, and Roger Waters, the remaining members of the Floyd, decided to analyze the social and psychological pitfalls of the dream of youth culture by using the tricks and trades of their profession. That, mainly, is what *The Dark Side of the Moon* is all about (Harris, 2003). Sure, the Floyd were not the only ones to explore the changing winds of time, and not even the first ones to do it by means of a concept album. There had been other records in the charts over the years before with the same theme, or one that was at least similar. Just to recall a few: the Pretty Things with what reputedly was the first concept album ever, *S.F. Sorrow* (1968); the Band with *Stage Fright* (1970); the Kinks with *Lola vs. the Powerman & the Money-Go-Round, Part 1* (1970); and the Who with *Who's Next* (1971). All of these records have their merits, but, as the sales figures show, Floyd's musical achievement made the deepest and most lasting impact on the rock audience.

Parts and pieces

In the past, many good things have been said of *The Dark Side of the Moon*. Reviewers praise the associative power of the lyrics, the strength of the interacting guitar solos, the rich texture of the music, and the transparency of the sound production. However, the theme itself and the consistency of its musical and lyrical presentation is, no doubt, its foremost quality. This truly is a concept album, blessed with a remarkable unity. One can mark a rock album as a concept album when its songs share the same frame of mind, still better, have a linking theme, or ultimately – albeit loosely – fit into an ongoing narrative. In its final state, *The Dark Side of the Moon* seemed to fulfil all of these criteria. Its initial building blocks, though, were quite uneven (Jones, 1996a).

One does not have to wonder about the consistency of the phrasing as all the lyrics were written by Roger Waters. The tracks, however, bear different credits for the music, have quite different lengths, and, especially, show different keys. Looking at their histories, one can even say that the whole was somewhat pieced together from some earlier songs, originally made for different purposes. 'Us and Them', for instance, was taken from 'The Violent Sequence', originally written for the score of the film *Zabriskie Point* (1970) on youth rebellion. Rejected by director Michelangelo Antonioni, it was performed by the Floyd during some of their concerts in 1970, and resurrected for the occasion. 'Breathe', in turn, originated from the score, co-written by Waters and avant-garde composer Ron Geesin, for *The Body* (1970), a surrealistic medical documentary directed by Roy Battersby. The soundtrack *Music from The Body* (1970) shows its embryonic form in an acoustic performance by Waters. Moreover, the tracks differ quite a lot in style. Strictly speaking, *The Dark Side of the Moon* includes only six 'songs', the other five tracks being instrumentals or ambient sound collages. The whole album is a fusion of psychedelic rock with some clear jazz-fusion and blues-drenched rock.

Looking at the overall structure, one can make an educated guess about its actual construction. 'Brain Damage', certainly, is the song on which the whole album has been built. The song, as Bill Janovitz (n.d.) argues, clearly refers to Barrett's case, as indicated by its reference to childhood memories – one of Barrett's favourite subjects – and the ongoing concerns of Pink Floyd after Barrett had left the band. It was conceived during the *Meddle* sessions in 1971, under the working titles 'The Lunatic Song' and 'The Dark Side of the Moon'. In due course that last title was transferred to the album, while the song itself was turned into its finale. One may safely assume that 'Breathe', hinting at someone being born or wakening up to reality, was next taken as an intro, while the other songs were adapted to fit in between, arranged so as to sketch in a background and outline the causes to the effect. 'Eclipse' was added to provide an appropriate closure for the suite, and some sound collages were fitted in to strengthen the whole. The other songs introduced a broader perspective and, as an effect, the case of Barrett was generalized into a description of the downfall of the initial hopes and dreams of 1960s youth culture in general.

In true Pink Floyd style the composition was tried out and elaborated during live performances. It was first played as the first half of their show during their 1972 British tour and presented in the programme as a new piece, fully titled 'The dark side of the moon. A piece for assorted lunatics'. At that time Waters himself qualified it as 'a definite piece' (Pollock, 1972), but as we know, it would still change considerably. Despite the mixed origins of the source material, the process of reworking resulted in strong balance.

On stage the song cycle was played as a whole. In its final form, however, it can be divided into sections, though opinions may differ about the precise location of the cutting points. Due to its release on the by now traditional double-sided vinyl record, one may argue that there are only two parts to the composition. (Remember, in the old days you had to turn the record over midway between the tracks.) Indeed, when listening to *The Dark Side of the Moon* on the record, one is easily inclined to locate the cutting point right between the songs of the A-side and those of B-side – that is, between 'The Great Gig in the Sky' and 'Money' – a cut that has been preserved on the later CD-reissue by a 15-second pause. However, some critics have pointed out that this causes some unbalance. To them, the way the A-side ends, makes Wright's composition 'The Great Gig' seem out of place, even superfluous; and at the time some people even maintained that this song could have been better left out (Grossman, 1973). The CD-reissue, in contrast, is not hindered by this problem. Here one is forced to perceive three sections (Table 7.1). The first two of those open with 'Breathe' and its reprise respectively; the third one starts with 'Any Colour You Like'. In the official guitar tablature book, this last song is listed as 'Breathe (Second Reprise)' (Pink Floyd, 1992). If we go along with this title, each section opens with a 'Breathe', acting as a kind of prelude, with the first of these having itself a prelude in 'Speak to Me'. And, as we shall see later on, at least logically 'The Great Gig' now forms a necessary part of the composition as a whole.

The sections are like the movements of a symphony, or rather the acts of a theatre play. Indeed, *The Dark Side of the Moon* is 'theatrical', as Waters himself said at the occasion of its first presentation during the British tour of 1972 (Pollock, 1972). As indicated by the opening call 'Speak to Me', the tale of his downfall is told by the protagonist himself, speaking to outsiders who are willingly trying to understand his condition. The story of his life, told in a slightly incoherent but evocative, associative prose, takes us through the narrative in a chronological order. The first act describes the initial condition of a young man, growing up in the restrictive world of the 1950s and the resulting feeling of boredom and misery. Next, the second act highlights his decision to choose for individual freedom instead, and describes the anxieties caused by the conflicting powers he experiences while growing up in the welfare state: the struggle with the social conventions of religion ('The Great Gig in the Sky'), the lures and

Table 7.1 The overall structure of *The Dark Side of the Moon*

Section	Song	Composer	Length	Key
I	1 'Speak to Me'	Mason	1:13	–
	2 'Breathe (in the Air)'	Waters, Gilmour, Wright	2:57	E dorian
	3 'On the Run'	Gilmour, Waters	3:40	–
	4 'Time'	Gilmour, Wright, Mason, Waters	5:36	F♯ dorian
II	1 'Breathe (Reprise)'	Waters, Gilmour, Wright	1:10	E dorian
	2 'The Great Gig in the Sky'	Wright	4:47	G dorian
	3 'Money'	Waters	6:32	B minor
	4 'Us and Them'	Wright	7:40	D major
III	1 'Any Colour You Like'	Gilmour, Mason, Wright	3:25	D dorian
	2 'Brain Damage'	Waters	3:48	D major
	3 'Eclipse'	Waters	2:03	D major

temptations of the new consumer society ('Money'), and the massing social and political counter forces ('Us and Them'). Finally, the third act depicts the lost battle and the resulting mental short-circuit. Thus, we are led from misery to madness via the intervening struggle to maintain one's sanity. Though this story line constitutes a narrative unity, it is rather hidden. First and foremost, it seems to be the harmonic unity of music itself, that allows the listener to discover it. How did the Floyd succeed in forging such an impressive harmonic unity from their disparate song material?

Diagonal substitution

All of their compositions were firmly rooted in the field of pop and rock music, and the Floyd mastered and used all of the musical means of this style. From its very beginning, though, their music had some important characteristics of its own. The most obvious clue to their compositional approach, when looking at *The Dark Side of the Moon*, undoubtedly is their predilection for the dorian mode. Only 'Us and Them', 'Brain Damage', and 'Eclipse' – at the end of the second and third parts – are, more or less, in straight major, more especially D major. The other songs and tracks, however, harbor quite different keys, which prove rather difficult to pinpoint. For 'Breathe', for instance, the key signatures we usually find in sheet music indicate D major or B minor. In fact, the key of this song is E dorian with a short modulation towards the key of C major. 'Time' shows the key signature of F♯ minor, but sometimes wavers to E major while parts of it also favor the key of D major. Overall this song, again, is dorian-oriented, in this case towards F♯ dorian. At least two other tracks on the album show the same inclinations. 'Any Colour You Like' favors the key of D dorian, while 'The Great Gig in the Sky' is mainly in G dorian, though the intro initially may suggest the key of F major. Next to D major and B minor ('Money'), this leaves us with a whole range of dorian keys.

An important part of unifying a composition is linking the keys of its constituent elements. In Western music, pop music included, the key of a composition is important because it defines the actual pitch of the available tone material. Basically, scales and chords are built out of pure thirds and fifths. The greater their harmonic distance from the tone centre or key, the more these pure tones will deviate from their counterparts in even temperament. That is the reason why the key is so important in harmonic music, as is a restricted use of tone material. Too abrupt transitions to remote chords run the risk of making a composition sound false. Therefore, conventional harmonic music is usually restricted to the three basic chords – the tonic, the subdominant and the dominant, whose tone material can be expanded by means of an incidental deviant chord, standardized progressions, and more or less conventional modulations to nearby keys, usually over the intervals of a third or a fifth.

From the very beginning, composers of popular music enjoyed playing with related keys, more specifically relative or parallel keys. These keys are related because the former share the same tone material, while the latter have their tonics in common. In many popular songs in a major key, for example, the middle eight is by convention shifted towards the relative minor key. Pop music revolutionized the idiom by taking this modal practice one step further. It extended the available harmonic material by introducing the principle of the diagonal replacement of related chords. In a pop song in the key of C major, the tonic C (I) can be traded for its relative minor Am (vi), as well as for its parallel minor Cm (i). Occasionally, one even finds the tonic's place taken by the A (VI) and E♭ (♭III). The same goes for subdominant and the dominant (Figure 7.1). The resulting, extended chord material is glued together in individual compositions by surprising leading notes, which in turn often are exploited in the melodies. That is why pop songs often show such a strong relationship between harmony and melody.

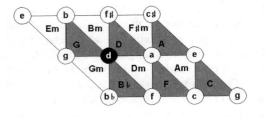

Figure 7.1   Diagonal relations between chords (tone centre D)

The Beatles were masters of this art of diagonal substitution (Tillekens, 1998). They applied this principle not only within, but also between songs. Ordering the tracks of their records, they seemed to prefer the diagonally related keys of A major, A minor and C major, combined with the key of E major. As a showcase, Alan W. Pollack (1995) points at their *'Abbey Road* Medley'. Except for the second section, the tracks forming the song cycle of *The Dark Side of the Moon* do not display any clear relationships of this kind. Here, the initial F major key of the intro of 'The Great Gig in the Sky', the B-minor key of 'Money', and the key of D major of 'Us and Them' can be interpreted as diagonally related to each other. Within and between the songs themselves, Pink Floyd also use these related chords lavishly and apply them to modulate to other keys. In 'Breathe', for instance, one notices an impressive sounding transition from the subdominant to the flat-submediant: I IV I♭VI I. These triads can be seen as ad-lib replacements of each other. Opening the song's middle-eight, Pink Floyd here uses the transition to modulate from E dorian to C major. In the later 'Reprise' of this song the same modulation in the end even, finally, lands in B minor, a fifth away from the initial E dorian. Harmonic acrobatics like these may seem wild, but still conform to what was almost standard practice in pop and rock music at that time. However, there is far more to say about the harmonic characteristics of Pink Floyd's music.

Sliding through the harmony

Diagonal substitution, mainly, is what gives pop and rock music its modal tinge. Pink Floyd, however, added some supplementary modal qualities to the idiom of rock music, by expanding on some other tricks. The background to their particular sound unarguably lies in the distinctive guitar technique of Barrett and Gilmour, who were both masters of the slide guitar. From the very start of his musical career, Barrett was inspired by the shining examples of Steve Cropper and Bo Diddley, and practiced the technique side-by-side with Gilmour. Instruments and instrumental techniques can, and sometimes do, change the existing musical idiom and in the hands of Barrett and Gilmour the use of the slide technique clearly enhanced the formula of rock music. Using the bottleneck or slide guitar technique, chord changes are mostly effected by sliding up or down the finger settings of the whole left hand over one or more frets of the guitar neck. In a recent interview, Daevid Allen of Soft Machine fame recalled his visit to the legendary '14 Hour Technicolour Dream' event, held at the Alexandra Palace on 29 August 1967: 'I saw Syd playing a curious sort of slide guitar with the Floyd at the Ally Pally in 1967 and he looked rather embarrassed by it. But out front it sounded spectacularly Wagnerian! I was impressed' (Ward, 2001).

One may easily understand Allen's amazement at seeing and hearing Barrett's slide guitar. Historically, the slide guitar technique is closely allied to the blues, a style that cultivates simple harmonies and looks for the necessary complexity by introducing non-standard 'blue notes' in the riffs, guitar solos and melody lines. Here the sliding technique was exploited mostly for its melodic effects, as it was perfectly suitable for adding tone material with deviant microtonal pitches. Barrett and Gilmour, however, mainly applied the technique to achieve harmonic effects. 'The Great Gig in the Sky' offers an excellent example of how this is done with some conventional and some less conventional progressions. Going further were the previous reprise of 'Breathe' had left things, the intro of this harmonically rather complex song starts for a full measure with a B-minor chord on the piano that subsequently leads to a three-measure sequence of | F | B♭ | F |, thereby temporarily constituting the key of F major. Then the line is taken up with some simple slides on the guitar's neck of the acoustic and electric slide guitars, delineating a twice repeated sequence of | Gm7 | C9 | and taking us into the key of G dorian. What follows next is a startling move that seems to bring us back to the key of F major: | Fmaj7 | B♭maj7 | E♭maj7 | Cm7 |. This progression is not as strange as it may seem at first sight, as these chords form a circle of consecutive fifths with an enharmonic shift at the end (Figure 7.2).

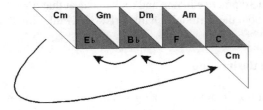

Figure 7.2   A circle of fifths in 'The Great Gig in the Sky' (measures 9–12)

By itself the circle of fifths is a well-known and long-time standing harmonic progression in popular music. Pink Floyd wheels through this sequence by simply sliding the finger settings of a partial, two-note chord simply up over five frets on the neck of the electric guitar (Figure 7.3).

Figure 7.3   Sliding through a circle of fifths in 'The Great Gig in the Sky' (measures 5–12)

The outcome is the glissando guitar style we know so well from Pink Floyd's music. The length of the slide over five frets equals an interval of five semitones. Larger intervals can be achieved as easily. The finale of the same song, for instance, ends with a long concluding slide over an octave, spanning twelve frets and taking us from the B♭ chord to its relative minor Gm7. And, of course, a similar treatment can be applied for minor and major third intervals. The step of three semitones, going from the flat-mediant III downward to tonic I, implied in the modulation in 'Breathe (Reprise)' we mentioned before, even appears to be one of the favorite intervals of Barrett and Pink Floyd; it occurs, for instance, at the end of the verse of the group's first song to reach the charts, 'Arnold Layne' (1967).

Of course, what can be done with the circle of fifths or third intervals, can be done with even smaller distances, like whole-tone or even semitone intervals. Though technically more simple to perform, harmonically these intervals are rather complex and can result in chords that are difficult to label. For instance, in another Barrett composition 'Astronomy Domine', the first track of *The Piper at the Gates of Dawn*, we find a transition from the E major towards a dissonant Em(maj7)add♯4 chord. The intricate label of the last chord may bewilder the musicological novice; the beginning guitarist, however, can master it quite simply by moving the usual, simple finger settings of the E chord one fret down along the neck of guitar (Marshall, 2001, p. 9). Besides their labels, there is more to be said about the harmonic characteristics of these smaller intervals, especially when they are related directly to the tonic.

Whole-tone and semitone shifts around the key

Their use of the slide guitar must have given the Floyd a taste for small harmonic intervals. At least, in their song material we find many of those, though, technically speaking, they are not always real slides. The definite feeling of small diatonic or chromatic shifts appears to have been more important. Barrett, in particular, seemed to relish chord changes and key shifts one semitone or whole-tone apart, as again is shown by 'Arnold Layne' – just listen to the verse of this song. This heritage has been neatly preserved in later Floyd compositions, and – what is more important here – it also accounts for the way in which most of the songs on *The Dark Side of the Moon* so easily edge into one another. The album is largley a combination of adjacent keys, welded together with semitone and whole-tone key shifts which let the tracks morph – segue, as it is called by musicologists – into one another.

Harmonically, these small intervals are more distinctive than transitions over intervals of a third or a fifth, especially when they entail the tonic. When the tonic is involved in a harmonic transition that is greater than one whole-tone step, the actual key tends to become unclear and there is a danger that some notes may even sound slightly off-key; in the case of a semitone step, the key may even glide towards the tonic of the other chord. However, as was only to be expected, daring pop musicians just viewed it as a challenge with possibilities to be exploited. Their experiments furnished the idiom of pop music with some special tricks and a special key: the backing, the use of dorian twin tones, and the tone trap.

Of these three harmonic tricks, the backing is undoubtedly the one best-known to practicing guitarists, as we use this term to refer to a typical guitar trick: the technique of shifting the finger settings of a whole chord stepwise over the frets within the short space of one single measure. Though not often heard on record, this trick was widely used during live performances in the early days of rock and roll – sometimes to establish a new key for a while, sometimes to return directly to original key. A recorded example is the Beatles' song 'Please Please Me', where the harmony at the end of the first line of the verse, is quickly pushed up by subsequent whole-tone steps: I ♭III–IV–V–V I I I. In the coda of 'It Won't Be Long' the group applies the same trick, but now stepping downwards by semitone intervals: I IV–♭III–II–♭II I I I. As these examples make clear, according to its character, the backing can have the effect of either energizing or, conversely, calming down the general atmosphere (Kramarz, 1983, p. 133; Tillekens, 1998, p. 164)

The use of the dorian mode, we encounter in *The Dark Side of the Moon* is another way of cultivating adjacent keys (Tillekens, 2002). Here, however, these keys are bound together in a special way. E dorian, just to pick an example, is a minor scale that has the same tones as the scale of D major and consequently shares its key signature. Therefore, where the usual scale of E minor has a C for its sixth step, E dorian instead comes up with a C♯. This tiny mutation preserves the scale's minor flavor, but changes the interval between the fifth and sixth steps of the scale as well as the interval between the sixth and seventh. As a result, the subdominant chord of E dorian is the triad of A major instead of A minor; and as A major is also the subdominant of D major, the two scales will easily mix. Harmonically, though, the two tonics lie far apart and that makes their combination slightly ambivalent. This ambiguity, moreover, is strengthened by the fact, that the tonic of E dorian relates as easily to two D chords (Figure 7.4). Their difference in pitch amounts to 21.5 per cent in timbre, over 10 per cent of a whole-tone step.

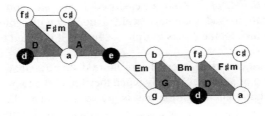

Figure 7.4   The dorian tone system with tonic E and co-tonic D

Therefore, the dorian mode constitutes a tonal system with two tonics, or rather, one tonic and a somewhat ambivalent co-tonic, which melodically are close neighbours but harmonically only distant friends. Combining them results in some typical progressions – mainly the repeated ostinatos of tonic and flat-seventh (i–♭VII) or tonic and subdominant (I–IV) – that give dorian songs their distinctive mood and feeling. We can hear the effect in songs like 'What Shall We Do with a Drunken Sailor' and 'Scarborough Fair' that were early staples of the skiffle and folk movement in the British Isles. In fact, the dorian mode was imported into the field of pop music by way of folk singer Martin Carthy's arrangement of 'Scarborough Fair'. Bob Dylan, for example, derived his 'Girl from the North Country' (1963) from this song, while Simon and Garfunkel (1966) took the song itself into the hit charts. The Moody Blues' hit 'Nights in White Satin', that entered the UK charts at the end of 1967, undoubtedly had a tremendous influence on the field of pop music. This song clearly shows the effect of the dorian harmonic ostinatos, with the repeated sequence I–♭VII supplying a harmonic oscillation that seems to stop time itself, making it as though the 'nights in white satin' are indeed, as the lyrics go, 'never reaching the end'. In fact, it is the distance that separates both tonics of the tune, which causes this effect of a fluctuating wave, rolling back and forth. On *The Dark Side of the Moon*, this particular ostinato is only sparsely used. 'Time' offers the best example. Here the dorian ostinato I–♭VII fittingly underscores the lyrics: 'Waiting for someone or something to show you the way', thereby suggesting that no one will show up for a long time. That way the ostinato is used only once. Most songs on the album prefer the subdominant IV as the designating chord instead. The alternating progression i–IV even constitutes a basic, recurring pattern in songs like 'Breathe' (| Em | – | A | – |); 'The Great Gig in the Sky' (| Gm7 | C9 |); 'Any Colour You Like' (| Dm7 | G |), which are all in the dorian mode (Woody, 2002). A similar harmonic pendulum also returns in the songs in a major key, such as 'Brain Damage'. Like the sequence I–♭VII, the alternating i–IV pendulum seems to stop the flow of time. However, instead of waiting in vain for some external event to happen, it rather evokes a feeling of someone endlessly dallying over some inner decision.

Both the backing and the dorian mode concern the way in which music lets us experience the flow of time. That also goes for the harmonic contraption we referred to as the tone trap. Seen from the perspective of harmonics, the tone trap is even bolder, and, though rather simple, it is most effective. In essence, it is a transition directly leading from the tonic chord towards a minor chord a semitone interval below. Paul McCartney's daring composition 'Yesterday' (1965), where the opening chords themselves already take us from F major to E minor, may offer the best example. Because of the small distance between the tonics of both chords, the original key of F major is momentarily made indecisive, as if caught in a trap and seemingly shifting towards E minor. In respect to the lyrics, the tone functions like a sort of time machine, bringing us back or forth in time into the actual moment to which the lyrics are referring. In 'Yesterday', this effect of actualizing an experience regards the day before, when 'all my troubles seemed so far away'. In 'Breathe', right after the modulation from E dorian towards C major already discussed, Pink Floyd apply the same harmonic trick to the same end, but now pointing to future expectations (Figure 7.5).

Though, just a semitone apart, the move from C major to B minor is effected by moving the finger settings on the guitar five frets downwards – just like we saw before with the circle of fifths. And, while the harmony is taken from C major to B minor, the wish 'Long may live …' is actualized in the promised emotional experience of giving smiles and crying tears. This 'Yesterday'-effect of actualizing a past or future experience, makes itself even more strongly felt in 'Time', where we find a temporary excursion in D major, starting in measure 65. After the twice-repeated sequence | Dmaj7 | – | Amaj7 | – |, we hear a descending progression (Figure 7.6).

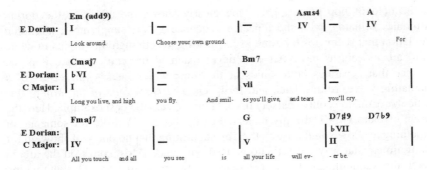

Figure 7.5   Modulation and tone trap in 'Breathe' (measures 54–65)

Figure 7.6   Tone trap in 'Time' (measures 73–80)

Here, though harmonically complex, the guitar technique in itself is again rather simple, as Gilmour plays the sequence with partial open chords and basic barre chords (Marshall, 2001, p. 51). The effect is no less impressive, though, moving the listener in time towards that fatal day when the realization breaks through that 'ten years have got behind you'. This short excursion, moreover, is repeated at the end of the song, but there the chord C♯m7 is followed by four measures of | Bm | – | Bm7 | F | that subsequently segues to the reprise of 'Breathe' in E dorian. This last move can be seen as a tone trap by itself, which takes us back to the question of how the tracks of *The Dark Side of the Moon* are welded together.

A journey through time

In the idiom of pop and rock music, the backing, the dorian mode and the tone trap offer some subtle means to manipulate the perception and experience of time passing by. The backing – and by implication the whole-tone key shift – helps in energizing or slowing down the flow of time, while the use of the dorian mode even seems to stop it. The tone trap, in turn, actualizes past or future experiences. Of course, as music history shows, these harmonic contraptions were not new at the time Pink Floyd applied them to their songs on *The Dark Side of the Moon*.

However, by combining them so closely in the compact format of their composition, the Floyd turned it into a unique journey through time, leading from childhood misery to adult madness.

The first part of the album is a dreamy sequence, indicating some preconscious, blurred childhood memories. Just like most childhood memories that linger in one's mind, the lyrics are rather vague; the words, though, clearly hint at the double bind by juxtaposing the feeling of happiness with the dark prophecy of daily boredom. 'Speak to Me' introduces the listener to the core opposition with its helicopter sounds and screaming seagull, suggestively representing the threatening system of the social machinery and the call for individual freedom. The lyrics of 'Breathe' – 'dig that hole, forget the sun' – next echo the Protestant work ethic, that teaches even little children the principles of hard work, self-discipline and postponement of gratifications as a means to a blissful afterlife in heaven. It is a choice each person has to make for her- or himself and, here, the dorian mode makes clear that someone is waiting for our decision to be made. The short modulation within the song, from E dorian towards C major, wakens us up to reality, urging us to make an actual choice. The song ends with the same modulation, now jumping a fifth from a G to a D chord, underlining the warning words 'race towards an early grave', indicating we have only been given one lifetime on earth and will have to spend it the best way we can. Next, the song ends by falling back into E dorian again and segueing to 'On the Run', a sound-collage of footsteps evoking the nightmarish urge to escape some invisible threat.

With some 40 seconds of clocks, alarms and bells, 'Time' wakes us up from this frightening dream and tells us we have waited too long and missed the chance to comply with the expectations – 'you missed the starting gun'. Initially this track seemingly takes the key from E dorian to E major by an alternating sequence of E and F♯m chords, each four measures long. As the lyrics start, however, with a four-measure sequence of | F♯m | – | A | – | E | – |, the key lands down in F♯ dorian. That is one whole-tone step upwards, thereby energizing the atmosphere. Still, the dorian mode lets us know that we are waiting in vain for a decision to be made. Again, the modulation towards the sixth, D major, mirroring the previous modulation in 'Breathe', is used to warn us of this stasis. Just like 'Breathe', the song ends with the modulation part, but now taking the original key a semitone lower towards F major. Subsequently segueing to E dorian, the implied tone trap takes us into the reprise of 'Breathe' and into the second section of the composition, actualizing the experience of youth, now 'ten years have gotten behind you'.

The dream of childhood is now over. The second section describes the youth of the songs' protagonist and his battle with the three opposing forces of religion, money, and politics. These three elements are presented consecutively in separate songs, the styles of which vary from jazz-rock by pop-rock to psychedelics – thus nicely fitting in with the periods of the 1950s, and the early and mid-1960s. The reprise of 'Breathe (Reprise)' rekindles the feeling of waiting for something to happen. The modulation at the end now ends up with B minor, segues into the first measure of 'The Great Gig in the Sky' and next climbs over F major to the new key of G dorian. This last step works as a backing, energizing the atmosphere. It is difficult to impute the precise meaning of the song from the scarce, spoken lines of the lyrics. By and large, it can be inferred from the angelic vocals of Clare Torry and from the song's working title 'Ecclesiastics'; which evokes Bible passages telling us that we should work hard as long we are able, because we have no certainty we can still better ourselves beyond the grave. The most important clue to the song's meaning is given by the protagonist's decision to shake off the paralyzing spell of the Protestant work ethic, if only by failing to meet its standards: 'I'm not afraid of dying'. Its key makes this song stand out among the other tracks, but deservedly so as it signals an important turning point.

This time there is no segueing into the next song. 'The Great Gig in the Sky' ends quite suddenly, because it seems to be one measure short, with 50 beats of silence as powerful as the dramatic silence at the end of the Beatles 'A Day in the Life'. It is as if we are waiting for the consequences of the choice to show up, keeping silent to hear the sound of the forces that are massing for a counterattack. These are represented first by 'Money'. Whereas 'The Great Gig in the Sky' left us in key of G dorian, 'Money' takes us to the key of B minor, telling of the lures and false promises of consumer society. Next, a short organ and saxophone intermezzo leads us into 'Us and Them'. This song is in regular D major but also shows strong inflections to the parallel key of D minor while the middle eight switches to the relative key of B minor. The combination of these relative and parallel keys underscores the melancholic atmosphere of the song and also, helped by the saxophone of Dick Parry that is heard on both tracks, links it with 'Money'. 'Us and Them' clearly suggests the sad feelings, evoked by the outside world's violent reactions against the counter culture, that are destroying the dream of a peaceful cultural revolution. The song ends with a sudden transition, a whole step upwards, from D major into C major, only to fall back, almost immediately, into D dorian in 'Any Colour You Like'.

There is no way out, as the dorian mode indicates. So the third section of *The Dark Side of the Moon* presents the lost battle and its inevitable outcome: madness. In respect to its keys, this is the most uncomplicated part of the composition, as it comprises only the keys of D dorian and D major. 'Any Colours' simply takes up the final C-major chord of 'Us and Them' and transforms it into its dorian counterpart, D dorian. This whole-tone step again stirs things up as we hear the sound of fighting guitars, struggling in vain to solve the prisoner's dilemma in which the song's protagonist is caught. The song appropriately finishes with a long confusing chord sequence, blurring the actual and leaving us with an open ending at the dominant of F major: | Dm7 | G | B♭maj7 | Am | E♭maj7 | F–C7♯9 C7♭9 |. Segueing into 'Brain Damage' and again taking a whole-tone step, the key is transformed into a clear D major, where it stays for the final tracks. Having started in E dorian, we end up in its co-tonic, D major. Though the key's triteness indicates that life has returned to normal, other musical devices point out there is still something wrong. In 'Brain Damage' it is the frightening, sharp-sounding arpeggio, built on the straightforward, alternating | I | IV | ostinatos. In 'Eclipse' it is a recurrent progression which provides the song with a lamenting, Gregorian tinge and turns it into a kind of litany (Figure 7.7).

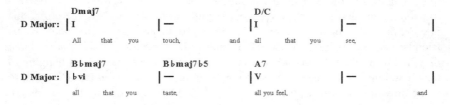

Figure 7.7   Litany sequence in 'Eclipse' (measures 9–16)

Having been told the whole story, the onlookers now express their grief, falling into silence at the end into which the sound of heartbeats is heard again, indicating that they all will have to live with this loss.

A requiem for youth culture

The dorian mode and it associated keys, which glue the tracks of *The Dark Side of the Moon* to one another, is by itself pre-modern. Over time, it has been preserved not only in folk music, but also in religious music. From the Middle Ages to the present, the dorian mode comes to the fore in a whole series of masses, ranging from De Machaut's *Messe de Notre Dame*, by Tallis's *English Service Music* and Monteverdi's *Mass for Four Voices*, to Beethoven's *Missa Solemnis* and Howells' *Mass in the Dorian Mode*. In his mass, Beethoven, for instance, consciously blends the keys of D major, B minor, and D dorian – the same combination of keys we find in *The Dark Side of the Moon*. The association with religious music is even strengthened by the album's finale, as 'Eclipse' with its litany-like repetition and its allusion to Gregorian chant, even resembles the Agnus Dei of the Catholic Requiem Mass. Indeed, the songs of *The Dark Side of the Moon* show many of the marks that the musicologist Philip Tagg (1993) lists for funeral music as it is understood in the tradition of Western music: a minor key, low volume, slow tempo, a restricted melodic ambit and short, repetitive phrases, a low tessitura, and descending movements. The songs on the album lack only the aeolian pendulum – a harmonic or melodic oscillation between a minor tonic and submediant major triads or between a minor sixth and perfect fifths – an omission to which Tagg attaches great significance, though it can be heard in 'Money'. All in all, because of this association, *The Dark Side of the Moon* can be taken as some sort of requiem, a secular ceremony, mourning the loss of the hopes and dreams of 1960s youth culture.

The theme of *The Dark Side of the Moon* circles around the opposition between boredom and fun, between drudgery and art, that was articulated, even constituted, by the idiom of pop and rock music itself (Grossberg, 1992). By establishing this opposition, pop and rock music located itself at the core of youth culture, defining this domain as a free port for the products of artistic self-expression, far beyond the boundaries and exigencies of everyday life. Like many other free ports, this one too proved to be a dangerous place for a prolonged stay. Seeing some of his friends succumb to the risks, British SF-author John Brunner (1973) realized that they had been playing outside too long. The stone that had been kept hanging in the air so long by the sheer power of youth culture's dreams and fantasies, had to come down in the end. In the same vein, Greil Marcus (1975, p. 45) confessed: 'We had gone too far, really, without getting anywhere.' Though not going to any real analytical depth, remarks like these point at the fact that the absolute freedom youth culture claimed for itself, was intrinsically a part of the problem itself. The same message is conveyed by Pink Floyd in *The Dark Side of the Moon*, but with music as the means. It is part of their art, we can add, that Pink Floyd succeeded in reaching such a large audience, thereby mending somehow the rift that had developed between pop and rock, while preserving the tensions.

The members of Pink Floyd were not the only ones to make a musical reassessment of youth culture. At about the same time, Jim Jacobs, for instance, released his musical *Grease* (1971), a nostalgic celebration of 1950s rock and roll culture, which turned it into the scenery of timeless adolescent interplay. Looking back at Syd Barrett's defeat, Pink Floyd, on the other hand, clearly recognized that the utopian perspectives of 1960s' youth culture themselves were the inevitable outcome of the 1950s. In Pink Floyd's musical presentation, the 1960s surface, so Marcus (1991, p. 384) put it in his column for the magazine *Artforum*, 'as a true curse: no grand, simple romantic time to sell to present-day teenagers as a nice place to visit, but a time that, even as it came forth, people sensed they could never really inhabit, and also never leave'. Marcus was referring to Oliver Stone's movie *The Doors* (1991), describing the life and times of Jim Morrison, yet another victim of rock music's overstatement of its wish for individual freedom. His statement, however, applies as well, maybe even better, to *The Dark Side of the Moon*.

Part III

'There's no dark side of the moon'
Theoretical discussions

Chapter 8

Reversing us and them: anti-psychiatry and *The Dark Side of the Moon*

Nicola Spelman

The mind of man has been poisoned by concepts. Do not ask him to be content, ask him only to be calm, to believe that he has found his place. But only the madman is really calm.

– Antonin Artaud (1925)

From the imprudent humor of Napoleon XIV's novelty song 'They're Coming To Take Me Away (Ha, Ha)' (1966), to the disturbing account of depression in Napalm Death's 'Dementia Access' (1992), portrayals of madness in popular music have shown it to be a wide-ranging and powerful medium for facilitating and communicating extremes of emotion. In terms of thematic content, the most common depiction of madness offered appears to be that which places madness as the antithesis of rationalism and mental coherence. Madness can thus be found to embody behavior ranging from the violent, deviant and criminal (for example, Ugly Kid Joe's 'Madman', 1991) to the less threatening, yet nevertheless unsettling and bizarre (for example, Queen's 'I'm Going Slightly Mad', 1991).

Such widespread yet sadly limited assumptions have not always dominated, however, for in the late 1960s and early 1970s an effective challenge was instigated by a number of prominent and influential artists – including Pink Floyd, David Bowie, Lou Reed, Alice Cooper, and Elton John – who attempted a more sympathetic treatment of the subject. Since it is clearly not coincidental, I assert that the principal reason for this departure may be found once the music is related to the dissemination of the innovative and often extreme anti-psychiatric theories of R.D. Laing, David Cooper, and Thomas Szasz.[1] As such, my intention in this chapter is to present a close reading of Pink Floyd's *The Dark Side of the Moon* exploring their indebtedness to anti-psychiatric ideas, and analyzing the ways in which those ideas are embodied in specific songs both verbally and musically.

An appreciation of the way in which perceptions of madness have changed throughout history is crucial when examining the relationship between a musical text and contemporary medical, social, and cultural beliefs surrounding mental illness. While it is likely that contemporary beliefs will manifest themselves in entirely observable ways (for example, with reference to specific treatments that may or may not be considered beneficial), there are often additional themes contributing to the depiction offered that are drawn from much earlier historical periods, notions that have, for whatever reason, remained prominent within the public conception of mental illness despite evident developments in psychiatric opinion. One such example, relevant to *The Dark Side of the Moon*, is the notion that those labelled madmen are, in fact, enlightened individuals capable of perceiving the true reality of human existence and experience. It is an assumption that first became popular in fictionalized mode within the farces of the Middle Ages, wherein the character of the fool or madman would appear 'center stage as the guardian of truth' (Foucault, 1965, p. 14). Although its portrayal was initially intended for comedic value, the enduring fascination of the mystery of madness has ensured it is a theme that has continually reappeared.[2]

The opinion that madness could possibly constitute a heightened state of awareness certainly became more prevalent during the late 1960s and early 1970s when, for once, the stark opposition between reason and unreason was used not to ostracize the madman, but to draw attention to the sickness within a society seemingly bent upon its own destruction. Those who mourned the 'insanity' of society itself frequently enforced their claims by following this reversal to its natural conclusion; if behavior generally believed to be 'normal' could be proven insane, then surely conventionally labeled 'mad' behavior could conceivably be sane. It was a reversal of conceptions that held particular favor within the work of R.D. Laing, and is, I would argue, the very axis upon which *The Dark Side of the Moon* communicates its critique of contemporary society and promise of a more meaningful existence.

Initially, the album appears to focus upon the fatuous, routine, and temporal nature of life as both 'Breathe' and 'Time' illustrate the various ways in which normal man is blinded by a false existence. The effective communication of this message relies upon the way in which the listener's expectations are continually yet subtly denied. 'Breathe', for example, begins with a variety of timbral and melodic gestures that appear to connote sublime predictability and comfort. The slide guitar is suitably unhurried in its smooth transition between notes (aided by the use of slow attack), its pure tone contributing to the bell-like arpeggiated motif of the Hammond organ and mellowness of the bass timbre to offer a warm textural ambience. In contrast to this, the slightly distorted accompanying guitar plays descending, picked arpeggios that lead effortlessly on to the beat where the tones are left to ring and pulsate; the kit adds to this shimmering quality with the use of ride cymbal quavers and occasional soft cymbal crashes. The first vocal statements of section A are perfectly suited to such accompanying gestures, responding in an agreeably lazy fashion through the delayed entry of phrases and use of appoggiaturas over the A-major chords to suggest sighs of contentment on the words 'air', 'care' and 'me'. The alternating I–IV progression in E dorian imposes no fixed sense of direction, and with the major sixth degree offering an attractive brightening to what would otherwise be a natural minor, the harmony maintains an appealing sense of stasis and security.

Once the B section is underway it would appear, however, that such contentment is misplaced. The use of a descending bass and kit fill results in a perceived decrease in energy level at the pivot junction between sections, preparing for the depressing revelation that the price to pay for such contentment is a life without meaning or distinction: 'And all you touch and all you see is all your life will ever be.' While brief in duration, the four bars of section B are given prominence through the sudden lack of fluency in the kit part as it appears to pause on its first crotchet following the activity of the preceding fill and proceeds to use toms to punctuate at the half bar rather than relax back into a continual pattern. Its crotchet-beat emphasis in the final bar, while evoking a slowing of time, helps to emphasize the contrasting increase in harmonic rhythm as the chords push downwards to the inescapable repetition of section A. The chord progression of section B is also significant, allowing a descending line – symbolic of the dissipation of section A's deceptive invulnerability – to be traced from the first two bass notes through to guitar and Hammond organ:

Section B chords:	Cmaj7	Bm	F	G	D7#9	D#dim7
Descending movement:	C	B	A	G	F	E♭ (D#)
	Bass …			Guitar & organ …		

The vocal motif equally descends to emphasize harmony notes (C, B, A) across the first three bars and, while more continuous than the melodic statements of section A, the line's unrelenting repetition and certainty of stress upon beat one works to suggest an unstoppable/inescapable truth (Example 8.1).

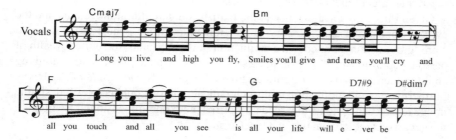

Example 8.1   'Breathe', Section B lead vocal and upper harmony vocal

As the song progresses, the repeat of section A begins to evoke a distinct element of misfortune as subtly disruptive gestures such as the organ glissando, and melodic syncopation with repetition (derived from the phrasing of section B) convey a dawning awareness of the need to awake from the opening reverie alongside a realization of the futility of work itself. The final prophetic statement of section B indicates the inescapability of man's mortality: it is possible to maintain an unconscious approach to life's progression in which case 'all you touch and all you see is all your life will ever be', but try to 'catch up' and commit yourself to the drudgery of work, and you face only 'an early grave'.

Such criticism of 'normal' man's existence, in which he is perceived to be restrained, even trapped, by Western society's necessity for conformity and an illusory world of contentment, formed a key premise for R.D. Laing and his theory of man's estranged state which he first articulated in *The Politics of Experience*, writing: 'The condition of alienation, of being asleep, of being unconscious, of being out of one's mind, is the condition of normal man' (1967, p. 24). Laing supported this belief by claiming that, for many people, their 'true self' is lost behind a 'false self' acquired to deal with a society that is profoundly estranged from reality. Furthermore, he made it clear that coercion was the source of this pitiful state: 'What we call "normal" is a product of repression ... The "normally" alienated person, by reason of the fact that he acts more or less like everyone else, is taken to be sane' (ibid., pp. 23–4).

During the late 1960s such views had, in fact, become commonplace in the New Left's attempts to highlight the necessity for social change; a change that would require involvement on a personal level to overcome what Roszak referred to as 'the deadening of man's sensitivity to man' (1970, p. 58). David Cooper, the psychiatrist who first employed the term 'anti-psychiatry', was especially vehement in his appeals for a reawakening of man's true potential, insisting, like Laing, that 'the well-conditioned, endlessly obedient citizen' could 'without metaphorical sleight-of-hand' be regarded as being 'out of his mind', and asking in dramatic conclusion: 'How do we turn around the signs at the entrance of the psychiatric prison so that we can see ourselves as the violently disturbed inmates of a rather larger bin?' (1971, pp. 13, 138).

Given Pink Floyd's allegiance to the British countercultural movement and the evident appeal of Laing's theory to the Bohemian fringe, who Roszak claimed were 'grounded in an intensive examination of the self' and 'the buried wealth of personal consciousness' (1970, p. 62), it is perfectly plausible that such thinking could influence the nature of critique favored within *The Dark Side of the Moon*. Furthermore, an identification with such radical opinion could convey a desirable image for the band – to be regarded as 'normal' and 'one-dimensional' is, after all, the very worst indictment one can level at an artist:

> normalcy can be destructive to the imagination, to creativity, to the intellect, to the soul. The only way we grow as people is through confronting our dark side, because if all you want is the quiet and safety, you're giving up reality… (Carpenter, 1997)

The opening of 'Time' quite literally demands the aforementioned desire for wakefulness as the cacophony of bells, chimes, and alarms enter in unpredictable discord, lasting for what seems an interminable duration of 30 seconds. Like 'Breathe', the song is divided into repeated A and B sections, although here the A sections are more direct in their criticism of life's rituals: 'And you run and you run to catch up with the sun, but it's sinking, and racing around to come up behind you again'; while the B sections lament wasted opportunities: 'And then one day you find ten years have got behind you, no one told you when to run, you missed the starting gun'. David Gilmour's strained-throat voice produces a more assertive vocal delivery, and his occasional use of melisma (for example on the words 'day' and 'way') suggests an attempt to break free from the confines of the phrase, thereby enhancing the suggested frustration of the lyric content. The strength of the vocal is also conveyed through its reliance upon the root notes of the chords on accented beats, yet its confined nature, utilizing a repeated alternation with the seventh degree, draws attention to the tedious dissipation of time. While the rhythm section's activity (bass and kit working in rhythmic unison) creates the impression that time is passing, the repetition of melodic motif and repeated F♯ aeolian chord progression suggest that life itself remains uniform/unchanged (Example 8.2).

Example 8.2   'Time', Section A vocal, bass and kit

The B sections of 'Time' are reminiscent of the comfort witnessed in the A sections of 'Breathe'. The change in drum pattern and shift to a more sustained bass line establish a half-time feel that, alongside Richard Wright's softer vocal timbre and calming choir gestures, creates a relative tranquillity. The simple alternation of tones within the melody continues through the change in harmony to provide an unassuming, lazy feel over the brightness of the major seventh chords (VI–III in F♯ aeolian). Once again, however, it appears that the listener has been lulled into a false sense of security, for there follows a subtle break in the expected continuity of phrase that draws attention to the twist in the lyric content: the result of such laziness being that ten years have passed without notice. The harmonic descent from Dmaj7 to C♯m then Bm appears to illustrate this depressing shift before rising up to deliver the final revelation: 'You've missed the starting gun!'

'Time' then is significant in the way in which it embellishes the aforementioned theme of a false existence, but it also forms a crucial part of the album's conceptualization of time itself. From the very beginning, the heartbeat and diverse ticks of three clocks in 'Speak to Me' encourage the listener to ponder their own mortality and the transient nature of time. 'On the Run' offers a more subtle expression of time, the repeating synthi-A riff representing a sense of eternity/timelessness, while auxiliary sounds punctuate and move around the spatial dimension, occasionally descending in pitch to represent the Doppler effect and underpin the spoken vocal statement 'live for today, gone tomorrow, that's me'. Whereas the activity of clocks at the opening of 'Time' pre-empts the returning concept of the dangers associated with a life of 'lying in the sunshine', the spaciousness achieved in the remainder of the introduction (through excessive reverb on the roto-toms, wide gap in frequency range between bass and xylophone, and apparent freedom of the pitched motifs) encourages further reflection upon time's all-encompassing nature. The following vocal sections (as outlined above) capture feelings of both frustration and regret at the inability to halt temporal movement and recapture missed opportunities.

In this instance, one is reminded of the character Billy Pilgrim in Kurt Vonnegut's *Slaughterhouse-Five*, who becomes 'unstuck in time': 'The second hand on my watch would twitch once and a year would pass' (1969, p. 20). This recognition is, however, a source of awakening for Pilgrim, as Patrick Shaw explains: he is then able to comprehend the 'negligibility of death, and the true nature of time' (1976, p. 94). This was also a view held by Laing who claimed that 'We are socially conditioned to regard total immersion in outer space and time as normal and healthy. Immersion in inner space and time tends to be regarded as anti-social withdrawal, deviancy ... in some sense discreditable' (1967, p. 103). In the inner world he claimed that 'Mundane time becomes merely anecdotal, only the eternal matters' (ibid., 1967, p. 109), and that one way to access this was through an impulsive curative process involving some of the people whom society labels schizophrenic. Thus, madness was conceived by Laing as a possible pilgrimage to rediscover inner space and time, destroy the false self, and be reborn through the re-establishment of a new ego:

> 'Instead of the mental hospital, a sort of re-servicing factory for human breakdowns, we need a place where people who have travelled further, and consequently may be more lost than psychiatrists and other sane people, can find their way *further* into inner space and time, and back again ... This process may be one that all of us need, in one form or another. This process could have a central function in a truly sane society. (ibid., pp. 105–7)

While the first half of *The Dark Side of the Moon* makes no reference to this view of an enlightened form of madness, the numerous references to time that expose the folly of being either too blasé or, conversely, too absorbed in its external passing, and the evident encouragement to ponder its inner, eternal existence, appear to support Laing's premise.

Moving on from 'Breathe' and 'Time' the album offers more specific examples of society's sickness, as the negative themes of commodity fetishism and war are explored within the tracks 'Money' and 'Us and Them'. Initially, 'Money' reminds listeners of their restricted existence within modern capitalist society; the opening irregular 7/4 loop of sound effects (each paper tear, dropping money bag, opening of cash register, and so forth, representing a single crotchet beat) determines the meter of the ensuing bass riff and vocal sections, acting as a metaphor for man's perfunctory existence. The deviation from regular meter is significant, for it evokes a sense of unnatural progression, enhancing the mechanistic nature of the sound effects and their unrelenting repetition. Once the bass riff and kit enter, the beat grouping of the meter (3+3+1) is also consequential as the final crotchet appears as a turnaround device. The effect is produced by the way in which the bass reaches its tonic goal on beat 6 and then utilizes beat 7 to flip up to the third before returning to the tonic once more for beat 1 of the following bar; the intervallic shape of the riff and cymbal crashes on both beat 7 and beat 1 offer the impression that the loop's repetition is being mechanically activated.

While the first half of verse 1 appears to condone a reasonable amount of financial striving (getting a 'new job' with 'more pay' so that you're 'okay'), subsequent passages reveal the attendant pressures and levels of deception as people become divorced from the functioning reality of life. Desire for the procurement of material wealth as opposed to the more substantive attainment of emotional wealth is evident in the pronouncements 'Grab that cash with both hands' and 'I'm all right, Jack, keep your hands off my stack', the accompanying guitar and organ gestures serving to highlight the vocal's authoritative nature through alternating crotchet stabs. The manipulation of bass riff, coupled with the vocal's refusal to conform to regular phrase patterning (beginning on beat 7 as opposed to the anticipated beat 1) further enhances the comfortless sentiments of such self-serving beliefs.

A number of musical devices help to illustrate the greedy accretion of material goods, the unstoppable force of the capitalist ideal. One such example occurs in the final two lines of verses 1 and 2 where, while listing the various possessions that money can buy, the vocal, doubled by guitar and bass, appears to run away with itself, providing a continuous stream of ascending and descending pitches with no breaks in delivery. The meter becomes ambiguous at this point, adding to the sense of unbridled movement by moving to two bars of 4/4 and a bar of 6/4. Moreover, the brief departure from Bm to F♯m then Em suggests that the only means of establishing a sense of individual direction (signified by the break with the bass riff) is through pursuing the ambition of furthering one's economic status within society. As such it is merely an illusory freedom, the individual imagining that they possess a life defined by the style of the commodities purchased: 'I'm in the hi-fidelity first class travelling set and I think I need a Lear jet' (Example 8.3).

Example 8.3   'Money', final two lines of verse 1

The critique of capitalism offered in 'Money' is, as Whiteley observes, 'all-inclusive. None of us is free from this social disease, the sentiments are universal' (1992, p. 111). Being the most acerbic critic of capitalism among those termed 'anti-psychiatrists' Cooper repeatedly called for a revolution that would involve 'both an external, mass-social, and internal, personal and private, divorce from all the mechanisations of capitalist-imperializing society' (1971, p. 139). The belief that an obsession with material wealth would overshadow, even negate, the pursuit and experience of life's true pleasures was equally shared by Laing who asked, 'What is to be done? We who are still half alive, living in the often fibrillating heartland of a senescent capitalism – can we do no more than reflect the decay around and within us?' (1967, p. 11). Again, there appears to be a similarity between such thinking and the sentiments exhibited in 'Money', as further evidenced by Waters's admission in the *Washington Post* of 28 April 1993: 'I'm obsessed with truth and how the futile scramble for material things obscures our possible path to understanding ourselves, each other and the universe'.

'Us and Them' continues the aforementioned critique by drawing upon the 'anti-war philosophy of the counter-culture' and 'fears of manipulation' (Whiteley, 1992, p. 114). Given the social climate of the time, such choice of subject matter is hardly remarkable, and yet the make-up of the critique deserves further mention, bearing, as it does, remarkable similarities in its exploration of human nature to Laing's chapter of the same name.[3] The title, 'Us and Them', is used in both texts as a means of questioning the possible methods and reasons by which humans label (Them) and hence disconnect from each other to generate and secure a sense of identity (Us). Laing articulates this idea by claiming: 'The invention of Them creates Us, and We may require to invent Them to re-invent Ourselves' (1967, p. 76), this being similar to anti-psychiatrist Thomas Szasz's opinion that: 'Social man fears the Other and tries to destroy him; but …

paradoxically, he needs the Other and, if need be, creates him, so that, by invalidating him as evil, he may confirm himself as good' (Szasz [1970] 1973b, p. 319).

In the song 'Us and Them', a sense of opposing identities is established through use of both lyrics (us/them, me/you) and harmonic language – 'us' and 'me' being accompanied by the tonic major (D major), while 'them' and 'you' works in dialectical opposition, moving to the relative minor chord VI (B minor). The use of echo results in six audible statements of each word and serves to signify the collective identity of the group, while panning – most noticeable on the word 'them' – to left, center, then right, suggests the imagined threat of the encircling Other. The sincerity of the following absolving statements: 'And after all, we're only ordinary men' and 'God only knows it's not what we would choose to do,' is undermined by the ensuing progression to tonic harmonic minor (Dm, maj7), an unexpected and uncertain chord (due to its minor third and major seventh construction), which is finally resolved by a deceptively soothing plagal cadence (G–D). Such statements are akin to the song's introductory spoken vocals in which the participants attempt to justify their use of violence – 'I was in the right / I certainly was in the right' followed by the admission and repetition of 'I don't know, I was really drunk at the time' – and once again bear a striking similarity to the opinions expressed by Laing in his chapter of the same name, wherein he bemoans man's apathetic existence and lack of personal responsibility:

> We are all caught in the hell of frenetic passivity ... Everyone will be carrying out orders. Where do they come from? Always from elsewhere. ... They are created only by each one of us repudiating his own identity ... each person claims his own inessentiality: 'I just carried out my orders. If I had not done so, someone else would have.' ... Yet although I can make no difference, I cannot act differently. No single other person is any more necessary to me than I claim to be to Them. But just as he is 'one of Them' to me, so I am 'one of Them' to him. In this collection of reciprocal indifference, of reciprocal inessentiality and solitude, there appears to exist no freedom.' (Laing, 1967, pp. 65, 66, 70, 71)

The dramatic crotchet descent of distorted guitar, bass, and piano, accompanied by a semiquaver drum fill, marks the arrival of the B section wherein the texture immediately swells, to signify the sense of combined endeavor suggestive of the forward movement of troops. As the lyric content becomes descriptive of military action, various musical gestures serve to evoke the impending sense of doom, the bass and piano pushing down with pounding crotchets towards the principal point of tension on the word 'died' where the sevenths and ninths in the backing vocals eventually resolve to chord tones of the following C chord. The kit punctuates the texture with dynamic cymbal crashes on beats 3 and 4 adding further emphasis to the lyrics 'forward,' 'cried,' 'rear,' 'front,' 'rank,' and 'died', while a triplet semiquaver snare fill, suggestive of gunfire, follows the lyric 'the general sat', serving to highlight his inert posture. The fruitlessness of the struggle is confirmed not only by the lyric content – 'forward he cried from the rear and the front rank died' – but equally by the insinuated modulation to G major that fails to achieve due recognition. The section begins ominously enough in B aeolian, and progresses to chord VII (A major) before falling to chord VI (Gmaj7) which, when followed by the unexpected C-major chord, may be understood as a pivot (functioning as both chord VI in B aeolian and chord I in G major). However, despite the I–IV movement of the Gmaj7 to C, the root of B appears only momentarily undermined, and with the repetition of the entire phrase alongside the lyrics, 'The General sat and the lines on the map moved from side to side', the emptiness of the gesture, both physically and metaphorically, becomes clear.

In Laing's text, he too chooses the brutality of war to illustrate the senselessness of human division and asinine fear of imaginary enemies, writing:

> In the name of our freedom and our brotherhood we are prepared to blow up the other half of mankind, and to be blown up in turn … it is on the basis of such primitive social phantasies of who and what are I and you, he and she, We and Them, that the world is linked or separated, that we die, kill, devour, tear and are torn apart …' (1967, p. 79).

The sense of futile struggle is summed up in the following statement: 'As war continues, both sides come more and more to resemble each other … We are Them to Them as They are Them to Us' (ibid., p. 83) – a view that is echoed in the second verse of 'Us and Them', with these lines: 'Black and blue, And who knows which is which and who is who, Up and down, And in the end it's only round and round and round'.

Returning to my opening premise concerning the possible reversal of conceptions of madness and sanity, and how this may be the very axis upon which *The Dark Side of the Moon* articulates its critique of contemporary society, it is now necessary to identify the ways in which the final two songs establish the possibility of a more meaningful, enlightened existence. 'Brain Damage' appears, at first, to conform to stereotypical representations of madness, reliant upon the belief that madness is a condition which reveals itself through unreasonable behavior and, as such, is diametrically opposed to reason and sanity. The musical text communicates the Otherness of madness through a number of compositional devices, each constituting a form of opposition to conventional, functional, and logical musical processing. Scott's examination of demonic signifiers is useful here, reminding us that:

> In music, terms that form binary oppositions are rarely of equal status. One term is usually the negative rather than the opposite of another, its identity is, as it were, that of the other term with a minus sign. Dissonance is a lack of consonance, yet consonance is not a lack of dissonance (Scott, 2003, p. 129).

As such, it is possible to identify chains of signifiers (for example, non-functional harmonic progressions, rhythmic phrases that challenge the structural beat, undirected melodic constructions, and so forth) that are dependent upon the listeners' understanding of utilitarian musical devices in order that their illogical character may be read as representative of the irrational identity of madness.

Initially, the verse of 'Brain Damage' utilizes a non-functional progression (D–G7) that repeats without evident purpose/direction and incorporates descending chromatic tones (F#–F). As outlined above, the lack of 'rational' progression is significant, but so too is the use of chromaticism, for unlike the dialectical opposition located in 'Us and Them', the lunatic is effectively positioned as neither major nor minor. Consequently, by drawing upon the frequently diagnosed behavior of the psychotic, the lunatic is portrayed as lacking a binary opposite, and thus existing as neither 'us or them', but rather as both an 'us and them'.[4]

Seemingly devoid of emotion, the vocal delivery is soft and relaxed, utilizing chest tone within a comfortable, yet noticeably limited, range. The rhythmic construction, being heavily syncopated, evokes a further sense of disconnection, the effect being that of an observer commenting upon events from a distance. The reference to lunatics in the first two lines harks back to the mid-19th century, when in 1845 the Lunatics Act was introduced in an attempt to alleviate the poor, unregulated conditions of private madhouses. Considered an acceptable term for the insane then, by the 1970s it would be recognized as a stigmatizing vulgarism: a term utilized to conjure up negative images of insanity that may be attached to certain actions and put forward as a benchmark from which to maintain and uphold popular beliefs.

Two further stereotypes underpin the remainder of verse 1, the first alluding to the long-established idea concerning madness and its connection with childishness ('Remembering games and daisy chains and laughs'), while the second promotes the necessity of policing the insane ('Got to keep the loonies on the path'). The simplicity of the accompanying gestures, particularly the lilting guitar arpeggiation and naive bass fills, appear to support the childish sentiments, although the bass's refusal to acknowledge the eventual chord change to E (continuing instead to sound octave Ds) along with the tritone interval of the vocal harmony, results in an unexpected dissonance that suggests a sense of foreboding despite the innocence of the lyric 'daisy chains and laughs'. Harmonically, the brief departure from the uncertainty of the alternating D–G7 to the functional movement of D, E7, A7, D (I, VofV, V, I) serves to reinforce the statement 'Got to keep the loonies on the path', implying both the reasonableness of such action and, through the use of a perfect cadence, the legitimacy of the path itself (Example 8.4).

Intensifying the ominous undertones, the beginning of verse 2 builds upon our conventional fear of madness: the lead guitar's eerie 4–3 appoggiatura that echoed the vocal's F#–F movement a tritone higher in verse 1, now becomes a direct repetition of the vocal pitches resulting in a dissonant clash between the major (F#) and minor sevenths (F) of the accompanying G7 chord. This disturbed response to

Example 8.4 'Brain Damage', verse 1

the enclosing madness, 'the lunatics are in the hall', is further stressed through subtle variation in the vocal's rhythmic phrasing, whereupon the revelation that they are in 'my hall' is emphasized through a slight, yet noticeable, delay in the delivery of the word 'hall' until beat 1 of the following bar. It is just after this point, where a keen sense of anticipation has been created, that the listeners' expectations are denied and the notion of reversal – and through this a reinterpretation of the song's opening – is revealed.

Initially, the verbal text alone is responsible for the sudden turn of events, the final two lines, 'The paper holds their folded faces to the floor and every day the paper boy brings more' revealing that 'the real madmen are not the ones you label mad, but the politicians on the front pages of the morning papers' (Whiteley, 1992, p. 116). The statement dissolves the supposed threat of the imaginary 'loonies', and exposes the more likely danger of those who hold the power of life and death, summarizing, as it were, Laing's cautionary tale:

A little girl of seventeen in a mental hospital told me she was terrified because the Atom Bomb was inside her. That is a delusion. The statesmen of the world who boast and threaten that they have Doomsday weapons are far more dangerous, and far more estranged from 'reality' than many of the people on whom the label 'psychotic' is affixed. ([1960] 1964, pp. 11–12).

Following this revelation, the chorus serves to normalize such fears, by engendering an emotional high that supports the positive sentiments of the lyric content. The preceding bar allows the listener a brief pause for reflection while enhancing the build in energy levels through the addition of organ with rotary speaker effect, giving rise to a whirling crescendo. The harmonic pivot into the chorus is equally assertive, the D7 chord moving with evident purpose onto G (V–I).

The major chord progression of the chorus (G, A, C, G) connotes strength and, through its lydian inflection (the A chord introducing the augmented fourth of G lydian), a sense of striving.[5] Instead of appearing directionless, the descending chromaticism discernible within the vocal harmonies appears purposeful, progressing D–C♯–C–B while being complemented by ascending, contrary-motion bass movement to resolve on a plagal cadence. The vocal is rhythmically more secure and continuous than in preceding sections, resulting in an expressive increase in momentum. Moreover, it employs greater use of chord tones, thereby enhancing the harmony's assured advance from the insecure verse statements. The smooth consonant movements and lush texture of the vocal choir help to soothe feelings of anxiety resulting from the knowledge of society's ills: 'And if the dam breaks open many years too soon, And if your head explodes with dark forebodings too.' There is also a suggestion of intertextual meanings: the lyric 'And if there is no room upon the hill' being reminiscent of The Beatles' 'Fool on the Hill' (1967), which is similarly implicative of the fool's heightened powers of perception. The final statement of the chorus is one of welcoming reassurance, the unison vocal phrase 'I'll see you on the dark side of the moon' evoking feelings of combined endeavor and collective strength (Example 8.5).[6]

The first chorus of 'Brain Damage' thus marks a critical moment in the album's reception; to rouse oneself from society's illusory sphere of contentment and comprehend its numerous afflictions may result in accusations of deviancy and mental abasement, yet the resulting awareness of truth and appreciation of potential experience will provide a form of sanctuary and solace. While previous songs question the sanity of society's actions, 'Brain Damage' shifts the focus toward an exploration of madness itself, encouraging listeners to ponder its definition and the methods by which it is 'treated'. Most importantly, the final lines of verse 2 and the ensuing chorus suggest an identification with what has been termed the conspiratorial model of madness:

Mental health … has come to mean conformity to the demands of society. According to the common sense definition, mental health is the ability to play the game of social living, and to play it well. Conversely, mental illness is the refusal to play, or the inability to play it well. (Szasz, [1963] 1974, p. 205)[7]

Exercise 8.5   'Brain Damage', chorus

No critic has been more vocal and persistent in their attack upon the medical model of psychiatry than Thomas Szasz. In his book *The Myth of Mental Illness* (1961) he asserts that what the majority of society and the psychiatry establishment refer to as mental illness is fundamentally separate and distinct from organic brain disease: 'Strictly speaking, disease or illness can affect only the body; hence there can be no mental illness. "Mental illness" is a metaphor. Minds can be "sick" only in the sense that jokes are "sick" or economies are "sick"' ([1961], 1972, p. 275). In Szasz's opinion, so-called mental illness should thus lose its mythical identity and be correctly defined as 'personal, social and ethical problems in living' (ibid., p. 269). The most crucial argument he offers in an attempt to elucidate the creation and perpetuation of this myth concerns the way in which mental illness serves as justification for the authority of the psychiatric profession, while providing society with a means of labeling and hence repressing individuals whose behavior is deemed undesirable. The relevance of his beliefs to *The Dark Side of the Moon* becomes clear when one considers the musical and lyrical text of the third verse of 'Brain Damage', where references to psychiatry's employment of physical 'treatment' and restraint imply covert forms of social conditioning.

The transitionary chord progression at the end of the first chorus serves to dispel the previous dynamism, utilizing minor chords III and VI in G major followed by a firm V–I cadence in D to signal a return to the joyless sentiments of the verse. While the harmonic and intervallic construction is similar, the rhythmic delivery is subtly manipulated in verse 3 to suggest a sense of confusion regarding the latest revelation: that 'the lunatic is in my head'. Both statements of the phrase involve a slight delay in the enunciation of the word 'head', whereas the uniform phrasing and literal repetition of the following lines: 'You raise the blade, you make the change' lack the rhythmic variety witnessed in previous verses and illustrate the clinical sterility of psycho-surgery. The implied hesitancy in acknowledging the presence of the lunatic, and the skilful way in which the listener is inculpated in the action of lobotomy[8] – '*you* raise the blade, *you* make the change, *you* rearrange me till I'm sane' (my emphasis) – serve to generate feelings of culpability and uncertainty concerning the acts of diagnosis and enforced therapy. The laughter (first heard in the opening 'Speak to Me') that interjects the first two vocal phrases – due to its inappropriateness of expression – may be read as either a stereotypical signifier of lunacy, or a mocking riposte to the protagonist's admission of 'illness'. Either way, its inclusion effectively contrasts the sombre, sustained organ accompaniment (which now lacks rotary speaker effect to allow a more fitting metaphor for the suggested death of the self), encouraging further empathy on the part of the listener.

Suspicion surrounding the possible means by which the state might manage deviant behavior, rather than act in the individual's best interest, was at a peak in the early 1970s:

> complaints of abuses, as well as a growing suspicion of government's big-brother role and the social pressures for conformity, now make it necessary to explore the history and workings of the therapeutic state, which is steadily acquiring the tools for control and, indeed, the modification of man. (Kittrie, 1971, p. 4).

As such, Waters's use of the term 'rearrange' as opposed to 'cure' suggests a particular identification with contemporary critics who questioned the validity of extreme physical treatments. The fact that prefrontal lobotomy had resulted in changed personalities was common knowledge, as Kittrie explains: 'Research disclosed that the operation destroyed the capacity to form abstract thought and robbed the individual of ambition, conscience, and planning abilities. The lobotomised person could react quickly to stimuli but was unable to reflect before reacting on the wisdom or effects of his response' (ibid., p. 306). Despite his reluctance to criticize 'treatments' in detail, lest it enforce the notion that such a thing as mental illness actually exists, Szasz frequently referred to treatments as 'tortures',[9] while Laing was understandably quick to denounce any intervention that dealt with behavior to the exclusion of experience: 'Any technique concerned with the other without the self ... and most of all, with an object-to-be-changed rather than a person to be accepted, simply perpetuates the disease it purports to cure' (1967, p. 45).

Further evidence of the possible influence of anti-psychiatry is apparent within the repetition of the verse's B section, which enables a continuance of imputations regarding the management of mental illness, this time drawing upon fears of involuntary incarceration: 'You lock the door and throw away the key, there's someone in my head but it's not me.' Since the late 1950s, Szasz had continually demonstrated his fervent opposition to such treatment, writing in 1970: 'For some time now I have maintained that commitment – that is the detention of persons in mental institutions against their will – is a form of imprisonment' (1973, p. 113). Equally pertinent was Laing's renunciation of established psychiatric institutions in favour of the Kingsley Hall therapeutic community, which in 1965 posed a particularly visible attack upon conventional medical intervention.

In response to the distressing content of the third verse, the final chorus brings a resurgence of comforting emotion that is heightened by the choir's improvised embellishments. The possible reference to former band member Syd Barrett has been well documented,[10] but it is the reassurance concerning the importance of individual expression and conviction that is most evident. The voices aren't perfectly balanced, allowing scope for individual assertion, while the cracked/strained delivery supports the previously discussed harmonic vigor suggestive of sustained endeavor: 'If the cloud bursts thunder in your ear, you shout and no-one seems to hear.' Conceptually, the notion of striving may have two possible motives, the first focusing upon the necessity for maintaining faith in one's own beliefs irrespective of conventional opinion, hence drawing upon Szasz's view of the so-called mentally ill as 'society's official and principal scape-goats' ([1970], 1973b, p. 271); the second relating to Laing's conceptualization of mental illness as a possible journey to potential enlightenment, a journey that was likely to be both arduous and frightening: 'In our present world, that is both so terrified and so unconscious of the other world, it is not surprising that when "reality", the fabric of the world, bursts, and a person enters the other world, he is completely lost and terrified' (1967, p. 103).

The final instrumental passage of 'Brain Damage' appears to demonstrate an identification with Laing's belief that madness may well constitute a form of personal redemption: a rebirth that would embrace an appreciation of innocent, true pleasures long since lost to 'grown-up' sensibilities. The bass lead in, moving in stepwise ascending motion (A–B–C♯–D) from the A7 chord to the D chord (and repeated upon the two subsequent statements of this chord progression), is reminiscent of early country music, serving to connote simplicity, honesty, and genuine values. In addition, a sense of playful nostalgia is introduced through the synthesizer's smooth articulation and rhythmically unhurried parallel chromatics in sixths (typical of the sentimental Tin Pan Alley ballads that country absorbed). Despite utilizing the uncertain chord progression of previous verses, the sense of foreboding is effectively banished as the bass complies with the eventual shift in harmony to the E chord and the prominent tritone intervals no longer appear (Example 8.6). The spoken vocal segments seem facile in both content and delivery, and the new laughter lacks the mocking, oppressive undertones characteristic of the old. In lamenting the loss of personal experience Laing stressed that: 'As adults we have forgotten most of our childhood, not only its contents but its flavour ... an intensive discipline of un-learning is necessary for *anyone* before one can begin to experience the world afresh, with innocence, truth and love' (1967, pp. 22–3). It is thus possible to view the final section of 'Brain Damage' as a momentary indulgence, an opportunity to evoke an imaginary utopia – a glimpse of the untainted existence that may await those journeying to the 'dark side of the moon'.

Example 8.6   'Brain Damage', final instrumental passage

As mentioned previously, the belief that madness could constitute a heightened state of awareness was not unique to the period in question. And yet, evidence points to a definite escalation of such ideas prior to the album's conception. 'Madness is a tentative vision of a new and truer world to be achieved through de-structuring – a de-structuring that must become final – of the old, conditioned world', wrote anti-psychiatrist David Cooper (1971, p. 85). Unsurprisingly, such beliefs occasionally adopted a pseudo-religious quality, elevating the notion of increased insight into a form of mystical, divine power: see, for example, Laing's description of the 'madman' as 'the hierophant of the sacred. An exile from the scene of being as we know it, ... a stranger, signalling to us from the void ... a void which may be peopled by presences that we do not even dream of' (1967, pp. 109–10). As such, it is perhaps not coincidental that the transition into 'Eclipse' encapsulates an impassioned feeling of spiritual ascendancy. The meter change to

6/8 (while maintaining the same quaver pulse) results in an increased occurrence of accents that produces a more driven feel. There is a noticeable dynamic growth aided by the return of full rotary effect on organ and half-bar kit fills which capitalize upon the use of toms and cymbals. Despite essentially descending in stepwise motion (D–C–B♭–A), the bass activity is equally vivid in terms of its presence and role in strengthening the anticipated sense of arrival/accession. Its use of an ascending octave slide below the final A7 chord serves to emphasize the eventual cadential movement into D major, a progression that represents the end of the suggested journey towards the dominant of G (initiated by the use of the augmented fourth – leading note of D major – during the choruses of 'Brain Damage').

In many respects, 'Eclipse' encapsulates the overriding message of the album, its list of potential experiences marking a final, climactic appeal to its listeners. In drawing our attention to the collective significance of every thought and every action, the enormity of individual responsibility becomes clear, and once more we are reminded of the choice that must be made between a life of sublime ignorance or pained awareness. The musical text imparts the strength necessary to align oneself with the latter, utilizing a lead vocal melody based upon the root or fifth of each chord and a strong functional progression D–B♭maj7–A–A7 (I–II–V–V7 with tritone substitution of chord II to allow smooth semitone movement onto the A chord). The amount of literal phrase repetition and gradual accretion of vocal layers secure a palpable build in tension that appears to reach its zenith upon the final statement: 'and everything under the sun is in tune, but the sun is eclipsed by the moon'. This final phrase, due to the density of texture, slight *rallentando*, and varied harmonic construction, appears stronger in terms of reiterating a sense of arrival than attaining mere closure. The dominant chord is omitted in favour of a B♭maj7–D progression that, while not cadential, offers a slight moment of uncertainty before the F and B♭ move inwards in semitones to form a welcome point of condensation upon the F♯ and A of the D chord.

Despite the apparent strength, even celebratory, connotations of the musical gestures within 'Eclipse', the use of the word 'but' has led many writers to suggest a more pessimistic reading of the album's closing statement. The final spoken vocal is often referenced as a means of affirming this conclusion, although it has the possibility to be viewed, alongside many of the earlier examples, as a defensive posture. And yet, there is a further conceivable interpretation, one that appears to fit more comfortably within the established tradition of esoteric meanings witnessed throughout the album's progression. That the immense power of the sun may be eclipsed by the infinitely smaller body of the moon may well be viewed as a metaphor, propagating the value of personal endeavor. The notion of mystical power is, once again, implicit and may be linked to Laing's remark that: 'The light that illumines the madman is an unearthly light. It is not always a distorted refraction of his mundane life situation. He may be irradiated by light from other worlds' (1967, p. 114). Moreover, once the sun is eclipsed by the moon, the 'dark side' is actually resplendent with brightness, a phenomenon that prompts an interpretation more in keeping with the exhilarated character of the musical text. Thus, the album acknowledges the ultimate sadness resulting from an awareness of society's ills, while simultaneously revealing the possible reward of self-realization – gaining access to our inner consciousness, reaching, as it were, the metaphorical dark side of the moon.

Notes

1. While unified by a desire to eradicate the medical model of psychiatry, one should be aware that anti-psychiatry has never been a universal discourse and distinct differences in theoretical approach exist between Laing, Szasz, and Cooper. For a more detailed overview, see Z. Kotowicz (1997), *R.D. Laing and the Paths of Anti-Psychiatry*, London: Routledge, ch. 6.
2. See, for example, P. De Broca (1966), *The King of Hearts*, MGM United Artists, which is set in France during the First World War. Here, the 'mad' are portrayed as perceptive, innocent, and truthful, while the supposed 'sane' are unable to comprehend the folly of war and have no regard for the beauty and preciousness of life.
3. The fourth chapter of Laing's 1967 book *The Politics of Experience* and *The Bird of Paradise*, is likewise entitled 'Us and Them'.
4. For further theoretical discussion of this matter, see G. Deleuze and F. Guattari (1984), *Anti-Oedipus*, trans. R. Hurley, M. Seem, and H.R. Lane, London: The Athlone Press.
5. Deryck Cooke's interpretation regarding the function of the augmented fourth is useful here: 'the sharp fourth ... acts as an accessory and more powerful major seventh on the dominant, its semitonal tension towards the dominant being alone capable of performing the 'heroic' task of lifting us into the key of the dominant. ... Functioning in this way, the sharp fourth expresses the same violent longing (upward semitonal tension in a major context) as the major seventh, but not in a context of finality; rather in a context of pushing outwards and upwards, aspiring towards something higher' (1959, p. 81).
6. The syncopation of the phrase is also significant in that the word 'moon' anticipates beat 1 of the concluding G chord, intensifying the aforementioned sense of harmonic striving.
7. This requires listeners to understand Szasz's basic premise that 'The sick role in psychiatry is typically other-defined' ([1961], 1972, p. 194).
8. Lobotomy, like EST (electroshock therapy), was introduced in the 1930s and widely administered up until the early 1950s, when reservations concerning its effectiveness and the introduction of drug therapy (sometimes referred to as chemical lobotomy) resulted in it becoming almost obsolete. It is interesting that Pink Floyd make reference to the operation some 20 years after its decline, although, due to the extreme nature of the procedure and its much publicized detrimental effects (illustrated in, for example, Kesey's *One Flew over the Cuckoo's Nest*, 1962), it is not surprising that it should remain so prominent within the public conception of mental illness and its treatment. The following quote provides a brief description of the procedure and what it was expected to 'cure': 'In its more primitive form it involved the removal or destruction of nerve fibres in the frontal lobe of the brain in an operation known as the "standard leucotomy" ... As with every new technique, psychosurgery was initially

hailed as a wonder treatment and was used for a wide variety of problems: "schizophrenia", alcoholism, learning disabilities, depression, anxiety, phobias, personality disorders, for shell-shocked war veterans and even for problem children' (Johnstone, 2000, p. 154).

9. See, for example, the following quote: 'The mental patient, we say, *may be* dangerous: he may harm himself or someone else. But we, society, *are* dangerous: we rob him of his good name and of his liberty, and subject him to tortures called "treatments"' (Szasz, [1970], 1973b, p. 308).

10. 'Although Syd was the trigger for the song, providing inspiration for the line "And if the band you're in starts playing different tunes …" Waters later gave the song a broader perspective' (Jones, 1996a, p. 101). 'The final chorus draws heavily on Syd Barrett's breakdown … Here there is a subtle change in rhythmic emphasis from the last chorus as if to underline Syd's lack of co-ordination – "and if the band you're in starts playing different tunes …"' (Whiteley, 1992, p. 116).

Chapter 9

Prismatic passion: the enigma of 'The Great Gig in the Sky'

Sheila Whiteley

It is now some ten years since my book *The Space Between The Notes: Rock and the Counterculture* (1992) was published,[1] and thirty years since I first heard *The Dark Side of the Moon* and was completely awed by its stunning beauty. It is something I return to again and again, in moments of sadness, in my moments of hesitation, in moments of joy. As such, the opportunity to provide, in the next section, a more detailed discussion of 'The Great Gig in the Sky' was compelling. It is undoubtedly one of the most erotic tracks ever to close the first side of an album, not least because Clare Torry's enigmatic solo raises questions concerning the tensions between sexual/religious ecstasy, the fear of dying and the seduction of eternity. The opportunity to meet her, and discuss further her intentions and feelings when recording the track is clearly an added bonus, and the following section provides an edited transcription, so opening out many of the points raised in my interpretative analysis.

I begin with an exploration of the tensions between sacred and profane love, and how these relate to the sense of euphoria promised by 'The Great Gig in the Sky'. Within human nature, the relationship between death (*thanatos*, or the destructive principle) and love (*eros*, or the creative principle) is not necessarily distinct. Both can evoke and celebrate sensuality – the erotic its joyous, the thanatic its darkest manifestations. Both work in the imagination, in the *not said*. It is this sense of the unspoken that drives Clare Torry's vocal and its evocation of the ecstatic. Suggestive of both the penetration of the unknown and the orgasmic of *jouissance*, her wordless vocal entices the listener into the seductive potential of the imaginary, responding to the enigma of death through an erotic exploration of sonic space.

More specifically, the first section explores the paradox raised by the question: Why, is 'The Great Gig in the Sky' the most made-love-to track in the world when it is ostensibly concerned with mortality and the fear of dying?

'The Great Gig in the Sky'

> I could not love except where Death
> Was mingling his with Beauty's breath
>
> – Edgar Allan Poe, 'Introduction' (1832)

The aesthetic, psychological and ideological fascination with the theme of dying is one that emerges throughout *The Dark Side of the Moon*. As Roger Waters observed, 'The fear of death is a major part of many lives and ... the record was at least partially about that'.[2] From the 'run rabbit run', through to the eclipse of the final outro, life is shown to be transitory and meaningless. For the young, the optimism of the 1960s was over, its heroes dead or at best scarred by the psychological uncertainties that had emanated from a hedonistic lifestyle. For them, the 'I'm not afraid of dying' that presages 'The Great Gig in the Sky' was more than a personal statement of acceptance: it was central to their realization that the dream was over.

'The Great Gig in the Sky' is pivotal to the album's exploration of life and death. In a society that had, by 1972, experienced two major wars, the controversy surrounding Vietnam, Watergate, and the controlling influence of multinational corporations, religious certainty was, at best, conjectural. Metanarratives had fragmented into the illusory of postmodernism, and the metaphysical had become little more than a sleight of hand. For the counterculture, the realization that religion was political, immersed in the trappings of ideology, sanctioning war and Third World deprivation, had led to an exploration of Eastern mysticism and hallucinogenics. Highs, however, gave way to lows and the stark realization that life was little more than a race towards death. The reprise of 'Breathe' that presages 'The Great Gig in the Sky' is, then, both structurally and emotionally contemplative, and a reminder that the approach of death ('Breathe'; Example 9.1)

Example 9.1   'Breathe'

necessitates a reassurance that it is only a beginning ('Breathe – Reprise'; Example 9.2). The supporting harmonies (G–D7(+9)–D♯o7–Em), however, are at best equivocal. There is no grand final cadence, rather a realization that religion is the opium of the masses, that the magic spells are grounded in the uncertainty of

Example 9.2   'Breathe – Reprise'

superstition, that transcendence is both a leap into the unknown and a quiet acceptance of the inevitable. It is, then, no surprise that the muttered 'Why should I be afraid of dying? There's no reason for it. You've got to go sometime' is set deep in the mix, the words compressed and dynamically fixed. The positive of the written statement is thus undermined by what is almost a 'fingers crossed' monotonal utterance of negativity. When mortality is inevitable, being afraid is no way out.

This sense of reconciliation to the unknown is integral to the opening of 'The Great Gig in the Sky'. Shaped by the tranquillity of Rick Wright's piano chord sequence, there is an evocation of contemplative space that envelops mortality within a feeling of transcendence. If the faithful need reassurance, then the textural simplicity and spacing of the chords, the slow heartbeat of the bass octaves, the ebb and flow of the inner melody against the gentle rise and fall of the upper voice, promise both a sense of stability and order and a rebirth of cosmic beauty, with subtle modulations of colour effected through the movement from minor to major to minor and the use of added sevenths and ninths (Example 9.3). While the

Example 9.3   'The Great Gig in the Sky', bars 1–4

contemplative has always been an aspect of the religious life, the death of the body and the release of the soul have inspired both the ecstatic of spiritual union (the *In Paradisum* of the Requiem Mass) and a comparison with orgasm, with the 'little death' of *jouissance*. As the one moment when all other senses are blurred and defused, and where time no longer has meaning, the euphoric of 'heavenly bliss' fuses with the erotic of orgasm. It is, for me, this tension between the spiritual and the erotic that most characterizes 'The Great Gig in the Sky'.

Presaged by the slow rise and fall of the piano arpeggio, the evocative slide guitar of Dave Gilmour echoes the melodic line first heard in 'Breathe' before it surges upwards, building the momentum and moving the listener from the reflective of *plaisir* to the ecstatic of *jouissance*.[3] The modulation from the warmth of the preceding Bb-major harmonies to the enigmatic of Gm7 provides a momentary tension before lift-off as the listener is swept into the full-color spectrum of the vocal. Loosely tethered by the underlying pulse of the alternating two-bar harmonies (Gm7–C9), the impact of Clare Torry's voice is electrifying as it surges upwards, each phrase an ecstatic rush of arousal as she moves the listener into the erotic intimacy of sensual pleasure. It is a sound that invites a heightened, active response. It is both spontaneous and passionate, powerful and primal, a rapturous, spiritual and sexual communion between the erotic and death as the passivity of 'Why should I be afraid of dying?' is transformed into the euphoric of ecstatic flight.

Here, the female cries that prefaced 'Breathe'[4] – which suggested an unfulfilled anguish as they subsided into the alternating Bm9–A harmonies of the opening track – are finally released. Impelled by an electrifying snare after-beat  and the glissando surge of the slide guitar, the vocal soars upwards in a sonic stream, exploring and re-exploring the erotic potential of the alternating harmonies, creating an almost physical sensation of female arousal that responds to the teasing dynamic and ever-mutating riff of the drums and bass over the swell of the Hammond organ. It is a musical language that embodies both intimacy in the supportive interaction of vocal/instrumentals, and gathering passion as the increasing momentum of the toms and the eddying thermals of the Lesley[5] provide a musical metaphor for the ecstatic rushes of orgasmic sensation. The climactic is heightened by the harmonic movement which moves from the alternating two-bar harmonies to a point of tension on Gm7/D and final release (Go7/Db) that gradually subsides to the Gb7–Bm harmonies, where the solo piano re-enters in a falling arpeggio that moves to a re-statement of the opening motif. The effect is to free the voice, to create the musical space for the surge towards climax. Initially rising upwards to top A, the sensual waves of female orgasm are reflected in both the fixation on gasps of ecstasy on the heavily punctuated top Gs, lapping waves of sensation as the voice moves against the momentum of the drums, rising once again to the top A before subsiding to the F♯ leading note in a gentle diminuendo that only hints at resolution as the solo piano leads once more into the contemplative reprise of the opening motif (Example 9.4).

Example 9.4   'The Great Gig in the Sky', bars 32–37

It is no mystery that the female orgasm is more suffuse than the male. It is both physical and dynamic, cyclical and sustained, overlapping and multiple. The temporal experience of tension and release in the first section of 'The Great Gig in the Sky' (bars 18–37) is thus replaced by the deeper and more introspective warmth of the middle section (bars 38–53) where there is a more gentle sense of re-arousal. The flight into the unknown that characterized the first section involved risk-taking (in the wide vocal leaps), strength (in the ecstatic highs), and spontaneous interaction. In contrast, the middle section explores the deeper realms of secondary arousal, the ebb and flow of sensation, and the resurging waves of bodily desire that characterize female erotic pleasure.

Initially, the vocal is tentative and musing, focusing in on the tensions between the Bm harmonies and the chromatic move to B♭ that inflect the opening bars of the middle section to 'The Great Gig in the Sky'. The vocal tone is warm, pitched on the lower register of the voice, explorative in its focus on the narrow intervals that signal the transition from minor to major before the stepwise move upwards from middle C to B♭, and the momentary breath that precipitates the rise to top A. This is colored by the shift from the Gm7 to C9 harmonies which, in context, provides only a momentary high before the gentle fall to the G triplets, where repetition serves only to stimulate a more expansive and measured high as the vocal slows to a gentle crotchet beat before it gradually diminishes, lost once again in the descending piano arpeggio that seems, always, to presage arousal. The impression throughout is of a beautifully constructed eroticized space. Punctuated by rests which provide momentary points of tension, the compression and extension of motifs, and the tonal contrast between the resonating upper body and head registers of the voice, the effect is a musical texturing both of temporality and the transcendence of time. In essence, Clare Torry's voice becomes a metaphor for the internal subjective world of the individual, exploring the speculative of sacred and profane sexuality through nuanced motivic development.

The final section of 'The Great Gig in the Sky' (bars 54–66) opens with an evocative return to the opening phrase of the vocal solo. This time, however, the vocal begins on the second beat of the bar, and the soaring ecstasy of the first flight is replaced by a more musing and thoughtful exploration of the primal motif. The high is still there in the leap to top G but the ebb and flow is more spaced out, punctuated by momentary reflective rests. The second phrase takes the listener deeper into space. Here, the rise to top G, which was earlier characterised by an elaboration of the deep structure (D–B♭–G–C–B♭–G), is finally revealed (Example 9.5).

Example 9.5   'The Great Gig in the Sky', bars 58–60

The stripping of the motif, the gradual diminuendo, and the slowly subsiding phrases initially suggest a move towards resolution, but the more measured pulse on the tonal center (G), triggers a final high as the vocal moves once again to the octave before it gently fades into the subsiding chords of the piano ostinato before a final, barely audible top G that gently subsides over the Gm7 harmonies. The plagal acceptance of the final cadence is thus given an underlying feeling of transcendence through the fading vocal as it dissolves into the ether of the final chord. The full color spectrum, that had earlier characterized Clare Torry's exploration of tonal flight, is finally transformed into a purity of sound that evokes the prismatic transformation of color into white light of the album's sleeve. It is, at one and the same time, an ending and a beginning, absorbed in the temporality of the final chord, yet reflective and reflexive in its transformative communication of bliss.

If 'The Great Gig in the Sky' is the ultimate performance, the best trip ever, the subliminal of the female voice 'I never said I was afraid of dying' (which is heard submerged deep in the mix of bar 58) says it all. The actuating spirit of the *animus*, which had earlier accepted death as 'the end' ('you've got to go sometime') is replaced by the *anima* of the soul which, within the context of the track, has experienced the ecstatic (literally 'over the moon') of free flight. It is for this reason, that I find Clare Torry's vocal solo so compelling. The *anima* is feminine, in contrast with the more hostile spirit of the *animus*,[6] and the choice of a female voice on 'The Great Gig in the Sky' creates a space of possibility. 'Because it is the Enigma, it doesn't explain itself, it makes itself heard' (Cixous, 1983, p.79). Not least, the vocal is self-involving in its erotic exploration of tonal space, whilst engaging in an intimate yet spontaneous evocation of sexuality that arouses listening desires. It is, in effect, impossible not to become actively involved in the floating waves of female yearning that suffuse 'The Great Gig in the Sky', and the thought that the release of the soul is a transformation of the more human experience of orgasm is, like Clare Torry's vocal, irrepressible. At the same time, it raises, once again, the equivocal of the erotic/spiritual, the tensions inherent in sacred/profane love, so returning me to my initial question: 'If 'The Great Gig in the Sky' is about mortality, then why is it the most made-love-to track in the world?'

The initial answer must lie, surely, in its wordlessness. There is no fixed meaning, no literalness in its exploration of sonic space. Thus, while the clues inherent in the reprise of 'Breathe', with its focus on 'what next', are given a certain focus in the piano introduction, which imparts an underlying chorale-like structuring to the Gm–C9 harmonies, the move to a Hammond organ in the middle section which creates a soul-inflected mood to the transformative vocal motifs, and the reprise of the piano in the final recapitulation which returns once again to the contemplative of the opening statement, the mood, overall, is enigmatic. In part, this is due to the mutating and transformative character of the solo vocal where the principal motif is evocative both of the shape-shifting of metamorphosis and the realization that 'Our souls are deathless: always, when they leave our bodies / They find new dwelling places ...', that 'We are not bodies only, But winged spirits ...' (Ovid, *Metamorphoses*).

The surge towards freedom of spirit (musically connoted by the leap upwards to the top Gs and As of the vocal solo) is thus comparable to the irrepressible ecstatic of release and while there is, as yet, no empirical evidence that tracks the journey of the soul, the comparison with the *jouissance* of orgasm is persuasive.

Here, the consuming waves of sexual pleasure that center on the erotic zones of the body are given full flight as consciousness is replaced by a *dérèglement de tous les sens*, an out-of-body experience that is both self-absorbed yet free. It is, above all, this sense of consummation that draws together the ecstatic of sexual orgasm with the release of the soul, or the essence of life. Both are grounded in the *'petit mort'* of the body; the erotic the momentary loss of consciousness that accompanies orgasm; the sacred, the release of the spirit that heralds the conclusion of life.

There is, then, a sense of optimism that, for me, is in stark contrast with the final outro of *The Dark Side of the Moon*. The first half of the album reads more like a parable of 'what could be' in its focus on the transitory of life. Life is shown to be predictable in its 'race toward an early grave', and while the sweetly tonal music of 'Breathe' and the relaxed mood of 'Time' lull the listener into a false sense of security, the feeling of warmth and stability is shadowed by the tensions of dissonant harmonies and lyrics that focus on the circumscribed nature of life as 'all you touch and all you see is all your life will ever be' ('Breathe') and the futility of 'hanging on in quiet desperation' ('Time'), sentiments that are given a forceful resonance in the paranoia of the 'On the Run'. 'The Great Gig in the Sky' thus offers a release into a transcendent bliss – a hint of what could be – if the warnings are taken to heart. In contrast, Side 2 evokes the realities of contemporary life – the obsession with money, the lunacy of war, the imprisonment of those who do not fit, the lunatics and brain-damaged whose heads 'explode with dark forebodings', and the polarization of self-interest v. humanity inherent in 'Us and Them'. 'Eclipse' thus frames the ultimate paradigm: 'everything under the sun is in tune, but the sun is eclipsed by the moon'. Circumscribed by the opening and closing heartbeat that begins and ends *The Dark Side of the Moon*, the tug between life and death and the final outcome is one of choice. Ignore or heed the warnings: be eclipsed or soar upwards to that final 'Great Gig in the Sky'.

An interview with Clare Torry

My interview with Clare was both wide-ranging and focused in its discussion of her personal involvement with the recording of 'The Great Gig in the Sky'. In the interests of clarity, I have edited our discussion in an attempt to tease out and elaborate on some of the key points raised in my interpretation of her vocal. What was compelling was her modesty and her humor – rare qualities in an artist whose musical realization of 'The Great Gig in the Sky' has inspired so many. I remain her most ardent fan.

Sheila Whiteley: Were you brought in specially for 'Great Gig'? Sort of 'We need someone special for this'. How had the band heard about you? What was your brief prior to recording 'Great Gig'?

Clare Torry: It was the beginning of 1973 so I was in the background of the music business, I was just really starting out. I'd done a few bibs and bobs here and there and unbeknownst to me, I'd obviously done a session at Abbey Road where Alan Parsons was engineering. When Floyd wanted a singer (this is so I'm told) they didn't want any of the usual people they knew, and it was Alan, apparently, who had suggested me. I knew nothing of this. I wasn't aware of Alan Parsons other than he worked on Harry's[7] first album, would you believe it? So I knew nothing about this. I wasn't involved with Floyd and, as I've told you, I wasn't a particular fan, and it was just, as far as I was concerned at the time, another booking and there we are. What was the other question?

Sheila: You were saying you were actually out that evening and you'd given them three hours that Sunday evening …

Clare: Well, actually what I did say was that I was rung up on the Friday by Dennis from EMI, from Abbey Road, and he said could I do a session and I said 'No. I'm very sorry, I'm working' – which was a lie because I was going to see Chuck Berry – and the weekend really was taken up and I couldn't possibly do it, and 'Who's it for, by the way?' 'Oh, Pink Floyd.' Didn't really make me feel 'Gosh! I must drop everything and do it,' to be perfectly honest, and Dennis, bless him, went on and on and I said 'OK'. Well, the only time I could do it was 7 to 10 on Sunday night and he said 'I'll check and see if that's suitable', and rang back five or ten minutes later to say that's fine, and I think my feeling was 'Bugger!' So I had to do it.

So I went up to the studio on the Sunday evening. I walked in and the four guys were there, and Alan, and obviously the tape op. always in the background, scurrying around in the shadows and making cups of tea. So they said, 'Well, we've got this track we'd like some singing on.' And I said, 'Oh yes, oh fine, and what have you got in mind?' And they said, 'Well, we'd better describe to you the concept of the album.' And they described it – what was really birth, living and all its bibs and bobs and aggros, and death – and I thought at the time, I have to be honest, I thought it was rather a lot of pretentious rubbish. That is exactly how I thought, and they played me the track a couple of times and I said, 'The best thing for me is to go out into the studio, put the headphones on and do something.' They didn't know what they wanted, I didn't know what they wanted.

I went into the studio and started singing and it was basically 'Ooooh, baby, baby, oooh, baby, baby' – typical soul-type singer stuff – and I suppose I went on for half the track, I don't know, and when it suddenly stopped they said, 'No, no, no, we don't want any words.' Now, that was when I thought 'Bloody 'ell, what do you do if you don't want words?' and then I thought 'Bloody 'ell, what do *I* do?' And I do remember Gilmour saying, 'Would you like me to write out the chords?' I said, 'No, no, no. You don't have to do that,' because to be perfectly honest it wouldn't have made any difference. Because I have to say that usually, when I sing, I have my eyes closed, other than reading 'oohs and ahs' on a session. So if I'm doing something solo I have my eyes closed, so it wouldn't have made any difference coz I wouldn't have read 'em. So, I said, 'No, no, no. I'm getting to be *au fait* with the chord sequence.' But when he said, 'There's no words,' I do remember feeling that it would be better if I went home, because I was starting to feel slightly embarrassed, really I was slightly embarrassed about it, and that's when I suddenly thought, 'Come on Clare, pull yourself together!' and I thought, 'Well the only way is to pretend I'm a musical instrument and take it from there.' At least I had a direction to go in and it sort of clarified my mind. So I said, 'OK.' I said to Alan Parsons, 'Put the red light on', coz usually the first take, the first and second take is the best and I'd learnt that during my few years in the music business. Maybe it's to do with being a Gemini, but I get bored basically, you know, 'I'm fed up, I've had enough of this. On to the next,' that's the way I am; and so Alan recorded it and I just thought of myself as an instrument. And they said, 'We really like that, that's definitely in the right direction.'

So we continued and it happened very quickly. It wasn't a long drawn-out thing. There are some sessions I look back on and I think 'Bloody hell, that was blood out of a stone.' This was not. It was very, very quick, because – as I told you before – I was back in King's Road having supper before 10 o'clock in the Chelsea Kitchen. It certainly wasn't Chelsea Kitchen at 3 o'clock in the morning and I think if you read anything that Alan Parsons has written, it was done pretty quickly. After a couple of takes, we started doing the third – we're not talking about 20 takes at all. I did say I was starting to repeat myself, and some of the melodic lines – I was thinking about them, instead of them coming off the top of my head in a spontaneous way. I was starting to think of the melody and so it was starting to become contrived, and then I felt it was time to say, 'I think you've got enough, thank you very much and goodnight.' Really! But I have to say the one thing I said to my boyfriend at the time after I'd done it, I never thought I could sing that high – and that's what excited me – but I honestly, truthfully, never ever thought it would see the light of day. I thought they'd just say, 'Thank you very much,' and really you could have knocked me down with a feather when it was released.

Sheila: But the excitement was not so much with what they had put down in terms of the keyboard line, the drums etc., part of it was the excitement of exploring your own voice and partly the excitement of hearing a really good sound coming out.

Clare: As I've said to you, it's very important to any musician. It sounds so basic, but if you have a marvellous can balance it sometimes can be inspirational and I do remember that the sound in my headphones that Alan Parsons provided me with was wonderful. In fact, the vocal sound was such that I honestly felt that I could soar because it was inspirational. If that sound in the cans had been with much less echo, it would have been 'Oh God, this is boring.'

Sheila: But it is transcendent, it is an 'out-of-body' sound.

Clare: I've got it in some magazine somewhere where Roger said 'It was just one of those happy things, it just worked' – and who knows why. I don't know why it worked. I never thought it would. I honestly didn't think that it would ever be heard again.

Sheila: And so what was your feeling when it actually came out and you bought it and you heard it for the first time?

Clare: My initial feeling was 'Gosh. They've spelt my name right!', but I think my initial reaction, if you really want the truth, when I opened the album up – because we didn't have cling film or what have you – was 'Ooooh!' So, to be quite honest, if it had only been one bar, I would have bought it simply because my name was on it. Pathetic. Does anyone know that the scream, right at the beginning, is me?

Sheila: I thought it was.

Clare: Nobody talked about that. I have one of the takes. It's on there. It's right at the very beginning.

Sheila: Of course it's your voice.

Clare: Yes. But nobody ever talks about that. They say, there's a scream at the beginning and nobody says it's mine. Funny that.

Sheila: And was it Roger the Hat saying 'I'm not afraid of dying?' Was it their roadie?

Clare: No … Turn it off, turn it off … [Clare looks for magazine.] This is *Mojo* 1998. I did ring them up to ask.

Sheila: So it wasn't Roger the Hat?

Clare: No. It was Jerry Driscoll announcing 'I've always been mad. I know I've been mad.' The crazed laughter is from Peter Buddy Watts, Floyd's late executive road manager, who was recorded on a previous session.

Sheila: Oh, right. So, who's the one that leads into you, Clare, on 'Great Gig', who says

Clare: 'Are you afraid of dying?'. 'I never said I was'. They're probably in *Uncut*.

Sheila: But had you heard these other tracks?

Clare: No. I hadn't heard any. I didn't hear anything. They certainly didn't sit me down …

Sheila: Because what's incredible is the way in which it goes into this very Lutheran quality just before you come on which suggests a religious side. But your religious side is so erotic, it's much more like the 1960s eroticism of that relationship of religion to orgasm –

Clare: Referred to as 'Home Again'. In the recordings, it was simply the third verse of 'Breathe', attached for emotional and structural reasons. Yes, [reads from *Mojo*, March, 1998] where Waters refers to the 'Are you afraid of dying?' 'The fear of death is a major part of many lives and as the record was at least partially about that, that question was asked but not specifically to fit into this song. I don't remember whose idea it was to get Clare, in, but once she sang it was great. One of those happy accidents. The slide guitar was just something that Dave was into at the time. A brilliant sound. Early tags for the piece while the concept was being developed were the mortality sequence and the religious theme. Early live versions incorporated taped Bible readings and the Malcolm Muggeridge speech.' (I did a thing with Malcolm Muggeridge, you know, in the mid '60s. 'Road to

Canterbury' it was called, and I wrote my little songs for it. I think it's probably been erased.) 'Based around a Rick Wright chord progression, it remained an instrumental with some spoken inserts until a couple of weeks before the Album was finished.'

Well, I was told about birth, living and death and all things in between like money, you know, all that stuff and I did think, I mean I thought it was pretentious nonsense. I mean, I really ... how old was I? 23 and (whispered: sorry, 16) and it meant nothing. For me, it was a job of work and it was a session. I had no idea, and I wonder if any of them, the guys in the band, knew that in 30 years' time people would still be talking about it and you would be writing an academic piece on it. For goodness sake!

Sheila: My second piece. I wrote about it in 1992 as well.

Clare: Can I just quote something from Alan Parsons [again, from *Mojo*, March 1998] – 'I had worked on a session before with Clare and suggested that we tried her out on this track. I think one has to give Clare credit, she was just told to go in and "do your thing", so effectively she wrote what she did. She wailed over a nice chord sequence, there was no melodic guidance at all apart from "a bit more wailey here" or "more sombre there." The vocal was done in one session, three hours, no time at all then a couple of tracks were compiled for the final version. Torry was an EMI songwriter, straight out of school who had just started doing a few vocal sessions.'

If I'd known then what I know now, I would have done something about organizing copyright or publishing. I'd be a wealthy woman now. The session fee in 1973 was £15, but as it was Sunday I charged a double fee of £30 – which I invested wisely of course! So there we are ...

Sheila: So, returning to the track. The drummer, Nick Mason. Was he down when you did it?

Clare: Yes, yes ...

Sheila: Because for me, that first section of Great Gig is almost an erotic duet between drums and vocals.

Clare: I wasn't aware, other than I've said to you – but I do have good lungs.

Sheila: And they didn't say anything about the dynamic shaping that went with the drums and the organ pad ...?

Clare: Well, I probably listened to that, and subconsciously did it. Really, you know.

Sheila: Who had the decision on the final cut? They did, presumably?

Clare: Well, I had nothing more to do with it.

Sheila: Did you sing on any of the other tracks, or was that left to Doris Troy and the other session singers?

Clare: No, what I can gather from reading all the bumf was that the album was virtually finished. They'd virtually finished it. Now, I'd heard on this radio interview, that Rick Wright had written this chord sequence, which I think was from somewhere else, some film that he'd written, got an idea, and they'd done a track, and Gilmour said something like, 'Well it would be nice to share the publishing royalties around, so we'll give Rick another track on the album', and it was a chord sequence. It's possible that Dick Parry could have gone in and done a sax solo on it, but it wouldn't have – I don't know, who knows what he would have done? I don't know. Dave Gilmour could have done a guitar solo over it. And maybe somewhere, maybe he did, who knows?

Sheila: Yes. If it hadn't hacked, you'd have to have something …

Clare: I was talking to Kay Garner (a friend) a couple of weeks ago, and I said, if I could turn the clock back, if I had a time machine and went back, and said 'No! Categorically, I am working, I cannot do it and tomorrow I'm going skiing …'

Sheila: What would have happened?

Clare: We were trying to decide who they would have got in, and we decided it could have been Vicki Brown, and that Vicki would have done her own interpretation, but it wouldn't have been what I did. You see, that's the whole thing.

Sheila: I'd love to ask about the erotic side of the track

Clare: It's about orgasm and virginity. (Oooh, I'm so embarrassed!!!) Um, what I have done, the few things live, if a band, or the drummer, or the guitar player's got a riff going, I will follow it. Then, it's a bit like jazz, then you play off each other and that is obviously …

Sheila: So, who played off who?

Clare: It was already done. The whole track was there – it was a fait accompli – the track was there. 'Do something on top of it.' So I did something on top of it. I mean, unbeknownst to me – it sounds a bit odd to say 'it came naturally', but I suppose it did. Completely, subconsciously, I sang to what I heard.

Sheila: But if someone had said to you, 'Come on Clare. Sing us an erotic track!'!

Clare: You know, over the years you wouldn't believe how many times I've had the mickey taken out of me. Because it's always been … well, 'Oh, oh, oh, oooooh' [takes off opening vocal to 'Great Gig'] – it was always that sort of thing. But it's been a very good thing because we've all taken the piss out of it, and that's been nice. Well it makes you realize …

Sheila: What I find is interesting that you get people like Madonna, Kylie for her bum, lots of women put down as sex goddesses, and you surely *are* a sex goddess.

Clare: I am a sex goddess … Blimey! You should see me in Waitrose. They drop at my feet.

Sheila: I'm sure they do!

Clare: Bloody 'ell, it's Clare Torry. She's a sex goddess!!!

Sheila: But it is a highly erotic track – it's the most made-love-to track in the world.

It not only builds to climax, but it sustains the climax. Absolutely ideal. And yet there's that underlying death thing which links it (for me) with all the religious iconic things that were going through in the 1960s which, at the time, I wasn't altogether aware of. I went to see the *Marat Sade*, went to see Glenda Jackson with her bare bum in Earls Court, and here is a track that is arguably the most erotic track that has ever been made ...

Clare: Yes, I do remember Harry saying to me, and I met him in March 1968, and I was a virgin. I always remember Harry saying, 'You'll never be able to sing a song like Sinatra, or Ella Fitzgerald or anybody until you've been in love.' And you could substitute the word lust for love and I think he was right. And he told me that.

Sheila: So, going back into the studio, there was certainly no eroticism whatsoever?

Clare: No, other than my boyfriend being the other side of the glass. So could that have had something to do with it?

Sheila: Quite possibly.

Clare: But I wasn't aware of it. But when you think of those films of faking the orgasm ...

Sheila: So what does it feel like to be a sex goddess?

Clare: Oh, I feel overwhelmed. Very underpaid. I mean, to be perfectly honest, we're talking about 30 years, and it is the 30th anniversary now and it rears its ugly head and I'm aware of it, but years ago and the year before that and the year before that, it never entered my head from one month to the next. And it hasn't really.

Sheila: Have people thought you're black?

Clare: Yes. There was something. A girlfriend brought her lap-top up, and we logged on to whatever and Pink Floyd, and there was this ongoing conversation between some guy in Wisconsin and some chap in Italy and they were saying, 'Does anyone know what Clare Torry looks like, or anything about her?' And then somebody joined in and said, 'I'd heard she was an African-American black woman,' and somebody else said, 'If you look at the concert Roger Waters did in 1992, he had three backing vocalists and I think Clare was the one in the middle.' And so somebody else says, 'No, no, no, no! They were all Black and Clare's White.' Which is wonderful. Nobody knows. And I quite like it actually.

Sheila: Have you been on any live performances of *The Dark Side of the Moon?*

Clare: Yes, just at Knebworth when it pissed down with rain, and I remember looking at Dave Gilmour, and his fingers were wet and I thought 'Shit! we're all going to be electrocuted'.

Sheila: And what we all want, all your fans. Where's this recording of all your stuff that you've done?

Clare: Well, they're endless. Thirty years is a hell of lot of stuff, a lot of it rubbish, other things that at the time I thought were not bad, but listening to them now, I think they're pretty acceptable. Compared to what's going on at the moment in the music business I think they're bloody marvellous. I know I'm very critical, and I've listened to some things and I feel quite embarrassed, and in fact, to be perfectly honest, when I listen to 'Great Gig' I feel rather embarrassed, and I think somewhere, one of these magazines, one of the fans says I was a little bit cringey. I think I felt rather embarrassed, but that's probably my middle-class upbringing. Seriously. You know. That's why I never thought it would see the light of day.

Sheila: Where did you get your voice from, Clare?

Clare: I've no idea. I went to Currys [electrical store] in the early years, down in Uckfield in East Sussex, and I said 'Do you have any voices?' and they said, 'We've got this old Elizabethan voice that might be good' and I said, 'I'll have two of those,' and that's where I got it from. (Mega joke!)

Sheila: You didn't go to the Royal College or anything?

Clare: No. I didn't want to. My mother wanted me to be trained, purely because when I was about three somebody where we lived in London said, 'And what are you going to do when you grow up?' and I said, 'I'm going to be an opera singer.' Well, that's what I didn't want to do, coz I didn't want to sing, I wanted to be a songwriter. Singing wasn't uppermost in mind, and I didn't ever take it on board at all. Writing songs, I'm going to be a songwriter, that was it. But when I did start, at EMI as a staff songwriter, I used to sing my own demos and then some of the guys, the boy songwriters, said 'I've just written a song for a girl. Could you do the demo, coz you sing quite well' and I said 'Oh yes, sure.' So I used to do some of their demos without even thinking about it. But my maternal grandmother was at the Royal College in the late 1800s and she was, in fact, very hand-in-glove with John Christie – who started Glyndebourne – so she was very much at the beginning of Glyndebourne and she was in fact one of the first people to go to the Royal College. Unfortunately she married a vicar and her music went by the board. That was it.

Anyway, back to *Dark Side of the Moon*. I also heard, or read somewhere, that they played *Dark Side of the Moon* when they went round on the shuttle. I said to my mum, I said, 'Christ, just think, just think throughout the radio waves going out to Betelgeuse, *Great Gig in the Sky*, all that way.'

Sheila: Well, you're an important woman.

Clare: But it hasn't entered my life. You know, I don't have people banging at my door. But then, as Roger Waters once said, I've got a quote from him somewhere … 'It's like serendipity, it was one of those things, that going into the studio.'

Coda

So, has my interview with Clare Torry affected my interpretation of 'The Great Gig in the Sky'? The honest answer is 'Not really'. My response to the track will always be one of wonder, absorption and loss in the sound of her voice as it weaves around the fundamental Gm harmonies, like a moth attracted to a light. The acknowledgment that she was excited by the sound of her voice, as it came through the cans, is also telling: 'The vocal sound was such that I honestly felt that I could soar because it was inspirational.' It is this quality that invites the listener to engage with vocal flight, with the thrill of soaring, the *jouissance* of ecstasy. Her briefing also provided some guidance prior to the recording – 'birth, living and all its bibs and bobs and aggros, and death' that inform the conceptual of *The Dark Side of the*

Moon. Above all, it is evident that I am not alone in my response to the erotic dimension of the vocal. It is, after all, the most made-love-to track in the world.

Notes

1. *The Space Between the Notes. Rock and the Counterculture* (London: Routledge, 1992) is concerned with the relationship between hallucinogenics and progressive rock. There is a full discussion of Pink Floyd's *The Dark Side of the Moon* on pp.103–18). I have also written on Pink Floyd in 'Altered Sounds', in A. Melechi (ed) (1997), *Psychedelia Britannica. Hallucinogenic Drugs in Britain*, London: Turnaround, pp. 120–42.
2. From Classic Albums. *The Dark Side of the Moon.* BBC 2, 3 May 2003.
3. The difference can be explained thus: '*Plaisir/jouissance.* English lacks a word able to carry the range of meaning in the term *jouissance* which includes ... crucially the pleasure of sexual climax. The problem would be less acute were it not that *jouissance* is specifically contrasted to *plaisir* by Barthes in his *Le Plaisir du Texte:* on the one hand a pleasure (*plaisir*) linked to cultural enjoyment and identity, to the cultural enjoyment of identity, to a homogenizing movement of the ego; on the other a radically violent pleasure (*jouissance*) which shatters – dissipates, loses – that cultural identity, that ego ... I have no real answer to the problem and have resorted to a series of words which in different contexts can contain at least some of that force: "thrill" (easily verbalized with "to thrill", more physical and potentially sexual, than "bliss"), "climactic pleasure", "come" and "coming" (the exact sexual translation of *jouir, jouissance*), "dissipation" (somewhat too moral in its judgement but able to render the *loss*, the fragmentation, emphasized by Barthes in *jouissance*).

   Barthes has also introduced the term *signifiance* (a theoretical concept initially proposed and developed by Julia Kristeva) as a process in which the "subject" of the text ... struggles with meaning ... entering, not observing – how the language works and undoes him or her ... Contrary to signification, *signifiance* cannot be reduced to direct communication, representation, expression: it places the subject in the text not as a projection ... but as a "loss", a "disappearance". Hence its identification with the pleasure of *jouissance*: the text becomes erotic through *signifiance* (no need, that is, for the text to represent erotic "scenes").' (Stephen Heath, Translator's Note', in R. Barthes (1982), *Image, Music, Text*, London: Fontana Paperbacks, pp. 9–10.)

   It is this sense of 'losing oneself' in the vocal (*signifiance*) – where there are no words that represent or describe the erotic – and *jouissance* – lost in the sound of the vocal/climactic pleasure – that inform my interpretative response to 'The Great Gig in the Sky'.
4. As Clare Torry observed in her interview, her cries that precede 'Breathe' are never mentioned: 'Nobody talked about that. I have one of the takes. It's on there. It's right at the very beginning.'
5. The Lesley is an attachment to the Hammond Organ and activates a swirling sound that can be accelerated by the use of a pedal. The shift from analogue to digital provides a point of comparison where low-frequency oscillations produce rhythm – holding down one note on a keyboard, while adjusting other parameters to produce a swirling effect (for example, 'Still Walking' by Throbbing Gristle).
6. *Anima, n.* the soul, the innermost part of the personality. *Anima mundi*, the soul of the world. *Animus n.* intention: actuating spirit: hostility (*Chambers 20th Century Dictionary* (1985), ed. E.M. Kirkpatrick, Edinburgh: W. & R. Chambers Ltd).
7. Band leader Harry Roach, Clare Torry's husband.

Chapter 10

The whole of the moon: 'Brain Damage', 'Eclipse', and the mythic narrative of the Pink Floyd

Peter Mills

Too high, too far, too soon
You saw the whole of the moon

– The Waterboys: *The Whole of the Moon*

You reached for the secret too soon
You cried for the moon

– Pink Floyd: *Shine On You Crazy Diamond (Part One)*

Howard Devoto, frontman and lyricist for the post-punk band Magazine, once commented on why he had only made one solo album after that group's dissolution: 'People think, just because you've made *one* record, that you're *always* going to make records, like a job. Well, it's not true.'[1] It's now a critical commonplace to praise Syd Barrett as a great lost genius of English pop, but this assumed significance is, arguably, based at least as much on the mythological narratives that have attached themselves to him as it is on the music he made, being (as his old friend Roger Waters has pointed out) modest in quantity if nothing else; a handful of Pink Floyd singles and one full album, a single track on another and two fragile, about-to-dissolve solo albums. The tale of the great visionary who walked away, Rimbaud style, from his muse and, retrospectively viewed, his audience, is a powerful one, and has acquired the status of a richly seductive mythopoeic archetype. In Barrett's case it was not only his 'muse' that was abandoned (although we should note that he was still trying to record a third solo album as late as 1974) but also, even though they (according to the myth) effectively excluded him in early 1968 by simply ceasing to collect him on the way to gigs, the Pink Floyd themselves. We can at this point note wryly that, in losing Barrett, they also lost their definite article, an important little detail of self-assertion frequently overlooked. Little was expected of the post-Barrett group – announcing that he had just got the full-time Floyd gig to a friend in a Cambridge pub, David Gilmour was told to 'Make the most of it … without Barrett, they're going nowhere'.[2]

In this piece I seek to explore some of the socio-cultural contexts which surrounded the conception and birth of this album, and investigate the final two cuts on *The Dark Side of the Moon* as in part evidence and in part summation of this. Perhaps more directly, we shall consider what they reveal about Roger Waters's relationship with both the Roger Barrett he had known since childhood and also 'Syd Barrett', the mythic figure whom he would subsequently explicitly eulogize on *Wish You Were Here*. I shall attempt to trace how the search for corrective images of this kind, seeking harmony and empathy, have been both goal and driving force in the work of Pink Floyd, and also try to explore how this urge to go forward and the compulsion to look back, drawing in both cases upon a mythologized past, both unified and fragmented the group. In the construction and the music of *The Dark Side of the Moon*, light and shadow collide and collude. It wasn't only Barrett who was changed utterly by his apparent 'abandonment' of music; Pink Floyd's work was changed forever too.

Something out of the 'Return of the Son of Nothing'

After Barrett's assisted departure from the group – the dissolution exemplified by the catch-me-if-you-can game of the infamous 'last number' 'Have You Got It Yet?', in which he played different chords each time around, the band trying to follow him, explicitly working *against* the idea of group-as-coherent-unit in a way unknown even to, say, the wildest shores of late Coltrane – the group drifted hazily between soundtracks and expensively indulged experiment and, by their own retrospective admission, stumbled forward not quite sure of their direction: for evidence of this, I refer you to David Gilmour's 1999 evaluation of *Atom Heart Mother*: 'A pile of shit'.[3] This drift continued, I would argue, until *Meddle*, released in the autumn of 1971. That album (my own favorite Pink Floyd record, incidentally) is interesting here in how it provides a blueprint for some of the structural ideas on *The Dark Side of the Moon*, most directly on 'Echoes' (working title: 'The Return of the Son of Nothing') which occupied Side 2 of the vinyl LP. The constructive model both suggests likenesses and emphasizes differences between the two pieces. The likeness being a sense of purpose and rigorous structuring over an audacious single work, serial in content but unified in experience, which was missing from preceding works; 'Echoes' anticipates, while never quite attaining, the clarity and flow of *The Dark Side of the Moon*. The key difference is encoded within the thematic content as *Dark Side*, of course, focuses on socio-cultural manifestations of madness, while 'Echoes' harks back to the *UmmaGumma* world of impressionistic word pictures, lush and poetic, but drifting, pointedly unfocused. *The Dark Side of the Moon*, for all its reputation as a hazed, stoner classic, snaps right into dazzling, telescopically crystalline focus. What 'Echoes' does pick up on, and in doing so provides a signpost towards our main subject, is the tendency toward forming images of empathy: 'I am you and what I see is me'. This combination of close self-examination and extrapolated abstraction, the introduction of inner and outer modes of reality, feeds directly into the paradoxical dynamics of *Meddle*'s successor. In *The Dark Side of the Moon*, Pink Floyd found their signature musical voice, definitively post-Barrett in its sense of languid, uncluttered, near-epic space. While developing the long-standing key elements of their work, they also found their subject, the thing that would keep them 'always making records', to quote Howard Devoto: that subject was effectively their own story, and how it might be used to illuminate the world beyond itself, thereby beginning a process of self-mythologization which, for better or worse, I would suggest, characterized their work thereafter and extended right on up to Waters's own 'departure' after *The Final Cut*.

But why did Waters, sole lyricist for *The Dark Side of the Moon*, suddenly alight upon this theme of what constitutes 'sanity' and 'madness', and the extrapolation from the particular to the universal? A glance at the contemporary contexts offer some insight; suffering badly from a Swinging Sixties hangover, the Britain of 1971–73 was a grim place to be. A Conservative government was flexing its muscles, building up for long-coming confrontation with the Trades Union movement, laying the ground for the crushing of the unions by force and legislation under the Thatcher government which came in on 4 May 1979 as, coincidentally or not, the group were working on that monument to bleak socio-cultural prognoses, *The Wall*. In this theater of class antagonism, with the patrician grandees and the proletariat tilted against each other, neither side was particularly interested in compromise, rather the disturbance and destruction of 'the other'. British society was suffering from a form of schizophrenia which had lain deep in its collective DNA and the political pulse of the period hauled it, painfully, to the surface where it could no longer be overlooked, or ignored. Most plainly, social discourse was functioning on the level of 'us' and 'them'.

'Us and Them'

I remember clearly as a child the 'Three Day Week', imposed by Conservative Prime Minister Edward (Ted) Heath in 1973 and the power cuts which came, in our house, for example, each evening from 7.25 to 9.15, as the power stations (including Battersea, which featured, of course, on the sleeve of 1977's *Animals*) were running at low capacity. So the population of the world's fifth-richest economy would light candles each evening, until power was restored. These cuts were due to both industrial action (primarily by the National Union of Miners, led by Thatcher's eventual bête noire Arthur Scargill) and the global 'Energy Crisis' precipitated by the threat of a great hike in oil prices by OPEC, the consortium of Middle East oil producers. The crisis was the central subject of public discussion, even in the culture industries; Ian Hunter of Mott the Hoople commented in a special 'Energy Crisis' issue of the British music weekly title *Melody Maker* (already venerable in 1973 and now defunct), 'It's like being in the Dark Ages'.[4] Note that 'Dark'; that same spring, Pink Floyd were delivering *The Dark Side of the Moon* at London's Earls Court, power cuts permitting. This, then, was the fulminating, fearful, disrupted and hostile discourse that passed for 'normal life' (or 'the English way') in Britain in the period of *The Dark Side of the Moon*'s composition, rehearsal, and recording.

The films which accompanied the early performances of the piece and which still sometimes turn up on TV – bowdlerized, for example, into a 'conventional' video for 'Money' – featured all the main British political party leaders of that time intercut with images of riot, chaos and disorder. Such juxtapositions might seem old hat to our hyper-sophisticated post-MTV deconstructivist sensibilities but the fact remains that they represented direct and radical attempts to connect the music to the social and political disturbance, or even borderline madness, that British society was collectively suffering under at that time, and which, I would suggest, was instrumental in giving birth to this music. Tapes of early performances of the piece reveal a far more avant-garde work, much more like the Floyd people already knew. There was extensive, disorientating use of recorded voices including a disturbing, double-voiced recitation of 'The Lord's Prayer', making much more explicit throughout the idea of as it were 'hearing voices' and, just beyond the horizon, the coming assault of the information revolution. The recordings included the voice of PM Edward Heath, and my bootleg tape of a 1973 show records a mighty audience cheer at the moment when Heath appears on the screen above the group coinciding with the line from 'Brain Damage', 'there's someone in my head, but it's not me'. For all the undoubted richness and complexity of the music, these messages, these connections, were direct, plain, and plainly understood by their contemporary audience. So I would argue that, far from being some prog-rock codified cosmic fantasy suite, *The Dark Side of the Moon* is as rooted in traditions of music as an agent of dissent, of social comment, and of protest as was, say, the punk movement (which, I should point out, was 'my' subcultural moment in the sun, as a teenager) which infamously claimed to 'hate' Pink Floyd. It's that combination of being street-level grounded yet encompassing cosmic scales, showing how apparently opposed elements are connected, discerning the local in the universal and the universal in the local, which is central to the record's musical success and enduring commercial appeal.

Now, the connection between the disturbances convulsing British society while Pink Floyd were working on what would become one of the music industry's greatest money-spinning (and apparently infinitely recyclable) products, Roger 'Syd' Barrett's personal turmoil, and the music of Pink Floyd seems to have something to do with the release of a modest LP in Britain on 14 May 1971. *Relics*, issued on 'Starline', one of EMI's range of budget labels, provided the opportunity to assess Pink Floyd's contemporary status in a number of ways. It might be said that it was somewhat early to be harking back, at cut price no less, maybe in some way suggesting that they were experiencing creative stasis, perhaps even hinting that their best work was already behind them. Yet it also enabled critical re-evaluation, the juxtaposition of material from the Syd and post-Syd periods being instructive, and, perhaps most importantly, discovery by a whole new, younger audience – partly due to the pocket-money-affordable price tag (99 pence in the then-new decimal currency). It's worth reminding ourselves that at this time it was very unfashionable for 'proper' rock groups, such as Pink Floyd, to release singles in the UK – it was 'unthinkable' that they would issue one in Britain, according to the publicity material which accompanied the US 45 of 'Free Four',[5] and there wouldn't be a Floyd single in the UK between 1968 and 1979, although they, alongside the likes of Led Zeppelin, were always happy to issue 45s in the States and Europe. Hence, *Relics* gave a younger audience a chance to hear the group, and, of course, the sense of fun in much of the Barrett-era material is fantastically appealing to the imagination of a child: just play 'Bike' to a ten-year-old and you'll see what I mean. It was certainly the first time I heard Pink Floyd, and the album was an unexpectedly big, steady seller. Suddenly, at least in the playgrounds of Leeds in summer 1972, Pink Floyd were being discussed, alongside David Bowie (who would cover 'See Emily Play' in 1973), Slade, and the rest. Thus an album retailing for little more than the price of the much-despised single format had effectively delivered them a new audience, which was now waiting for their next move.

For the group, *Relics* was useful in other ways too; it gathered together some early singles (on LP for the first time), various album cuts from scattered sources, and one previously unreleased number entitled, appropriately for a period apparently characterized by a form of creative drift, 'Biding My Time'. The last word of that title resurfaces on *The Dark Side of the Moon* of course, and the urgency and paradoxically rational expression of deep, mortal panic within the later song is, it seems to me, driven in part by the fear that Pink Floyd were becoming 'relics' themselves: 'waiting for someone or something to show you the way' ('Time'). I'd also argue that *The Dark Side of the Moon*'s sense of focus and urgency, as well as its thematic flow, is at least in part a consequence of the success of *Relics*, and their refreshed exposure to their younger, more energetic direct incarnation, throwing their current inertia and unfocused lack of direction into harsh relief, perhaps reminding them of the virtues of precision in form. Much of the material on *Relics* was Barrett's; all of a sudden he found this five-year-old work generating large sums of money for him as the royalties started to flow in. This also had an impact. At the time *Dark Side* was being worked up, Syd Barrett was rehearsing with his so-short-lived-it-barely-happened band 'Stars' in Cambridge rehearsal rooms and brief, chaotic shows in the city. (The temptation to flag up the connection between the lunar/solar imagery prevailing on *The Dark Side of the Moon* and the name of Barrett's band is irresistible.) The money from *Relics* in some senses made the option to withdraw from the game more real for Barrett, and its success led Roger Waters to reflect upon where the group had been, and where he could see it going. The combination of the emergent Barrett/Floyd mythologies alongside the social chaos prevailing in the UK at that time gave Waters his subject: how the inner and outer spheres of experience might clash and, equally powerfully, harmonize. These elements were prismatically drawn together into the focused, urgent, beam of light represented by *The Dark Side of the Moon*.

The final cuts (I)

'Brain Damage' and 'Eclipse' are the last two tracks on *The Dark Side of the Moon*. Since *Revolver* established the principle of the 'final cut', as it were, as the signpost position on an album, pointing to possibilities beyond the world we currently inhabit (a cultural habit of signification which still holds, as it happens), the final track on a rock album has borne or been expected to bear the added burden of an expectation of significance. 'Tomorrow Never Knows' sets the bar high, but these two songs, which we shall treat as a unit, deliver. They represent a culmination of the overt and covert lyrical and musical themes which thread through the album as a coherent whole, while also hinting at parallel fragmentations and breakdowns. The songs offer both a sense of thematic conclusion and a narrative direction back into the text; like James Joyce's *Finnegan's Wake* the conclusion leads us back to the beginning, via the heartbeat-fade-outro which suggests, again like the *Wake*, that we are both encountering and participating in an eternal circle, a cycle in which birth, death, creation and extinction, harmony and discord are continually co-present, gathered up into the present instant (witness 'Eclipse': 'All that is *now*, all that is *gone*, all that's to *come*'; my emphasis). What we have, then, is not simply the commonplace that endings are beginnings, but that suggestion that there is a continuity of experience which is both circular and spiral. The end is indeed the beginning for this created soundworld, but the circle spirals: the escalating arrangement and upward changes of Gilmour's guitar in 'Eclipse' provide the upward lift underpinning that song's mesmerizing circular riff.

'Brain Damage' is key to our understanding of the record as a whole. It trails little sparks of significance in its wake; for example, it originally bore the album's title and is the only place on the album where the phrase is used. It has its roots in a song also called 'The Dark Side of the Moon' which Waters wrote around the time of *Meddle* but which was never recorded. It was also, somewhat prosaically, known at the working-title stage as 'The Lunatic Song', showing its hand fairly directly, making plain the intention to import, exploit and explore the culturally embedded connective resonances between lunar phases and phases of madness/disturbance within the human brain. 'Brain Damage' stood for some time as the finale of the piece, during the period in which the piece was 'played in' during the group's touring, which, while not quite neverending, was by comparison with what followed a remarkably busy live schedule. Their habit, which surely would now not be tolerated by the industry, was to work material up via live shows and then go into the studio and record it. Hence they knew it well, and the audiences knew it well. The Floyd tried much of the material out first in Italy, where they were frequent visitors, first to work with Antonioni in 1969, then touring thereafter. (They were much loved there – this of course led to Adrian Maben's 1972 *Live at Pompeii* movie and also provides evidence of the entirely unpredictable Italian appetite for what we might unashamedly call English Prog Rock: Van Der Graaf Generator and Genesis were hugely popular there in the early 1970s, and the lovably otiose PFM remain Italy's best known rock export. Tapes from these Italian shows see the piece developing out of the vein they struck with *Meddle*.)

Waters has intimated that 'Brain Damage' refers at least in part to Barrett, and draws both on the mythologized narratives surrounding him (already in place by 1972, we must note) and, more particularly, on their personal friendship. Thus the local and universal models are drawn in to the song's sense and structure; witness the intimate, near-confidential verses and the expansive multi-tracked vocal, full-band bridges and lush backing vocals forcefully emphasizing the album's title phrase. As a production number, it's some way from 'Alan's Psychedelic Breakfast'. Further, this is a song without a chorus, emphasizing the apparently naturally-occurring flow of the piece as a whole. This holding together of the local and universal spheres is a vital, urgent balance characteristic of the entire record, and something which, I would argue, is lost from their post-*Dark Side* recordings, where the vision rendered up feels far more solipsistic, the flow far more forced. A key part of *The Dark Side of the Moon*'s appeal lies in its emotional impact, which bears the force and simplicity of truth.

Waters has called 'Brain Damage' 'a defence of the notion of difference'[6] and it's my contention that *The Dark Side of the Moon*, and these tracks in particular, represent the starting point of Waters's public mourning for the loss of the original vision of the group, and, implicit within that, the image of Barrett as its visionary. There's guilt here too, of course; in 1968, Barrett had very quietly been 'dropped' from the group. We can argue that henceforth the group's 'vision' becomes more and more inward-looking; consider the explicit messages addressed by Waters to his old friend on *Wish You Were Here*, throughout which Waters cajoles, quotes (the 'cold steel rail' of the title track runs from Barrett's own 'Dark Globe'), flatters, and implores his former comrade to re-enter the fray. In his litany of encouragement and praise, on the title track and 'Shine On You Crazy Diamond', Waters deliberately uses and thereby reinforces the language of mythologization, both local to Pink Floyd ('come on you piper') and of universal models of creative heroism ('come on you painter … you legend … you martyr, and shine!') Anything, we note, but 'come on you rock star'. A laughter sound effect is used early in 'Shine On', as are images of the sun and moon, and 'black holes in the sky', explicitly referencing *The Dark Side of the Moon*'s use of such effects and images, and equally clearly linking Barrett with both albums. He urges Barrett to resist the extinction of creative eclipse, and to 'shine on'. By suggesting that they 'bask in the shadow of yesterday's triumph', Waters is, typically, doubly reflective, deliberately invoking the trope of light and dark exploited so effectively on *The Dark Side of the Moon*, and also summoning up their early, mutual days. Are they now simply 'relics', even in the face of the group's unimaginable success?

Let's return to 'Brain Damage'. The lyric here has very deliberate, simple, direct movements and progressions within it: the central focus for the narrator is the observed/perceived 'lunatic', and each verse begins with a shift of locale for this figure, each time moving more deeply into the personal space of the narrator. The locations are very important to our understanding of the song – 'the grass' that Waters had in mind was the lawn at King's College Cambridge, and the grassy banks between the College and the River Cam ('the grassiest grass I could imagine', he notes, rather sweetly[7]) where, pre-Floyd, the two Rogers would sit, talk, and dream. In this locale, clearly indicative of the class split central to British society we considered earlier (the public have access to the grass leading down to the river, but not to the College lawns themselves), we can also detect a related split between ways of seeing; an enforced and thereby 'normalized' distinction between forms of intelligence: high learning and 'madness', 'genius' and 'disturbance'. If you go to look at the turf at King's College, you see the 'Keep off the Grass' signs, but in 'Brain Damage' the lunatic is *on* the grass – a very English transgression. Waters signposts this world of his friendship with Barrett, and the early days of the group, via nods to 'See Emily Play' and its genesis as music for the 'Games For May' event: 'Remembering games, and daisy chains and laughs'. We can see how the music supports the emotional thrust of the lyric: there is a slight dissonance introduced into this phrase – 'Remembering games'/ 'You lock the door'/ 'You raise the blade' – caused by the maintaining of the D bass against the E-major chord: the E is perfectly harmonious, although maybe slightly unusual in something in D, and adding the D makes for an E7, but we note that holding the D down at the bottom in the bass causes a momentary disorientation, before the return of the A and D, the perfect cadence hauling us back into harmoniousness. Thus the music reflects the ebb and flow of the state of mind investigated in the lyric itself.

The intrusion of the (supposedly sane) outer world which cuts across this ambiguous idyll arrives daily via the letterbox, into the hall, with the faces of those in the news serving as the faces of the lunatics: 'The paper holds their folded faces to the floor / And every day the paper boy brings more.' Yet the power of the song's key symbolic figure is concentrated by its representative singularity: there is no mob of assorted lunatics who stray from the path, simply this single and singular figure, who moves, over the verses, from the path, to the grass, to the hall, to the inside of the narrator's head. The outsider becomes the insider, the two becoming fused, yet also distinct – 'There's someone in my head, but it's not me'. The figure is both spotlit and particularized whilst remaining faceless, perhaps in the manner of the businessman offering us 'Pink Floyd' product from the sleeve of *Wish You Were Here*. The bridge – remember, this is a song without a chorus – offers some release, shifting from a D via D7th briefly into the key of G, then back via A to D. The bridge offers a more telescopic view, turning the gaze away from the lunatic to the broad sky above the head, connecting the inner chaos of the 'lunatic' to a wider, more material manifestation of the same process of breakdown ('And if the dam breaks open ...'), connecting this narrative to the broader contexts of the album, the epic and the particular, the outer and the inner co-present. These are both reflective of a shading of mood and, of course, central to the setting of such an atmosphere, hence the tonality is uneasy throughout, with the change from verse to bridge providing and emphasizing a startling shift in musical and narrative perspective.

This brings us to another key element of Pink Floyd's work, present from the first recordings but made explicit in *The Dark Side of the Moon* and, in particular, these final two songs on: the centrality of disturbance to their lyrical vision of the world, and the paradoxical striving toward a centralizing of marginal characters. This effort in some ways takes the Floyd back to their beginnings – here, we see Waters picking up a central element of Barrett's writing technique: consider the journey into the mind of an 'outsider' of 'Arnold Layne', or the imaginative empathy we find in 'Scarecrow'. The twist is, of course, that Barrett himself later becomes the subject of his own characteristic compositional technique. We also see it in less well-known corners of the Floyd catalogue such as 'Point Me At The Sky: 'isn't it sad we're insane ... a game we've been playing for thousands of years'. Waters, to return to his 'defence of the notion of difference', is trying to describe a natural form of unnaturalness. 'Brain Damage' identifies and makes plain this co-existent moment, via the image of a duality of mind, within the central dichotomies of madness and creativity, disorder and clarity. We can see therefore how these themes have as it were been creeping up on Waters, even in the (I would argue) relatively directionless years 1969–71, like the plotted movements of 'the lunatic' in 'Brain Damage'. They contribute now to this moment of breakthrough.

Here meanings slip, and are shifted by their contexts – the recorded laughter of their sound engineer Pete Watts is employed to suggest disturbance rather than happiness or contentment (as deliberate contrast to the song's 'daisy chains and laughs', from the idyll of memory), discord rather than harmony. Here we have a change of meaning, where gestures are reinterpreted, understandings rearranged – what *is* the madcap laughing at? This is part of a discrete but continuous strand of thought in Pink Floyd's work, and we can alight swiftly on illuminating examples: Arnold Layne looks at himself in the mirror and sees only a 'distorted view' – the narrator's voice asks, 'why can't you see?', suggesting an obscurity of vision and comprehension. Arnold is posited as 'a nasty sort of person', and is judged and punished according to the laws that prevail, and finally incarcerated. We are reminded of 'Brain Damage's image of imprisonment: 'You lock the door, throw away the key'. The final admonition, 'Don't do it again', suggests (or hopes?) that Arnold's conduct was a momentary lapse of reason, and less an outbreak of the true self, a hope that the rearrangement will work. Similarly, and more brutally, in 'Careful With That Axe, Eugene' and *Meddle*'s 'One Of These Days' we find figures, suggested via music and title only in the first case, music and a single-line lyric in the latter ('One of these days I'm going to cut you into little pieces'), again on the cusp of doing something terrible. We might also remind ourselves of the key question during the 'voice gathering' for *The Dark Side of the Moon,* which provoked several of the most memorable responses; 'When were you last violent, and were you in the right?' The question makes plain both an interest in human interaction, and a consequent effort to understand *why* people behave in the way they do. This is clearly related to the gravitational pull exerted by images of empathy. Now this empathetic model may seem perverse, given that Pink Floyd, and Waters in particular, have been routinely called for their alleged misanthropy, but I'd argue that the evidence is there, from Arnold Layne ('it's not the same, it takes two to know ... why can't you see?) resonating through 'Echoes' ('I am you and what I see is me') up to *The Dark Side of the Moon,* via 'Us and Them', 'Speak to Me', and, of course, 'Brain Damage'.

Waters, then, is interested in exploring, understanding and expressing images of this transformative moment of transgression, of thresholds, of ideas of crossing the line; this is the man, lest we forget, who, during the last show of their 'In The Flesh' tour, at the Montreal Olympic Stadium on 6 July 1977, spat in the face of a fan. (History does not record whether it happened during a performance of 'Dogs', with its line about a man who 'was trained not to spit *in* the fan'.) We could say much about this; I'll note that it is a remarkable variant on the rules of performer/audience interaction. Further, it was a piece of 'line-crossing' that in my view easily outdoes the (contemporary, almost to the week) brawls between the Sex Pistols and audience members in small, tight clubs, or Kurt Cobain's taunting his post-*Nevermind* audience with the opening chords of 'Smells Like Teen Spirit', then going into another number. Sid Vicious shooting into the audience during his go at 'My Way' in Julien Temple's 1979 movie *The Great Rock 'n' Roll Swindle* is by comparison merely a staged, kitsch fantasy. Can such transgressions, then, be undone, can the transgressor make it back, or are we witnessing the eclipse of reason by the occluding disc of lunacy? This brooding upon the fragility of the surfaces and apparently harmonious structures which hold 'normal' society together, while defending deviation as a legitimate form of 'difference', is key to Waters's post-Barrett creative vision, and thus to our understanding of *The Dark Side of the Moon.* Waters's lyrics 'about' Syd are of course also at least as revealing about him, – are all his observations of 'difference' a response to the myth of Syd? Much has been made of Waters's fierce and iconoclastic rejection of the star system (specifically the spitting incident), but we need also to remind ourselves that he was responsible for arguably the most radical, biggest production-value stage show in rock history (or, dare we say it, show business) 'The Wall', in order to comment on the process itself. So we had the spectacle of popular culture's most palpable image of self-loathing and alienation being cheered to the rafters by vast stadium crowds.

I would argue that Waters desperately admires, even envies the 'difference', or the courage, that enabled Barrett to walk away, throwing off the identities that others were creating for him. Yet that gesture, that letting go, being a relaxation, was also a consequence of brain damage; hence the brain that works 'differently' is one which is worthy of admiration (and one, thereby, which provided a referential template for other musicians thereafter, such as Howard Devoto). Barrett was able to be quite relaxed and self-aware about his situation, playing as well as living the role for inquiring journalists: he told one in 1972 that he was 'disappearing, avoiding most things' and that he was 'full of dust and guitars. The only work I've done in the past two years is interviews. I'm very good at it.'[8] Waters's inability to 'disappear' and to 'transgress' in that way, in part drove his loathing for the process, for the audience, and for the self that both produces and consumes the 'product'. The force of his interest in transgression comes from the fact that he is continually seeking and striving for harmony and harmonious construction – he wants, despite all the evidence to the contrary, to construct images of harmony. In the case of *The Dark Side of the Moon*, the image which interests him is the eclipse, the alignment, the high point of cosmic harmony, which proves and provides the symbiosis of light and dark – Jerry Driscoll's qualifier to 'As a matter of fact, it's all dark', being 'It's only the reflected light from the earth that makes it look bright' was, tellingly, omitted. Driscoll's 'last word' was thus deliberately constructed while appearing to happen and flow naturally; likewise, Waters constructs the wall, builds it up, synchronized, harmonized, complete, and then tears it down. He brings the elements together for a harmonious instant – the climax of 'Eclipse' and *The Wall* are both symbolic of concord and discord – and both moments pass, but not without the moment at which 'everything under the sun is in tune' ('Eclipse'). The moment is touched, via imaginative construction, while Barrett intuitively saw 'the whole of the moon' without the labor, the literal and metaphorical 'bricklaying'. 'Brain Damage' makes use of the album's title, and indeed, as noted, briefly bore it, and Waters has observed that the image of the dark side is used in part to establish empathetic links between those who perceive themselves to be 'full of dust and guitars', at odds with the times, or the world, or themselves.

Pipers, legends, martyrs

How then does the figure of the 'mad artist' influence these songs? Further, is such a paradigm in some way a cultural necessity? Dylan Thomas said, 'I'm not a bard or anything like one; but they want me to be one, and so I try to behave like one.'[9] The idea of the 'mad artist' is itself a stereotype, or we might say an archetype, just as *The Dark Side of the Moon* is the archetype of the themed/concept album, arguably even over *Sgt. Pepper*. In some ways we can see Barrett's retreat as an act of wisdom, like Don van Vliet's withdrawal to the trailer in the Navajo desert once music stopped being the central means of expression for him. Waters's post-Floyd output can most generously be described as variable in impact, although 2002's UK live shows at least had more vigor and engagement with ideas of his own performance than previous stints. It may be that we see Waters as the antithesis of the piper-legend-martyr figure, and indeed he may see himself that way too, but he has succeeded in placing the debates, tendencies, ebbs and flows, propulsions and withdrawals which move him *within* his work, in some senses ridding himself of them, externalizing them there.

A brief comparison between Roger Waters and Kurt Cobain might prove instructive: both men experienced deep self-loathing after great commercial success, and, extremely uncomfortable with their 'new' identities as rock stars, both planned career-sabotaging follow-ups to breakthrough albums, both of which were ultimately abandoned. Pink Floyd's idea for a deliberately uncommercial successor to *The Dark Side of the Moon*, 'Household Objects', was aborted when the group (very sensibly, tellingly) decided that there was no point spending days trying to make a rubber band sound like a bass guitar when you could just use a bass guitar; instead they made a high-production-value album eulogizing their former bandmate and castigating the music industry. In Cobain's case, an earlier, even more abrasive version of what became *In Utero*, the in-itself-hardly-easy-listening follow-up to *Nevermind*, was produced by ex-Rapeman leader and professional controversialist Steve Albini. A slightly more MTV-friendly version was mixed from the same sessions. Waters had the advantage of an interpretive sensibility which allowed him to place some distance between himself and the situation he perceived himself to inhabit, a kind of emotional intelligence and melancholic articulacy ('the English way'). He was able to construct models, via self-mythologizing images (Barrett as lost visionary, the use of doubles and masks at the start of 'The Wall' shows – an idea lifted by U2 on their 'Zooropa/ZOOTV' tours – the image of 'The Wall' itself), which would express and release his tensions. He could, as it were, spit it out. Waters has commented about the spitting in Montreal: 'What was going through my mind – my whole body – was an enormous sense of frustration ... a feeling of what are we all doing here, what's the point? And the answer that kept clanging monotonously back was: cash and ego. That's all it's about.'[10] We note here how the inner and outer (the mind and the body) are held to be equally expressive of his 'sense of frustration'. *The Wall*, in all its totality, arguably had its genesis in this eruptive moment.

While Waters employed his eclipses, crazy diamonds, animals, and walls to absorb and express his fear and loathing, Cobain's cauterizing directness, even via such extraordinary statements as *In Utero*'s working title, 'I Hate Myself and I Want to Die', or the Teen Spirit taunts, didn't seem to offer him a shape or a model to help him 'spit it out' as Waters had. In some ways the internalization finally consumed him – his most frequent physical complaint was of stomach trouble, feeling as though there was something he couldn't eject. The title of the last Nirvana album speaks volumes; *In Utero* imagines and desires a withdrawal away from the world, back into the womb, the creative darkness, behind another, more profound and fundamental kind of barricade. Ultimately, he was dragged down by the stone, and destroyed himself, instead of 'the wall'. The inside and the outside could not be reconciled. Cobain was of course brutally flung into the spotlight in a way that Waters never was, via MTV and 'overnight success'; Nirvana did not offer its members the anonymity which 'Pink Floyd' offered and which, broadly speaking, they have clung on to as a virtue. Yet I'd argue that, while Waters has undeniably charted a more cautious and businesslike course between the extremes of withdrawal (Barrett) and self-destruction (Cobain), he has clearly inhabited much of the same creative territory, breathing much of the same high, thin air.

The morning after his funeral, on Sunday 10 April 1994, a tape recording of Cobain's widow Courtney Love was played in public, to the great number of mourners who had gathered close to Cobain's house in Seattle. In the tape, she read extracts from his suicide note and communicated her own reactions to what her husband had written. Her righteous, loving rage blazed brightest with her aside to his comment in the note that he 'couldn't be a rock star' as he would feel he was betraying his audience by playing a role, and her comment strikes me as deeply loving and naturally wise: 'Then don't be a rock star, asshole!'.[11] Syd, like Cobain, was in some ways broken by a potent combination of a personal fragility culturally associated with refined levels of creativity and industrial levels of narcotic abuse – 'Kurt was *always* smoking or speeding'[12] – and the need to be continually somewhere, or someone, else. Syd's infamous stare at the TV camera when refusing to mime on Dick Clark's American Bandstand expressed not simply the apparent blankness of drug damage but subversiveness and self-knowledge: he *couldn't* play that game. Waters's own admiration of Barrett, and his old friend's ability to choose to 'not be a rock star', is illuminative of his own vexation about his own 'success'; it is grounded in part in Barrett's refusal to conform and Waters's own ability (or willingness?) to do the same.

Waters's work with Ron Geesin, on *Atom Heart Mother* and subsequently on the incidental soundtrack music for Roy Battersby and Tony Garnett's 1970 documentary film *The Body*, is also worth a glance (we might also recall Gilmour's dim view of *Atom Heart Mother* – another volley in their long battle, perhaps). Here again, Waters took some of his collaborators' methods on board. Geesin, now a Senior Research Fellow in Sound at the University of Portsmouth in the UK,[13] had a fresh eye for experiment in the studio, via tape loops and ambient effects, for example, and Waters learned much from him, using the experience to bring about a clearer and more emotionally resonant approach to his own songwriting. We might note with interest that *Music From The Body* includes a song called 'Breathe'. It's not truly an early version of its more famous successor, but shares the same opening line, 'Breathe in the air'. We see again the development of interior monologues, a journey described. For Pink Floyd, a sense of conceptualization within a single album was not new, but *The Dark Side of the Moon* offers a fresh rarefaction of focus. Waters once more takes from the 'eccentric' collaborator, processes the experience, and adds to it his remarkable melodic, more formally musical skill. This method incorporates dynamic and resonant ambiguities into his work.

Though figures such as Barrett, Brian Wilson, or Roky Eriksson provide an often intensely moving templature of the intersection of clinical disturbance and creativity, the referencing of madness in rock music repertoires and performances is notably stylized, flirting with images and gestures associated with it. These signs are either 'performed' or 'experienced' via a catalogue of acts who buy into it the paradigmatic mythology with varying degrees of serious-mindedness, and success. Sometimes, it does seem to prove a successful vehicle for a genuinely off-kilter creative sensibility – consider the work and persona of Captain Beefheart, and his would-be successor Tom Waits, or some periods of David Bowie's work. Frequently, however, the representation is cartoonish and little more than a usefully 'dissident/outsider' discourse to attach as a marketing tool, such as in the highly theatrical puppet-show/comic-book worlds accompanying the meat-and-potatoes rock of Ozzy Osbourne or Alice Cooper. Likewise, Prince's 'Let's Go Crazy' (from *Purple Rain*) means, to coin a phrase, something else; it references partying, and embracing the material world via very sane and deliberately marketable music, although his later career undeniably bears some of the hallmarks of a dissident mindset which is permitted to function within the industry only by dint of his previous market value.

Compare this rich theater to the English (as opposed to British) middle-class existential aesthetics of, say, Peter Gabriel (notably on his remarkable third album with the 'melting face' cover, which hit the shops six months after *The Wall*) and, more recently, Radiohead and their own acolytes, Coldplay, both of whom clearly bear the influence of Pink Floyd in their work. Now it's not the job of this essay to examine the role of the English public school in developing codifications of psycho-social disturbance via rock, with Waters, Gabriel, Radiohead's Thom Yorke and Coldplay's Chris Martin all being products of that system – although it's a nice gig for someone – but a song like Radiohead's 'Creep' (chorus line: 'I'm a creep / I'm a weirdo') clearly, if somewhat crudely, via a post-Nirvana slow grind, reflects a use of discourses arguably introduced to popular music via the Pink Floyd mythic narrative and, in particular, by *The Dark Side of the Moon* itself, newly equipping the form of the popular song with methods via which to express otherness (cf. Waters: 'a defence of the notion of difference'). Gabriel's work has seen lunacy as it were 'made musical', notably in the track 'Lead a Normal Life' (from '3'), via the loops, repetitions, and atonal leaps leading to the fade, where 'Brain Damage' employs a very direct, arpeggio-driven, musically harmonious model. Fear of, or the portrayal of, mental illness and any attendant slippage of identity is not untypical of English middle-class aesthetics, and the key question is, what is the distinction between 'performance' and 'experience'? This swings us right back to 'Brain Damage', where the narrator experiences anxiety about his own identity, reminding himself that he has 'Got to keep the loonies on the path', and where the line 'And if the band you're in starts playing different tunes' links directly to the last days of Syd's tenure in Pink Floyd, and the mutiple torments of 'Have You Got It Yet?'. Yet here was a 'concept' song; and here we are praising the mother of all concept albums. Syd, again. Like Waters said, crazy, but like a diamond.

The final cuts (II)

One of the virtues and difficulties in writing about individual cuts from *The Dark Side of the Moon* is that it is such a powerful and coherent whole that to isolate elements might be said to reduce them. Yet to listen to, say, the old US Harvest 45 of 'Money' on which I spent my pocket, er, money in 1974 is to hear it clear and fresh – like Waters revealing in the 'Classic Albums' documentary performance the song's roots as a very basic blues clothed in a bizarre time signature (7/8). The idea of an album as a single piece was in some ways both perfected and destroyed by *The Dark Side of the Moon*, appropriately dichotomous in its effect upon how popular music is constructed. It's no mystery why Pink Floyd were, according to the ebb and flow of fashion, revered by the ambient/conceptual acts of the early 1990s such as The Orb. So is it so hard to imagine, as *The Rough Guide to Rock*[14] suggests, any of the songs played independent of the others? I'm not sure, but not unlike The Beach Boys' *Pet Sounds* the songs work together in a way which provides cumulative propulsion up to the emotional climax, musically reinforced, in 'Eclipse'.

The transition from 'Brain Damage' is startling, but also musically slick, conforming to certain conventions of rock dynamics – listen to Mason's floor tom literally count the band in, on four, into the change to 'Eclipse' – while simultaneously, via the album's internal narratives, reconfiguring them. 'Eclipse' moves forward while utilizing a hypnotic, churning mantric cycle (D–B♭7–Gmin6–A), driven by Wright's orbit-shakingly powerful slabs of organ chords and Waters's dominant walking bassline (D–C–B♭–A and round again) with the perfect cadence (A–D) again giving a sense of resolution each time the phrase is repeated. The sense of escalation comes in part via the increasingly complex arrangement. The first repetition is a very simple statement of the chord progression, then in turn are added a small chorus (second repetition); the female vocalist in the gospel choir style familiar from the album as a whole alongside more guitar and drum embellishments characterize the third time round, the arrangement building to a climax at the start of the fourth repetition. During the fourth-last bar the arrangement strips back again and the last three bars are suddenly back to the simplicity of the beginning which reinforces the sense of resolution and completion. The last time the progression is repeated, instead of the A–D (perfect cadence) we find Gmin6–D – effectively a plagal cadence, which, refusing to give such a sense of resolution as the perfect, contributes to the intoxicating, metathematic sense of completion and ambiguity, of harmony and discord, co-present in a single moment.

'Eclipse', referred to on the original half-inch master tape box as 'End', was written to order by Waters to, as it were, provide what Nick Mason called 'something climactic, the real ending' for the work overall. Waters remembers: 'I suggested it all needed an ending, I wrote "Eclipse" and brought it into a gig, at the Colston Hall in Bristol, on a piece of lined paper with the lyrics written out ...'.[15] So it is separate from the rest of the album in that it was written explicitly to provide a conclusion to it; the piece had been performed as 'Eclipse' and/or 'Piece For Assorted Lunatics' before it was added, toured into shape, and the tape box, marked 'The Lunatic Song/End', was subsequently annotated to the titles they now bear. Moving away from the particular, internal domestic contexts of 'Brain Damage' to the music of the spheres, yet persuading by force of assertion and the cumulative flow of the music that the contexts are closely connected, 'Eclipse' provides a conscious conclusion, drawing together all the elements of the album, be they sonic signifiers (the female voice, musical textures, the recorded voices, employment of favored keys and chord sequences – the last three cuts on the record are in D) and emotional resonances (the symbiosis of the individual life and cosmic harmony, empathy, inclusivity, '*All* that you ...'). 'Eclipse' brings these elements together. Its sense of both light-speed movement and meditative stillness is reinforced by the mesmeric cycle of chords making up Rick Wright's organ motif, foregrounded in the mix for the first time, leading the surging, churning riff, while Gilmour's guitar covertly creeps up the scale in order to provide both stillness and escalation, continuity and change, providing a musical match to the emotional force of the album's climax. 'Eclipse' relates symbiotically to the rest of the record, pulling together narrative strands in a way expressive of the effort to construct images of empathy that drives the album as a whole. 'Time', 'Money', 'Us and Them', 'Speak to Me': these titles also stand as representative thematic strands within the text as a whole, and 'Eclipse' finally focuses them. Most remarkably, it does this in 90 seconds.

The lyric moves through couplets and triplets which deal with an escalating, cumulative scale of perception, intuition and experience, leading to a moment of creation in which Manichean/dualistic models of both the external and internal cosmos (*The Dark Side of the Moon* – 'outer space' is also 'Music from the Body' – inner space) sublimate, where light and dark meld, transforming and confirming each other, and a climactic moment which seems to pass as soon as it arrives. It confirms the cyclic theme by picking up its lyrical cue from the album's opening vocal, 'Breathe' ('And all you touch and all you see, is all your life will ever be').[16]

The lyric moves thus, acknowledging in its content the central concerns of the record:

i   'All that you …'
ii   'All you …'
iii   'Everyone you …'
iv   'All that is …'
v   'And everything … but the sun'

i, ii   Sensory perceptions (four lines):   (touch/see/taste/feel)
i   Emotional experience (two lines):   (love/hate)
ii, i   The material world (four lines):   (distrust/save/give/deal/buy/beg/borrow/
          steal)
ii   Art as sanity/madness/myth (two lines):   (create/destroy)
i, iii   Empathy, human conduct (four lines):   (do/say/eat/meet)
i, iii   Discord (two lines):   (slight/fight)
iv   Philosophical meditation (three lines):   (now/gone/come)
v   Harmony: unifying transformative symbols and contexts (two lines):
          (tune/moon)

Each statement in the lyric finds its equivalent and counterpoint, drawing together the key themes of the record; the opposition is necessary – like a culture's need for madness, or 'difference' as opposed to sanity, or 'sameness'. Thus Barrett's visionary 'madness' and Waters's devastating 'sanity' informed this work ('now') and all that flowed up to it ('gone'), and subsequently flowed from it ('to come'), and thus the dynamic represents the process in action in the very moment it finds an image to describe it – the description brings on the understanding and brings the process into being. These key terms (now/come/gone) are reinforced by sonic emphasis, via the escalating, multiple voices, here in declamatory harmony, as opposed to the codified Babel of voices running through the rest of the album; in its earlier, live incarnation, the song was played 'over' a frenzy of taped voices. This freedom from the background noise offers an image of potential for change, via focus and empathy; note that the only line echoed by the female voice is the most empathetic in import – 'Everyone you meet'. The final image is ambiguous, cautious, but emotionally positive: the 'moment' of possibility is glimpsed. Again, it's a big production number, yet one which communicates its purpose both richly and plainly; we don't notice the machinery. The simplest rhyme of 'tune' and 'moon' is therefore transformed by its context, by the meanings brought to the terms by the rest of the record and the journey undertaken to arrive at the climax of the record. This is indeed a transformative moment, like the moment of total occlusion during an eclipse. The plagal cadence (Gmin6–D) provides, as is its wont, an almighty, just-out-of-the round 'Amen' at the climactic moment, bringing us to an instant, held, which then passes, ('but …') followed by the heartbeat which leads us back to the start of the cycle. So we have, it would seem, a set of binary oppositions, apparently wholly separate yet which depend on each other for definition; therefore, if we know how to read them, these apparent oppositions reveal themselves as expressions of complex systems of exchange. There are indeed hidden harmonies within the discord.

'Eclipse' questions and sublimates the bi-polar identities we have seen at work within the text (light/dark, illumination/extinction – Waters would later revisit this imagery to implore Barrett to resist the 'eclipse', and to 'shine on' – past/present, vision/blindness, sanity/madness, self/other) concentrating them into a single moment in which identities are both forged and lost. At the moment of realization, the realizer is changed. 'Pink Floyd' was/were changed forever by this music that they had made. This then is their problem just as it is their triumph; the start of self-mythologization, where the moment of totality in creativity passes into the phase of self-consciousness.

'Brain Damage'/'Eclipse' represents the moment at which Pink Floyd's musical and lyrical topography is both newly and freshly discovered and most intuitively mapped and understood, before the simulacra begins to be overlaid, the map preceding the territory on *Wish You Were Here* ('running over the same old ground'): a shock of insight and discovery and focus, of revelatory vision represented musically and lyrically as being poised in perfect, deadly balance ('And everything under the sun is in tune') yet one which acknowledges its own impermanence ('but the sun is eclipsed by the moon'). As such it represents the high-watermark of their creativity as a unit in its truest sense: they see the whole of the moon, clear, vivid and lucid. Paradoxically that creativity burns most brightly at the moment of its eclipse. These final cuts provide a conclusion, but one which is still on the run, a resolution both linear and cyclic, like the groove of a record, or the phases of the moon.

Notes

1. *New Musical Express*, 23 May 1988.
2. *Uncut*, no. 73, June 2003, p. 64.
3. *Mojo,* December 1999.
4. *Melody Maker*, 12 February 1973, p. 3.
5. Quoted in R. Sanders (1976), *Pink Floyd*, London: Futura, p. 82.
6. Classic Albums series: *The Dark Side of the Moon* (Matthew Longfellow for Isis/Eagle Rock/BBC, 2003).
7. Ibid.
8. Sanders, 1976, p. 48.
9. C. Fitzgibbon (ed.) (1988), *The Collected Letters of Dylan Thomas*, London: Dent, p. 345.
10. *Mojo*, December 1999.
11. Charles R. Cross (2001), *Heavier Than Heaven: A Biography of Kurt Cobain*, London: Hyperion, p. 267.
12. Ibid., p. 348.
13. Ron Geesin website address: www.rongeesin.com
14. *The Rough Guide to Rock* (2001), ed. M. Ellingham et al., London: Rough Guides/Penguin, p. 622.

15. *Uncut*, no. 73, June 2003, p. 47.
16. The closing moments of U2's 'Walk On' from *All That You Can't Leave Behind* (2001) deliberately reference the cumulative emotional force of 'Eclipse' and its status as a concluding statement of resolution: for example, 'all that you see, all you create, all that you wreck, all that you hate, all that reason, all that you speak …'.

Musical works cited

Pink Floyd

'Arnold Layne' (UK single, Columbia DB 8156, March 1967)
'See Emily Play'/'Scarecrow' (UK single, Columbia DB 8214, June 1967)
'Point Me At The Sky'/'Careful With That Axe, Eugene' (UK single, Columbia 8511, December 1968)
From *Meddle* (Harvest /EMI, 1971):
  One Of These Days
  Echoes
From *The Dark Side of the Moon* (Harvest/EMI, 1973):
  Breathe
  Time
  Brain Damage
  Eclipse
From *Wish You Were Here* (Harvest/EMI, 1975):
  Shine On You Crazy Diamond
  Wish You Were Here
From *Animals* (Harvest/EMI, 1977):
  Dogs
Atom Heart Mother (Harvest/EMI, 1970)
Relics (Starline/EMI, 1971)
The Wall (EMI, 1979)
The Final Cut (EMI, 1983)

Other artists

Barrett, Syd: 'Dark Globe' (from *The Madcap Laughs*, Harvest, EMI, 1970)
Beach Boys, The: *Pet Sounds* (Capitol, 1966)
Gabriel, Peter: 'Lead A Normal Life' (from *Peter Gabriel* aka '3', Charisma, 1980)
Nirvana: *Nevermind* (Geffen, 1991)*; In Utero* (Geffen, 1993)
Prince: 'Let's Go Crazy' (from *Purple Rain*, Warner Brothers,1984)
Radiohead: 'Creep' (from *Pablo Honey*, Parlophone/Capitol, 1993)
U2: 'Walk On' (from *All That You Can't Leave Behind*, Island, 2001)
The Waterboys: 'The Whole of the Moon' (from *This Is The Sea*, Ensign, 1985)
Waters, Roger and Geesin, Ron: 'Breathe' (from *Music From The Body*, Harvest/EMI, 1970)

Chapter 11

Pink Floyd's Levinasian ethics: reading *The Dark Side of the Moon*'s philosophical architecture

Kenneth Womack

From the album's unforgettable musical landscapes and its deeply philosophical lyrics to its cover artwork and its signature spoken asides, Pink Floyd's *The Dark Side of the Moon* (1973) offers a sustained ethical vision predicated upon goodness and Levinasian notions of alterity and otherness. On the album, Pink Floyd ask us to open our hearts and minds to new avenues of living, to 'breathe, breathe in the air / Don't be afraid to care'.[1] In addition to exploring ground-breaking sonic dimensions in popular music, the album poses significant existential questions about human identity and the vexing nature of interpersonal relationships. As Roger Waters remarks in the DVD documentary *Pink Floyd: The Dark Side of the Moon* (2003), the album 'was an expression of political, philosophical [and] humanitarian empathy that was desperate to get out'. With songs such as 'Time' and 'Money', the band – via Waters's intentionally unambiguous lyrics – debates two of contemporary life's most fractious issues, specifically, the manner in which we devote ourselves to pecuniary interests at the expense of our human relationships and the ways in which these diversions mitigate our capacity for perceiving the inherent beauty in living.[2] Even more importantly, tracks such as 'Us and Them' and 'Eclipse' discuss the ethical significance of other beings in relation to the needs and desires of ourselves.

Reading the album in terms of Emmanuel Levinas's philosophies of otherness and alterity provides us with an illuminating system for understanding Pink Floyd's ethical stance.[3] As Jill Robbins observes in *Altered Reading: Levinas and Literature* (1999, p. xiii), Levinasian ethics 'denotes the putting into question of the self by the infinitizing mode of the face of the other'. With *The Dark Side of the Moon*, Pink Floyd's ethical imperatives include an expansive analysis of the self's relationship to the larger worlds in which we live, as well as the ways in which those worlds impact the self's capacity for enjoying goodness and comprehending otherness. In addition to Levinas's critical matrix of alterity, a reading of *The Dark Side of the Moon* within the philosophical context of Iris Murdoch's postulation of goodness underscores Pink Floyd's stridently humanistic agenda for addressing the recuperative powers of alterity and otherness – concepts, in themselves, that oblige human beings to realize our responsibilities for perceiving otherness.

Such philosophically vexed issues as obligation and responsibility are perhaps most usefully considered via Levinas's conceptions of alterity, contemporary moral philosophy's *sine qua non* for understanding the nature of our innate responsibilities to our human others. In 'Is Ontology Fundamental?' (1966) Levinas discusses the ethical significance of other beings in relation to the needs and desires of ourselves. Our ethical obligations to others, Levinas reasons, find their origins in our inability to erase them via negation. Simply put, unless we succeed in negating others through violence, domination, or slavery, we must comprehend others as beings *par excellence* who become signified as 'faces', the Levinasian term that refers to the moral consciousness and particularity inherent in others. For Pink Floyd, *The Dark Side of the Moon* provides an ethical forum in which to consider the collective interrelationships that human beings share with one another. In 'The Trace of the Other', Levinas argues that 'the relationship with the other puts me into question, empties me of myself' (1986, p. 350). More importantly for our purposes here, Levinas describes the concept of the face as 'the concrete figure for alterity' (quoted in Robbins, 1999, p. 23). The notion of alterity itself – which Paul-Laurent Assoun characterizes as 'the primal scene of ethics' (1998, p. 96) – refers to our inherent responsibilities and obligations to the irreducible face of the other. These aspects of our human condition find their origins in the recognition of sameness that we find in other beings. This similarity of identity and human empathy establishes the foundation for our alterity – in short, the possibility of being 'altered' – and for the responsibilities and obligations that we afford to other beings. By authoring a song cycle that elevates alterity and otherness over social bifurcation and excess, Pink Floyd challenge listeners to embrace alterity and establish a genuine sense of interpersonal ethics and renewal.

In Levinas's conception, alterity implies a state of being apprehended, a state of infinite and absolute otherness. Alterity's boundless possibilities for registering otherness, for allowing us to comprehend the experiences of others, demonstrates its ethical forcefulness. Its exteriority challenges us to recognize an ethics of difference – and, hence, an ethics of otherness. Such encounters with other beings oblige us, then, to incur the spheres of responsibility inherent in our alterity. When we perceive the face of the other, we can no longer, at least ethically, suspend responsibility for other beings. In such instances, Levinas writes in 'Meaning and Sense':

> the I loses its sovereign self-confidence, its identification, in which consciousness returns triumphantly to itself to rest on itself. Before the exigency of the Other (*Autrui*), the I is expelled from the rest and is not the already glorious consciousness of this exile. Any complacency would destroy the straightforwardness of the ethical movement. (1996b, p. 54)

In this way, the Levinasian notion of exteriority underscores the value of alterity as a means for engendering ethical knowledge.

In addition to their illuminating intersections with Levinasian ethics, Pink Floyd establishes an ethical perspective in *The Dark Side of the Moon* through the band's incorporation of what amounts to a fairly traditional philosophy of goodness. In her important volume of moral philosophy *The Sovereignty of Good* (1970), the late English novelist and philosopher Iris Murdoch elaborates upon the concept of goodness and the ways in which our personal configurations of it govern human perceptions regarding the relationship between the self and the world. Murdoch's paradigm for understanding goodness functions upon the equally abstract notions of free will and moral choice. 'Good is indefinable,' she writes, 'because judgments of value depend upon the will and choice of the individual' ([1970] 1985, p. 3). Postulating any meaning for goodness, then, requires individuals to render personal observations about the nature of this precarious expression and its role in their life decisions. Although Murdoch concedes that goodness essentially finds its origins in 'the nature of concepts very central to morality such as justice, truthfulness, or humility', she correctly maintains, nevertheless, that only individual codes of morality can determine personal representations of goodness (p. 89). 'Good is an empty space into which human choice may move' (p. 97), she asserts, and 'the strange emptiness which often occurs at the moment of choosing' underscores the degree of autonomy inherent in the act of making moral decisions (p. 35). Individuals may also measure their personal conceptions of goodness in terms of its foul counterpart, evil, which Murdoch defines generally as 'cynicism, cruelty, indifference to suffering' (p. 98). Again, though, like good, evil finds its definition in the personal ethos constructed by individuals during their life experiences in the human community. Because such ontological concepts remain so vitally contingent upon personal rather than communal perceptions of morality, Murdoch suggests that their comprehension lies in the mysterious fabric of the self. 'The self, the place where we live, is a place of illusion,' she observes, and 'goodness is connected with the attempt to see the unself, to see and to respond to the real world in the light of a virtuous consciousness' (p. 93). In Murdoch's philosophy, goodness manifests itself during the meaningful pursuit of self-awareness and self-knowledge.

Drawing upon Levinas's critical matrix of alterity and Murdoch's postulation of goodness, a reading of *The Dark Side of the Moon* underscores Pink Floyd's considerable humanistic agenda for 'altering' our interpersonal perspectives and affording us with a means for registering otherness. In *Shadows of Ethics: Criticism and the Just Society* (1999), Geoffrey Galt Harpham observes that 'ethics does not solve problems, it structures them' (p. 37). With *The Dark Side of the Moon*, Pink Floyd structures the album's ethical dimensions via a carefully orchestrated song cycle. As Waters remarks:

The album uses the sun and the moon as symbols; the light and the dark, the good and the bad, the life force as opposed to the death force. I think it's a very simple statement saying that all the good things life can offer are there for us to grasp, but that the influence of some dark force in our natures prevents us from seeing them. (Quoted in MacDonald, 1997, p. 207)

Interpreted in sequential order, the album narrates the self's transformative journey from a worldview marked by madness, paranoia, and greed toward a sense of ethical renewal based upon alterity, goodness, and the recognition of otherness. In short, *The Dark Side of the Moon* depicts the self as it reconsiders its place in the larger human community that exists beyond the confines of selfhood.

In addition to the album's innovative lyrics and music, *The Dark Side of the Moon*'s cover art – designed by Storm Thorgerson and Aubrey Powell of Hipgnosis fame – contextualizes the song cycle by affording the listener (or reader) with a visual concatenation of the album's tracks. The cover itself depicts a ray of light as it enters a prism, producing a rainbow spectrum that continues onto the album's back cover, which features an inverted prism through which the rainbow is transmogrified once more into a ray of light.[4] This complex of visual imagery can be read in terms of the ray of light's alteration into a rainbow of virtual otherness. The prism, with its attendant electrocardiogram, also evokes the sound of a beating heart that both begins and concludes the album. 'The heartbeat alludes to the human condition and sets the mood for the music,' David Gilmour observes, 'which describes the emotions experienced during a lifetime' (quoted in Schaffner, 1991, p. 176). The album's interior artwork includes a ghostly photograph of the ancient pyramids of Giza.[5] In themselves, the pyramids represent humankind's incredible penchant for erecting monuments to our own vanity and boundless ambition. Like the 'lifeless things' in Shelley's 'Ozymandias' (1817), the pyramids that adorn *The Dark Side of the Moon*'s cover exist as decaying memorials to our enduring inability to recognize the limits of mortality and, even more significantly, the necessity for perceiving otherness in the here and now. The album's title denotes the seemingly inescapable madness that exists just beyond our ken: 'I'll see you on the dark side of the moon,' Waters sings on 'Brain Damage', referring to the paranoia and psychosis that threaten to overwhelm us. Simply put, the pressures of modern life, coupled with our insatiable desires for financial reward and interpersonal dominion, set us on a collision course with insanity.

The Dark Side of the Moon's opening track, 'Speak to Me', provides the verbal and sonic script for the ensuing song cycle. As the album's de facto overture, 'Speak to Me' features an admixture of sound effects and musical motifs that will appear throughout the subsequent tracks.[6] Taking the form of a verbal invitation for the listener to engage in quasi-conversation with *Dark Side*'s ethical imperatives, 'Speak to Me' includes Jerry Driscoll's spoken aside: 'I've always been mad. I know I've been mad, like the most of us'. With Driscoll's words, 'Speak to Me' not only impinges upon the theme of insanity that will be explored throughout the album, but also self-consciously encourages the listener to participate in a potentially transformative experience.[7] The next track, 'Breathe', ushers in the album's prevailing argument that contemporary life – with its consumeristic barrage and overarching success myth – renders people, for all intents and purposes, insane. With the phrase 'all you touch and all you see / Is all your life will ever be', Pink Floyd underscores life's inherent corporeality and general mundanity in contrast with the fecundity that consumerism and self-indulgence promise. 'When at last the work is done,' Gilmour sings, we search for new vistas of gratification rather than pausing to reflect upon our place in the world. Seeking to 'balance' ourselves on the 'biggest wave', we 'race towards an early grave'. The ensuing instrumental 'On the Run' continues this theme by shifting the scene to a busy airport, where an announcer calls out departures and arrivals as members of the business class sprint to catch their flights and play their part in commerce's unyielding progress into oblivion. Roger the Hat's cryptic aside, 'live for today, gone for tomorrow', demonstrates the fleeting nature of our existence, as well as the philosophy of presentness that plagues our condition. As the song comes to a close, Gilmour's fiery guitar crescendos into the sound of a crashing jet plane. Sudden, unexpected death, it seems, has ended our desires before we have even begun to live them out.

One of the album's most thematically prescient tracks, 'Time' examines the ways in which temporality controls our every move. A fusillade of chimes, watches, ticking clocks, and Nick Mason's hurried drumbeat establish the song's mind-numbing pace. Listless and suffering from a diffuse sense of identity, we find ourselves 'ticking away the moments that make up a dull day', Gilmour sings, while 'waiting for someone or something to show you the way'. If we don't know ourselves, how can we possibly recognize the face of otherness? Waters's lyrics also belie the vanity of youth and our self-delusional notions of immortality: 'You are young and life is long and there is time to kill today,' Gilmour sings. Yet suddenly, 'you're older, / Shorter of breath and one day closer to death'. During the song's final stanza, Waters invokes the Thoreauvean dictum that the 'mass of men lead lives of quiet desperation' with little hope of altering their plight in the future. Before you know it, Gilmour sings, 'the time is gone [and] the song is over'. Even more perplexing, life becomes void of meaning, and the speaker finds himself bereft of the necessary language to explain his state of being: 'Thought I'd something more to say.' A life lived in pursuit of empty dreams has robbed the speaker of his humanity. How can anyone achieve genuine selfhood in a world in which we remain continuously on the run, attempting to thwart the uncompromising power of time? Can we really enjoy a sense of goodness when we never stop and smell the proverbial roses?

Pointedly, the brief reprise of 'Breathe' that follows 'Time' finds the speaker retreating to the warm glow of 'home, home again': 'When I come home cold and tired', Gilmour sings, 'It's good to warm my bones beside the fire.' As with time's artificiality and the hollow rewards of unchecked self-indulgence, even our comforting conceptions of home exist in a transitory space. In itself, the notion of home connotes feelings of solitude and withdrawal. Yet these very same images – while peaceful and reassuring – ultimately serve to mitigate the speaker's capacity for fully engaging with otherness. As the song comes to a close, the speaker hears a tolling bell in the distance, a bell that will 'call the faithful to their knees' to bow before the unswerving presence of death and the limits of our mortality. Accompanied by Rick Wright's mournful piano, 'The Great Gig in the Sky' – a not-so-subtle metaphor for death itself – explodes our notion of home's ostensible permanence. Clare Torry's ethereal – and, significantly, *wordless* – vocal illustrates humankind's fear of dying.[8] Indeed, we have no words for something that we cannot even begin to fathom. For all of our knowledge and technological innovations, we simply cannot imagine a world in which we cease to exist. Torry's wailing vocal genuflects (at least musically), as we do (and ultimately *will*), before the shadow of death. As 'one of the most extraordinary vocal performances ever captured on record', 'The Great Gig in the Sky' brings *The Dark Side of the Moon*'s first half to a breathtaking close (Jones, 1996a, p. 98).

As if to suggest that human beings never truly allow themselves to comprehend death's invariable role in our lives, 'Money' reminds us of our insatiable appetites for wealth and our easy capacity for lapsing into the vacuousness of materialism. A bitter satire about the dangers of greed and its tendencies to erode our value systems, 'Money' opens with the unmistakable sounds of cash registers, the veritable engines that drive our culture of consumerism. Waters's lyrics variously tell us that money is a 'gas', a 'hit', and, ultimately, a 'crime'. 'Get a good job with good pay and you're okay,' Gilmour sings, underscoring our culture's clear-cut, unapologetic philosophy of capitalism. In addition to deriding the wisdom of philanthropy – 'Don't give me that do goody good bullshit' – 'Money' lauds the self-serving pleasures inherent in pursuing wealth for wealth's sake: 'I'm in the high-fidelity first-class travelling set / And I think I need a Lear jet.' The song provides the listener with not one – as the title might imply – but two satirical targets: money itself, of course, but also the song's speaker, who proudly asserts that he deserves a life of prosperity and privilege. Murdoch observes that 'the world is aimless, chancy, and huge, and we are blinded by self' (1985, p. 100). There is little question that the song's speaker is overwhelmed by an ongoing need for self-gratification. Interestingly, 'Money' ends with a chorus of verbal asides in which the respondents proclaim their shared sense of 'rightness': 'I was in the right!'; 'Yes, absolutely in the right!'; 'I certainly was in the right!'; and, finally, 'You was definitely in the right'.[9] More importantly, the song's speaker remains profoundly unable to perceive the face of the other. He is, as Murdoch suggests, in a state of interpersonal blindness.

With its steady, unhurried cadence, 'Us and Them' decelerates the momentum created by 'Money' – and the song's intricate 7/8 time – into a more soothing tempo. Like Ravel's *Boléro*, 'Us and Them' slowly establishes *The Dark Side of the Moon*'s pace so as to provide a dramatic backdrop for the song's interludes about an insular general's inability to recognize his soldiers' senses of particularity. Much of the song concerns the dichotomous systems that often characterize human relationships: 'us and them'; 'me and you'; 'black and blue'; 'up and down'; 'down and out'; 'with [and] without'. Waters's lyrics demonstrate the semantic failure inherent in such binaries. How, indeed, do such easy distinctions account for the innumerable variations of truth that exist, for example, between 'us' and 'them'? Why, moreover, do human beings resort to such simple dichotomies in order to categorize their relationships with one another?[10] 'Us and Them' reaches its dramatic pitch in the portions of the song that narrate a general in the act of sending his army into battle: 'Forward he cried from the rear / And the front rank died,' Gilmour sings. For the general, the soldiers exist as mere pawns on an impersonal battlefield: 'And the general sat and the lines on the map / Moved from side to side.' As with the speaker in 'Money', the general cannot, for the life of him, recognize otherness. For him, the soldiers exist as nothing more than inhuman, insensate 'lines' on a map.

'Us and Them' segues into the free-form technicolor virtuosity of the instrumental 'Any Colour You Like', which, as its title suggests, argues for coming to terms with life's inevitable conflicts and compromises, rather than attempting to mitigate them via the artificial strictures of money and social status.[11] With the next track, 'Brain Damage', Waters illustrates the degenerative nature of an environment in which people elevate fame and commerce over the interpersonal needs of the self.[12] In short, we experience a form of brain damage rooted in the incongruity between our carefree childhood experiences and our more complicated, success-driven adult worlds. 'The lunatic is on the grass,' Waters sings. We remember 'games and daisy chains and laughs' from the past, while in our adult present we've 'got to keep the loonies on the path' as it is defined by our prevailing socio-economic systems. The pressures of contemporary life are both complex and relentless, Waters reminds us. We are imprisoned by paper – whether that paper be currency or the endless paper trails generated by the unremitting bureaucratic engines of modern society: 'The paper holds their folded faces to the floor / And every day the paper boy brings more.' Suffocating under the sheer weight of our existence, is it any wonder that we have become lunatics of one sort or another? As 'Brain Damage' comes to a close, Waters argues that we have no choice but to retreat into the vortex of our disintegrating psyches:

And if the dam breaks open many years too soon
And if there is no room upon the hill
And if your head explodes with dark forebodings too
I'll see you on the dark side of the moon.

In this way, the 'dark side of the moon' emerges as a metaphor for our collective insanity. It exists as a netherworld in which we've been forced to sacrifice our souls and our identities for the larger, universal 'good' of our society: 'You raise the blade, you make the change / You rearrange me 'til I'm sane.' It seems that our sanity – the sense of normalcy that so many of us crave – is merely a socially constructed illusion. In the end, Waters sings, 'There's someone in my head but it's not me.'

During 'Eclipse', *The Dark Side of the Moon*'s final cut, goodness and alterity finally coalesce. A virtual smorgasbord of emotions, sensations, and ethical conundrums, 'Eclipse' marks the climactic moment on the album when Pink Floyd challenges the listener to celebrate unity over division, alterity over individualism. The concept of the moon eclipsing the sun – with the 'simple image of the tiny, dead, barren moon blocking out the huge life-force of the sun', in Jones's words (1996a, p. 101) – suggests that humankind can conquer the constricting mechanisms that rule our lives if we establish a genuine sense of community among 'lunatics' across the globe. In 'Eclipse', life's binaries – love and hate, giving and taking, creation and destruction – exist side by side, daring us to make the ethical choices that might yet change the world. Universality looses time's power to control the texture and quality of our lives. In 'Eclipse', the past, present, and future become conjoined in the eternal here and now of humanity's existence:

> All that is now
> All that is gone
> All that's to come
> And everything under the sun is in tune
> But the sun is eclipsed by the moon.

In this manner, Waters's lyrics dreamily imagine a world in which earth's fecundity has been made manifest once again. Life's promise and possibility have become restored by the recognition that, like it or not, we all share in the peculiarities of the human condition. The boundaries between us and them might just be erased. In the utopian fantasy of 'Eclipse', we possess the capacity, Waters argues, for achieving unblemished otherness.

As a work of art, *The Dark Side of the Moon* evinces the kind of bold vision espoused by centuries of literary texts. As Murdoch observes: 'Art transcends selfish and obsessive limitations of personality and can enlarge the sensibility of its consumer. It is a kind of goodness by proxy' (1985, p. 87). Pointedly, the final verbal aside that concludes the album serves to temper Pink Floyd's overarching conceptualization of a universalizing goodness: 'There is no dark side of the moon really. Matter of fact, it's all dark,' Driscoll famously remarks. While *The Dark Side of the Moon* generally provides listeners with hope for the future, Driscoll's words provide a cautionary note about the ideas of optimism and unity that pervade the lyrics of 'Eclipse'. While Levinasian alterity implies a realization of otherness and an understanding of our larger responsibilities to other human beings, the notion of becoming altered also suggests that we might not be successful in our quest, that we may fail in our ethical mission to register the face of the other. Driscoll's words imply that negativity might ultimately trump the album's philosophy of revitalized selfhood and ethical renewal. Is it already too late to save humanity from interpersonal ruin despite our best efforts to the contrary? As Waters observes, *The Dark Side of the Moon* 'talks about the illusion of working towards ends which might turn out to be fool's gold. The philosophy that's embodied in it has got a little meaning for a lot of human beings. It deals with the Big Picture' (quoted in Schaffner, 1991, p. 182). Perhaps our only saving grace exists in the fading heartbeat that ends the album, only to begin once more – in the circular fashion of James Joyce's *Finnegans Wake* (1939) – as 'Speak to Me' comes alive yet again and the heart beats anew. Perhaps we, too, will get a second chance to overcome the cultural brain damage that threatens to destroy us.

Notes

1. Waters borrowed the phrase 'Breathe, breathe in the air' from the opening words on the soundtrack which he composed with Ron Geesin for Roy Battersby's documentary film *The Body* (1970).
2. Waters recalls that 'I had something definite I wanted to say. People were always misinterpreting the lyrics, so I thought it was time to make it as direct and specific as I could' (quoted in Jones, 1996a, p. 94).
3. In *Ethical Criticism: Reading after Levinas* (1998), literary critic Robert Eaglestone argues, rather unconvincingly, that 'Levinas's thought cannot be turned into a methodology: it is not a philosophy that can be *applied* ... To ask for a Levinasian critical method is to ask for something that cannot and should not exist' (p. 176; italics added). In fact, Eaglestone offers little evidence demonstrating the thrust of his contention beyond his observation that 'there is obviously no one critical process which embodies Levinas's ideas, no one answer' (p. 176). Yet Levinas's ethical philosophy quite obviously posits its own terminology – including such concepts as 'adequation', 'alterity', 'the face', and 'negation', among a host of others. Simply put, Levinasian philosophy, despite Eaglestone's misgivings, can easily be *applied* as an interpretive matrix in much the same interdisciplinary fashion as gender studies, psychology, history, and sociology – to name but a few of literary criticism's multitudinous allied disciplines, each of which possesses its own contingent of thinkers with their own critical vocabularies.
4. Waters provided Thorgerson with the original idea of a spectrum, while Rick Wright requested that the artist create a concept that was 'simple, clinical, and precise' (quoted in Schaffner, 1991, p. 177).
5. The pyramids were originally produced as posters for the album's LP release. Thorgerson remembers travelling to Egypt in order to photograph the pyramids: 'That was very spooky. Going up to the pyramids at night, under a full moon. *Very* scary. But great' (quoted in Schaffner, 1991, p. 177).
6. 'Speak to Me' finds its origins in the phrase that the band's renowned engineer Alan Parsons used while assembling the verbal asides that would adorn the album. These recordings provided responses to such questions as 'Do you fear death?'; 'When was the last time you hit anyone?'; and 'Is there a dark side of the moon?' The respondents

included Jerry Driscoll, the janitor and doorman at Abbey Road Studios; Henry McCulloch, a guitarist with Paul McCartney and Wings, and his wife; and a selection of the band's roadies, including Liverpool Bobby, Chris Adamson, Puddy Watts, and Roger the Hat (Jones, 1996a, p. 96).

7. Pink Floyd also investigate the deleterious effects of madness, paranoia, and desperation on such later albums as *Wish You Were Here* (1975) and *The Wall* (1979), recordings that plumb the depths of loneliness, isolation, and despair.

8. As Torry remembers, Pink Floyd 'didn't know what they wanted – just said it was a birth and death concept. I looked suitably baffled and just sang something off the top of my head. I got such a shock when the album came out and became a massive hit' (quoted in Jones, 1996a, p. 217).

9. Our potential for unchecked hubris is perhaps best illustrated by the words of Ishmael Reed, who remarks that 'in the twentieth century we've seen a lot of disasters happen because of people who thought they were right and everybody else was wrong' (1995, p. 338).

10. As if to underscore yet again the vital need for human beings to recognize the face of the other, one of the respondents offers the following verbal aside during 'Us and Them': 'Good manners don't cost nothing, do they?' In the documentary *Pink Floyd: The Dark Side of the Moon*, Waters contends that 'Us and Them' is 'about whether or not the human race is capable of being humane'.

11. The phrase 'any colour you like' finds its roots in Pink Floyd roadie Chris Adamson's maxim, 'you can have it in any colour you like', which he would employ when asked to perform an impractical or unpleasant task. As Jones explains, 'It was his way of saying, "You can make do with what you're given", and originates from Henry Ford's famous boast of the 20s that Ford cars were available in any colour you like, as long as it was black' (1996a, p. 100).

12. As with such songs as 'Shine on You Crazy Diamond' and 'Wish You Were Here', 'Brain Damage' also refers, of course, to Syd Barrett's psychological demise during the late 1960s and beyond. Yet, as Waters observes, the song has larger implications: 'It would be easy to say this song was influenced by what happened to Syd, but I guess it's more particularly about the real human being living inside the outer being that the rest of the world sees. In other words, the lunatic is really us, here, that we're trying to keep inside this box. An awful lot of us stop being able to respond to the child in us because the adult takes over and holds sway of the controls, and we obey those instructions' (quoted in Jones, 1996a, p. 100).

Part IV

'Speak to me'
The influence of *The Dark Side of the Moon*

Chapter 12

The moons are eclipsed by the moon: covering the dark side

Russell Reising

Do not mistake the finger pointing at the moon for the moon itself.

– Zen proverb

The remarkable range and varied quality of cover versions of *The Dark Side of the Moon* and some of its individual songs indicates the resilience and flexibility of Pink Floyd's musical vision, one capable of inspiring glee clubs, head bangers, hard rockers, lounge acts, jokers, banjo pickers, cellists, reggae toasters, string quartets, and symphony orchestras. In fact, on a St Patrick's Day episode of Dave Attel's popular Comedy Central television program *Insomniac*, Attel roamed around Dublin all night chatting up the celebrating locals. When in one pub he met two musicians jamming on a long-necked Irish bouzouki and bagpipes, Attel immediately requested *The Dark Side of the Moon*. Bob Dylan's 'All Along the Watchtower' may be the most covered song from the rock tradition (as well as the one most frequently used in television and film soundtracks), but no other album in rock history has been covered as much, from as many different angles, or as interestingly as has Pink Floyd's classic.

The Dark Side of the Moon cover versions come in three varieties:

1. performers doing one or two songs (Government Mule doing 'Money', the Austin Lounge Lizards on 'Brain Damage') or selections from *The Dark Side of the Moon* on tribute albums (*The Reggae Tribute to Pink Floyd*, *The Chillout Tribute to Pink Floyd*, the London Philharmonic's *Us and Them: A Symphonic Tribute to Pink Floyd*);
2. *The Dark Side of the Moon* tribute albums on which different performers cover the album in its entirety (*The Moon Revisited; The* Dark Side of the Moon *Revisited*); and,
3. full-blown performances of the album suite by a performing ensemble (Phish, the Squirrels, Out of Phase, the Easy Dub All-Stars *Dub Side of the Moon*, the Section's string quartet homage to *The Dark Side of the Moon*).

Short of performing conventional cover versions, a number of performers have sampled fragments of *The Dark Side of the Moon*. While Jethro Tull released *A Passion Play* in July of 1973 and, therefore, probably could not have been influenced by *The Dark Side of the Moon*, the heartbeat and collage of sounds that opens that ill-fated concept album sounds unmistakably in Pink Floyd's debt. Even the pathetic Milli Vanilli jumped on the Pink Floyd bandwagon when they framed their song 'Money' with the sound collage that begins Floyd's 'Money', and Marky Mark and the Funky Bunch similarly dip into 'Money' on *Music for the People*. And, as one dedicated fan from the UK notes on a website, Big Void 'filled their *The Floor or The Other Side of the Room* album with more Floyd (and particularly *The Dark Side of the Moon*) references than you could shake a stick at'.[1] Of course Pink Floyd tribute bands regularly offer up more or less convincing renditions of the entire Floyd corpus, including a hillbilly cover of *The Wall*, but what concerns us here are the ways that *The Dark Side of the Moon* appeals to a broad spectrum of other musical ensembles.

Crescent moons: or, A Brief History of 'Time' (and other cuts from *The Dark Side of the Moon*)

Cover versions of individual songs range from the brilliant homage to the truly bizarre, with every single cut from *The Dark Side of the Moon* being covered at least once since 1973. As unlikely as it might seem, even 'Breathe' has received attention from a wide variety of performers. Robin McAuley contributes a lovely, guitar-intensive rendition to *The Songs of Pink Floyd*; David West picks out a bluegrass version on *Pickin' on Pink Floyd: A Bluegrass Tribute*; and 50 Cent Haircut does a blisteringly fast country version on *A Fair Forgery of Pink Floyd*. Open Door jazzes the piece up with electric piano and whispery lounge vocals on *Rewind*, one of the many 'various artists' compilations of Pink Floyd cover songs. D.I.N. match Richard Wright's intensity, sense of velocity, and bizarre electronica in their version of 'On the Run' from *The Other Side of Pink*. Canadian post-grunge rockers Sea of Green cover 'Breathe' on their *Time to Fly* disc in an incredibly massive Teutonic interpretation. 'On the Run' gets two treatments on *The Electronic Tribute to Pink Floyd*, one by Cracker G. and another by George Sarah: the first anchoring something akin to Floyd's original synthesizer experiment with a thuggish backbeat, while the second never ascends beyond sluggish noodling, although a surging and robust riff near the conclusion almost rescues the piece. Neither version captures, or seems remotely interested in, the frantic menace and noisy desperation of Pink Floyd's original, and, far from evoking the 'travel section' of *The Dark Side of the Moon*, both Cracker G. and George Sarah seem to be spinning their respective wheels, waiting for someone or something to show them the way out of their relentless digital grooves.[2]

'Time', with its tense percussion lead in and ferocious guitar licks and vocals would seem an ideal, if daunting, piece for cover artists, and it has, in fact, generated some remarkable interpretations. On *Echoes of Pink: A Pink Floyd Tribute* (Reverberations, 2002), a collection of covers by twelve 'up and coming acoustic female vocal singer/songwriters', *The Dark Side* selections are among the most interestingly interpreted. As the liner notes suggest, 'stripped of their old bodies, these new takes on Floyd classics showcase the art and caliber of Pink Floyd's songwriting through its many incarnations'. Notable for their restraint and relative commitment to the original ethos of *The Dark Side of the Moon*, these covers offer engaging acoustic renditions rather than anything obviously 'female'. Melissa Quade's 'Time' (*Echoes of Pink*) is a case in point. Her 'Time' explodes out of the speakers in ways that capture the frenetic edge of David Gilmour's vocal and guitar performance, which virtually sizzle with desperate, almost sacred, rage. Quade's vocal range re-creates the highs and lows of 'Time', each paying tribute to Gilmour's performance, including the double-tracking of her voice, while also feminizing the autobiographical drift of Waters's lyrics. Particularly lovely is her wordless singing during the 'Breathe Reprise' conclusion, where, during the guitar interlude, it effectively complicates that passage in the music and also pays homage to Clare Torry's singing – no other approximation of which graces *Echoes of Pink*. On *The Royal Philharmonic Plays the Music of Pink Floyd*, the orchestra sustains the tension of the drum introduction to 'Time', coaxing it out to astonishing, and taut, lengths and then reproduces much of the menace and pressured anxiety of the song with a wide array of symphonic instrumentation. In another orchestral collection, *Us and Them: Symphonic Pink Floyd*, the London Philharmonic offers two different versions, one saturated with eerie string effects and foreboding bass notes, and another called 'The Old Tree with Winding Roots Behind the Lake of Dreams Mix' that features electronic effects rather than conventional orchestral instrumentation. The *Electronic Tribute* includes Motor Industries' 'Time' with uninspired synthesizer riffs (that sound like toys!) and an incredibly slow pace that, in spite of its restraint, lacks all of the menacing energy of the original. I can't be sure, but I also believe that Nightnoise, the Celtic new age ensemble, pay tribute to 'Time' on their intriguingly titled album *Something of Time*. 'Timewinds', the first cut on the disc, begins with a quiet clock ticking before a synthesizer blasts the same note with which David Gilmour opens his guitar introduction to Pink Floyd's song.

Of all the covers of 'Money', Government Mule's live versions rock hardest, especially at the high volumes characteristic of their shows. A group credited as 'the Project' contributes a hard-core 'Money' to the 2003 film *The Italian Job*, versions of which kick in at both the beginning and end of the film as the soundtrack for thrill-packed heists, and the film explores the dark side of money nearly as well as Floyd's song. Leslie King's 'Money' (*Echoes of Pink*) kicks off with a peppy acoustic bass line virtually identical to Waters's, and then eases into a bluesy version replete with very rhythmic picking and strumming, and sultry vocals. King models her phrasing perhaps too closely on the original, although her sexy vocalese interlude evokes some of the untrammeled eroticism of Clare Torry's performance on 'The Great Gig in the Sky'. The Ben Perowsky Trio stretches their eerily austere and trippy jazz version out to almost eight minutes.

British soul chanteuse Elkie Brooks belts out a throaty 'Money'. Both Tommy Shaw (on *The Songs of Pink Floyd*) and Gary Hoey (*Money*) showcase their guitar skills on their respective treatments of 'Money'; while Shaw's sounds edgy and harsh, the way Stevie Ray Vaughn might have played it, Hoey drenches his version in wah-wah effects. On the *Electronic Tribute*, Dynamichrom delivers a typically echoey and drum-machine heavy techno version, replete with really cynical, but occasionally powerful, vocals and a synth groove that treads a fine line between funky and tedious. Dynamichrome's layering of their lush electronic assault, their infectious danceability, and occasional allusions to a vast array of Floydian sounds lends credibility and interest to their contribution. However, any interest their interpretation may have generated vanishes under the weight of their having resorted to a typical 4/4 beat, thus domesticating all of the rhythmic interest at the heart of the song's appeal. Whatever 'Money' is, it isn't just a clichéd dance tune!

Not surprisingly, 'Us and Them' has received two different symphonic treatments, from both the Royal Philharmonic and the London Philharmonic. Also not surprisingly, both versions tend towards sappiness rather than pathos and anguish. The Royal Philharmonic loads its lumbering version up with lots of flutes and other light woodwinds, while the London ensemble also settles for a saccharine rendition with plenty of violin bowing substituting for Floyd's instrumentation. The majestic oceanic flourishes of 'Us and Them' would seem ideally suited to a large-scale orchestra, but both groups fail to capitalize precisely where their strengths might reveal something profound in the music. Brielle Morgan's very melodic 'Us and Them' (*Echoes of Pink*) also lovingly re-creates the atmosphere of the original, down to the echoing vocals and graceful keyboard arpeggios. The fullness of Morgan's voice nicely communicates the ironic pathos of Floyd's lyrics of death and slaughter, just as the sensuousness of her presentation harkens back to the female voices that embellish *The Dark Side of the Moon*. Jimmy Haslip pretty much destroys the song with Kenny G.-sounding sax playing and quiet, almost hushed, vocals (*The Songs of Pink Floyd*). I've also heard a bad live recording of the parody band Mr Bungle working its wacky but lugubrious way through 'Us and Them' with occasional symphonic crescendos, but the quality of the MP3 recording prevents positive identification.[3] Tony Franklin (*The Songs of Pink Floyd*) gives 'Any Colour You Like' a very lively psyche-pop interpretation, filled with impressive synthesizer climbs and crescendos reminiscent of 'Us and Them'.

'Brain Damage' has been covered from the widest range of musical perspectives. The Austin Lounge Lizards have coupled the cut with 'Eclipse' in a fast-paced and humorous bluegrass medley on *Lizard Vision*; Purdymouth W.V. performs a hillbilly version on *Just Don't Kiss Her*; Bim Skala Bim blazes through a frenetic acid-ska rendition on *Bones*; and Texas Faggot has fashioned a rumbling techno rendition – all interesting interpretations and all very much worth hearing. Candid Daydream and Alice in Chain's Jerry Cantrell perform hard ballad 'Brain

Damage's live in concert. The Bugs Bunny Foundation stretch their uneven electronic version out over seven minutes of distorted chanting (*Electronic Tribute to Pink Floyd*). The brooding distortion and obsessive-compulsive atmospherics of their 'Brain Damage' capture some of the maniacal drift of the song, and the wall of confusion, punctuated with industrial eruptions, escorts the listener into the nether regions of Floyd's original. Unfortunately, Nikki Boyer's 'Brain Damage' is the weakest *Dark Side* cover from *Echoes of Pink*. The speeded-up pace, dance-hall piano performance, and flippant lyrical presentation all trivialize 'Brain Damage', communicating nothing of interest or innovation. Even the laughter that concludes the piece sounds more like the giggling that would accompany a pillow fight rather than the dark, desperate, and anguished clinging to sanity that closes Floyd's work. In one of my personal favorites, the Tufts University Beelzebubs offer a surrealistic glee-club rendition of 'Comfortably Numb' coupled with 'Brain Damage' and 'Eclipse', both introduced and concluded by the *Dark Side of the Moon* heartbeat.[4] The Beelzebubs' lush harmonies and glee-club sanitizing of *Dark Side of the Moon*'s concluding songs resemble Pink Floyd's version about as much as Pat Boone's 'Tutti Frutti' resembled Little Richard's, although their attempt at creating the ominous atmospherics underwriting the tunes, including some laughter that never quite reaches lunatic proportions, surely represents one of the most ambitious flights of glee-club imagination ever. The Bugs Bunny Foundation, which had so successfully reimagined 'Brain Damage', doesn't quite measure up in their version of 'Eclipse', which maintains the shattered feeling in a bizarrely morbid waltz but unfortunately whimpers to a close, never having quite grasped the piece's sense of finality.

Half moons

The Moon Revisited (Magna Carta, 1995), in association with *Brain Damage – The International Pink Floyd Magazine*, is one of the compilations that collect various artists contributing to a performance of the entire album. Situating the album in the context of social and political unrest in the United States, Jeff Jensen, editor of *Brain Damage*, declares *The Dark Side of the Moon* 'A Record of Hope' and finds hope in the fact that Roger Waters's belief in human potential in the face of dark forces remains as 'relevant and influential now as it was' when Pink Floyd recorded it in 1973. As he puts it in his essay on the CD sleeve:

> Thematically, *Dark Side of the Moon* is simply the story of life. With the beginning heartbeat representing birth to the final heartbeat of death ending the record, the lyrics warn of life's tragedies such as the passage of time (Time), greed (Money), war (Us and Them), and death (Great Gig in the Sky). There are endless interpretations, and part of the magic is listening and determining what this record means to you.

Most artists choose to remain relatively true to the original, with notable exceptions such as Magellan's addition of spoken-word passages to 'Money'. The album also concludes with each of the contributors adding a vocal line to Robert Berry's instrumentation of 'Eclipse'. Rather than reproducing Floyd's signature heartbeat, Cairo's 'Speak to Me' and 'Breathe' feature thunderous and ominous knocking, like something out of *Macbeth* or the original film version of Shirley Jackson's *The Haunting of Hill House*. Their straight reproduction of the instrumental intro keeps the lyrics in the background, so that the first utterance of 'Breathe' is barely distinguishable from its lush background, highlighted by subtle guitar ornamentation in the upper registers. Rob LaVaque's 'On the Run' passes some of the surging sounds from channel to channel, an effect that approaches the massive auditorium-filling jolts from 1972's original live performances.

Shadow Gallery's 'Time' explodes with an ear-shattering jangle of clocks and alarms, but once the roto-tom beat comes up, the song slips into pale-imitation land. The guitar notes don't have any of the menacing clarity of Gilmour's original, and the vocalists' attempt to add melodic and harmonic embellishments to the mix detracts from the song's overall ethos. This very competent cover version indicates just how precise and subtle the album's hold, including the cameo performances by Clare Torry and Dick Parry, on our consciousness can be, with even the subtlest variations frequently registering as failures rather than mere differences. A group listed as Dark Side of the Moon offers up 'The Great Gig in the Sky' with five female vocalists who can really wail, moan, and soar their way through the material. While their vocalese lacks the visceral force of Clare Torry's original, its range, fluidity, and clarity make for a very satisfying and emotionally complex conclusion to the first half of the suite.

Magellan takes great liberties with the Floydian original of 'Money', inserting various vocal and instrumental effects more or less in place of the syncopated coin sounds. The distorted vocal presentation, complete lack of funky rhythmic sense, and general sense of lumbering takes it almost immediately out of the race. In fact, it's on their 'Money' that the centrality of subtle tonal and atmospheric changes is most manifest. Magellan's 'Money' sounds monolithic and one-dimensional, whereas the performance and production of Pink Floyd's songs sometimes leaps out, sometimes jumps off, and sometimes lurks in the multidimensional crevices of aural space. Enchant's 'Us and Them' quite simply doesn't – enchant us, that is. Flat and insipid rather than floating, beautiful, and pleading, the song misses out on the depth of Wright's playing and Mason's drumming. Certainly not percussion heavy, 'Us and Them' nevertheless benefits tremendously from Nick Mason's deft touch, especially in the militaristic flourishes and intensity of his contribution. World Trade performs 'Any Colour You Like' with different keyboard effects and, once again, guitar, bass, and drum interjections that fail to step forward in the performance or the mix. Robert Berry's 'Brain Damage' captures some of the song's haunting quality and tranquillized segues, but, whereas Gilmour's guitar touches add to the emotional poignancy and sonic interest of the original, here they barely reach audibility. 'Eclipse' is performed by a grand collection of the various musicians who perform the other cuts, encapsulating both the strengths and weaknesses of *The Moon Revisited* in general.

Full moons

Internet debates rage as to who has performed the so-called 'Limited Edition Trance-Remixes' of many Pink Floyd albums, most frequently attributed to self-professed Floyd-fanatics the Orb. Whoever has recorded and released the ambient cover of *Dark Side of the Moon* tries to stay faithful to Pink Floyd's original, as faithful as a complete electronification can be. This isn't exactly a case of carrying coals to Newcastle, as Pink Floyd is commonly cited as a dominant influence on the contemporary ambient scene and as the trance/ambient interpretations do reimagine much of the suite. But, in general, the dance/ambient translation lacks inspiration and settles in for mere soporific noodling and over-sampled mimicry. The lush keyboards, vocal lines run through various echo programs, mechanical-sounding drum machines, and computer effects that dominate the 'trance remix' explore the spaciness of the suite with minimal success, but more often than not turn Pink Floyd into little more than either soaring faux-symphonic crescendos, electrified waves of sound, or clichéd dance grooves. While 'Us and Them' does reach some majestic heights, the 'trance remix' really confirms Roger Waters's comment from the *Live at Pompeii* disc to the effect that, just as giving somebody a Fender Stratocaster doesn't turn them into Eric Clapton, giving them computers and synthesizers certainly doesn't turn them into Pink Floyd.

On 2 November 1999, Phish performed a faithful version of *The Dark Side of the Moon* in its entirety as a variation on their annual tradition of covering significant albums during their Halloween concerts. They introduce it with a brief narrative of their ubiquitous friend 'Jimmy', from a small town surrounded by mountains. Jimmy leaves town, looking for action, and heads to Vegas. Finding Sin City too crazy and crowded, Jimmy decides to hitch to Salt Lake City, which just happens to be where Phish is performing that evening. As they cruise, the driver puts on one of Jimmy's favorite albums, and they career along, at sunset, through the desert, listening to music they love so much. (For more information on Phish's performance, see the interview with Phish bassist Mike Gordon, Chapter 14 in this collection.)

Phish remain fairly true to original throughout their performance, even down to solo and harmonic singing; they use what sound to be original recorded effects from *The Dark Side of the Moon* throughout the concert, as at the beginning of 'Time'. 'On the Run', filled with guitar and keyboard effects, also nicely mimics Floyd's original. Phish, in fact, capture the drama of Pink Floyd's transitions and segues; their introduction to 'Time', for example, builds with the same kind of ominous interplay between Jon Fishman's percussion and Trey Anastasio's guitar work. Nobody can quite equal Gilmour's vocal work, and, in 'Time' as in some other vocal sections, it's Phish's singing that never quite reaches Floydian intensity, anxiety, or exuberance. On the other hand, they do pump up the funk on the jam segments of the suite, as in the rocking section of 'Time' immediately following the guitar solo, which Anastasio handles with deft inventiveness. One of the great elements of Phish's performance is the anticipation listeners feel about just how they're going to approach 'The Great Gig in the Sky'. I think it's enough to say that Anastasio puts plenty of heart into each wail and scream, and about 20,000 fans respond with generosity.

Bassist Mike Gordon thunders into 'Money' with admirable power, setting the sonic tone for one of the more impressive phases of Phish's *Moon*. Indeed, the fusion of rock, funk, and jazz that is 'Money' seems ready made for Phish's interpretation/tribute, and their coherence as a band shines on as they rock and jam their way through the most improvisation-friendly section of *The Dark Side of the Moon*. I've seen Pink Floyd, the reconstituted Pink Floyd of *Pulse*, and Roger Waters all perform 'Money' more than a few times, and their ability to jam on 'Money', even within the tightly framed context of the album, always amazed and impressed me. Phish's version captures every bit of that musical freedom within boundaries.

Page McConel's lustrous organ work ushers Phish's glide into 'Us and Them', shifting the musical tempo and emotional valence with consummate smoothness. Phish's melodic and harmonic vocal presentations work best on 'Us and Them', capturing both the austerity and the soaring majesty of the song, revealing the intricate interplay of Pink Floyd's composition, and interfacing most seamlessly with the music and vision of Floyd's original. Phish work through 'Any Colour You Like' and 'Brain Damage' competently, with nice vocal and guitar flourishes, leading finally up to the exhausted closure of 'Eclipse'. Phish's one-time performance constitutes one of the great tributes to Pink Floyd's masterpiece. Unfortunately for many Phish/Floyd fanatics, Phish's *The Dark Side of the Moon* now exists only in a few thousand memories of the limited audience who were lucky enough to be at the E Center that night, and probably scores of thousands of bootlegs and computer files.

Out of Phase covers the album in its entirety on *Dark Side of the Moon 2001* (Hypnotic, 2001). 'Speak to Me' opens with what sounds like a washing machine agitating, but which the credits list as an ingenious touch, an actual child's heartbeat – 'Rosa (still in the womb)'. Quite a promising opening, enhanced by various spoken words, laughs, and other electronic effects eventually morphing into a version of 'Breathe' dominated by lush acoustic guitar picking and, in the background, a woman wailing à la 'Great Gig in the Sky'. Eventually 'Breathe' shifts into a percussive and heavily synthesized mode, and sweet, overly sweet, vocals gradually emerge out of the sonic background. Warning sirens dominate the early bars of 'On the Run' before it eases into an electronic segment reminiscent of Floyd's original, albeit with some dainty alterations. 'Time' opens with a minimalist ensemble of clock ticking, alarm clock buzzing, and a cuckoo clock, and then slides into an impressively surging instrumental build-up to the lyrics. Heavy on percussion, the rendition nevertheless manages to capture the ominous sounds of Gilmour's guitar, but the vocals, entirely too smooth and harmonious, detract from whatever sense of foreboding, lost opportunities, and pressure the instrumental introduction establishes. The heavy techno drumbeat fails to restore the song's sense of fated inevitability, giving it more a sound of dance hall or rave club programmed anonymity. The weakest vocal rendition on the entire disc comes with the insipid presentation of 'Home, home again. I like to be here when I can', which misses all of Gilmour's vocal intensity and range. 'Great Gig in the Sky' fails to add much to the mix, until it fades out to the sounds of a thunderstorm and winds reminiscent of 'One of These Days'.

A brilliantly conceived and performed 'Money' takes off to the sounds of an adding machine (the credits list a cash register) rather than jangling coins and leads into a heavily synthesized voice. In a manner fully consistent with Roger Waters's lyrics, this huge departure from Pink Floyd's original introduces a sense of the mechanization of human life, the prefabrication and automation of existence, that 'money' inflicts on our species. The sax and guitar solos really capture the jazzy and funky essence of the original, but they are left too far back in the mix to explore new terrain with any real claim to visceral excitement. After the solo, the synthesized effect on the vocals escalates, erasing all traces of humanity. Unfortunately, 'Us and Them' lumbers in with a plodding synthesizer beat and vocals that are insipid rather than anguished. 'Any Colour You Like' recaptures some of Floyd's intensity and relentlessness with a distorted guitar, incantatory drumbeat, and synthesized symphonic presentation. Just where Floyd began a transition into their final songs, Out of Phase crank up the originality and power of their rendition, which builds and soars until their guitar segue into 'Brain Damage'. Here, the metallic echo effects combine with an industrial sound reminiscent of a punch press to underlie and threaten the distorted vocals. The peppy interludes sound jarring rather than rehabilitory, but the chaotic background and tranquilized vocals offer an interesting take on the idea of brain damage and lunacy. Alas, the saccharine vocals of 'Eclipse' abandon all of that interest, and the album degenerates into an unremarkable conclusion.

For all its limitations, *Dark Side of the Moon 2001* possesses some remarkable interpretive touches as well as some passages true to but expanding on Pink Floyd's original version. Most importantly, it represents a genuine interpretation rather than mere mimicry of Floyd's material. In terms of vision, performance, and production, the album contributes something new and innovative, though not necessarily 'updated' as promised by its ambitious title. In this respect it stands head and shoulders over the tedium of *The Moon Revisited* and the foolishness of the Squirrels' *The Not So Bright Side of the Moon*.

The Not So Bright Side of the Moon, the Squirrels' 'tribute to Pink Floyd', opens with hiccups, a rubber ducky, mooing cows, sound effects, and a 'silly' voice declaring 'I've always been mad' before jumping into a very jazzy 'Breathe', whose promising instrumentals collapse under the weight of another silly voice. The project never fulfills the promise of its interesting takes on Storm Thorgerson's original cover art, with the ray of light and prismatic effect filtered through a human head on the front and the 'wacky' performers crammed into a triangle. Sounding something like an amateurish Weird Al Yankovich – but without Yankovich's humour or insightfully parodic vision – the Squirrels plow their way through *The Dark Side of the Moon* with competent musicianship, but with a vision wholly lacking in comprehension and cluttered with many disastrous passages intended, I can only suppose, to 'lighten' the suite with humorous nuances.

The Squirrels do launch into 'Time' with an extraordinary mix of percussive effects (in place of Mason's roto-toms) and glowering chords, by far the strongest segment of the album. Once again, however, the vocals sound like singers who, unable to engage the material in a meaningful way, settle for a limp attempt at parody. 'Great Gig in the Sky' embodies most of these same limitations, with a competent instrumental mimicry of the original playing behind a whining dog (Shamus revisited?) in lieu of Clare Torry and a chorus singing 'the torture, the torture, the torture never stops'. Listeners must feel the same, and subjecting oneself to the second half of *The Not So Bright Side of the Moon* surely constitutes something akin to masochism.

Indeed, when 'Money' begins with syncopated rubber-ducky squeaks, the coughing up of phlegm and spitting into a spittoon, and a cash register sound, the insulting, because completely irrelevant, attempt at humor tempts one simply to chuck this one aside. But the Squirrels then pump out an instrumentally brilliant fusion of Pink Floyd's 'Money' and the rock standard 'Money (That's What I Want)'. 'Us and Them' wraps the chintzy sound of a disco-era synthesizer around mocking vocals, relieved only by a majestic-sounding bridge. 'Brain Damage' as a 1930s-style Spike Jones piece works quite wonderfully, jettisoning the somber austerity of the original, but maintaining the warped sense of lunacy, paranoia, and rage. Nevertheless, as 'Eclipse' fades out to the sounds of a carnival calliope and hiccups, the only sure thing is that 'a splendid time was not had by all'.

Torn between parody and musical ambitions, the Squirrels plod their way through *The Dark Side of the Moon* with cartoon sound effects and sophomoric attempts at humor. The mishmash of lovingly re-created and occasionally clever interpretations dragged down by the stone of the Squirrels' uninspired vocals and failed attempts at novel sound effects results in a mere hodgepodge of aggravating antics. There's plenty of room and material for a competent, witty, and interesting dismantling of Floyd's magnum opus, of course, especially after so many performers and movements which, in the name of minimalism, punk energy, roots authenticity, or some other trendy slogan, have repudiated the much maligned 'excesses' of Pink Floyd and progressive rock in general. Alas, the Squirrels have none of those qualities, and *The Not So Bright Side of the Moon* wallows in almost completely unrelieved mediocrity and unimportance. These rodents needed somebody in charge to tell them to 'put down the ducky' and to break the news that there are no chickens on the dark side of the moon.

Figure 12.1 Cover artwork for the Easy Star All-Stars' *Dub Side of the Moon* **(2003).** Reproduced by permission of Michael Goldwasser of Easy Star Records

Or are there? The Easy Star All-Stars' *Dub Side of the Moon* creates a profound, cross-cultural analysis and interpretation of *The Dark Side of the Moon*, and it does so with chickens! Touches of Jamaica bathe their *Dark Side* in Caribbean sunlight and in an agrarian cultural climate seemingly incompatible with the crystalline soundscapes created on Abbey Road's high-tech networks. They begin, not exactly with heartbeats, but with percussion, replete with echoic effects from the club tradition, leading into a lively reggae translation of 'Breathe', which fuses a Floydian guitar with Jamaican keyboards and rhythm section. The All Stars' vocals remain true to the general drift of Pink Floyd's throughout their rendition, but they impart a warmth and intimacy resulting both from their vocal styles and from their slightly accented inflections. 'On the Run' exploits reggae mixing skills fused with synth work and appropriately frenzied drumming to both capture and reinterpret Floyd's original. If Pink Floyd's version reminds one of dashing through Heathrow, surely the All Stars capture what, if any, anxiety must accompany a rush through Freeport International.

'Time' begins, à la Floyd, with clocks ticking and bells ringing, but with the lively and rural addition of rooster crows and bugle blasts. It is here that the leisurely pace of Floyd's introductory section picks up a Jamaican touch. Most interestingly, the All Stars toast their own interpretation of the pressures of time over Pink Floyd's original vocals, Rastafarianizing the philosophical edge of

Waters's lyrics. If you haven't already heard *Dub Side of the Moon*, imagine for
yourself Waters's lyrics with the following lines, usually chanted with prophetic
urgency, interspersed throughout the song:

> Tick-a, tick-a tock
> Look at the clock
> Got to move it on the dot
> And don't you know man that time will come
> When time is the master
> And time can be a disaster
> Got no time to play
> Time is the master
> And time is the master
> I say you can't change the hands of time
> You could never turn back hands of time
> Got no time to play
> Got to get on the go and move it right away
> There's no time to delay when I tell you say
> Cause time is the master[5]

The Easy Star All-Stars perform 'Time' with that inimitably lively reggae lilt,
creating a lively and breezy atmosphere, while still insinuating and actually
expanding on the philosophical depth of Floyd's original. But the headiness,
heaviness, and darkness of their version never descend into morbidity, almost as
though their own orientation vis-à-vis 'time' as a master lightens the burden of
mortality. Maybe 'toking away the moments that make up a dull day' makes all
the difference. 'Time' slides imperceptibly into an echo-heavy 'Great Gig in the
Sky' wailed to a heavy bass accompaniment. While many of the vocal effects
recall Clare Torry's own, they never reach the level of anguished eroticism of her
impassioned contributions, largely as a result of the irreducibly up-beat reggae
beat laid down behind.

The seriously whimsical (and whimsically serious) Jamaican vision of *The
Dark Side of the Moon* blossoms with their witty replacement of the synchronized
coin and cash register sounds with those of a match lighting, a bong hit, and post-
toke coughs. This reggae 'Money' exploits the playful side of Waters's lyrical
irony, and the reggae beat almost persuades one that these luxuries purchased with
the filthy lucre of the song's title might not ultimately condemn one to hell.
However, the addition of some serious toasting pushes the boundaries of Waters's
original lyrics and reconfigures the imminent threat money poses to the soul.

> Money will make a good man bad (yeah, yeah)
> Money will make nuff man mad (yeah, yeah)
> Money will make bredren and bredren go to war

Forget about the good times
No bother make it change your ways
You no careful it will make you lose your mind
If you worship it, destined for a fall
Very addictive, watch the selective
No bother sell your soul just fi the money
When Jah Jah come, ain't nothing funny
Can't bear your weight inna Mount Zion
…

Never remember when them used to beg a dollar
Never remember when them used to beg fi hunger
Now them get rich and gwan like big timer
Burn down them bridge that them cross over
Boy, you can be rich today and broke tomorrow
Don't you know that's the way life goes
…

It a the root of all evil[6]

This spoken word embellishment, like that on 'Time', creates a probing cross-cultural exploration of another response to 'money', one that bridges the trans-Atlantic distance between England and Jamaica. As Michael Goldwasser of Easy Star Records comments in my interview with him (Chapter 15 below):

Remember that Jamaica was a British colony until just over forty years ago, and the British influence is still there. Also, many of the lyrical concepts of the album are universal: life, death, time, money, war, insanity. You definitely find plenty of songs about those subjects in reggae.

'Us and Them' is a slightly jazzy interpretation warmed by very mellow sax playing and spacey percussion effects. While the All-Stars stop short of the orchestral majesty of Wright's soaring keyboard passages, they restore the austerity of the 'Violent Section' he originally scored for Antonioni's film *Zabriskie Point* and out of which the *Dark Side of the Moon* 'Us and Them' evolved, resembling a chamber interpretation more than full symphonic volume and range. With the exception of some lovely ska-saturated trombone flourishes, the All-Stars' 'Any Colour You Like' functions, as does Floyd's, as a bridge between the heart of the album and its concluding medley.

The All-Stars accentuate the lunacy of 'Brain Damage' by distorting and distancing the vocal line behind the most austere reggae beat and some synthesizer embellishments and vocalese intended to approximate inner instability. The lightness of the reggae atmospherics belies the desperation of the lyric, granting them an even more disconcerting and sonically oxymoronic sense of dislocation than does Pink Floyd's original. Unfortunately, 'Eclipse' fails to close the All-

Stars' *Dub Side of the Moon* with anything like the grandeur and haunting finality of Floyd's *Dark Side*. Even this weakness, though, fails to detract from the overall power and interest of *The Dub Side of the Moon*. Throughout their performance of the suite (and in the four alternative tracks included on the CD) the Easy Stars All-Stars reveal a completely different rhythmic and tonal universe on the dark side of the moon, one that seems so coherent and sympathetic to Pink Floyd's, you have to wonder whether 'hanging on in quiet desperation' might also be the Jamaican way.

The Section's *Dark Side of the Moon* begins with an old Floydian trick, the sound of a door opening and footsteps across a room, followed by the nicely dissonant notes of a string quartet warming up, and settling into a combination of the percussive introduction to 'Time' meshed with a heartbeat sound reproduced on the body of a cello. All in all, an impressive announcement that what follows will be simultaneously interpretation and variation, but under the auspices of a sincere tribute to the original *Dark Side*.

Popular music arranged for string quartet understandably suffers from some inherent handicaps. Often an arranger takes an authentic approach to the music, faithfully trying to re-create the exact distribution of melody and harmony and following the patterns of verse/refrain in the original version. Without lyrics, however, popular music tends to lose its sense of motion through time, and the repetition of the same music without different words becomes quite boring. In rare instances, the combination of musically rich original material and an arranger sensitive to elements that are idiomatic to the medium for which they are arranging can create something new and exciting. This is the case with the Section's *Dark Side of the Moon*.

Music can often represent, almost onomatopoeically, visual and/or conceptual images in sound. Sometimes this is achieved simply by making the melody go higher in pitch when talking about heights (for example, John Mayer: 'Someday I'll fly, someday I'll soar' from 'Bigger than my Body') or by stopping the music when talking about nothing or stopping (James Taylor: 'I just wanna stop, and thank you baby' from 'How Sweet It Is'). The Section's version of 'Breathe' achieves this in a more abstract way. It opens up quite viscerally, giving us an unmistakable sound of breathing. The breathing is made tangible first by the quartet as a whole, with accordion-like swells through dissonance and consonance that sound like strong, deep inhalations and exhalations. Next, the Section's violin rendition of Gilmour's slide guitar solo is able to achieve a sense of breathing not found in the original. Indeed, a well-played violin is inherently more capable of producing this effect than a slide guitar. Although both can achieve fluidity of pitch, the violin is able to use more or less bow to produce crescendos and decrescendos and warm the tone in the middle of a sustained note with vibrato to make it come 'alive'. Such expressive playing, magnified by the entire ensemble doing similar things, can create a very convincing effect.

'On the Run' is surprisingly similar to the sounds and techniques used by contemporary composers and performers. The use of artificial harmonics is reminiscent of John Adams's 'Shaker Loops', and the repetition of an ostinato (around which are placed various sounds) that changes over a long period of time is central to the minimalists' exploration of phase. Although the strings are not able to imitate the changes in timbre in exactly the same way as on the original, they create changes by varying who plays the ostinato and when. Throughout, the reference to the Kronos Quartet's recording of 'Black Angels' by George Crumb is unmistakable. One notable similarity is the groaning sound of 'pedal tones', where the violinist presses the bow with such force on the string that the tones that emit from the instrument are well below the actual pitch and sound like groaning. At the end of the 'Run', the Section bend pitch in a way that achieves a Doppler effect similar to that produced by Pink Floyd on the album.

It is on 'Time' that the realization of a wordless version of *The Dark Side of the Moon* takes on interesting nuances. Although the first verse of 'Time' has plenty of excitement, what with changing pitch, harmony, and driving rhythms, without the lyrics the second verse ('tired of lying in the sunshine staying home to watch the rain') is rather boring. Ironically, this is an asset. What better way to text-paint boredom than with a melody that doesn't move, harmony that feels suspended and repeats, and has very little rhythmic variation? Whereas this lack of motion actually serves the meaning of 'Time', it hurts the rendition of 'The Great Gig in the Sky'. But again, while the most prominent feature on the original, the vocals, drives the piece from beginning to end, the string quartet version has other elements that come to the perceptual fore and reorient the composition. A circle of fifths progression is much more prominent in the Section's version, moving the music forward with a sense of inevitability. In addition, and probably more a feat of arranging than anything, is a nod to 'Breathe' in their 'Great Gig in the Sky' with faster and more labored, even rushed, breathing effects; the strings sigh together as though old age has approached and death is knocking.

'Money' opens up with perfectly timed plucks, scratches, and tortuous bowings of the Section's stringed instruments re-creating the original sound effects with remarkable ingenuity, wit, and authority. Just where you might think a string quartet interpretation of *The Dark Side of the Moon* will get derailed, the Section kicks into high gear, allotting instrumental and vocal lines among its four instruments with convincing subtlety and verve, and changing tempos and feels with pinpoint accuracy. And they rock hard on the jam section, until they float effortlessly into 'Us and Them', where they showcase the strengths of a string quartet and demonstrate their ability to capture the true nature and beauty of a piece of music. Although Wright's sustained, even-sacred sounding, organ and Dick Parry's melancholic sax solo are gone, the beauty of the quartet version is still stunning. Rather than having one instrument try to imitate the echoes in the original, the effect is created by stereophonic panning between the first violin and viola, a lovely way that something as traditional as a string quartet can evoke the high-tech effects of Pink Floyd. In addition, the harmonic progression in the verse is a real highlight of the collection, made more real and tangible as played by strings. The harmonic progression of this ten-bar segment is outlined by the second violin mimicking the guitar part. 'Us', and the echoes that follow, is supported by tonic harmony (I); 'and Them' (and the echoes that follow) is supported by submediant harmony (in first inversion – vi^6), both consonant to the ear. When the lyrics reach 'and after all, we're only', the underlying harmony is an augmented triad built on the flatted mediant ($\flat$III$^+$), a very dissonant sound. For the lyrics 'ordinary men,' the harmony moves to a more consonant subdominant seventh chord (IV^7). The sequence ends with a return to tonic harmony before starting over. All of this occurs over a repetitive 1, 5–1 pedal point in the cello, adding to the relative sense of consonance and dissonance experienced through the passage.

When the Section slide into 'Any Colour You Like', they, like Pink Floyd (and like some of the other cover versions) usher us from one musical universe into another, while at the same time segueing into the finale of *The Dark Side of the Moon*. The Section pulls out all the stops to render mental illness aurally on 'Brain Damage', using consonance and dissonance and creating a truly bizarre feel with a variety of effects: sul ponticello and trills (alternating between two notes while placing the bow on or very near the bridge to create a glassy/surrealistic sound) glissandos, and artificial harmonics. When they return to more orthodox playing for 'Eclipse', they demonstrate the reason why Waters and company added the concluding track after sensing incompleteness in early performances.

The Section's *Dark Side of the Moon*, like the Easy All-Stars' *Dub Side of the Moon*, embodies the essences of both 'cover' and tribute, revealing previously unexplored depths and recasting even our favorite passages into new musical vocabularies. Both cast light on *The Dark Side of the Moon*. And in the end, this is precisely the reason we listen to our favorite music in different formats – to hear something that we didn't before or in a way that changes our perception and makes the original more meaningful.[7]

Visual interlude

Of course, as Storm Thorgerson realized when he conceived of the famous prismatic effect that graced the cover of *The Dark Side of the Moon*, Pink Floyd's classic was about more than sound. Into that breach comes the marketing of Lumonics Videos' VHS release *The Light Side of the Moon* as 'a magical blend of astonishingly beautiful imagery – a richly textured variation of colors and shapes, that dance with the music … designed to transport you to a state of energized relaxation and pleasure' (VHS liner notes). Given the history of Pink Floyd's light shows, up to and including the brilliant pyrotechnics as produced and filmed for their *Pulse* performance of *The Dark Side of the Moon*, the Lumonics effort seems to capitalize on what Floydians might well regard as an integral dimension of the *Dark Side* experience. Their liner notes, in fact, suggest such a natural connection:

'if you have enjoyed listening to *Dark Side of the Moon* through the years, you owe it to yourself to "see the music" through this extraordinary visualization.' Unfortunately, *The Light Side of the Moon* offers up little more than generic, computer-generated geometric pulses and squiggles, never really motivated by or in synch with Pink Floyd's composition. Moreover, its generic quality is further belied by Lumonics' claim that their video also syncs perfectly with *Enigma* and *Fleetwood Mac*. I haven't tested it with other albums, but I suspect it might also provide a tantalizing video accompaniment to Savoy Brown, Uriah Heep, and the Backstreet Boys. Trying to out-visualize the visual environment for a Pink Floyd concert might be doomed from the start, rather like trying to follow up the cannons in Tchaikovsky's *1812 Overture* with toy pop guns.

These cover versions succeed and fail in many ways, from grand visions and inspired translations to limp and pathetic parodies. However, the sheer scope of these efforts – parody, tribute, imitation, translation – and the different visions brought to bear – feminine, Afro-Caribbean, symphonic, electronic – and the fact that most of the full-blown cover versions have been recorded in the last ten years, register the enduring power *The Dark Side of the Moon* still wields over contemporary musical culture, a culture not known for the endurance of its artifacts. Neither the turning of the millennium nor the album's 30th anniversary can account for such staying power. Consider the fact that no other albums of similar significance (the Beatles' *Sgt. Pepper's Lonely Hearts Club Band*, the Rolling Stones' *Beggar's Banquet* or *Let It Bleed*, Stevie Wonder's *Songs in the Key of Life*, Cream's *Disraeli Gears*, the Who's *Tommy*, the Byrds' *Notorious Byrd Brothers*, Joni Mitchell's *Ladies of the Canyon*, the Jimi Hendrix Experience's *Electric Ladyland*, or other monuments of the rock era) have received anything like the same ongoing reinterpretation and homage as *The Dark Side of the Moon*. Of course, songs like 'All Along the Watchtower' and 'Voodoo Chile (Slight Return)' receive plenty of cover treatments, but the albums as a whole remain largely unexplored territory. *The Dark Side of the Moon*'s enduring hold over our collective consciousness as well as over the creative projects of contemporary musicians seems a more significant testament to the album's importance than its staggering sales record from 1973 up to the present.

Notes

1. http://pages.eidosnet.co.uk/johnnymoped/musicforthemasses/musicforthemassesd arksideofthemoon/musicforthemassesdarksideofthemoon_facts/musicforthemasses_ darksideofthemoon_facts_covers.html
2. Shplang perform 'Breathe' on their album *Journey to the Center of Mirth* (1996), but I was not able to locate it.

3. Versions of 'Us and Them' also exist by Italian sax crooner Fausto Papetti in an album also entitled *Us and Them* (1998), by Switch (*Switch*, 2000), and by Innovations (*Innovations Plays Pink Floyd*, 1998), but I was unable to find any of those recordings.
4. Many of these versions are commonly available as bootleg recordings, and are downloadable from various peer-to-peer file-sharing programs.
5. The rest of the lyrics for this toast go as follows:

Tick-a tick-a tock
Move it on the dot and don't you look-a back
Serious time
This a terrible time yeah
This a serious time yeah
Got to know what you do in this time
Tick-a tick-a tick-a tick-a tick-a tock
Move it on the dot I say you could a never stop
Got no time to play I said no time to delay
Move it right away
Cause time is the master
Time is the master, time can be a disaster
So you got to move it on the go
Keep on coming through my door…

6. I want to thank Michael Goldwasser of Easy Star Records for his generous assistance and for his permission to quote these toasts. Michael was also generous in all his exchanges with me during my work on this project. I send him my thanks and respect. The complete text of the 'Money' toast runs as follows:

Money will make a good man bad (yeah, yeah)
Money will make nuff man mad (yeah, yeah)
Money will make bredren and bredren go to war
Forget about the good times
No bother make it change your ways
You no careful it will make you lose your mind
If you worship it, destined for a fall
Very addictive, watch the selective
No bother sell your soul just fi the money
When Jah Jah come, ain't nothing funny
Can't bear your weight inna Mount Zion
Haffe have nuff love inna you heart me friend

Never remember when them used to beg a dollar
Never remember when them used to beg fi hunger
Now them get rich and gwan like big timer
Burn down them bridge that them cross over
Boy, you can be rich today and broke tomorrow
Don't you know that's the way life goes
Money a money and friend a friend
Me nah put no money before my bredren
Them a worship and a kill fi the dollar
For the love of money man a kill him own a brother
Power is money, money is power

Materialistically them get conquer
It a the root of all evil
Ghetto youth, Dollarman, mi a beg of you
Don't bother mix up inna bwoy dem sumpin
Boy, if a trouble, you a get it pon the double
Pon the paper chase, boy, a watch no face
Any likkle thing them want fi dun the place
Man a different from the dollars and cents
Don't bother play with yuh life now mi friend
Money will make a good man bad
Money will make nuff man mad

Money

7. I want to thank Gerry MacDougall for contributing many of the ideas and some of the writing in this discussion of *The String Quartet Tribute to Pink Floyd's The Dark Side of the Moon*. Himself an excellent cellist ('There's always room for Cello'), Gerry teaches music and music theory at Solon High School in Ohio.

Chapter 13

Eclipsing: the influence of *The Dark Side of the Moon* on the next generation's music through Radiohead's *OK Computer*

Ben Schleifer

Life begins with a simple, quiet heartbeat. Some might say that a musical beat mimics a heartbeat and reminds us of a time we cannot remember. This might be why everyone under the sun enjoys some form of music. Those 'softly spoken magic spells' charge me with many emotions, through both lyrical and musical splendor. Few popular bands do both consistently. One of these bands is Pink Floyd; another is Radiohead. Some bands balance melody and poetry, but they seem to lack Pink Floyd's and Radiohead's psychological edge, their dynamic use of a variety of sounds, and their visual artistry. Many of rock's classic albums don't speak to today's youth (I was born in 1984 in Norman, Oklahoma, and I believe my generation is unique), but I would contend that Pink Floyd's *The Dark Side of the Moon* does, and speaks to it quite strongly. As does Radiohead's *OK Computer*. In this essay, I will examine *OK Computer* as a representative example of the Floydian influence, both musically and lyrically. *The Dark Side of the Moon*, thus, influences contemporary youth both directly, with the themes it explores, and indirectly, by shaping part of our musical taste, Radiohead.

Autobiographical

Before I proceed, I should clarify this problematic notion of 'my generation' – with the emphasis on 'my'. I would like to offer myself as a representative specimen of 'my generation' with which I share both a historical moment and a philosophical outlook. Born in a roughly ten-year span – around 1978 to 1988 – in the United States, we tend to think of ourselves as independent and outside of 'the norm', and we endeavor to look different. We shy away from sports and other competitive ventures and prefer instead to engage in artistic activities and dialogue. My generation remains socially aware and concerned, but tends towards passivity. We have a hint of cynicism and rely far too much on television and movies for entertainment, although we do find social psychology terribly fascinating as well. We are neither 'the MTV generation' nor 'Generation X'; actually, we try to avoid labels altogether. This is my generation, or at least a significant subculture within it.

Whereas we encountered the Beatles or Rolling Stones fairly early in our lives, many of us discovered Pink Floyd late in adolescence, most commonly through either the song 'Another Brick in the Wall Part II' or the supposed synchronization of *The Dark Side of the Moon* with the motion picture *The Wizard of Oz*, which has been aptly named the 'Dark Side of Oz'. One of my friends turned me on to *The Dark Side of the Moon* while we were playing video games. I loved it, and bought and listened to it the very next day. Roger Waters's lyrics and David Gilmour's gorgeous melodic taste coupled with the mesmerizing vocals of Clare Torry and Doris Troy (and even the comments of Roger the Hat) combined perfectly to stir my emotions. The album depicts how the journey through everyday life leads to insanity, which gave me greater sense of my own vulnerable individuality.

Shortly after *The Dark Side of the Moon* stirred my emotions, my brother stirred me by playing *OK Computer* for me. By the time *OK Computer* came out in 1997, Radiohead had achieved great success among my generation (Doheny, 2002, p. 59). This success came out of adopting the same techniques Pink Floyd used to address its generation. *OK Computer* is Radiohead's own experiment with new musical and poetic endeavors, their *Dark Side of the Moon*, so to speak. This album also coheres better than either *Pablo Honey* or *The Bends*, Radiohead's previous albums, in both thematic ideas and musical connection. Songs can be isolated, but the album functions better as a whole. After hearing the conclusion of *OK Computer*, with the slowly resolving sound of 'The Tourist' ending with a quiet heartbeat, I began to draw parallels between these two albums.

These parallels can be best seen by analyzing the albums together, first by describing what Pink Floyd accomplished and then by giving examples of how Radiohead addressed many of the same ideas. This is not to say that Radiohead consciously imitated *The Dark Side of the Moon* when working on *OK Computer*. But *Dark Side* is a crucial ancestor in the conception and production of *OK Computer*, so powerful, in fact, that, without it, we might never have had *OK Computer*.

By the way: which head's radio?

One might argue that Pink Floyd's impact on popular music, especially with and after *Dark Side*, is far too great not to have influenced Radiohead. Even when putting the music and style aside, Radiohead frequently reveal their debts to Floyd's sonic and electronic influences. Johnny Greenwood, the lead guitarist and music-smith of Radiohead, admires what Floyd has done and even covered the song 'Wish You Were Here'. Floydian imagery also informs the artwork on *OK*

Computer. The illustration of two little black men shaking hands recurs throughout the CD's cover art and appears strikingly similar to the two people shaking hands on the cover of *Wish You Were Here*. Towards the back of the CD booklet of *OK Computer*, there appears not only a floating pig (*Animals*) but also a heartbeat line running through the page, the same heartbeat line Storm Thorgerson immortalized on *The Dark Side of the Moon*.

Both *OK Computer* and *The Dark Side of the Moon* portray one theme, which each song addresses in separate ways. According to Jones, 'The album's premise is that modern life is a recipe for insanity, and that a human has to fight hard to escape it' (1996a, p. 93). Waters wanted to address the mental decline of original Floydian Syd Barrett; he did it in the forum of an album, rather than just a single song. Radiohead's theme is harder to identify precisely. The dream of escaping modern life shows itself again and again in *OK Computer*. At no time in *OK Computer* is everything, or even anything, OK. Radiohead shows us how we can become a machine, a 'Paranoid Android', as we stifle the inner ravings of the mind to conform to the outside. Both themes show how the creative individual loses the ability to function in the world. Radiohead add a twist on this alienation and anxiety by addressing in their lyrics and music the new technologies we find in this era, much as the Floyd did back in 1973.

For my generation, or perhaps for any generation living in confusing times, these feelings of anxiety and alienation provide a cynical outlet. The fact that Pink Floyd already addressed this theme reassures us that we aren't isolated in our thoughts. *OK Computer* suggests that my generation will continue to address such concerns, and this gives us at least the comfort of conscious awareness. Ironically, the album actually removes the feeling of estrangement by showing that many people, including these artistic rock bands, have this 'emptiest of feelings'. Both Waters and Yorke know exactly what kind of anxiety comes from isolation, and both use the opposition of dichotomies to animate their alienation and anxiety themes. The resistance of the dichotomies sets up a natural tension, which in turn leads to anxiety, and the rift between the dichotomies causes each aspect to seem very remote. *The Dark Side of the Moon* explores such dichotomies as us/them and moon/sun, while *OK Computer* recasts them as paranoia/'fitter-happier' and quiet life/climactic death. Both Yorke and Waters draw on their personal experiences to deal with such issues. These dichotomies, however different, actually balance the themes, and allow each album to reach some kind of equilibrium.

The first Radiohead song I heard was their grunge hit, 'Creep', but I never thought much of the group until I heard one of their complete cyclic albums, those on which the melodies, style, and effects sound very similar throughout the album so that it becomes one long song where each track becomes crucial in conveying the ideas, both musical and thematic. A Wagner opera, with its endless melody, is a good way of approximating a concept album of popular music. Any concept albums made today (there are a few) had to be somewhat affected by Floyd. The

Beatles' *Revolver* was arguably the first concept album, but Pink Floyd mastered the approach with *The Dark Side of the Moon*, which weaves these beautiful elements into a tapestry that the Beatles approached but never quite equaled, at least at the level of coherence. Anyone who listens to *The Dark Side of the Moon* can grasp the basic concept and the sound that Pink Floyd created. The same is true for *OK Computer*, one of the most impressive accomplishments in the recent history of pop music.

With reference to as many songs as possible, I will examine various elements in Floyd's work on *The Dark Side of the Moon* and then demonstrate Radiohead's parallel accomplishments on *OK Computer*. Since some of these elements pervade both albums, the parallels I draw between two particular songs do not preclude other important interconnections. Again, rather than implying a conscious effort on the part of Radiohead to imitate Pink Floyd or model *OK Computer* on *The Dark Side of the Moon* (though such might, at least in part, be the case), my goal is to show how Pink Floyd continues to influence popular music long after the creation of its greatest album.

The dark side of the computer

Both albums start the journey with a birth intro. Nick Mason starts the life of *Dark Side of the Moon* in 'Speak to Me' with a heart beating, followed by a screaming crescendo, and finally by adding breath and so giving the album life. Radiohead's first song, 'Airbag', also thematizes a rebirth at the beginning of the album. Yorke tells of his remarkable resurrection when 'an airbag saved my life', and now 'I am [he is] born again'. The swelling scream begins life, and employs the musical technique that Doheny refers to as 'jump cutting' (2002, p. 62), a quick jump from one musical idea to another contrasting one, and this device reoccurs in both albums. The best example of jump cutting in popular music would be the transition in The Beatles' 'A Day in the Life'. The jump cut from birth of 'Speak to Me' takes us right into 'Breathe'.

'Breathe, breathe in the air': Waters begins his night journey with this calming, reassuring advice (or command?). The thematic concept of 'Breathe' can be seen in *OK Computer*'s 'Exit Music (for a film)'. Both melancholy songs share motifs of breathing and air. In the third verse of 'Exit Music', 'Breathe, keep breathing/ Don't lose your nerve / Breathe, keep breathing / I can't do this alone', Thom Yorke echoes the first three lines of the *The Dark Side of the Moon*, 'Breathe, breathe in the air / Don't be afraid to care / Leave but don't leave me'. By the end of 'Exit Music', the two star-crossed lovers (the film is the Modern *Romeo and Juliet*) are unable to 'escape' because they choke on the air. The two lovers are trapped in 'everlasting peace', a phrase sung with such passion and loathing that peace seems quite impossible. In a similar vein, 'Breathe' speaks of how one's life choices will only become a race 'towards an early grave'.

Now that the race is on, we come next to 'On the Run', a musical depiction of a hurried individual trying to catch a plane, but ironically crashing like a plane while trying to reach an impossible destination. 'On the Run' has no lyrics aside from the occasional comment by Roger the Hat and the announcer listing flight departures, but even the lyrical *OK Computer* has a similar song both musically and conceptually in 'Lucky'. This song 'effectively plays "fantasy 70s rock bands" by persuading Jimmy Page to join a heartfelt but already unsettled Pink Floyd ... [It employs] hi-tech "nails down the blackboard" guitar weirdness' (Doheny, 2002, p. 80). The weirdness Doheny mentions refers to the reverberating guitar on the background of 'Lucky', which he later claims starts the song's production. This new effect resembles Gilmour's cyclic guitar crash in 'On the Run' if it were slowed down. Regardless, both were relatively new constructs. Also, both 'Lucky' and 'Airbag' are about crashes and the anxiety caused by modern transportation systems. 'On the Run' addresses how airports can cause a mental air crash; it reflects the fact that Pink Floyd collectively hated planes and flying (Jones, 1996a, p. 97). The same crash can be heard in the crescendo of 'Lucky' as Yorke pleads for someone to pull him out.

After the plane crash at the climax of 'On the Run', the listener is jolted out of the silence by surprising alarm, 40 seconds of chiming clocks erupting in planned chaos. This eternal chime leads into 'Time', the zenith of musicality for Pink Floyd. Waters explains the concept of the song best when he tells of his misspent youth, 'I spent an awful lot of my life – until I was about 28 – waiting for my life to start ... I thought that, at some point, I'd turn from a chrysalis into a butterfly and my real life would begin' (ibid., p. 98). *OK Computer* visits this chrysalis motif in Yorke's song 'Let Down', when he begins the second verse with: 'Shell smashed / Juices flowing / Wings twitch / Legs are growing'. Although more optimistic than 'Time', the lyrics of 'Let Down' portray the same longing and waiting that Waters recalls. Even the person Yorke writes about in 'Let Down' seems to be animated by the notions in 'Time' – time and waiting. Yorke sings that 'One day / I'm going to grow wings / A chemical reaction / Hysterical and useless', but he describes a person who is 'Waiting for someone or something to show [him] the way'. Waters's lament in 'Time' warns against becoming that exact person Yorke describes in 'Let Down'.

OK Computer also revisits the quiet desperation evoked in 'Time'. In the early 1970s, 'Hanging on in quiet desperation [was] the English way' (Waters), but Radiohead highlights the quiet desperation that also plagues the 1990s. All of 'No Surprises' is a plea to live a quiet life. Yorke softly begs, 'I'll take a quiet life / A handshake some carbon monoxide / No alarms and no surprises / Silent.' In 'Fitter, Happier', a machine voice tries to convince himself to live without emotion. With an eerie lack of intensity, the robot describes himself as 'Concerned, but powerless / An empowered and informed member of society / Pragmatism not idealism / Will not cry in public.' This resistance to emotion is the quiet desperation of trying to find stability.

Nick Mason's drumming in 'Time' remains ahead of the beat (Jones, 1996a, p. 98), emphasizing a lack of stable rhythm. When coupled with the surprising clock explosion and the haunting bass line, the music doubles the lyrical theme. Radiohead employ similar techniques in 'Paranoid Android'. Johnny Greenwood unleashes the speed by changing the meter from 6/8 to 7/8 in the subsection of this song (Doheny, 2002, p. 62), which gives the music the same rushed uneasiness of the faster drumming in 'Time'. The guitar intro to 'Paranoid Android', although much more complex and faster than Waters's bass line, haunts the listener with its hollow feel. Leading up to the purging section, Greenwood slams his guitar with tremendous force, creating small explosions of sound. After the line 'God loves his children', musical hell breaks loose with the change in meter and an assorted array of sonic assaults. The monster guitar riff ends abruptly, but the next chord, in the beginning of 'Subterranean Homesick Alien', provides welcome relief from the chaos.

When 'Time' segued into 'The Great Gig in the Sky', Pink Floyd took the listener on an unprecedented sonic journey, or at least this was so in 1973. Radiohead embarks on the same kind of journey with the song 'Fitter Happier'. 'Though wordless, 'The Great Gig in the Sky' still manages to convey mind-blowing poetry. Floyd wrote this song as a sort of requiem, with just one vocalist singing her heart out. There is only a voice whispering, 'First you hear whispers, and then you die'. As its name implies, 'The Great Gig in the Sky' sings for the dead who have moved beyond words, beyond earthly shackles. Clare Torry's otherworldly whines express almost all the themes of *The Dark Side of the Moon,* yet she does not say one word. She improvises against Wright's accompaniment, but follows Waters's conducting to achieve the ambiance he intends (Jones, 1996a, p. 99). This wordless song about death has the highest climaxes and lowest depths of the human psyche rolled up in a jazzy little number of a woman singing to the piano.

Radiohead's 'Fitter Happier', on the other hand, has no melody (to the words at least), and yet still manages to be a strikingly moving song. 'Fitter Happier' is for those who are dead on the inside. The music has left the words like passion leaving a life. Some musical ideas erupt around the words, but the speaker cannot feel them. 'Fitter Happier' wants to be music, but it cannot. All that is left is 'A pig / In a cage / On antibiotics'. 'Fitter Happier' is an undistinguished little poem that lacks both the music and human vocal inflections of 'The Great Gig in the Sky'. A computer voice reads the words: 'No paranoia ... No longer afraid of the dark ... No chance of escape ... A pig / in a cage / on antibiotics.' Removing the emotional components of song – the voice and the music – reveals the full extent of the emotionally charged words. This voice, literally a paranoid android, excites the most extreme of emotions as it tries to deny and destroy them within itself.

Music lacking words and words lacking music – both of these songs are supercharged with emotions, but neither resolves the emotional struggle. Nor would either piece actually fall under the definition of a song in popular music. A song with a singer needs words, especially in popular music, even if they make no sense. Jazz scat singers use nonsensical words when they sing to turn their voice into a musical instrument. Clare Torry uses no words at all. Her singing evokes the 'Queen of the Night' aria from *The Magic Flute* more than it resembles Ella Fitzgerald's scat singing. A song also requires music and a melody. Some poems actually have a natural rhythm and melody to them, but Yorke removes any chance of music by making a computer read his words.

The songs also mirror each other in their placement as central, eerie tracks around which the respective albums revolve. *The Dark Side of the Moon* leads up to 'The Great Gig in the Sky' and falls away afterwards; 'Fitter Happier', likewise, is the location that *OK Computer* is going to and coming from. Two thematic fixtures cross at 'Fitter Happier'. Doheny describes the fixture as a 'positive stream', initially strong but slowly winding down as a second 'negative stream' gets progressively stronger (2002, p. 78). The songs bounce back and forth, but meet at equilibrium in 'Fitter Happier'. The transition occurs in the floating music heard in the background: a piano plays the soft introduction to 'Let Down', then morphs into the exit for 'Exit Music', which says, 'We hope that you Choke' (ibid., p. 73). The chord progression in the piano part, from major tones to minor ones, is a transition independent of the lyrics. This cyclic song has a *Revolver* feel in that one song recaps the entire album, yet the recap arises in the middle of the album just as with 'The Great Gig in the Sky'. 'Fitter Happier', like 'The Great Gig in the Sky', is the glue that makes the album so cohesive.

One, two, three, four, five, six, seven. Easy enough, right? Well, with respect to music, seven is a very hard number to work around. But the song that follows 'The Great Gig in the Sky', 'Money', uses a rotating beat in seven to create an unmistakable, and very mature, rhythmic loop. This 'money loop' is Pink Floyd's most distinct and recognizable rhythmical concoction. Seven seems to be a rare number in popular music, but, as mentioned above, Radiohead also has a meter change into 7/8 in 'Paranoid Android'.

If the 7/4 time in 'Money' is not bizarre enough, Floyd employs sound effects to augment this strangeness. 'The song's opening is just a single sound effect of the hard, cold, yet rhythmic sound of a cash register. The dynamic sound effects of the 'money loop' still amaze the new generation listener. By syncopating the sounds of a cash register, tearing paper, and dropping 50p pieces (Jones, 1996a, p. 100), Pink Floyd create a fantastic rhythm that many daring popular musicians try to mimic, yet never truly succeed.

Radiohead, like Floyd, incorporate the appropriate sound to fit thematically with their songs. Just as the mechanized 'money loop' makes 'Money' become a chaotic factory of harsh and inhumane sounds, the computer voice in 'Fitter Happier' is appropriate to the song's harsh, inhumane world. In sharp contrast, the twinkling lightness of Radiohead's glockenspiel gives both 'No Surprises' and 'Let Down' an innocent, childlike flavour. 'Subterranean Homesick Alien' uses a 'swooshing psychedelic guitar swirling around' (Doheny, 2002, p. 64) to create a very spacey noise, lending it an unmistakably Floydian feel.

Radiohead's 'Electioneering' has the same thematic bluntness as 'Money'. Both songs explore the selfishness underlying money's existence, and both songs expose the harsh reality of politics and 'voodoo economics'. Moreover, both songs also address the reasons why 'hanging on in quiet desperation is the English way'. The 'new car, caviar, four star daydream, and ... football team' (Waters) can only be had through 'riot shields / voodoo economicks ... cattle prods and the IMF / I trust I can rely on your vote' (Yorke). Radiohead describe the means for commandeering the pointless luxuries of 'Money' in terms of intriguing lyrical images that show the brutal underbelly of material success and 'business as usual'. Both tracks highlight the dichotomy between moral beliefs at the heart of the contemporary system. Yorke epitomizes this dichotomy in the conclusion of 'Electioneering': 'When I go forwards, you go backwards, and somewhere we will meet.'

Waters dedicates a song to these opposing forces that is aptly named 'Us and Them'. An epic anti-war song, it depicts a conflict when 'there is no reason for it' (Waters). *OK Computer*, although not specifically focused on war, depicts an equally powerful inner conflict of trying to overcome societal pressures. In fact, *OK Computer*'s themes about societal pressures can be encapsulated by this line in 'Us and Them': 'Down and out / It can't be helped but there's a lot of it about.' Yorke engages in his own 'battle of words' in *OK Computer*, and his fight has an ambiguous antagonist. The ache felt by the speakers in 'Let Down', 'Karma Police', 'No Surprise', and even 'Fitter Happier' seems to arise from their feeling of being controlled by outside forces. 'Us and Them' addresses the problem of either fighting alongside the large group or of resisting it. When the man with the gun says, 'There's room for you inside', do you go with him? These cuts crystallize the concept of being unsettled, alone, and unable to escape that pervades both albums.

Both 'Us and Them' and 'Exit Music' contain slow-moving, thinly orchestrated sections culminating in hell breaking loose. In 'Us and Them', this jump cut occurs four times in a organized orgy of sound, including a piano slamming chords, a jazzy saxophone improvisation, a chorus wailing to match the sax, and devastatingly biting lyrics which hit and then recede like heavy waves. In 'Exit Music', the single climax, which surprises the listener with similar effects using different instruments, is preceded by background sounds that resembles waves on a beach with gulls. Very heavy drum beats and powerful chords lead in to both crescendos, where the listener hears a loud bellyache of each chorus and synthesized tones that carry us until we hit those resolving peak notes. The backup choir and synthesized tones make a huge sound larger until they finally release on a single repeated word: 'die' ('Us and Them') and 'choke' ('Exit Music'). Both words are far cries from the vital heartbeats of the albums' respective musical visions.

As *The Dark Side of the Moon* draws to a close, the madness takes hold, and the lunatic is loose. 'Brain Damage' is Waters's sparsely shrouded musical plea to reunite with his, now schizophrenic, partner Syd Barrett (Jones, 1996a, p. 101). Waters wishes to see his lunatic on the darker side of the lunar body. 'Climbing Up the Walls' is Radiohead's treatment of a similar theme. Both 'Brain Damage' and 'Climbing Up the Walls' occur towards the end of each album, and the creepiness bubbles up from the presence in each song of faceless being that is unwelcome, but always there. Waters commented on the universality of 'Brain Damage', 'I guess it's more particularly about the real human living inside the outer being that the rest of the world sees. In other words, the lunatic is really us, here, that we're trying to keep in this box' (ibid.). The same could be said about 'Climbing Up the Walls', with its image of the real or id persona that lives within the outer shell. Each song makes use of the metaphor of the mind as a room in a house.

Yorke's 'Climbing Up the Walls' opens with 'I am the key to the lock in your house', which provokes fear in the listener, who then asks, 'Who has the key to my house?' In 'Brain Damage' the lines 'You lock the door / And throw away the key / There's someone in my head but it's not me' ignite the same fear and questioning. Who is in my head if it is not me, and why can't I escape? In these songs even the image of being trapped in the head or skull is inescapable, returning over and over.

The end of 'Climbing Up the Walls' encapsulates three motifs – alienation, inescapability, and the head – that drive the two songs and even the albums: 'You'll get the loneliest of feeling that / either way you turn, I'll be there / Open your skull, I'll be there / Climbing up the walls.' In 'Brain Damage', Waters addresses this same alienation ('You shout and no one seems to hear') and helplessness ('The lunatics are in my hall / The paper holds their folded faces to the floor / And every day the paper boy brings more'). Those lunatics in my hall are not going anywhere; I cannot escape them. The lunatics in both songs are 'in my head' or 'my skull', and both writers imply that the way to change the madness is to brutalize the head. Yorke sings of '15 blows to the skull', while Waters refers to a lobotomy or worse: 'You raise the blade / You make the change / You rearrange me 'till I'm sane' and 'if your head explodes with dark forebodings too / I'll see you on the dark side of the moon'.

This last line of the chorus of 'Brain Damage' is an attempt at reassurance. Yorke also tries to neutralize the eeriness: 'Do not cry out or hit the alarm / We are friends till we die'. Both lines try to comfort the 'trapped head' and predict that there will be companionship until the end. Ironically, though, the reassurance in 'Climbing Up the Walls' is undercut by Radiohead's dissonant music and Yorke's unnerving vocalization.

The sound of 'Brain Damage' finds many parallels in the cuts on *OK Computer*. The introduction is remarkably like that of 'No Surprises', using a playful, childish melody to lead into emotionally mature lyrics. The airy guitar plays against some spacey background special effects akin to those in 'Subterranean Homesick Alien' and 'Let Down'. Waters uses the jump cuts already discussed as present in both 'Us and Them' and 'Exit Music'. The chorus in 'Brain Damage' swells like the background harmonics of 'Lucky'. Finally, Roger the Hat talks and laughs in an insane counterpart to the mechanical robot in 'Fitter Happier'.

At the end, 'Brain Damage' unobtrusively turns into 'Eclipse'. 'Eclipse' sums up everything that the word 'life' entails; it puts into words what 'The Great Gig in the Sky' expresses without them. The repetition of the word 'you' that occurs in 'Eclipse' also occurs in 'Let Down', which keeps repeating the line 'You know were [*sic*] you are.' Like 'Eclipse', this song argues compellingly that self-recognition and rootedness are the best ways to stay sane and whole. Waters also repeats the word 'all' in 'Eclipse'; Yorke employs the word 'no' in the same manner in 'Fitter Happier'. Yorke's 'no' implies the denial of Waters's 'all'. 'Eclipse' attempts to encompass all that is human while 'Fitter Happier' denies the things that make us human.

Final eclipse

Naturally, musical similarities also exist between 'Eclipse' and the songs on *OK Computer*. The heavy, slow drumming drudgingly pushes 'Eclipse' towards a climax, as with the drumming at the climax of Radiohead's 'Exit Music'. This slow pulse increases the length and sheer mass of the music, making the songs sound huge. The singing synthesizer of Radiohead resembles the vocals of Doris Troy in Floyd to give the piece a booming chorus. 'Eclipse' has a floating guitar scale over the melody, which occurs in 'Paranoid Android', allowing for the listener to follow *something* when the pulse moves so gradually. This layering technique makes 'Eclipse' very grand in scale, and Radiohead do the same with 'Let Down'. Spacey background sounds evoke the psychedelic feel of Pink Floyd; they also can be heard in 'Subterranean Homesick Alien'. The songs at the end of these albums wind the listener down into a relaxed feeling of conclusion; in 'The Tourist', Yorke explicitly says, 'Hey, idiot slow down / Slow down.' Both songs end with a chord that is hit loudly, and then dies, almost lovingly, away with a throbbing heartbeat fading into silence. Radiohead's 'The Tourist' uses a drum to emulate the heart stopping, but it has the same effect. Together, the sounds of those heartbeats appear in sync with each other, seemingly forever.

OK Computer is not, nor was it meant to be, the new *Dark Side of the Moon*. But it is the album that comes closest to achieving the effect that *The Dark Side of the Moon* had in its own time. Without *The Dark Side of the Moon*, no *OK Computer* could have bloomed. Both albums give the listener a look at the 'other side' that my generation needs and enjoys. Whether it is money or time, machine or politics, both albums also scream out, encapsulating what previous generations have seen, foretelling mine what might lie around the next corner, and hinting at what might wait for us all on the dark side of the moon.

Chapter 14

'And if the band you're in starts playing different tunes': an interview with Mike Gordon of Phish

Russell Reising

For some years now as part of their Halloween concert tradition, Phish have played a tribute version of one of their favorite albums. They have covered, for example, the Who's *Quadrophenia*, the Beatles' *The Beatles* (aka, *The White Album*), and Pink Floyd's *The Dark Side of the Moon*. Their *Dark Side* performance actually broke with tradition, as they chose to perform it the night after Halloween as a way of rewarding loyal fans who followed them from Las Vegas to West Valley, Utah for a show at the E Center on 2 November 1988. A one-shot deal, their cover of Floyd's achievement stays remarkably faithful to the original and represents one of the great cover versions of *The Dark Side of the Moon* – an achievement all the more remarkable given the fact that, as Mike Gordon, the band's bass player, reports, Phish learned the piece the day of the concert! Mike was kind enough to answer some questions about his and Phish's feelings about Pink Floyd and their version of *The Dark Side of the Moon*. I'd like to thank him and John Paluska, Phish's manager, for their generosity and time in helping me out with this dialogue.

Russ Reising: First of all, Mike, I want to thank you for considering these questions. Last year I published a collection of essays on the Beatles' *Revolver* (I've always thought it their most important album), and now I'm doing one on *Dark Side of the Moon*. I thought interviewing people involved in the recording of *Dark Side of the Moon* would be a great addition to the book project. But I thought it would be equally interesting to speak with folks like you guys about your performances and the general place *Dark Side of the Moon* plays in your tastes and lives as musicians and general hipsters about town.

I'd like to establish some basics first. I've read on various websites that your initial decision to perform *Dark Side of the Moon* was rather spur of the moment. Is this true? If so, could you please elaborate a bit? If not, please talk a little about what went in to your decision.

Mike Gordon: We've had a tradition of covering albums by other bands on Halloween. A few years ago we performed the Velvet Underground's *Loaded* (it was the middle set of three that night). We were playing in Vegas and fans came from all around. But many fans decided to skip our Utah gig the next night, and catch up with us in Colorado a couple of nights later. So we decided to pull a 'you snooze, you lose' gag. We learned the hugely monumental *Dark Side of the Moon* during the day and performed it, in its entirety the day *after* Halloween. It was unprecedented and unexpected for us to break our tradition like that.

Russ: How many times have you performed *Dark Side of the Moon*? Do you ever plan to return it to a concert play list? Did your performances change much over time? If so, how so and how did your sense of Floyd's and Phish's *Dark Side of the Moon* evolve?

Mike: We only played *Dark Side of the Moon* that one time in its entirety, and, since we don't like to repeat ourselves if avoidable, we don't intend on doing it again. But we've also covered several of the songs from the album on different occasions. Notably, our drummer comes out front sometimes and sings, 'Great Gig in the Sky,' complete with one of his signature Electrolux vacuum cleaner solos. It was only that one performance, but learning an entire album by another artist is a great way to get inside the music, and find new appreciation for familiar songs and sounds. I was reminded how well the songs on the album flow from one to the next to create an overall experience greater than the sum of its parts.

Russ: First, let me apologize for not knowing the history of Phish's performance of *Dark Side of the Moon*. On the disc I have, you mention some center: Fleet Center, United Center, Office Depot Center, Trojan Condoms ('Ribbed for her pleasure') Center – they all get mixed up in my mind. Do you recall exactly which year you did the show?

Mike: 1998.

Russ: You mention, 'learning an entire album by another artist is a great way to get inside the music, and find new appreciation for familiar songs and sounds.' Is there any way in which Phish's having done *Dark Side of the Moon* has had a lasting effect on the kinds of songs and sounds you guys now do? How about you as a bass player? I know that early reviewers found Roger Waters's bass playing incredibly bizarre. I've always found it wonderfully cerebral and funky at the same time. Has he had any impact/influence on your playing?

Mike: In the case of *Dark Side of the Moon*, we already were so ultrafamiliar, like most people are, that we already would have incorporated the influences into our music, subconsciously. That is especially true since we learned the album in two hours, just enough time to pull it off. We are inspired by the way the songs flow, and the sense of darkness. You're right about the bass playing. I did enjoy incorporating that sparse funkiness into my playing that night. It was too long ago to remember what I specifically would have gleaned.

Russ: Was there anything particular about either the lyrical or musical nature of *Dark Side of the Moon* that particularly stands out to you as a listener, and was there any particular quality of it that you guys tried to capture in your performance. There are lots of long musical passages without lyrics (maybe like 'Possum' or 'David Bowie'), but I also know that Roger Waters labored on the lyrical drift of the piece as well.

Mike: What stood out musically and lyrically that we wanted to capture? To me it was a chance to go on a real night-time adventure. And I wanted to capture the nightliness, and bring people through a dark tunnel, spruced with funkiness. If we really achieved the vibe, then it wasn't only a novelty that we were playing something so familiar. But since it was so long ago, I can't remember how the fans reacted.

Russ: What is your general feeling about the way you perform *Dark Side of the Moon*? It seems fairly true to the original, even in the vocalize section of 'The Great Gig in the Sky' where you wail your way through it. Where do you think you differ from Pink Floyd in emphasis, interpretation, effect, etc.?

Mike: For only a few hours of rehearsal, the harmonies and playing were surprisingly tight, as I remember. Of course, we had grown up listening to the album, so it was well engrained. Pink Floyd has an element of deep darkness, as the title of this album suggests. I think Phish, at its finest, can also get into some dark, scary places. But since our lives and family backgrounds have been so fortunate, we are graced by a positive world outlook. It's possible that a band like Pink Floyd has access to a darkness which only comes from experiencing some tragedies first-hand. Also, when a band covers another band, the result is innately post-modern.

Russ: I find your musings on the darkness in Floyd fascinating. You mention that 'since our lives and family backgrounds have been so fortunate, we are graced by a positive world outlook,' and you then speculate that perhaps some of Floyd's own ethos comes from first-hand tragedy. I wonder if your situation as a band (your other family) is similarly instrumental in creating a positive ethos. I know that struggles within Floyd grew increasingly tense. How about for Phish? Your collective work is incredible, and there are many numbers on which you seem to be functioning as one consciousness parceled out into four different instruments, five including the voice.

Mike: You're right: it seems evident that our high-spirited parents, with their upper middle class lack of tragedy, and the way all eight parents seemed excited to excel in different ways, contributed to the positive vibe in our music. We've always considered our offstage and offstage discourse to be part of the same continuum. We simply get along great, and after 20 years that says a lot. It's not that we don't have disagreements or opposing goals sometimes, but we have highly effective communication skills, it seems, when it comes to conflict resolution. The group dynamic thrives when we are shooting the shit as it does when we are on stage immersed in the chemistry of Ouija-style improvisation.

Russ: I love the little hitch-hiking story you use to lead into the Boston version I've heard. I loved my hitching experiences and they provided many bonds and many opportunities for adventure, and, one of the things I loved most, complete opportunity for reinventing myself. I really mourn the relative death of hitch-hiking these days.

Anyway, do you all share a passion for *Dark Side of the Moon*, or are there important differences among the band? I was a college sophomore when it came out – what a perfect time for me! I assume you guys all grew up with that forming part of the soundtrack of your lives. In general, where does *Dark Side of the Moon* figure in your tastes and in your pantheon of pop music?

Mike: I think we all share a passion for *Dark Side of the Moon*. I might listen to more bluegrass than classic rock or art rock, but in junior high I remember inviting my friend Ron over, turning off all the lights, and lying on the floor between two large speakers listening to all of the classic album. I think my bandmates and I would all agree that it's unquestionably one of the most significant accomplishments in the history of rock albums. It's no surprise that it was one of the top selling albums.

Russ: Is it possible to pin down the album's greatest appeal for you?

Mike: I love music that is at once spacey and rhythmic, and this effect is achieved with flying colors on *Dark Side of the Moon*. There is also an unfolding – from song to rhythm to sound effect and back to song – that is eloquent and makes the whole album feel like a dream. Dreaminess is my highest ideal for music. I think Phish has been very much influenced by this use of textures coming and going. *Dark Side of the Moon* is sonically superior to most other albums, with tight, crisply separated sounds. And that makes a perfect bed for its eloquent, tragic lyrics.

Russ: Your remark about your own musical tastes, music at once spacey and rhythmic and that 'dreaminess is my highest ideal for music' really got to me, and I couldn't agree more. I specifically remember an old San Francisco song, 'Just a Little' by the Beau Brummels. It came out when I was in about sixth grade, and I used to just lie on my bed and let it ripple over me. Now that you mention it, what got me *was* that quality of dreaminess that emerged out of the combination of instrumentation, production, and vocal effects. It's also my ideal for psychedelic music. In terms of psychedelia, of which I consider *Dark Side of the Moon* a definitive statement, what do you think about *Dark Side of the Moon* as a psychedelic work? I don't want to impose a narrow definition on it, of course, but I think that's partly what you're getting at.

Mike: Any music that takes you to a specific and new place in your brain could be considered psychedelic. And by that definition, *Dark Side of the Moon* does a good job of it. I sometimes find improvised music to be the most direct path to psychedelic enlightening, but for a more composed medium, *Dark Side of the Moon* would do the trick, it seems.

Russ: I've always thought Gilmour's solo on 'Time' to be one of the great moments in rock guitar history. Unfortunately, when I first saw them perform *Dark Side of the Moon*, they showed up to Detroit late, and they didn't really get the sound together until they did 'Echoes' for their encore. Much of that concert, including that guitar solo, was mangled by bad sound, a rarity for Pink Floyd's live performances. Are there parts of the album you really like more or respond to more than others – musically, lyrically, etc?

Mike: I like that high hat and sound effect vamp after the first song – it's a feeling of heading off toward a strange place. I love how *funky* 'Time' sounds when it starts. There are nice 'holes' in the rhythm – split seconds where no instrument is playing a note. That makes it lilt along, I think. 'Money' ingeniously uses an odd rhythm – seven. It sounds so inevitable, and you would never know the meter is odd. I've always loved the moment in the middle when the instruments sparse out for a few bars and, again, that space between the notes makes you really want to crank it up on your stereo.

Russ: *Dark Side of the Moon* has always seemed like a very 'English' album. You know, 'hanging on in quiet desperation is the English way' and all that. Moreover, given the composition history of the album as well as the way Floyd tended to perform, there's not much spontaneity or freedom to improvise (parts of 'Money' being the sole exception in the performances I've seen). The piece did evolve, of course, and changed in interesting and significant ways from its debut in 1972 to its release in '73. But during each touring phase, Floyd performed it by the books.

Phish strikes me as a having a very 'American' sound, open, exuberant, spontaneous, and wide-ranging, musically, lyrically, and emotionally. I think this possible contrast constitutes one of the wonders of your performances of the album. What impact or effect does the 'Englishness' of *Dark Side of the Moon* have, and how does it communicate itself to you guys either musically or lyrically? Does it feel like 'non-American' music in its construction or performance?

Mike: The influence of British rock in general on American bands is undeniable. I agree that Phish has an American spirit, but some of the song writing has also been informed by growing up listening to English bands. Though it was too long ago to remember our version, it seems that there were some spots in *Dark Side of the Moon* for improvisation to occur. The main spontaneity came from deciding to cover the album on the spur of the moment. We had covered the Beatles' *White Album* and the Who's *Quadrophenia* on two prior Halloweens, so we have no problem paying tribute to big influences from that country. Personally, I've had feelings in the past that certain sounds have felt 'too British' for me to be able to relate closely to, but *Dark Side of the Moon* is not an example of that. There is room in the American psyche for dark-sounding music.

Russ: One of the things I found interesting about the filmed version of *Dark Side of the Moon* in *Pulse* was the remaining Pink Floyd's transforming an album that many people feel is about personal issues, with occasional references to insanity into a very public, almost political, statement. They include footage of many US and world leaders, for example. This strikes me as similar to what Roger Waters did with his performance of *The Wall* in Berlin, where he similarly reimagines that work as one of intense public, communal, and political significance.

How does Phish think about this dimension of *Dark Side of the Moon*? Intensely private? Public and political? Both/and? Either/or? Neither/nor? Both both/and And either/or?

Mike: We appreciate music that seems to work on many different levels at once. I believe that music can be for the mind, body, heart, and soul. I also think the experience can be simultaneously private and public. Your inner feelings are stroked when you listen to such a pure and monumental album as *Dark Side of the Moon*, and at the same time some of those feelings are archetypal, and a song can connect you to other people around you who have similar concerns and emotions. And though Phish tends to avoid political affiliations, it also makes sense that any music could be interpreted as political, with social messages. I guess it's what you make of it.

Russ: You remark near the end of your initial responses that *Dark Side of the Moon* is simultaneously 'private and public', both personal and archetypal. I couldn't agree more, and I think Floyd's final performance of the suite a few years back worked more on that dimension. Their background film was often explicitly political, with scenes of world rulers doing buffoonish things to the 'Brain Damage' section. I think that interface between the private and the public, or the personal and archetypal, is also a signature element of psychedelia. It might also be true of all 'great' album statements. Would you care to chat for a bit on just how/where *Dark Side of the Moon* achieves that mystical fusion? Do you think this has something to do with *Dark Side of the Moon*'s enduring popularity and tidal pull on several generations? My students and my son still return to the album with all the intensity and interest I remember feeling 30 years ago.

Mike: The timelessness of the album probably indicates at least some mystical attainment. 'Ticking away the moments that make up a dull day' seems very personal for anyone to imagine. But the concept of 'Time' is universal. I often like music that is timeful rather than timeless. The album has timelessness, but once when I cranked it up in high school, lying on the floor in the dark between the two speakers, that experience was timeful. It shaped my musical development at that exact, particular moment.

Chapter 15

The Jamaican side of the moon: an interview with Michael Goldwasser of Easy Star Records

Russell Reising

Russell Reising: First of all, congratulations on a brilliant recording. I happened upon it by chance and was enthralled from the first notes through the final eclipse. When I was in the final stages of my book on the Beatles' *Revolver*, I encountered *Revolver: A New Spin* by Ann Dyer, who rearranged, edited, and covered *Revolver* in a variety of lush and insightful styles. For example, she records 'Good Day Sunshine' with beach sounds and rolling waves in the background, and she does one of the most soulful versions of 'Eleanor Rigby' ever. This time around I find *Dub Side of the Moon*. Makes me want to keep doing these books, if only to stumble on new wonders like your project.

Thanks very much for fielding some questions about *Dub Side*. Since this book is on *The Dark Side of the Moon*, I'd like to establish some basics about your orientation to Pink Floyd's work and then move into the specifics of your interpretation. I'd like you to give me some background on the Easy Star All-Stars and how you folks decided to reinterpret *Dark Side of the Moon*. Why that album? Did you consider any others?

Michael Goldwasser: Easy Star All-Stars is basically the house band for Easy Star Records. It consists of me and whoever else I can round up at the moment. For this record, it was basically me, Ticklah (who co-produced the album), and a bunch of sidemen.

My partner Lem from Easy Star Records came up with the idea for the album. He was a big *Dark Side of the Moon* fan since high school, and one day a few years ago he was listening to it and realized that it could work well as a dub album. He brought that idea to the rest of us, and we agreed that it could work because of the tempos, the lyrics, and the overall vibe of the album. Plus there's a lot of space for dubbing. So it's not as if we set out to do a reggae version of a rock album and decided on this one over others; we decided to do this project, and it just so happened to be a reggae cover of a rock album.

Russ: I don't imagine that 'hanging on in quiet desperation is the [Jamaican] way'! Nor does the kind of highly produced music and distant stage and performance style of Pink Floyd remind me of any reggae artists I know or performances I've attended. How do you situate Pink Floyd and *Dark Side of the Moon* within the world of Jamaican music and culture in general, and reggae and ska in particular?

Michael: Well, as I mentioned before, a lot of the lyrics do make sense in a Jamaican context. Remember that Jamaica was a British colony until just over 40 years ago, and the British influence is still there. Also, many of the lyrical concepts of the album are universal: life, death, time, money, war, insanity. You definitely find plenty of songs about those subjects in reggae.

On a musical level, yes, there are many differences between British rock and Jamaican reggae, but ultimately, it's all just music. If you do it well, people from all backgrounds will respond. While most of the Jamaican artists who performed on the album had never heard the stuff before, they all really appreciated the Pink Floyd version when we played it for them.

Russ: How do you think *Dub Side of the Moon* engages Pink Floyd's *Dark Side*? What kind of interpretation were you going for in your version? What were your most interesting and most difficult decisions to make as you put your own spin on Floyd's original? I love your intro to 'Money', as does probably everyone who's ever listened to it. It's clever, of course, but it also captures and reenergizes an already funky Floyd original.

Michael: We were trying to envision how the album would have come out if it had been recorded and mixed in Kingston in the late 1970s or early '80s – that's the interpretation that we were going for. I wanted to make it into an album that I could relate to, since I'm not a fan of Pink Floyd, but I am a fan of reggae.

We decided pretty early on to keep the structure of the album the same as the original, and to retain the harmonic structure straight through. So having those guidelines made it easier to work. The main decisions had to do with smaller details, like deciding whether to mimic a particular guitar or keyboard part from the original. The intro to 'Money' seemed like a no-brainer to me. We didn't have a choice!

Russ: How did you decide to embellish the original songs with your own toasting? I find your material on 'Time' absolutely spectacular. It meshes with the philosophical ideas, the emotional tone, and the musical essence of the piece perfectly, as though the song was written for you. What kind of meanings do you think your toasting contributes to the Floyd original? How do they extend, expand, change, or reinterpret the lyrics?

Michael: We wanted to give the album more of a reggae flavor, so toasting made sense. Also, we didn't want a lot of bombastic guitar solos; that's not reggae to us. So toasting became another way to replace those solos, and give the songs new twist. I've never really analyzed the lyrics, so I can't answer your last question.

Russ: What about the music and sound effects you offer? Were they created with any specific sense of how they related to Floyd's original album?

Michael: Well, we definitely wanted to reference the original as much as possible in regards to sound effects. But we also used them as a chance to bring in some more humor, like the bong hits in 'Money' or the roosters crowing at the beginning of 'Time'.

Russ: What kinds of things haven't I asked that you'd like to comment on about *Dub Side of the Moon*?

Michael: I just hope that non-reggae fans who check out *Dub Side* will think about buying some other reggae records the next time that they walk into a record shop. If we've opened up people's minds, then we've done a good job.

'Thought I'd something more to say': an annotated bibliography of selected reviews and commentary on *The Dark Side of the Moon*

Mathew Bartkowiak

'Back to Earth.' *Mojo*, #52, March 1998, 88–9.
  This small 'sidebar' feature was part of the larger article, 'The True Story of Dark Side of the Moon' (see *Sutcliffe* below). Alan Parsons, credited as producer on the album, recounts that the album took nine months to record due in part to a relaxed atmosphere: 'It was very relaxed, even lazy really. They were already becoming family men. And then at the studio they'd be watching football or Monty Python. Everything stopped for Monty Python.' Included too, is a recollection from Roger Waters of his feelings towards the album as production and recording were finishing up early in 1973.

Black, Johnny. 'The Long March.' *Mojo*, #96, November 2001, 72–82.
  'The Long March' is the first part of an extended look at Pink Floyd in Issue 96 (see *Bungey* below). Black's piece mostly deals with the post-Barrett era to the creation of *The Dark Side of the Moon*. *Meddle*, is specifically mentioned by Gilmour as a 'clear forerunner for *Dark Side of the Moon*, the point when we first got our focus.'

Bungey, John. 'Equilaterally Yours.' *Mojo*, #52, March 1998, 84–5
  This small 'sidebar' feature was also part of the larger article, 'The True Story of Dark Side of the Moon' (see *Sutcliffe* below). Bungey focuses specifically on the album art, pointing out the piece would actually be considered a 'mechanical tint lay,' as 'There was no original painting; just a black-and-white diagram with instructions to the printer about colours.' After being briefed on the thematic background of the album, the prism design was selected as one of six possibilities for the cover.

Bungey, John. 'Wish You Were There.' *Mojo*, #96, November 2001, 83.
  This single-page feature was part of a longer examination of the group (see

Black above). Bungey guides the reader through the 26 tracks featured on *Echoes – The Best of …* including four *Dark Side* tracks.

Charlesworth, Chris. 'Caught in the Act/Floyd – a perfect Moonshot.' *Melody Maker*, 26 May 1973, 63.

Charlesworth praises a performance given by Pink Floyd at Earls Court in London, citing it as a 'faultless' concert, which combined both musical and technical attributes to leave an audience of 18,000 'shaking their heads in bewilderment' as they exited the arena.

Charlesworth, Chris. 'Floyd: all Wright now!' *Melody Maker*, 16 November 1974, 6–7.

Compared to the other members of Pink Floyd, Rick Wright is said to be the 'complete mystery' of the group. Next Charlesworth comments on several aspects of the group's dynamic including the relative distance the band puts between itself and the media.

Clerk, Carol. 'Lost In Space.' *Uncut*, #73, June 2003, 40–66.

This cover feature on the 30th anniversary of *The Dark Side of the Moon* features four separate interviews with Roger Waters, Richard Wright, Nick Mason, and David Gilmour as well as various smaller features on such subjects as total sales and cover art. Several themes recur within each of the interviews, including a general agreement that the album was made in a relatively drug-free atmosphere (excluding alcohol use and/or some marijuana usage amongst group members).

In terms of the lyrical content of the album, the members all note their thematic importance, but disagree as to how much members generally regarded the quality of lyrics as a whole. Each member also allows for some very individual commentary such as Waters applying the lyrics. Small pieces are interspersed through the feature including a look at the 'Dark Side of the Rainbow' phenomena (that being the supposed connection of *Dark Side* to the *Wizard of Oz* film). Members also briefly weigh in on their opinions of each track in a feature entitled, 'The Rototoms Are Great.'

Cohen, Scott. 'Treading Waters.' *Spin*, September 1987, 64–7

Besides commenting on several aspects of his career, Waters explores what he feels allows for the staying power of *The Dark Side of the Moon* on the charts.

'Dark Side of the Moon.' *Library Journal*, 15 November 1985, vol, 110, #19, 44.

Suggesting to the reader that 'a replacement copy is probably in order by now', this short review states the album is 'still pretty chilly stuff, and in retrospect, it has a certain prophetic quality, although the vision is one of madness, greed, and oppression.'

Dallas, Karl. *Bricks In The Wall*, New York: Shapolsky Publishers, 1987.

Dallas's analysis of *The Dark Side of the Moon* allows for some insight to the recording of the album, as well as the stage show. Dallas states that the album, 'is a remarkable work by any standards' but especially in the way that 'natural sounds play a musical role.' Specifically he addresses the cash registers on 'Money' as well as the 'terrifying snatches of conversation' which run through the album.

Demorest, Stephen. 'Paranoid Floyd.' *Hit Parader*, #156, July 1977, 10–13.

Although the piece is focused mainly on the release of Pink Floyd's *Animals*, Demorest manages to explore many of the effects of *The Dark Side of the Moon* on the group.

DeRogatis, Jim. *Kaleidoscope Eyes: Psychedelic Rock From the '60s to the '90s*, Secaucus, NJ: Citadel Press, 1996.

Under the heading, 'Money Changes Everything,' DeRogatis briefly looks into *The Dark Side of the Moon*, stating, 'it is the Floyd's catchiest record. The power of the hooks can't be underestimated.' The album's 'luxurious psychedelic sound that deserves its vaunted reputation' is attributed to 'Years of knob twirling,' 'engineer Alan Parsons,' and 'Abbey Road's new twenty-four-track tape machines.'

Erskine, Pete. 'The lighter side of Gilmour.' *Sounds*, 1 June 1974, 7.

Erskine ponders (in reference to *The Dark Side of the Moon*) 'whether the nature of the previous album really is inhibiting them in what to do next,' and, along the same lines, discusses the band's plan to orchestrate an album.

Erskine, Pete. 'Thrills: Floyd void: lunar probe lost in space.' *New Musical Express*, 5 October 1974, 9.

Penned in the 80th week of *The Dark Side of the Moon*, appearing on the NME charts, Erskine asks what is next for Floyd. When asked of the possibilities of an outtakes album Gilmour replies, 'No, we never get anything finished to that point. We don't work on anything unless it's going to be used.'

'Floyd to Tour in November?' *Sounds*, 10 August 1974, 4.

The possibility of a British tour is dissected in this short piece, attesting to the need of the band being able to find 'suitable large venues'. The possibility of playing several nights in a single venue is posed as a possible solution to the large venue conundrum.

Fricke, David. 'Pink Floyd.' *Musician*, December 1982, 48–56.

The life of Pink Floyd is chronicled in this extended interview with David Gilmour, with a special emphasis on chronicling of the band's development up to *The Wall*. Specifically in context to *The Dark Side of the Moon*, Gilmour deconstructs the effects of the album on Pink Floyd's career. Gilmour shares with Fricke other candid comments about his dismay with the success of *Dark Side*, including in terms of being concretely labeled in the media and public's eye as, in Fricke's words, 'the last living truly psychedelic band, a "space band."' *Dark Side*'s technical background is discussed at length.

Fricke, David. 'Platinum Floyd.' *Rolling Stone*, 20 August 1998, 34.

Fricke enlists Roger Waters to reflect on the success of the album. Waters attributes the continued sales to the fact that the subject matter is 'simple idealistic stuff'. 'I think that has something to do with the longevity of the piece.'

Fusilli, Jim. 'View Music: Pink Floyd Sets a Record: *Dark Side of the Moon*, Now 25, Is Still On Charts – Sex, Drugs, and Lots and Lots of 'Money' Have Helped Make This Psychedelic Opus a Classic.' *Wall Street Journal*, 10 April 1998.

Fusilli sees the unprecedented success of *The Dark Side of the Moon* (by this time on the Billboard charts for 1,100 weeks to it being 'a mature, ambitious work, with a hefty dose of melodrama', which overall is capable of being 'Serious without being overbearing'.

Grossman, Loyd. 'Records: The Dark Side of the Moon.' *Rolling Stone*, 24 May 1973, 57.

'Dark Side' is described here as an 'extended piece' that 'seems to deal primarily with the fleetingness and depravity of human life ...' Grossman also shares what he believes are the potential 'weak spots'.

Hedges, Dan. 'Records; Pink Floyd hangs a moon.' *Rock*, 7 May 1973, 20.

Beginning with criticism of Pink Floyd's merchandising, Hedges paints a non-complimentary picture of *The Dark Side of the Moon*. The author states that Pink Floyd has become reliant on the 'same, repetitive, time-worn paraphernalia: clocks ticking, hearts beating, footsteps, miscellaneous mumbling – the whole gamut of Floyd sound effects.'

Hollingworth, Roy. 'The Dark Side of Floyd.' *Melody Maker*, 10 March 1973, 19, 54.

Hollingworth describes his experiences at a premiere party for *The Dark Side of the Moon* at the London Planetarium.

Jones, Cliff. *Another Brick in the Wall: The Stories Behind Every Pink Floyd Song*. New York: Broadway Books, 1996, pp. 93–101.

Jones fulfills the promise of his title and runs down each track on *The Dark Side of the Moon*. Before examining the album track for track, Jones also shares a bit about the album's premiere at the London Planetarium in February 1973, including the band's refusal to attend due to the lack of a quadraphonic mix and four-way speaker system for the premiere playing of the album. The examination of the tracks provides several key insights into the compositions as well as into the band.

Kent, Nick. 'The band who ate asteroids for breakfast.' *New Musical Express*, 18 May 1974, 26–7.

Described as a 'consumer's guide,' the article encompasses the career of Pink Floyd from their humble beginnings, to their release of *The Dark Side of the Moon*. Full releases, singles, bootlegs, compilations, and 'odds and sods' are chronicled and rated, including *Zabriskie Point*.

Lambert, Pam. 'Still On the Charts, This Big Album Arrived When Nixon Was in Office.' *Wall Street Journal*, 3 May 1984.

Written in honor of the upcoming 520th week on the Billboard pop charts; Lambert looks briefly into the longevity of the album.

Mabbett, Andy. *The Complete Guide To The Music Of Pink Floyd.* London: Omnibus Press, 1995, pp. 51–9.

Mabbett offers a short introduction to the album before going into a track by track analysis.

Mabbett, Andy. 'Everything You Ever Wanted to Know About Dark Side of the Moon But Were Afloyd To Ask.' *Q*, #79, 1993, 57–9.

Mabbett's piece is the second half of a feature by *Q* concerning *The Dark Side of the Moon*, and it, in fact, examines various interesting tidbits about the album and its history, such as 'It is estimated that one in every five households in Britain owns a copy of Dark Side of the Moon' and 'With so many copies of Dark Side sold, it now is virtually impossible that a moment goes by without it being played somewhere on the planet.'

Maconie, Stuart. '25 Million Gloomy Punters Can't be Wrong.' *Q*, #79, 1993, 52–5.

The legacy of *The Dark Side of the Moon* is examined in this retrospective piece. Roger Waters recalls a meeting in Nick Mason's kitchen in which he introduced the idea of a common theme to run throughout the album. Maconie states that the album's legacy has had a continuous impact over the last 20 years, even with the emergence of punk, and he explains the album's influence on the 'house and techno' scene.

Malamut, Bruce. 'Dark Side of the Moon.' *Crawdaddy*, June 1973, 80.

After an extensive walk-through of the album, which includes the observation that the ending of 'On the Run' closes 'with the explosion of an H-bomb'; Malamut begins to examine the album more aesthetically.

McCormack, Ed. 'New York Confidential.' *Rolling Stone*, 26 April 1973, 16.

With a heavy dose of disdain, McCormack chronicles Pink Floyd's appearance at Radio City Music Hall in this short piece.

Miles (compiled by). *Pink Floyd: The Illustrated Discography.* London: Omnibus Press, 1981.

Basic facts concerning the album – including release date, track listing, and album notes – are compiled here, together with four short paragraphs describing the band's schedule in late 1972 and early 1973, (including a 13–14 January 1973 break for work on music recorded for a ballet by Roland Petit). Also, the bands' fraying of relations with Capitol Records is touched upon, saying that their contract after the release of *The Dark Side of the Moon* went to Columbia Records.

Moore, Bob. 'Pink Floyd two years after the moon.' *Concert News*, vol. 3, #8, 11 July 1975, 1

A report on a Detroit Michigan date at Olympia Stadium. The author observes that, to the crowd of 17,000, the 'concert took on the effect of a living organism that breathed, endured and metamorphasised [*sic*] with the lyrics.'

Oldfield, Michael. 'Caught in the Act: … Floyd's finest hour.' 23 November 1974, 30.

Oldfield discusses his impressions of one of Floyd's British dates, voicing his frustration with the mass-spectacle crowd being 'ungrateful' to the band and their performance. Although the piece is almost entirely devoted to criticism of the crowd, Oldfield does take the time to chronicle Pink Floyd's performance of *Dark Side* as their 'best yet'.

'Pink Floyd – The Dark Side of the Moon.' *Billboard*, 10 March 1973, 52.

Billboard's short review of the album states that the album is a 'tour de force for lyricist Roger Waters.'

'Pink Floyd – The Dark Side of the Moon.' *Circus*, June 1973, 49.

Given a rating of 'one ear, one mouth' (translation: 'Worth one listen at least; Savory, but for special taste'), *Dark Side* garnered a mixed reaction from *Circus*, though in the end the album is still credited as being 'a natural high'.

'Pink Floyd's Flaming Plane.' *Circus*, September 1973, 58.

Pink Floyd are praised here for their performance at the newly opened 18,000-seat Earls Court arena in London. The author points out several key highlights in the stage-show including: Roger Waters's gong bursting into flames midway through 'Set the Controls for the Heart of the Sun' and 'an enormous model airplane' which skimmed over the audience's heads crashing 'in a blazing fireball behind Richard Wright's wailing synthesizers' during a two-hour version of 'Dark Side of the Moon'.

'Pink play for charity only.' *Melody Maker*, 14 April 1973, 5.

Announced in this small piece is the only English live performance date for Pink Floyd in 1973, 18 May. It proposed that the show be held at Earls Court with all proceeds going to a yet-to-be-determined charity.

Plummer, Mark. 'Producing The Goods.' *Melody Maker*, 7 April 1973, 28–9.

Melody Maker goes behind the scenes with this chronicle of producers Chris Thomas, who mixed *The Dark Side of the Moon*, and Tony Visconti, producer of Mark Bolan and David Bowie. Plummer states that the idea of mixing *Dark Side* had 'become a terrible chore' for the group.

Povey, Glenn and Ian Russell. *In the Flesh: The Complete Performance History.* New York: St Martin's Griffin, 1997, pp. 107–17.

The authors provide some detail of the inner workings of the early live performances of Pink Floyd's classic and also address the effects of the album's success on the group; first pointing out that Capital Records 'could do little to prevent Pink Floyd from moving on now that their contract had been fulfilled'.

'*Q* Sleevenotes: PINK FLOYD Dark Side of the Moon' *Q* (supplement), #56, May 1991.

This supplement to the magazine gives a basic overview of the recording and legacy of the record. Also of interest is that the album is credited with having EMI's 001 catalogue number and has been available on CD since August of 1984.

'Rock-a-Rama.' *Creem*, May 1973, 69.

(Quoted in its entirety): 'Woooooooo, Zeeeepraaahhmmmmmmmmmmmmm mmssic bluuuuuuuusctch quaaaaaaaaloooooooood faaaaaaaaaaaar ooouuuuuttt (to be read in quadraphonic sound).'

Schacht, Janis. 'Record Reviews.' *Circus*, June 1973, 20.

Schacht compares *The Dark Side of the Moon* to earlier Syd Barrett-era Pink Floyd, stating 'Floyd is almost a completely different group.' Confused by 'ten short pieces in the guise of a single unit' in a period where 'The Floyd had been getting more and more into long concept pieces', Schacht questions, 'Has one of the original underground progressive bands gone commercial on us?'

Schaffner, Nicholas. *Saucerful of Secrets: The Pink Floyd Odyssey.* New York: Harmony Books, 1991, pp. 134–5, 171–201.

Schaffner describes *The Dark Side of the Moon* as a 'masterpiece, the album Pink Floyd were *meant* to make: that hypnotic evocation of alienation, paranoia, madness, and death that has transfixed several generations of listeners...' One sees through featured quotations from group members that the creation of the album reflected the creative process of the group. Various interpretations are also showcased in terms of why the album was as successful as it was. Schaffner gives the group's 17 March midnight performance at Radio City Music Hall in New York in 1973 special attention. The book also notes the lasting effects of the success of the album on the group.

Stump, Paul. 'Spaced odyssey.' *Uncut*, May 2003, 112–13.

Chronicling the 5.1 remix release of the album in 2003, Stump labels *Dark Side* as 'a monument to turgidity and misguided ambition.' Also included is a short question and answer column with David Gilmour and Richard Wright, in which the specifics of the remastering are discussed.

Sutcliffe, P. and Peter Henderson. 'The True Story of Dark Side of the Moon.' *Mojo*, #52, March 1998, 66–89.

This extensive piece includes a detailed history and track-by-track analysis of the album with commentary mostly from Roger Waters and some from Alan Parsons. Several myths are deconstructed about the album including that, even though the album 'was widely enjoyed as great drug music, the soundtrack to a perfect trip on the listener's narcotic vehicle of choice,' it was thus, assumed that the group 'wrote and recorded the album while similarly loaded.' The formation and creation of the album is also examined. In terms of the recording of the album, the article discusses technical considerations (like Gilmour's self-admitted 'theft' of Eric Clapton's Leslie speaker sound from 'Badge' for 'Any Colour You Like', and borrowing the alternation of echoey and dry sounds on 'Money' from Elton John).

'Talent in Action.' *Billboard*, 21 April 1973, 20.

In this review Pink Floyd is praised for being able to handle the potentially dwarfing experience (according to the author) of playing at Radio City Music Hall, and capable of exploiting the Hall's attributes. The unidentified author states that the 'band awed the crowd with its electronic ("First in space") virtuosity and its command of production techniques.'

Wadholm, Richard. 'Dark Side of the Moon.' *Phonograph Record Magazine*, April 1973, 28.

Wadholm begins his reaction to the album by sharing a sense of tragedy that 'Pink Floyd, the band that used to eat neutrons for breakfast, has gone the way of the Moody Blues, King Crimson and Kurt Vonnegut. No neutrons are eaten on their new album. Not even a nibble.' Wadholm does note a 'poignancy' never tried before on a Pink Floyd album. 'We are ushered into the album through a heartbeat fading in to the dim voices of a bad dream.' He continues, 'In the end, we're ushered out again, like visitors in a hospital ward, by another heart beat.'

Walls, Jeannette. 'The Lunatics Are On the Web.' *Esquire*, July 1997, vol. 128, Issue 1.

Walls examines the fabled *Wizard of Oz/Dark Side of the Moon* phenomenon.

Welch, Chris. 'Floyd Joy.' *Melody Maker*, 19 May 1973, 36–7.

In this interview with David Gilmour, Welch explores a variety of topics from Gilmour's opinions of current musical acts to the meaning of *The Dark Side of the Moon*. *Dark Side* is chronicled specifically midway through the piece, beginning with Gilmour asserting: 'The heartbeat alludes to the human condition and sets the mood for the music, which describes the emotions, experienced during a lifetime. Amidst the chaos – there is beauty and hope for mankind.' Also of note in the article is Welch's question of what lay ahead for Floyd where Gilmour responds, 'We have vague ideas for a much more theatrical thing, a very immobile thing we'd put on in one place.' One may make a case that this is arguably a relevant early inkling/clue of what was to come specifically in context to the release of 1979's *The Wall* album and subsequent tour by Pink Floyd.

Welch, Chris. *Pink Floyd: Learning to Fly*. Chessington, Surrey: Castle Communications, 1994, pp. 88–93.

Welch powers through some of the basic facts along with analysis dealing with the evolution of *The Dark Side of the Moon*. Included are citations of: the 1972 Rainbow Theatre premiere performances of the piece in its entirety; the development of the album witnessed on *Pink Floyd Live at Pompeii*; the recording of Pink Floyd's associates and friends for the snippets of dialogue throughout the album; and an examination of Waters's lyrical messages of isolation and madness.

Welch, Chris and Jeff Ward. 'Keep on Truckin.' *Melody Maker*, 27 July 1974, 39.

Appropriately framed by advertisements for Budget Rent a Van, Avis Trucks, and Midlands British Road Services, this article discusses the 'steady growth in the support systems, not in the least in the transport division' of major touring rock acts. Pink Floyd, along with groups like Emerson, Lake & Palmer, and the Who, are examined in terms of the logistics of their storage and shipment of 'equipment, from instruments, and cases, to complete sound systems, lighting and stage props.'

Works cited

'100 Greatest Rock and Roll Albums of the 20th Century, The', accessed 15 December 2002 at http://members.tripod.com/~tcotrel/100rockalbum.html

Adorno, T. and Horkheimer, M. (1994), *Dialectic of Enlightenment*, trans. J. Cumming, New York: Continuum.

Adorno, Theodor W. (1991), *The Culture Industry*, London: Routledge.

Amatneek, Bill (1970), *In a Wild Sanctuary* (album review), *Rolling Stone*, **69,** 29 October, p. 46.

Artaud, Antonin (1925), *Manifesto In Clear Language*.

Ashcroft, B., G. Griffith and H. Tiffin (1998), *Key Concepts in Post-colonial Studies*, London: Routledge.

Assoun, Paul-Laurent (1998), 'The Subject and the Other in Levinas and Lacan', trans. Dianah Jackson and Denise Merkle, in Sarah Harasym (ed.), *Levinas and Lacan: The Missed Encounter*, Albany: State University of New York Press, pp. 79–101.

Bacon, Tony (1981), *Rock Hardware: The Instruments, Equipment and Technology of Rock*, Poole, Dorset: Blandford Press.

Barthes, Roland (1982), *Image, Music, Text*, London: Fontana Paperbacks.

Baum, L. Frank (1900). *The Wonderful Wizard of Oz*, Chicago: George M. Hill.

Belz, C. (1972), *The Story of Rock*, 2nd edn, New York: Oxford University Press.

Benjamin, J. (1978), 'Authority and the Family Revisited: Or, a World Without Fathers?', *New German Critique*: pp. 35–57.

Benjamin, Walter (1989), *Messiaanisen sirpaleita. Kirjoituksia kielestä, historiasta ja pelastuksesta*, orig. in *Gesammelte Schriften* (1972), trans. Raija Sironen, ed. Markku Koski, Keijo Rahkonen and Esa Sironen, Jyväskylä: Kansan sivistystyön liitto, Tutkijaliitto.

Bennun, D. (1993), 'Pink Floyd Meet The Orb' [*Melody Maker*], accessed 15 November 2002 at http://bennun.biz/musicint/floyd.html

Best, Steven and Douglas Kellner (2001), *The Postmodern Adventure: Science, Technology, and Cultural Studies at the Third Millennium*. London: Routledge.

Bourdieu, Pierre. (1984), *Distinction: A Social Critique of the Judgement of Taste*, trans. R. Nice, London: Routledge & Kegan Paul.

Bradby, B. (1990), 'Do-Talk and Don't-Talk: The Division of the Subject in Girl Group Music', in S. Frith and A. Goodwin (eds), *On Record: Rock, Pop and the Written Word*, New York: Pantheon, pp. 341–68.

Bradley, David (2000), 'Klaatu Identities and Beatles Rumors', retrieved 11 June 2003, from the World Wide Web: http://www.klaatu.org/klaatu1.html

Brunner, John (1973), *The Stone that Never Came Down*, New York: Doubleday.

Brunvald, Jan Harold (1981), *The Vanishing Hitchhiker: American Urban Legends and Their Meanings*, New York: Norton.

Buchbinder, D. (1998), *Performance Anxieties: Re-producing Masculinity*, New South Wales: Allen & Unwin.

Butler, J. (1990), *Gender Trouble: Feminism and the Subversion of Identity*, New York: Routledge.

Cadwallader, Allen and David Gagné (1998), *Analysis of Tonal Music: A Schenkerian Approach*, Oxford: Oxford University Press.

Campbell, Joseph (1949). *The Hero With A Thousand Faces*. Princeton, NJ: Princeton University Press.

Carpenter, John (Director of *Halloween*) (1978) quoted in Clive *Barker's A–Z of Horror* (1997), (mini) (UK). TV documentary hosted by Clive Barker, directed by Ursula Macfarlane, Production Companies: Arts and Entertainment Video, BBC. Distributor: BBC.

Castells, Manuel (1996). *The Rise of The Network Society*, Oxford: Blackwell.

Chambers, I. (1985), *Urban Rhythms: Pop Music and Popular Culture*, London: Macmillan.

Cixous, Helene, 'Tancredi Continues' ([1983] 1991), trans. and reprinted in '*Coming to Writing' and Other Essays*, ed. Deborah Jenson, with introductory essay by Susan Rubin Suleiman. Cambridge UK: Harvard University Press.

Claek, Carol (2003), 'Pink Floyd: Lost in Space', *Uncut*, 73 (June): pp. 40–66.

Clawson, M. (1999), 'Masculinity and Skill Acquisition in the Adolescent Rock Band', *Popular Music*, **18** (1), pp. 99–114.

Connell, R.W. (1995), *Masculinities,* Berkeley, CA: University of California Press.

Cooke, Deryck (1959), *The Language of Music*, Oxford: Oxford University Press.

Cooper, David (1971), *The Death of the Family*, London: Penguin.

Cooper, Gary (1985), 'An Interview with David Gilmour', in *The Wish You Were Here Song Book*, London: Pink Floyd Music Publishers, pp. 73–81.

Cross, Charles R. (2001), *Heavier Than Heaven: A Biography of Kurt Cobain*, London: Hyperion.

Cunningham, Mark (1999), *Live and Kicking. The Rock Concert Industry in the Nineties*, London: Sanctuary Publishing.

Curtis, Jim (1987), *Rock Eras. Interpretations of Music and Society, 1954–1984*, Bowling Green, OH: Bowling Green State University Popular Press.

Dafydd, R. and L. Crampton (1996), *Encyclopedia of Rock Stars,* New York: DK Publishing.

Debord, Guy (1995), *The Society of the Spectacle*, orig. La Société du spectacle (1967), trans. Donald Nicholson-Smith, New York: Zone Books.

Di Perna, Alan and Barad Tolinski (1997), 'Wall of Sound', (*Guitar World Presents) Guitar Legends*, No. 22, pp, 46–7, 95.

Doheny, James (2002). *Radiohead: Back to Save the Universe: The Stories Behind Every Song*, New York: Thunder's Mouth Press.

Duncombe, Stephen (1997), *Notes From Underground: Zines And The Politics of Alternative Culture*, London: Verso.

Eaglestone, Robert (1998), *Ethical Criticism: Reading after Levinas*, Edinburgh: Edinburgh University Press.

Eco, Umberto (1981), *The Role Of The Reader: Explorations In The Semiotics Of Texts*, London: Hutchinson.

Edmonds, Ben (2001), *What's Going On? Marvin Gaye and the Last Days of the Motown Sound*, Edinburgh: MOJO Books.

Eno, B. and P. Schmidt (1976), *Oblique Strategies: Over One Hundred Worthwhile Dilemmas*, accessed 8 January 2003 at: http://www.rtqe.net/ObliqueStrategies/OSintro.html

Enzensberger, Hans Magnus (1992), *Mediocrity And Delusion: Collected Diversions*, London: Verso.

Everett, Walter (1999), *The Beatles as Musicians:* Revolver *through the* Anthology, Oxford: Oxford University Press.

Fielder, Hugh (2003), 'Dark Side Of The Moon/The Dark Side of the Rainbow?' *Classic Rock*, March, pp. 64–8.

Fisher, Dana. R. (1998), 'Rumoring Theory And The Internet: A Framework For Analyzing The Grass Roots', *Social Science Computer Review*, **16** (2), pp. 158–68.

Fitch, Vernon (1997), *The Pink Floyd Encyclopedia*, Burlington, Ontario: Collector's Guide Publishing.

Fitch, Vernon (2001), *Pink Floyd. The Press Reports 1966–1983*, Burlington, Ontario: Collector's Guide Publishing.

Fitzgibbon, C. (ed.) (1988), *The Collected Letters of Dylan Thomas*, London: Dent.

Fong-Torres, Ben (1972), 'The Beaver and the Ex-Weaver', *Rolling Stone*, **102,** 17 February, pp. 16–18.

Foucault, M. (1965) *Madness and Civilization: A History of Insanity in the Age of Reason*, trans. Richard Howard, New York: Random House.

Foucault, M. (1974), *The History of Sexuality, Vol. 1: An Introduction*, New York: Pantheon.

Foucault, M. (1980), *Power/Knowledge: Selected Interviews and Other Writings, 1972–1977 / Michel Foucault*, ed. and trans. C. Gordon, et al., Brighton: Harvester.

Foucault, M. (1991), 'What is an Author?' in C. Mukerji and M. Schudson (eds), *Rethinking Popular Culture: Contemporary Perspectives in Cultural Studies*, Berkeley: University of California Press, pp. 446–64.

Freud, Sigmund (1953–74), *The Standard Edition of the Complete Psychological Works of Sigmund Freud,* 24 vols, trans. and ed. J. Strachey et al., London: Hogarth.

Frith, Simon (1981), *Sound Effects. Youth, Leisure and the Politics of Rock and Roll*, New York: Pantheon Books.

Frith, Simon (1988), *Music For Pleasure: essays in the sociology of pop*, London: Basil Blackwell.

Frith, Simon (1996), *Performing Rites. On the Value of Popular Music*, Oxford: Oxford University Press.

Frith, Simon and A. McRobbie (1990), 'Rock and Sexuality', in S. Frith and A. Goodwin (eds), *On Record: Rock, Pop and the Written Word*, New York: Pantheon, pp. 371–89.

Gardner, Todd (2002), 'Dark Side of the Rainbow', retrieved 11 June 2003, from the World Wide Web: http://www.turnmeondeadman.net/DSotR/DSotR Intro.html

Giddens, A. (1990), *The Consequences of Modernity*, Cambridge, UK: Polity.

Goodwin, Andrew (1990), 'Sample and Hold. Pop Music in the Digital Age of Reproducing', in Simon Frith and Andrew Goodwin (eds), *On Record: Rock, Pop, and the Written Word*, London: Routledge, pp. 258–73.

Green, L. (1988), *Music on Deaf Ears: Musical Meaning, Ideology and Education*, Manchester: Manchester University Press.

Green, L. (1997), *Music, Gender, Education*, Cambridge, UK: Cambridge University Press.

Grossberg, Lawrence (1992), *We Gotta Get Out of this Place. Popular Conservatism and Popular Culture*, New York and London: Routledge.

Grossman, Loyd (1973), *The Dark Side of the Moon* (album review), *Rolling Stone*, **135**, 24 May, p. 57.

Gunderson, Edna (1997), 'The Power of "Oz" lifts "Moon" Sales', *USA Today*, 6 June, p. 2D.

Harpham, Geoffrey Galt (1999), *Shadows of Ethics: Criticism and the Just Society*, Durham, NC: Duke University Press.

Harris, John (2003), 'Pink Floyd – Tales from the dark side of the moon, thirty years later. Interview with Roger Waters', *Rolling Stone*, **922**, 15 May, 145–50.

Harris, John (2003), 'Thirty Years of Darkness: The True Tales behind the Madness, Alienation and Brilliance of *Dark Side of the Moon*', *Rolling Stone*, **922**, 15 May, pp. 45–9.

Hawkins, Harriett (1990), *Classics and Trash: Traditions and Taboos in High Literature and Popular Modern Genres*, London: Harvester Wheatsheaf.

Hearn, J. (1994). *Men in the Public Eye*, London: Routledge.

Hebdige, Richard (1979), *Subculture: The Meaning of Style*, London and New York: Methuen; Helsinki: SKS.

Henderson, Peter, Phil Sutcliffe and John Bungey (1998), 'Pink Floyd's Dark Side of the Moon 4', originally appeared in *Mojo* (March 1998); retrieved 5 September 2002, from the World Wide Web: http://utopia.knoware.nl/users/ptr/pfloyd/interview/dark4.html

Hodges, Nick and Jan Priston (1999), *Embryo: A Fink Floyd Chronology, 1966–1971*, London: Cherry Red Books.

Hoggart, Richard (1957), *The Uses Of Literacy*, London: Chatto & Windus.

Holding, Eric (2000), *Mark Fisher. Staged Architecture*, Architectural Monographs no 52, Chichester: Wiley-Academy.

Holm-Hudson, Kevin (2002), 'The "American Metaphysical Circus" of Joseph Byrd's United States of America', in Kevin Holm-Hudson (ed.), *Progressive Rock Reconsidered*, New York: Routledge, pp. 43–62.

Humm, M. (1995), *The Dictionary of Feminist Theory*, 2nd edn, Hemel Hempstead: Prentice Hall.

Huyssen, A. (1986), 'Mass Culture as Woman: Modernism's Other', in T. Modleski (ed.), *Studies in Entertainment: Critical Approaches to Mass Culture*, Bloomington: IN, pp. 188–99.

Janovitz, Bill (n.d.), 'Brain Damage. AMG-review', *All Music Guide*, retrieved 3 May 2003, from http://www.allmusic.com

Johnstone, Lucy (2000), *Users and Abusers of Psychiatry: A Critical Look at Psychiatric Practice*, 2nd edn, London: Routledge.

Jones, Alison (1995), *Dictionary of World Folklore*, Edinburgh: Larousse.

Jones, Cliff (1996a), *Another Brick in the Wall: The Stories behind Every Pink Floyd Song*, New York: Broadway Books; reprinted 1999, London: Carlton.

Jones, Cliff (1996b), *Echoes: The Stories Behind Every Pink Floyd Song*, London: Omnibus.

Kärki, Kimi (2002), *Taiderockin naamiot teknologian teatterissa. Pink Floydin lavaesiintyminen 1965–1981*, unpublished MA thesis, Department of Cultural History, University of Turku, Finland.

Kennedy, Helen (1997), 'A Floydian analysis of "The Wizard of Oz"', *New York Daily News*, 13 May, p. 39.

Kent, Nick (1974), 'Crazy Diamond', *New Musical Express*, 14 April; reprinted in C. Heylin (ed.), *The Penguin Book of Rock and Roll Writing*, London: Penguin Books, 1993, pp. 578–93.

Kesey, Ken (1962), *One Flew Over The Cuckoo's Nest*, New York: Viking.

Kittrie, Nicholas, N. (1971) *The Right To Be Different: Deviance and Enforced Therapy*, London: The Johns Hopkins University Press.

Kortelainen, Anna (2002), *Albert Edelfeltin Fantasmagoria: nainen, 'Japani', tavaratalo*, Helsinki: SKS.

Kotowicz, Zbigniew (1997), *R.D. Laing and the Paths of Anti-Psychiatry*, London: Routledge.

Kramarz, Volkmar (1983), *Harmonie-Analyse der Rockmusik. Von Folk und Blues zu Rock und New Wave*, Mainz: Scott.

Krause, Bernard (1970), *In a Wild Sanctuary* (liner notes), Warner Brothers, WS 1850.

Krause, Bernard (1971), *Gandharva* (liner notes), Warner Brothers, WS 1909.

Krause, Bernard (1998), *Into a Wild Sanctuary: A Life in Music and Natural Sound*, Berkeley, CA: Heyday Books.

Kumar, Krishan (1987), *Utopia and Anti-Utopia in Modern Times*, Oxford: Basil Blackwell.

Laing, Ronald D. ([1960] 1964), *The Divided Self*, Harmondsworth: Penguin.

Laing, Ronald D. (1967), *The Politics of Experience* and *The Bird of Paradise*, Harmondsworth: Penguin.

Lambert, Mel (1998), 'Classical Sessions: Interview with Alan Parsons on the 25th Anniversary of Pink Floyd's "The Dark Side of the Moon"', retrieved 25 June 2003, from the World Wide Web: http://www.mel-lambert.com/Writer/Interviews/PAR. Alan_Parsons.html

Landau, J. (1972), *It's Too Late to Stop Now*, San Francisco: Straight Arrow.

Leach, E. (2001), 'Vicars of "Wannabe": Authenticity and the Spice Girls', *Popular Music*, **20** (2), pp. 143–68.

Levinas, Emmanuel (1986), 'The Trace of the Other', trans. Alphonso Lingis, in Mark C. Taylor (ed.), *Deconstruction in Context: Literature and Philosophy*, Chicago: University of Chicago Press, pp. 345–59.

Levinas, Emmanuel (1996a), 'Is Ontology Fundamental?', trans. Simon Critchley, Peter Atterton, and Graham Noctor, in Adriaan Peperzak, Simon Critchley, and Robert Bernasconi (eds), *Emmanuel Levinas: Basic Philosophical Writings*, Bloomington: Indiana University Press, pp. 2–10.

Levinas, Emmanuel (1996b), 'Meaning and Sense', trans. Alphonso Lingis, in Peperzak, Adriaan, Simon Critchley, and Robert Bernasconi (eds), *Emmanuel Levinas: Basic Philosophical Writings*, Bloomington: Indiana University Press, pp. 33–64.

Lewis, Lisa A. (ed.) (1992), *The Adoring Audience: Fan Culture And Popular Media*, London: Routledge, pp. 9–29.

Leydon, Rebecca (2001), 'Debussy's Late Style and the Devices of the Early Silent Cinema', *Music Theory Spectrum*, **23** (2), pp. 217–41.

Logan, Nick and Bob Woffinden (1977), *The Illustrated Encyclopedia of Rock*, New York: Harmony Books.

Longfellow, Matthew (dir.) (2003), *Pink Floyd: The Dark Side of the Moon*, Isis Productions/Eagle Rock Entertainment/Pink Floyd Music Limited.

Mabbett, M. and A. Mabbett (1980), *Pink Floyd: The Visual Documentary*, London: Omnibus.

Macan, Edward (1997), *Rocking the Classics. English Progressive Rock and the Counterculture*, Oxford: Oxford University Press.

MacDonald, Bruno (1997), *Pink Floyd: Through the Eyes of the Band, its Fans, Friends and Foes*, New York: Da Capo Press.

Mailer, Norman (1970), *The White Negro*, San Francisco: City Lights.

Maltby, Richard (1995), *Hollywood Cinema*, Oxford: Blackwell.

Marcus, Greil (1975), 'The Band. Pilgrim's progress', in his *Mystery Train*, 4th edn, London: Penguin, 1991, pp. 39–64.

Marcus, Greil (1991), 'A brief return of the 1960s. Real life rock top ten Spring 1991', *Artforum*, April/May; reprinted in his *In the Fascist Bathroom. Writings on Punk, 1977–1992*, London: Viking, 1993, pp. 383–7.

Marsh, D. (1999), *The Heart of Rock and Soul*, New York: Da Capo.

Marshall, Wolf (2001), *Pink Floyd: Early Classics. A Step-by-Step Breakdown of the Guitar Styles and Techniques of Syd Barrett and David Gilmour*, Milwaukee, WI: Hal Leonard.

Martin, Bill (1998), *Listening to the Future. The Time of Progressive Rock 1968–1978*, Chicago: Open Court.

McDonald, Kari, and Sarah Hudson Kaufman (2002), '"Tomorrow Never Knows": the contribution of George Martin and his production team to the Beatles' new sound', in Russell Reising (ed.), *'Every Sound There Is': The Beatles' Revolver and the Transformation of Rock and Roll*, Aldershot: Ashgate, pp. 139–57.

McDonald, Patrick (1997), 'Pink Floyd Meets Oz … Well, Almost', *The Advertiser* (Adelaide, Australia), 30 May, p. 13.

Mellers, Wilfrid (1988), *Man and his Music. Part III: The Sonata Principle*, rev. edn, London: Barrie and Jenkins.

Meltzer, R. (1970), *The Aesthetics of Rock*, New York: Something Else Press.

Moore, A.F. (2001), *Rock: The Primary Text: Developing a Musicology of Rock*, 2nd edn, Aldershot: Ashgate.

MTV.com News (1997), 'The Pink Floyd/Wizard of Oz Connection', retrieved 11 June 2003, from the World Wide Web: http://www.mtv.com/news/articles/ 1433194/19970530/story.jhtml

Mulvey, Laura. (1989), *Visual and Other Pleasures*, Bloomington and Indianapolis: Indiana University Press.

Murdoch, Iris ([1985] 1970), *The Sovereignty of Good*, London: Ark.

O'Donnell, Shaugn (1999), '"Mind Your Throats Please": Collage as Retransition in Pink Floyd's *Atom Heart Mother Suite*', unpublished paper presented at the Society for Music Theory Annual Conference, Atlanta, 11 November.

O'Donnell, Shaugn (2002), 'Sailing to the sun: *Revolver*'s influence on Pink Floyd', in Russell Reising (ed.), *'Every Sound There Is': The Beatles' Revolver and the Transformation of Rock and Roll*, Aldershot, UK: Ashgate, pp. 69–86.

Oldenburg, Ann (1997), 'Pink Floyd, "Oz" in Sync: Album Reveals "Dark Side" of the Rainbow', *USA Today*, 23 May, p. 2D.

Palacios, Julian (1998), *Lost in the Woods: Syd Barrett and the Pink Floyd*, London: Boxtree.

Palmer, G. (1997), 'Bruce Springsteen and Masculinity', in S. Whiteley (ed.), *Sexing the Groove: Popular Music and Gender*, London: Routledge, pp. 100–117.

Parker, David (2001), *Random Precision: Recording the Music of Syd Barrett 1965–1974*, London: Cherry Red Books.

Pink Floyd (1973a), *Dark Side of the Moon*, Harvest.

Pink Floyd (1973b), *The Dark Side of the Moon*, Hampshire House Publishing.

Pink Floyd (1975), *Wish You Were Here*, Harvest.

Pink Floyd (1979), *The Wall*, Harvest.

Pink Floyd (1992a), *Dark Side of the Moon, Shine On*, Columbia Records, CK 53184 / CXK 53180. [Remastered, originally Harvest Records SMAS-11163, 1973]

Pink Floyd (1992b), *The Dark Side of the Moon. Guitar Tablature Edition*, London: Pink Floyd Music Publishers; reprinted 1995.

Pollack, Alan W. (1995), 'Notes on Free As A Bird. Alan W. Pollack's Notes On Series, no. 194', *The 'Official' rec.music.beatles Home Page*, retrieved 3 September 2002, from http://www.recmusicbeatles.com

Pollock, Ian (1972), 'Travelling light. Pink Floyd: February 17, 18, 19 and 20', *Rainbow. The Free Programme of the Rainbow Theatre* (13), London.

Povey, Glenn and Ian Russell (1997), *Pink Floyd: In the Flesh. The complete performance history*, London: Bloomsbury.

Radio Hauraki (2003), accessed 21 July 2003 at www.radios.co.nz/radio_research

Raphael, Ray (1988), *The Men from the Boys: Rites of Passage in Male America*, Lincoln: University of Nebraska Press.

Reed, Ishmael (1995), 'The Many Battles of Ishmael Reed', interview with George Paul Csicsery, in Bruce Dick and Amritjit Singh (eds), *Conversations with Ishmael Reed*, Jackson: University Press of Mississippi, pp. 314–38.

Rees, Dafydd, and Luke Crampton (1996), *DK Encyclopedia of Rock Stars*, New York: Dorling-Kindersley.

Resnicoff, M. (1992), 'Roger and Me – The Other Side of the Pink Floyd Story', *Musician*, November; accessed at http.//www.ingsoc.com/waters/interviews/ waters_nov_92.html

Reynolds, S. (1999), *Generation Ecstasy: Into the World of Techno and Rave Culture*, New York: Routledge.

Reynolds, S. and Press, J. (1995), *The Sex Revolts: Gender Rebellion and Rock'n'roll*, London: Serpent's Tail.

Ritz, David (1991), *Divided Soul: The Life of Marvin Gaye*, New York: Da Capo Press.

Ritz, David (1994), 'Marvin's Miracle' (liner notes), *What's Going On*, Motown CD 31453-0022-2.

Robbins, Jill (1999), *Altered Reading: Levinas and Literature*, Chicago: University of Chicago Press.

Rolling Stone (1987), 'The Top 100: The Greatest Albums of the Last Twenty Years', 27 August, pp. 45–174.

Rose, Phil (2001), *Which One's Pink?: An Analysis of the Concept Albums of Roger Waters and Pink Floyd*, Burlington, CA: Collector's Guide Publishing.

Roszak, Theodore (1970) *The Making of a Counter Culture: Reflections on the Technocratic Society and its Youthful Opposition*, London: Faber.

The Rough Guide to Rock (2001), ed. M. Ellingham et al., London: Penguin/ Rough Guides.

Salmi, Hannu (1999), *Imagined Germany. Richard Wagner's National Utopia*, German Life and Civilization Vol. 29, New York: Peter Lang.

Sanders, R. (1976), *The Pink Floyd*, London: Futura.

Sarris, A. (1968), *American Cinema; directors and directions, 1929–1968*, New York: Dutton.

Schaffner, Nicholas (1991). *Saucerful of Secrets: The Pink Floyd Odyssey*, New York: Harmony; reprinted 1992, London: Delta.

Scott, Derek B. (2003) *From the Erotic to the Demonic: On Critical Musicology*, Oxford: Oxford University Press.

Sedgewick, Nick (1985), 'A Rambling Conversation with Roger Waters Concerning All This and That', in *The Wish You Were Here Song Book*, London: Pink Floyd Music Publishers, pp. 9–23.

Shaw, Patrick (1976) 'The Excremental Festival: Vonnegut's Slaughterhouse-Five', *Scholia Satyrica*, **2** (3), pp. 3–11; quoted in Tepa Lupack, B. (1995) *Insanity As Redemption In Contemporary American Fiction*, Florida: Florida University Press.

Sheinbaum, J. (2002), 'Progressive Rock and the Inversion of Musical Values', in K. Holm-Hudson (ed.), *Progressive Rock Reconsidered*, London: Routledge, pp. 21–42.

Shuker, Roy (1998), *Key Concepts In Popular Music*, London: Routledge.

Smith, G. (1995), *Lost in Music: A Pop Odyssey*, London: Picador.

Stacey, Jackie (1994), *Star Gazing*, London: Routledge.

Stephenson, Ken (2002), *What to Listen for in Rock: A Stylistic Analysis*, New Haven: Yale University Press.

Straw, Will (1997), 'Sizing Up Record Collections: Gender and Connoisseurship in Rock Music Culture', in Sheila Whiteley (ed.), *Sexing the Groove: Popular Music and Gender*, London: Routledge, pp. 3–17.

Stump, Paul (1997), *The Music's All That Matters. A History of Progressive Rock*, London: Quartet Books.

Stump, Paul (2001), 'The Incredible Journey', *Uncut*, 54, pp. 42–50.

Sutcliffe, Phil (1995), 'The 30 Year Technicolour Dream', *MOJO*, 20, pp. 64–80.

Sutcliffe, Phil and Peter Henderson (1998), 'The First Men on the Moon', *MOJO* 52, March, pp. 67–89.

Szasz, Thomas S. ([1961] 1972), *The Myth of Mental Illness: Foundations of a Theory of Personal Conduct*, first edition, London: Paladin. (New York: Harper & Row 1961; London: Secker & Warburg, 1962).

Szasz, Thomas S. ([1970] 1973a), *Ideology and Insanity, Essays on the Psychiatric Dehumanization of Man*, London: Calder & Boyars; original edn 1970, New York: Doubleday Anchor.

Szasz, Thomas S. ([1970] 1973b), *The Manufacture of Madness*, London: Paladin; original edn, 1970, New York: Harper & Row; reprinted 1971, London: Routledge & Kegan Paul.

Szasz, Thomas S. ([1963] 1974), *Law, Liberty and Psychiatry*, London: Routledge & Kegan Paul; original edn 1963, New York: Macmillan.

Tagg, Philip (1993), '"Universal" music and the case of death', *Critical Quarterly*, **35** (2), 54–98.

Theberge, P. (1989), 'The "sound" of music: technological rationalisation and the production of popular music', *New Formations*, 8, 99–111.

Thornton, Sarah (1995), *Clubcultures: Music, Media and Subcultural Capital*, Hanover and London: Polity Press.

Tillekens, Ger (1998), *Het geluid van de Beatles* [The Sound of the Beatles], Amsterdam: Spinhuis.

Tillekens, Ger (2002), 'Marks of the Dorian family. Notes on two Dorian double-tonic tunes', *Soundscapes*, **5** (3); retrieved 3 December 2002, from http://www.soundscapes.info

Tolinksi, Brad (1993), 'Pink Floyd: Wall of Sound', *Guitar World*, **14** (2), pp. 79, 121–3.

Torker, Frank (1990), 'Peter Watts, Road Manager interviewed by Frank Torker', in *The Dark Side of the Moon Song Book. Guitar Tablature Edition*, London: Pink Floyd Music Publishers, pp. 9–15.

Toynbee, J. (2000), *Making Popular Music: Musicians, Creativity and Institutions*, London: Arnold.

Tulloch, John and Henry Jenkins (1995), *Science Fiction Audiences*, London: Routledge.

Vattimo, Gianni (1999), *Tulkinnan etiikka*, trans. and ed. Jussi Vähämäki and Liisa Kunttu, Helsinki: Tutkijaliitto.

Vonnegut, Kurt (1969), *Slaughterhouse-Five: or, The Children's Crusade, a Duty-Dance With Death*, New York: Dell.

Waksman, Steven (1999), *Instruments of Desire: The Electric Guitar and the Shaping of Musical Experience*, Cambridge, MS: Harvard.

Walser, R. (1993), *Running with the Devil: Power, Gender and Madness in Heavy Metal Music*, Hanover, NH: University of New England Press.

Ward, Steve (2001), 'Interview with Daevid Allen', *Wondrous Stories. Magazine of the Classic Rock Society*, 117, October; retrieved 3 May 2003, from: http://www.planetgong.co.uk/octave/archive/classicrock.shtml

Watkinson, Mike and Pete Anderson (1991), *Crazy Diamond: Syd Barrett and the Dawn of Pink Floyd*, London: Omnibus Press.

Weber, M. (1970), *Protestant Ethic and the Spirit of Capitalism*, trans. T. Parsons, London: Unwin University Press.

Weinstein, Deena (2002), 'Progressive Rock As Text. The Lyrics of Roger Waters, in Kevin Holm-Hudson (ed.), *Progressive Rock Reconsidered*, New York: Routledge, pp. 91–109.

Welch, C. (1994), *Pink Floyd: Learning to Fly*, Chessington, Surrey: Castle Communications.

Whiteley, Sheila (1992), *The Space Between the Notes. Rock and the Counter-culture*, London: Routledge.

Whiteley, Sheila (1997), 'Altered Sounds', in A. Melechi (ed.), *Psychedelia Britannica. Hallucinogenic Drugs in Britain*, London: Turnaround, pp. 120–42.

Williamson, Nigel (2001), 'Notes From the Underground', *Uncut*, 54, pp. 54–62.

Willis, P. (1978), *Profane Culture*, London: Routledge.

Wolff, Janet (1981), *The Social Production of Art*, London: Macmillan.

Wood, Alan. 'How To Listen to Dark Side of the Moon': http://alam.wpi.edu/ +chekov/ds-howto.html

Woody, Dave (2002), *The Music of Pink Floyd*, retrieved 3 September 2002, from http://www.pchs1.com/ecourses/pinkfloyd/mainpage.htm

Zappa, Frank (1981), *Shut Up 'n Play Yer Guitar Some More*, Ryko RCD 10533/34/35.

Index

General Note to the Index:
Since the titles of these essays provide specific information regarding their contents, I have assumed that the reader interested in, say, 'psychiatric issues' will consult Nicola Spelman's piece; similarly, readers interested in Radiohead will read Ben Schleifer's contribution. Therefore, I have not indexed the general themes indicated by the titles of these contributions.

For groups other than Pink Floyd, I have not listed individual songs or albums; anybody interested in checking for individual songs or albums by performers such as the Beatles, Beaver and Krause, or Marvin Gaye, for example, should consult the entries under the names of the performers.

For the entries under Pink Floyd, I have included references to individual members of the band only when they are quoted or something noteworthy is said about them.